HAYWOOD COUNTY PUBLIC LIBRARY

gratefully acknowledges
the presentation of
this book

In Memory of

Lt. Col. (US Air Force Ret.)

Joseph L. Hannah

BY THESE DONORS

Waynesville Township High School

Class of 1954

DATE OF GIFT

February 14, 2018

C-130 Hercules:
A History

Martin W. Bowman

Pen & Sword
AVIATION

First published in Great Britain in 2017 by
Pen and Sword Aviation

An imprint of
Pen & Sword Books Ltd
47 Church Street
Barnsley
South Yorkshire
S70 2AS

Copyright © Martin Bowman, 2017

ISBN: 9781473863187

A CIP catalogue record for this book is
available from the British Library

Printed and bound in India by Replika Press Pvt. Ltd.

Pen & Sword Books Ltd incorporates the Imprints of Pen & Sword Aviation, Pen &
Sword Family History, Pen & Sword Maritime, Pen & Sword Military, Pen & Sword
Discovery, Wharncliffe Local History, Wharncliffe True Crime, Wharncliffe
Transport, Pen & Sword Select, Pen & Sword Military Classics, Leo Cooper, The
Praetorian Press, Remember When, Seaforth Publishing and Frontline Publishing

For a complete list of Pen & Sword titles please contact
PEN & SWORD BOOKS LIMITED
47 Church Street, Barnsley, South Yorkshire, S70 2AS, England
E-mail: enquiries@pen-and-sword.co.uk
Website: www.pen-and-sword.co.uk

Contents

Chapter One

By The Numbers

A C-130 was lumbering along when a cocky F-16 flashed by. The jet jockey decided to show off. The fighter jock told the C-130 pilot, 'watch this!' and promptly went into a barrel roll followed by a steep climb. He then finished with a sonic boom as he broke the sound barrier. The F-16 pilot asked the C-130 pilot 'What he thought of that?' The C-130 pilot said 'That was impressive, but watch this!' The C-130 droned along for about five minutes and then the C-130 pilot came back on and said, 'What did you think of that?' Puzzled, the F-16 pilot asked, 'What the heck did you do?' The C-130 pilot chuckled. 'I stood up, stretched my legs, walked to the back, went to the bathroom, then got a cup of coffee and a cinnamon bun.

Everyone knows the Hercules - even those who are unaware of its C-130 military designation know exactly what it is for and what it does, this bulky, squat, but lovable aircraft with the reassuring friendly face of a seal pup and whaled tail. In RAF circles it goes by the name of Fat Albert' and in Việtnam it soon earned sardonic affection as the 'trash hauler' - at least, that's what the 'fast movers' (fighter pilots) called it.

If the decision by Lockheed in the fifties to reject conventional piston engines in favour of the newer and less proven technology of turboprops had been a brave one, then the decision to create a state-of-the-art Hercules for the 21st century was an unparalleled step. Such technological advances were not even a remote possibility in the early fifties when the USAF developed requirements for a new tactical aircraft based on the lessons being learned in the Korean War. Even so, in 1950 an idea - a pipe-dream almost - for an aircraft that could carry a 30,000lb payload of freight or troops over a distance of 1,500 nautical miles and could land and take off from difficult terrain, was reportedly thrown into a brainstorming meeting at the Pentagon by an unknown USAF colonel. At this time the request was akin to trying to send a manned vehicle to the moon. Certainly, it was almost technically impossible, given the limit of engine and airframe development at this time. However, a more formal operational requirement developed from the original idea and requests for proposals were issued to Boeing, Douglas, Fairchild and Lockheed.

The Air Force demanded responses within two months. The Burbank advanced design department made its submission on time and the Model L-206, as it was called, was judged the winner out of the four contenders. Lockheed had opted for an uncomplicated, workmanlike design for the airlifter, but had made what it thought was a brave decision by rejecting conventional piston engines and going for the newer and less proven technology of turboprops.

The designers proved their detractors wrong. The first Hercules entered service in 1956 with the USAF Tactical Air Command. Ten years later, when America became involved in the Việtnam War, it was the Hercules that moved troops and equipment from the US base at Naha, Okinawa, to South Việtnam. At the peak of the war effort there were fifteen squadrons of C-130s permanently assigned for Tactical Air Command or temporary deployment duties. Although around fifty Hercules aircraft were lost in Việtnam, the C-130 had more than distinguished itself, not just in troop and cargo movements but in many other important roles, too. For instance, it was the last aircraft out of Saïgon in 1975 and was jam-packed with people: there were 475 reported on board, fifty of them crammed into the flight deck!

Since then, the Hercules has never been far from the front line. It has continued to prove to be a most flexible workhorse, while its humanitarian role may account for the great affection which the Hercules seems to inspire; it even boasts its own

C-130A assembly line with 53-3132 (c/n 3004) at the head of the line which was delivered in December 1956.

Line up of the very early production C-130As, the first seven of which were ordered by the Air Force in February 1953. (Lockheed)

civilian fan club!

The C-130's reputation was such that one US colonel proclaimed that it was the only airplane of which it could be said that if it had been grounded, then the war would have ended. Universally this 'Mr Dependable' is fondly referred to as the 'Herky Bird'. In the twenty years since the Việtnam War this priceless aircraft has written its own chapter in aviation history as the world's most successful military airlifter. For when military cargo and heavy equipment have to be delivered into trouble zones - or soldiers and paratroops, or people, relief supplies and medical aid, or if the need to be evacuated from war and famine, then the success of the operation depends on this immensely reliable and versatile airlifter. When there are labours to be done, whether they be military support or international relief, the Hercules is usually there, swirling the dust in the middle of desert wastes, being put down on a remote jungle strip, or landing on bomb-scarred runways at war-ravaged airports, delivering cargo or airdropping supplies.

For forty years the Hercules has come to the aid of countless thousands in every part of the world. Name a continent and the Hercules has invariably been there and usually more than once - seen it, done it and if it hasn't, is doing it tomorrow. Normally it is in the background, beavering away, earning its keep, not so much an unsung hero, but more a faithful friend we have all met somewhere

before and have begun to take for granted. Sometimes, though, at Khê Sanh, Entebbe and Sarajevo, to name but a few, the Hercules has taken centre stage. At Khê Sanh in 1968 6,000 marines were entirely dependent on air supplies and the C-130s delivered everything, often in foul weather conditions and in the face of enemy opposition, for seventy-one days almost non-stop. Pilots used what came to be known as the 'Khê Sanh' approach, a method whereby the aircraft stays high, only nose-diving towards the landing strip at the last moment so as to avoid anti-aircraft fire for as long as possible.

More than 2,100 of these much-loved aircraft have been built and yet the design did not please everyone when it first appeared in 1954 - Kelly Johnson, who generated many wonderful sleek designs - the Starfighter and the SR-71 'Blackbird' included - at the Burbank 'Skunk Works', called the Hercules 'ugly'. Granted, the C-130 has never been sylph-like and it can be un-comfortable, especially riding back there in the hold - but ugly? Never! Its rotund appearance has tended to hide several novel features, including four turboprop engines capable of reverse

Above: Samuel Marvin Griffin, Sr, the 72nd Governor of Georgia from 1955 to 1959, christening the first C.130 with a bottle of Chattahoochee River water.

Right: Sixty years later, Governor Nathan Deal got a little wet during the commemorative christening ceremony Tuesday, April 15, 2015 of the latest C-130J. The bottle contained Chattahoochee River water just as Governor Marvin Griffin used during the christening 60 years earlier. (both Lockheed Martin)

YC-130 prototype 53-3397. (Lockheed)

thrust, large low-pressure tyres semi-recessed into undercarriage blisters and a rugged, simple construction that was designed from the outset to operate from rough or semi-prepared grass- or sand-strips with the minimum of support. This 'ugly duckling' has undergone five major facelifts and countless modifications, while some show stretch marks having been lengthened to carry civil and military cargo in the L-100 configuration. These changes have resulted in a myriad number of successful variants, including gunship, bomber, air-to-air refueller, airborne command post, AWACS, fire-fighter and even airborne hospital: but the Hercules has always managed to retain the same familiar characteristics and proven pedigree that it has enjoyed since it first took to the skies on 23 August 1954.

In January 1951 Lockheed reopened Plant 6, a government-built factory at Marietta, fifteen miles from Atlanta, Georgia and the complex was used to revamp B-29s and then build 394 Boeing B-47E Stratojets. The vast 76-acre site was now destined

to build another aircraft in far greater numbers, because on 2 February 1951 the USAF issued a request for proposals (RFP) to Boeing, Douglas, Fairchild and Lockheed for a medium transport to replace the Fairchild C-119 tactical troop and cargo transport, which had proved underpowered and offering little improvement over the C-46 and C-47 transports. A replacement for the 'Flying Boxcar' was of paramount importance, particularly in view of the escalation of and American involvement in, the Korean War, which had broken out in June 1950. The new medium-size transport had to be able to carry 92 infantrymen or 64 paratroopers over 2,000 miles for tactical missions, or for logistic missions, a 30,000lb load (including bulldozers, trucks, road-graders and howitzers) over 950 nautical miles (all without refuelling). Also, it had to operate if required from short and unprepared airstrips; and it had to be capable of slowing down to 125 knots for paradrops (made through two side doors) and even more slowly for steep 'assault' landings. A critical requirement was

Prototype AC-130A 54-1626 *Vulcan Express* with camouflage paint applied. This aircraft was later retired to the USAF Museum in May 1976 and put on display. (USAF)

YC-130 prototypes YC-130 53-3396 and 53-3397 in formation.

that it had to perform with one engine out over the drop zone and this had to be taken into consideration.

At Lockheed-Burbank, Art Flock and his design team under the supervision of Willis Hawkins, head of the advanced design department, went to work on temporary design designation L-206. It would have to be an amalgam of jeep, truck and aircraft. Flock opted for four engines instead of two, even though this decision would make the L-206 more expensive than its competitors. No turbine-powered transports had ever been produced in the USA before and it was a surprise therefore, when the slim-line 3,750eshp Allison T56-A-1A turbine driving three-bladed, variable-pitch, constant-speed propellers was chosen. But these gave the L-206 a top speed of 360 mph, faster than any other tactical transport; and pitch could be reversed to enable crews to stop quickly and back up the aircraft on a short field. Pressurization was essential because was that, having delivered troops and cargo, the new transport had to be able to accommodate 74 litter patients and two medical attendants and evacuate them from the battle area. 'Kelly' Johnson did not favour the 'bulky' shape but the dependable, sturdy new transport was not designed to break the sound barrier. From the outset it was a thoroughbred, but a workhorse and not a steed, conceived only to toil and sweat down in the dust, ice lakes and jungle clearings, places where grace and beauty have no place - designed to get the job done and get out again, preferably all in one piece. However, the entire fuselage was air-conditioned and heated and the Hercules was one of the first aircraft to use air bled from the engines to supply the air-conditioning and pressurization systems. Its basic mission weight being only 108,000lb was due to the widespread use of machined skins with integral stiffening - one section for the upper and lower wing surfaces was 48 feet long - which largely eliminated riveting and in the process, produced a much stronger and more robust surface structure. More weight was saved by using 300lb of titanium on engine nacelles and wing flaps, while another new development in the form of high-strength aluminium alloys was used throughout the aircraft's overall structure. In an age when complexity in aircraft design seemed to be the byword, the simple Hercules design consisted of only about 75,000 parts.

The Lockheed proposal was submitted in April 1951 along with the three other manufacturers and on 2 July was declared the winner. There followed a contract for two YC-130 (Model 82) prototype/service-test aircraft, which would be built at Burbank and on 19 September 1952. And the Pentagon issued a letter contract for seven C-130A production aircraft (Model 182) which would be built in Marietta. On 10 February 1953 most of the design team moved to Georgia. Al Brown was chosen as C-130 project engineer. The first prototype was used initially for static tests. The

South Pole Ice (SPICE) Cores being loaded aboard LC-130H 93-1096 *City of Christchurch, N.Z.* of the National Science Foundation for transport to the National Ice Core Laboratory in Denver, Colorado at McMurdo Station in March 2015. (Leah Street)

second YC-130 prototype first flew at the Lockheed air terminal on 23 August 1954 with Stanley Betz and Roy Wimmer at the controls and Jack Real and Dick Stanton, flight engineers on board. 53-3397 was airborne in 800 feet from the beginning of its take-off roll and made a 61minute flight to Edwards AFB in the Mojave Desert in California without a hitch. Most of the subsequent trial programme was earned out at the Air Force flight test centre at Edwards. Soon the Hercules was turning in cruising speeds of up to 20 per cent faster, an initial rate of climb and service ceiling 35 per cent better, a landing distance down by 40 per cent and one-engine-out climb rate up by a very impressive 55 per cent.

In April 1954 the Pentagon ordered a further twenty C-130As and in September another order was issued for 48 more. The C-130A differed from the YC-130s principally in having provision for two 450 US gallon (1,703 litre) external fuel tanks outboard of the outer engines and in being powered by more powerful T56 engines. The first 27 aircraft were delivered without nose radome, but were later modified to carry AN/APS-42 or AN/APN-59 search radar. The first production C-130A-LM (53-3129) was rolled out at Marietta on 10 March 1955. Chief pilot Bud Martin and co-pilot Leo Sullivan flew it on 7 April and flight engineers Jack Gilley, Chuck Littlejohn and Bob Brennan checked out the systems. 53-3129 flew perfectly, but on 14 April at the end of a test flight in which each engine was feathered and air-started, an in-flight fire broke out in the No.2 engine during a landing at Dobbins Air Force Base. Leo Sullivan and co-pilot Art Hansen got the C-130 down safely but the fire took hold and broke off the left wing before fire crews extinguished the blaze; fortunately no-one was injured. The cause of the fire was later traced to a quick-disconnect fuel hose behind the engine firewall which had worked loose (the coupling was

C-130A 55-0023 *City of Ardmore,* the fiftieth Hercules built, was the first of three in the first delivery to Tactical Airlift Command at Ardmore AFB, Oklahoma, on 9 December 1956. It was retired on 9 October 1989 and displayed at Linear Air Park Dyess AFB.

Hercules 'Tanker 133' (57-0482, first delivered in August 1958) owned by Hawkins & Powers at Greybull, Wyoming used for aerial firefighting, from March 1989.

fitted to each engine to permit the USAF to change power plants quickly). The problem was soon rectified, a new wing was fitted and 53-3129 was flying again within a few months. *The First Lady* went on to complete a memorable career, seeing service as a JC-130A space-vehicle tracker at the Atlantic missile range, then as a transport and later as an AC-130A gunship in South-East Asia. 53-3130 took over as the new structural test aircraft, using much of the heavy instrumentation from 53-3129.

In August 1955 a fourth contract was issued for 84 Hercules. Total orders now stood at 159,

discounting the two prototypes. In June 1956 two C-130As were delivered to the USAF Air Proving Ground Command at Eglin AFB for Category II and operational suitability tests, which they passed with flying colours. The C-130s also came through gruelling tests in cold climates and a programme of heavy lift cargoes and air drops. Finally, on 9 December 1956 the first five including 55-0023 *City of Ardmore,* the fiftieth Hercules built were flown to the Tactical Air Command's 463rd Troop Carrier Wing, at Ardmore AFB, Oklahoma. During the acceptance ceremony, Robert E. Gross, the chairman of Lockheed, formally handed over the

L-100 (N9268R) which was acquired by Delta Airlines in August 1966. This aircraft was modified to L-100-20 in December 1968 and sold to Saturn in September 1973. It is now in storage at Marana Air Park, Arizona. (Lockheed)

Hercules to General Otto P. Weygand, chief of TAC. Addressing the 5,000 people present, Weygand said 'the C-130 will play a most important role in our composite air strike force, for it will increase our capability to airlift engines, weapons and other critical supply requirements'.

By the end of 1958 C-130As equipped six TAC squadrons in the US, three PACAF squadrons in the 483rd TCW at Ashiya AB in Japan and three USAFE squadrons in the 317th Wing at Évreux-Fauville in France. During 1958 the pioneer

Hercules squadrons of the 463rd Wing at Ardmore moved to Sewart AFB and this base became the hub of C-130 operations for the next three years. Altogether, 192 C-130As (and twelve ski-equipped C-130Ds) were delivered to TAC, while fifteen C-130As were delivered to the Air Photographic and Charting Service, Military Air Transport Service (MATS).

In December 1958 a contract was issued for 127 C-130Bs (Model 282) for TAC (C-130B 57-0525 first flew on 20 November 1958). The

KC-130F BuNo149798 *Look Ma, No Hook* taking off from the deck of the USS *Forrestal* during possible COD (Carrier Onboard Delivery) trials off the coast of Massachusetts in October 1963. The KC-130F carried out 95 take-offs and 141 landings using a simulated *Forrestal*-class carrier at Patuxent River; it was then used in carquals on board USS *Forrestal* during operations off the coast of Massachusetts on 30 October. Lieutenant (later Rear Admiral) James H. Flatley USN carried out 54 approaches, of which sixteen resulted in 'bolters' (touch-and-go landings). He later made more landings, stopping in a range of between 270 to 495 feet without using an arrestor hook and take-offs in the range of 745 feet or less, without using the carrier's catapults. Flatley demonstrated that the KC-130F could have delivered 25,000 lb loads to a carrier operating 2,500 nautical miles from the nearest land base but using a C-130 as a COD aircraft at sea would have involved clearing the deck of almost every other aircraft and the concept was not adopted. (Lockheed)

USN EC-130V/NC-130H. The EC-130V is an HC-130H modified to an early-warning aircraft with rotordome (radar AN/APS-125).

C-130B differed from the C-130A in that its internal fuel capacity was increased by 1,820 US gallons (6,889 litres), it had heavier operating weights and it was powered by 4,050eshp T56-A-7 engines. The US Navy received seven C-130F transports, the US Coast Guard twelve HC-130B rescue aircraft, the US Marine Corps 46 KC-130F tankers and MATS had five WC-130B weather

reconnaissance aircraft. A further 29 examples were ordered for the air forces of Canada, Indonesia, Iran, Pakistan and South Africa.

The C-130E (Model 382-4B), which first flew on 15 August 1961 was designed for longer-ranged logistic missions. Deliveries of the first 389 C-130Es for MAC began in April 1962. The US Coast Guard received one EC-130E electronics

C-130H 93-2042 of the 182nd Air Wing, Illinois Air National Guard undergoing maintenance by the 309th Maintenance Wing at the Repair and Refurbishment Depot at Hill AFB.

HC-130H 64-14855 of the 301st Rescue Squadron in the 920th Rescue Wing at Patrick AFB, Florida refuelling a US Air Force Reserve HH-60G Pave Hawk helicopter.

platform and the USN four C-130G TACAMO communications platforms. Argentina, Australia, Brazil, Canada, Iran, Saudi Arabia, Sweden and Turkey ordered 97 production Es to bring total C-130E production to 491.

The next major variant was the C-130H-LM (Model 382C), which was first delivered to the RNZAF in March 1965. A total of 1,092 C-130H aircraft was built. Basically similar to the C-130E they were powered by T56-A-15 engines, usually derated from 4,910 to 4,508eshp. Some 1,092 C-130H/K models were built. This includes 333 variants for the USAF, ANG, AFRes and USCG and 693 C-130Hs for the US armed forces and 46 countries excluding the UK. Sixty-six C-130K-LM

(Model 382-19B) examples with some components by Scottish Aviation, with British electronics, instrumentation and other equipment installed by Marshall Engineering, Cambridge were delivered to RAF Air Support Command. The C-130K first flew on 19 October 1966 and entered service as the Hercules C.Mk.1 in April 1967. Thirty C-130Ks were brought up to a standard approaching that of the L-100-30, with the fuselage stretched by 15 feet. C-130J/-30 (Models 382U/V) are being built to replace C-130s in service with the RAF, the launch customer and in the US, those with MAC, AFRes and ANG. N130JA, the C-130J (RAF Hercules C.4/ZH865) prototype was rolled out at Lockheed-Marietta on 18 October 1995 and flew

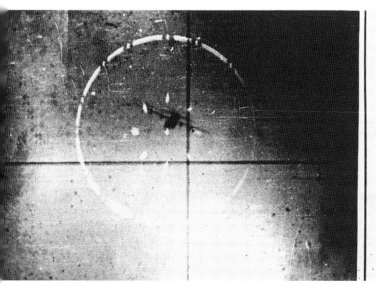

Ст. лейтенант Кучеряев

Gun-camera photo of C-130A-II-LM 56-0528 of the 7406th Support Squadron at Incirlik Airbase in Turkey which was shot down on 2 September 1958 by four Soviet MiG-17s 34 miles NW of Yerevan during a reconnaissance mission along the Turkish-Armenian border parallel to the Soviet frontier. The six flight crew were confirmed dead when their remains were repatriated to the United States, but the eleven intelligence-gathering personnel on board have never been acknowledged by the authorities.

An A-6 Intruder receives fuel from VMGR-252 KC-130R BuNo 160625 during a flight out of Marine Corps Air Station, Cherry Point, North Carolina. This Hercules was delivered in April 1978.

for the first time on 5 April 1996.

In March 1995 Lockheed Martin was formed by the merger of Lockheed Corporation with Martin Marietta and is an American global aerospace, defence, security and advanced technology company with worldwide interests. None of the earlier variants has been more significant or as far-reaching than the C-130J development of the aircraft: which was truly a model for the next millennium, with databus architecture replacing conventional wiring; a revolutionary new powerplant driving six-blade, scimitar-shaped composite propellers; and a cockpit with a digital autopilot, a fully integrated global positioning system, colour weather and ground-mapping radar and a digital map display, plus an advisory caution and warning system that allows for fault detection.

By the mid-1990s there were still in active service over sixty C-130As out of the 231 C-130As built, approximately 130 C-130Bs out of 230 delivered and of the 491 C-130Es built, more than 310 were in worldwide service with the US armed forces and about ninety others in operational use with armed forces of various countries. US government agencies were operating more than 300 C-130H models in a variety of special versions and about 350 standard C-130H model were in operation with the armed services of more than 46 overseas countries. About eighty of the 116 L-100, -20 and -30 aircraft built were also in service with military and non-military operators. By the dawn

of the 21st Century the airlifter that is without equal had been in continuous production for over forty-five years, through at least eighty-five original and modified versions. Today the C-130 is operated by seventy countries and 2,400+ have been delivered. Now that's versatility for you!

In 2000 Boeing was awarded a $1.4 billion contract to develop an Avionics Modernization Programme kit for the C-130. A total of 198 aircraft are expected to feature the AMP upgrade. An engine enhancement programme saving fuel and providing lower temperatures in the T56 engine has been approved and the US Air Force expects to save $2 billion and extend the fleet life.

As of January 2014 Air Mobility Command, Air Force Materiel Command and the Air Force Research Lab were in the early stages of defining requirements for the C-X next generation airlifter programme to replace both the C-130 and C-17. An aircraft would be produced from the early 2030s to the 2040s. If requirements are decided for operating in contested airspace, Air Force procurement of C-130s would end by the end of the decade to not have them serviceable by the 2030s and operated when they cannot perform in that environment. Development of the airlifter depends heavily on the Army's 'tactical and operational manoeuvre' plans. Two different cargo planes could still be created to separately perform tactical and strategic missions, but which course to pursue is to be decided before C-17s need to be retired.

Chapter Two

Trash Haulers -
The Workhorse of the Việtnam War

I believe the term 'hauling trash' predated the Việtnam War. The first time I ever heard anyone use it was in the spring of 1965 when I was on temporary duty at Ubon, Thailand on the flare mission. Willy Donovan, one of the other loadmasters, had come to Okinawa from C-135s in MATS. Willie was a big Beatles fan. One day he sang a little ditty to the tune of Yellow Submarine that went 'We all live in a green garbage can' etc and etc. It was about that time that I first heard the term 'trash hauler'. I have an idea the term may have originated in MATS. I started out in TAC at Pope and never heard it there. However, we rarely carried cargo except when we were TDY overseas or were on training exercises with the Army. In Việtnam, that was pretty much all we did. We had scheduled passenger missions every day but most of our missions carried general cargo - mostly ammunition and fuel, usually in barrels although some airplanes were loaded with bladders and pumps to haul it in bulk. Some missions were into forward airfields in the field and some were from the major supply bases to other facilities around the country. During my second overseas tour in 69-70, the common term for C-130s and C-123s was 'mortar magnet.'

Sam McGowan, loadmaster/flare kicker in the 35th TCS, 6315th Operations Group at Naha Air Base on Okinawa. He is the author of A*nything Anywhere Anytime and Trash Haulers and The Cave;* an exciting novel about a C-130 flareship crewmember who is shot down over Laos and declares his own personal war on the anti-aircraft gunners who shot him down.

US soldiers at Đà Nẵng Air Base in 1965.

Việtnam was formerly part of French Indo-China, together with Laos and Cambodia which lie along its western border and is bounded in the North by China. After the defeat of the French forces in July 1954 it was split into two countries, the Republic of South Việtnam and the Communist North, using the 17th Parallel as the dividing line. The victors were the Communist Việt Minh ('League for the Independence of Việtnam)[1] forces led by General Võ Nguyên Giáp and they planned to take control of the South using a new Communist guerrilla force called the Việt Công (VC) or the National Liberation Front (NLF). The VC campaign increased in intensity in 1957 until finally, in 1960, Premier Ngô Đình Diệm appealed to the United States for help. Special 'advisers' were sent in and in 1961 President Lyndon B. Johnson began the negotiations which led to total American involvement. In February 1965 the Việt Công stepped up its guerrilla war and the first American casualties in Việtnam occurred when the VC attacked US installations in the South. The US retaliated with strikes by US naval aircraft from carriers in the Gulf of Tonkin against VC installations at Đồng Hới and Vit Thu Lu. The guerrilla war escalated until in 1965, the South Việtnamese administration was on the point of collapse. The US responded with a continued build-up of military might, beginning with

Operation 'Rolling Thunder', as the air offensive against North Việtnam was called.

The first C-130 tactical transports were introduced in the Southeast Asia theatre in 1961 during the crisis in Laos. As at the outbreak of the Korean War fourteen years earlier, America was largely ill-prepared for 'conventional' warfare on the Asian mainland. PACAF was a nuclear-deterrent force, like the majority of US commands at this time, a third of its 600 aircraft being made up of F-100D/F tactical fighters. Only fifty-three C-54 and C-130A aircraft comprised its transport fleet, the majority of units being stationed in Japan, the Philippines and Taiwan. In Japan C-130As of the 815th TCS, 315th Air Division were based at Tachikawa Air Base or 'Tachi' as it quickly became known, northwest of Tokyo and those of the 35th and 817th TCS, 384th TCW, at Naha Air Base, Okinawa; a few aircraft of the 315th Air Division were also detached at Naha. In the Philippines, three squadrons operated in the 463td TCW at Clark Air Base and two others operated from Mactan Air Base. In Formosa (Taiwan) three C-130 squadrons in the 374th TCW operated from Kung Kuan Air Base.[2]

Before total US intervention in Việtnam, the PACAF Hercules had been used mainly for logistic support between the home bases and bases in Thailand and South Việtnam. After the spring of

A line up of USAF C-130As sits on the Lockheed-Georgia Company production flight line in Marietta, Georgia, in 1957 prior to delivery. One of the first Hercules built, complete with the original Roman nose, sits at the far left. The Hercules in the middle (55-0005) would eventually be left behind at Tân Sơn Nhứt AB, South Việtnam, as that country fell to Communist forces in 1975. The aircraft to its left (55-0007) was transferred to the Bolivian Air Force in 1988. The C-130A in the foreground (55-0009) was destroyed in a rocket attack at Đà Nẵng AB, South Việtnam in 1967. (Lockheed)

Paratroops of the 1st Brigade, 101st US Airborne Division during the airlift from Kontum to Phan Rang, South Viêtnam. During the spring and summer of 1966 the Brigade was transported on five occasions by the C-130s. Each deployment involved 200 Hercules lifts and each operation was mainly re-supplied by air. C-130B (58-0752) in the 463rd TCW, in the background, survived the war in SE Asia and was modified to WC-130B; later it reverted to C-130B and finally was sold to the Chilean Air Force in 1992. (USAF)

1965 however, the Hercules became the prime transport aircraft in the Pacific theatre. Its first task was to airlift troops and equipment to South Viêtnam from Okinawa: thus from 8-12 March 1965 C-130s deployed a Marine battalion landing team to Đà Nẵng; and on 4-7 May, they carried the Army's 173rd Airborne Brigade to South Viêtnam in 140 lifts. Casualties were numerous and the Hercules carried out many air evacuations.

From early 1965 C-130s from the PACAF and MATS wings were regularly rotated into South Viêtnam. More than any other aircraft, the Hercules was destined to become the workhorse of the Viêtnam War, just as the Dakota had proved itself to be in World War II. Beginning in the spring of 1965, Fairchild C-123 Providers and de Havilland Canada C-7 Caribous were stationed permanently in-country, but the transport-dedicated versions of the Hercules were rotated in and out of strips nearest the combat zones in South Viêtnam

from bases in the Pacific Air Forces (PACAF) region. Based mainly at the major airfields of Đà Nẵng, Tuy Hòa, Cam Ranh Bay and Tân Sơn Nhứt, the C-130 tactical transports were deployed to South Viêtnam on a temporary duty basis.

It soon became obvious that transports and their crews would be needed in large numbers to support US intervention in southeast Asia. The primary function of the Hercules was aerial transportation but they would have to perform many other roles besides; for infra-theatre aeromedical evacuation, as 'airborne battlefield command and control centres' (ABCCCs), AC-130 gunships, rescue aircraft, flare-dropping aircraft and even 'bombers'. In South-East Asia the Hercules was to see widespread service, not only with the USAF, but with the US Navy, the USMC (as the KC-130F), the Coast Guard and the VNAF (Viêtnamese Air Force), in what was to become a long and bloody conflict against a very determined and implacable enemy. Beginning in 1972 Project 'Enhance Plus' gave the VNAF over 900 badly needed helicopters, fighters, gunships and transports, including thirty-two hastily withdrawn C-130As from ANG units in the US. In addition, the RAAF operated C-130Es on airlift duties between Australia and South Viêtnam. These were from 36 Squadron and from 1966, 37 Squadron. From 1965 to 1975 40 Squadron RNZAF operated five C-130Hs on logistic flights between New Zealand and Saïgon and Vũng Tàu, South Viêtnam.

The only Hercules aircraft based permanently in Southeast Asia were the special mission aircraft such as flare ships, SAR aircraft, special operations aircraft and later, gunships. Starting in January 1965, C-130As and crews drawn from the squadrons at Naha, Okinawa, were attached to the 6315th Operations Group (TAC) control for use as flare ships in South-East Asia. Operating from Đà Nẵng, the flare-dropping C-130As and their crews were used mostly for the interdiction of the Viêt Công infiltration routes through Laos. The C-130As were designed to operate in conjunction with the 'fast movers' (fighter-bombers) such as the F-4 Phantom, in night strikes against VC convoys using the Hô Chi Minh Trail. Two code-names accompanied the start of the flare-dropping project.

Operations which were carried out over the 'Barrel Roll' interdiction area in northern Laos were termed 'Lamplighter', while those flown against targets in the 'Steel Tiger' and 'Tiger Hound' areas of southern Laos were known as 'Blind Bat'. (Eventually the two operational areas in Laos were merged into one and 'Blind Bat' was normally used to describe flare-dropping missions generally).

'No, bats are not blind' wrote Sam McGowan 'but we might as well have been on those dark nights over the Hô Chi Minh Trail in Laos and southern North Viêtnam. It's too bad we didn't have the senses of a bat because if we had, we might have been able to see something on the truck routes that wound their way through the dense forest beneath the wings of our C-130A. Operation 'Blind Bat' was perhaps one of the most interesting if not dangerous missions of the Viêtnam War in the years between 1964 and 1970, when the mission was terminated. Because the Communist infiltrators took advantage of the darkness of night to make their way south out of North Viêtnam, the US Air Force worked diligently to find a way to detect the nearly illusive trucks and other means of transportation by which the North sent supplies to their troops in South Viêtnam. Dropping flares from transports was nothing new in Viêtnam; the

Destroyed C-130A 55-0042 21st TCS flareship in its revetment following the mortar and sapper attack on Đà Nẵng at midnight on 30 June/1 July 1965 was evidently aimed at the ramp where there were three C-130A flareships. 55-0042 was destroyed and burnt, except for the tail section. 55-0039 was also destroyed and 55-6475 was eventually repaired and returned Stateside. Air Police Staff Sergeant Terry Jensen (35th APS) was killed in action.

A dramatic LAPES drop, somewhere in Việtnam. This tactic was a low level self-contained system capable of delivering heavy loads into an area where landing was not feasible from an optimum aircraft wheel altitude of five to ten feet above the ground. Their load, which could consist of two pallets with a total weight of up to 38,000lbs were resting on roller bearing tracks in the floor of the aircraft. Small parachutes were deployed at the proper time to jerk the cargo from the aircraft to land on the runway and theoretically come to rest in a short distance. These deliveries ceased after one eight-ton load of lumber skidded into a mess hall off the end of the runway crushing three Marines to death. Another LAPES delivery of artillery rounds ploughed through a bunker, killing two Marines.

technique had been used in World War II and Korea. In South Việtnam C-47s and C-123s flew nightly flare missions in support of ground installations that might find themselves under attack. But the C-130 'Blind Bat' mission was different; our targets were trucks, not enemy squads and we were flying interdiction missions, not support for ground forces.

'The C-130 flare mission had its beginnings sometime in 1964 when a detachment of C-130As was sent to Đà Nẵng Air Base, perhaps by way of Tân Sơn Nhứt, where the 6315th Operations Groups was maintaining a 'Southeast Asia Trainer'

mission at the time. According to the late Bill Cooke, who was one of the two navigators involved, the crews went in to brief for the night's mission and when they got back to their airplanes they discovered that they had been spray-painted black! Just when the first mission was flown is disputed. While it is known that missions were flown in November 1964 with Cat Z maintenance troops from the 21st TCS flying as kickers, the mission probably actually started many months earlier using only loadmasters who threw the flares out the paratroop doors. There is no doubt that in April 1965 the mission became semi-permanent at least and two or three C-130As were kept at Đà Nẵng until the project was cancelled and a new one was simultaneously established at Ubon AB, Thailand.

From Đà Nẵng, the C-130As of the 6315th Operations Group at Naha, Okinawa flew nightly missions out over Laos seeking out targets. The C-130s operated as part of a four-ship formation made up of the flareship, a pair of USAF B-57 Canberra attack bombers and a USMC EF-10 EWO aircraft known as 'Willy the Whale'. With the C-130 serving as a mother ship to lead the formation to the target, the team would leave Đà Nẵng and hit west and later north, to seek out the enemy and destroy him.

'Though automatic flare launchers were later developed (but never used by 'Blind Bat') the mission in the early days was very much a Rube Goldberg arrangement. The 'flare launcher' was actually an aluminium tray that had been manufactured in the Sheet Metal Shop back at Naha, while the flares were stored in wooden bins tied to an airdrop pallet. The crews were equipped with the 'finest' detection equipment - which consisted of the pilots' and navigator's eyeballs and a pair of binoculars!'

At peak strength, the 'Blind Bat' project numbered six C-130As and twelve crews, mainly derived from the 41st Troop Carrier Squadron. The first 'Blind Bat' loss occurred on 24 April 1965 (incidentally the first Hercules loss in Việtnam) when C-130A 57-0475 and its 817th Troop Carrier Squadron/6315th Operations Group crew at Korat RTAF Base hit a mountain during a go-around in

C-130B 61-0950 of TAC unloading a tank in Vietnam. This Hercules was finally retired from the Air Force in 1994 and was sold to Romania in 1996.

Coming in to land at Khâm Đức.

bad weather. The aircraft had lost two engines and was low on fuel and was carrying a heavy load. Major Theodore R. Loeschner and his five crew were killed.

'Even though the equipment was rudimentary at best, the mission evidently was a thorn in the Communist side, for on 1 July 1965 a mortar and sapper attack on Đà Nẵng was evidently aimed at the ramp where the three C-130 flareships were parked, waiting to go out on a mission. Two airplanes were destroyed in the attack and the third was damaged, along with an airlifter C-130B that had the misfortune to be parked nearby. The flareships were the first C-130s ever lost to enemy action.[3]

'The flareship mission was seen as limited successful by the Air Force, but research was begun to develop a new weapons system with both reconnaissance and attack capability that eventually led to the AC-130 gunship and the B-57G. Most of the techniques and much of the equipment used on the gunships had been developed and/or tested by 'Blind Bat' crews. Though there was still a mission for 'Blind Bat', cost considerations led the Air Force to terminate the programme in 1970 after the gunships came on the scene. Funding for the mission transferred to a new programme using modified B-57s that had been equipped with sophisticated detection equipment.

'In early 1966 the flare mission moved from Đà Nẵng to Ubon, Thailand and the flare mission changed somewhat. Instead of departing as part of a formation, the C-130 flareships began going out single-ship to patrol a specified area looking for targets. Each flareship was allotted a certain number of strike flights each evening and had the option of calling for more through the 'Moonbeam' Airborne Combat Command Centre which circled high over Laos each evening controlling airstrikes. And we received a new name as the 'Blind Bat' call sign came into use. Actually, 'Blind Bat' was one of two call signs used by the flareships with 'Lamplighter' being the other. 'Blind Bat' missions operated over Laos while the Lamplighters went north, across the Anamite Range into North Viêtnam. According to some veterans of the mission flareships at one time operated as far north as the Hànôi-Hảiphòng area, but increasing enemy defences forced the C-130s to operate further south in the 'Route Package One' and 'Two' areas south of Vinh. By 1967 the threat of SAM's in North Viêtnam caused a cessation of operations over the North.

'In the spring of 1966 shortly after I reported in to the 35th Troop Carrier Squadron at Naha, I had my introduction to the flareship mission. I was already a seasoned veteran after flying numerous airlift missions in Tactical Air Command C-130Es while on TDY from my previous base at Pope, next to Fort Bragg in North Carolina. I had even been on an airplane that took a few hits as we were landing at Đông Hà the previous November, when there was nothing there but a shack for passengers waiting to board Air Việtnam. I had flown one other mission over the north since I had reported in to my new assignment at Naha. That one had been a BS bomber missions dropping leaflets as part of Project 'Fact Sheet', the special mission my squadron bore sole responsibility for. Tonight would be different. While on previous missions we had sought to elude the enemy, tonight, on my orientation flight as an observer before our crew started missions the following evening, we were looking for him and there was almost a 100% chance we were going to find him; the chances were he was going to let us know he was there. I went in-country as the senior loadmaster of a 21st Troop Carrier Squadron crew commanded by Captain Bob Bartunek, with Captain Steve Taylor as co-pilot, Lieutenant Dick Herman as navigator, Staff Sergeant Cecil Hebdon as engineer and Airmen Mike Cavanaugh, Willy Donovan, Sam McCracken and myself as loadmaster/flare kickers. 'To say that our tour at Ubon was exciting is an understatement. Every other night our crew took off sometime between just before dark and midnight and headed northeast; out over Laos and sometimes up into North Việtnam. No, we were not shot at every time we flew, at least not that we could see, but we were certainly shot at enough! My introduction to North Việtnamese anti-aircraft came about within the first five minutes after we penetrated the skies of North Việtnam. Excitement

gripped the pit of my stomach as I heard the pilot say, 'Go ahead and depressurize, so the loads can put out the chute.

'I signalled to the rest of the crew to go ahead and open the aft cargo door slightly to extend the aluminium flare chute. As soon as the chute had been placed into the narrow opening between the raised C-130 ramp and the partially open door, one of the other loadmasters used the hand pump to pressurize the system and force the door down on the chute to hold it in place. I could feel the pressure in my ears as the flight engineer opened the outflow valve and allowed pressure to escape to bring the inside of the airplane up to the 10,000 feet of elevation at which we were flying. Even though there were mountains below us that reached to within a couple of thousand of feet of where we were, it was an elevation that was high enough to keep us clear of all the small arms and .50-calibre fire that the Army helicopter crews flying in South Việtnam thought was 'heavy' fire. There were big guns where we were going, dozens of 37 and 57mm anti-aircraft guns, all of which could reach us at 10,000 feet and even a few 85s, the same guns that had made the skies over Germany so deadly for my father and uncle as they flew missions in their B-24s.[4]

'When it was secure, one of the other guys climbed onto the door to take his place as the flare kicker while another stood by with a flare in his hand ready to put it in the chute when the pilot called for it.

'Since I was crew loadmaster with my own crew, I was on the interphone cord which is where

C-130B-LM 61-0969 of the 29th TAS/463rd Tactical Airlift Wing at Cam Ranh Bay in July 1969. This aircraft, which was delivered to TAC in January 1962, was sold to Argentina in February 1994.

KC-130F/R BuNo149789 of VMGR-152 which served with MAG-36 and MAW-1 at Biên Hỏa Air Force Base (Ken Roy).

I would be the next evening when we went up on our own. Tonight each of the eight members of my crew was on a mission in one of the four airplanes that were flying.

'When the pilot's words came through my headset 'load four flares' I held up four fingers. The other loadmasters put four flares in the chute and then set the fuses for an eight-second delay.

'We were approaching the Mu Gia Pass where we would drop a string to see if there were any targets in what was the most heavily defended place in southern North Việtnam.

'Drop four!'

'As the words came through my headset the guy on the door, who was also wearing a headset let fly with the four flares he was holding in place

On 28 February 1968 C-130E 64-0522 of the 779th TAS, 314th TCW was hit in the port wing by intense small arms fire on take-off from Sông Bé Army Air Field ALCE and MACV Compound in South Việtnam. Major Leland R. Filmore and his co-pilot, 1st Lieutenant Caroters, turned away and flew over a village south of the airfield but received more gunfire. The port wing tanks burst into flame that quickly engulfed the aircraft but the pilots were able to land the burning aircraft back on the runway where the courageous fire crew unsuccessfully fought to extinguish the flames though all five crew and five passengers escaped with only minor injuries before the Hercules and its cargo was completely destroyed. Major Filmore was awarded a Silver Star for his part in this event.

January 1967, South Việtnam. TAC C-130E 62-01841 of the 50th TCS at a forward airstrip having unloaded men of the 1st Infantry Division (the United States Army's oldest continuously serving in the Regular Army and officially nicknamed 'The Big Red One'). On 20 April 1974 C-130E 62-01841 departed Guam-Agana NAS on a training mission to perform touch-and-go's. Prior to one of the landings, the no. 3 or no. 4 engine had been shut down. The aircraft experienced a blow-out of tyres on the right hand main landing gear on touchdown. It yawed right, skidded across a taxiway and parking ramp narrowly missing a parked line of A-3 fighters. It finally came to rest against an embankment where the remains of the aircraft completely burned out. All six men on board were killed.

with his feet. A few seconds later the sky behind us lit up as the four flares burst into brilliance. And just as they did, I saw brilliant white winking lights on the ground somewhere below us. I was looking out the left paratroop door at the ground. Out of the lights came cherry-red balls like those fired by Roman candles. They rose slowly at first and then quickly accelerated toward us. 'I want my mother!' Those are the thoughts that went through my mind as I realized for the first time in my life that someone down there was trying to kill me.

'Our flares had no more than popped when we were greeted by cherry-red tracers, 37mm fire, coming up somewhere far below. 'I want my mother!' That was my thought when I realized someone down there was trying to kill me! But the burst of 37mm rose to burst harmlessly in the sky about 100 feet or so above us. The pilot said they

were off to our right by about the same distance, but I could have sworn they went right by my nose! It suddenly occurred to me that the next three months were going to be an exciting time.

'Now that 'Charlie' had made his presence known, we knew what area to avoid by just the right distance to keep out of the way of his shells and we went on to a typical night of flare kicking over North Việtnam. A few minutes later a flight of fighters, F-4s from Đà Nẵng arrived on station and we sent them down after the trucks that were making their way through the narrow pass.

'My tour started out during the dry season and we saw and attacked a lot of trucks, but then it went into the rainy season and truck traffic on the Trail became light. A lot of our missions were aimed at targets that had been identified from reconnaissance photographs taken earlier in the day. 'Suspected' truck parks and ammo dumps were usually the targets in such instances. Other times we would just patrol the skies looking for the lights of trucks on ground below. Since the NVA used shielded headlights, the trucks were difficult to spot. And as often as not when we did find a convoy, they would speed into the shelter of a 'village' where they were off-limits to air strikes. Yes, the US news media was lying when they told the country that 'unrestricted' air strikes were being conducted in Southeast Asia. The air strikes were very restricted, so much so that legitimate enemy targets were quite often spared.

'One of our best nights came about strictly through a series of mistakes, all of which linked together to become a triumph. We had been told during our briefing to look for a 'suspected' ammunition dump along the banks of a river in North Việtnam. Our intrepid officers had spotted the 'dump' and had called in a flight of USAF F-4s to take it out. But just about the time the fighters arrived in our area and right after Bartunek had told us to load six flares into the chute, the pilots lost sight of the target completely. If they couldn't see it, they couldn't tell the fighters were it was. The fighter pilots only had a few minutes of loiter fuel and they were starting to complain. Willy Donovan was sitting on the cargo door holding the flares in place with his feet and his legs were beginning to

ache. Bartunek was getting frustrated. Finally, Willy had had enough. He raised his feet and let the six flares slide out into the night, where they burst into a brilliance that turned the night beneath us into near-day. With the illumination, someone, I think it was Dick Herman, spotted the target again just as Bartunek was raking Willy over the coals for letting the flares go without being told to do so. Everyone settled down and got back to the business of trying to destroy the enemy.

'The first F-4, a Gunfighter out of Đà Nẵng, roared in over the target and dropped his bombs. They hit close to the target, but not close enough to do any damage. His wingman came along behind him. He not only missed the target completely, his bombs fell on the opposite side of the river nearly a mile away! But through a fluke of good fortune his bombs fell smack in the middle of the real ammo dump which was cleverly concealed and had not been detected. Even though he missed his aiming point by a mile (literally!) the errant fighter pilot destroyed the real ammo dump. We heard later that the pilot was put in for a Silver Star for the mission.

'Missing targets was a common occurrence on night missions by fighters in Southeast Asia. Every crewmember who flew the 'Blind Bat' or C-123 'Candlestick' mission can attest to the phenomenal lack of accuracy on the part of the fighter pilots,

USMC KC-130 BuNo148248 of VMGR-152 leaving Subic Bay on the island of Luzon in the Philippines for Đà Nẵng in 1969. From 1967 to 1975 the bulk of VMGR-152's missions were directly in support of action in South-East Asia. Detachments typically lasted five days and operated out of Đà Nẵng Air Base. In addition to aerial refueling and Marine Logistic (MarLog) cargo missions, VMGR 152 'GVs' dropped flares in support of ground troop operations at night. At its peak the squadron was flying 900 missions a month and continued this high tempo of operations well into 1967.

especially the F-4s. Of all the airplanes working over the Trail at night, the WW II vintage A-26 Invader was undoubtedly the best. One afternoon we went up early and worked with an A-26 near the Plain of Jars. For nearly an hour the 'Nimrod' pilot worked over the target, first dropping bombs, then napalm, then firing rockets, after that his guns and finally dropping his own load of eight flares on the supply dump. It was undoubtedly the best airshow I have ever seen.

'Along with the A-26s, the USMC and Navy A-4s were the most accurate bombers working the Trail. Air Force F-4s were undoubtedly the worst. The F-100s and A-1Es were pretty good, but they were flying mostly in South Việtnam in support of ground forces and not working over the Trail. (Navy A-1s operating from carriers operated over both North Việtnam and Laos.) The AC-47 gunship was tried over the Trail just before I got to Ubon but this was one mission the venerable old Gooney Bird was not suited for. In less than a week Charlie shot down both of the 'Spookies' and AC-47s spent the rest of the war working in South Việtnam or in the lesser defended areas of Laos. It was not until the advent of the super gunship, the AC-130 that an effective truck killer came on the scene.

'There was one area where the F-4s were good, though and that was with CBUs, or cluster bombs. The CBU had been developed for use against antiaircraft sites and the Communists were well aware that it they revealed their position, a flight of CBU-carrying F-4s would soon be on the way to take them out. Watching a CBU strike was something else. One night a particular gun made the mistake of firing on us when we were a little bit out of range. Bartunek called in a flight armed with CBUs. I watched as the F-4 drew red tracers from the enemy gun as he made his bombing run. Suddenly, tiny winking white lights erupted all over the place from which the red tracers were originating - and the red cherry balls suddenly ceased. I must admit it sort of did my heart good to witness the gun crew's destruction.

'Even though we were flying out of Thailand, we were not safe from enemy attack. One evening while my crew was out on a mission, an enemy team tried to probe the base - right outside the 'Blind Bat' enlisted men's quarters! A Chinese Nùng guard managed to sound the alarm.[5] He got off one shot with his shotgun as an NVA special ops soldier was cutting his throat. But the one shot was enough. A few shots were fired but the enemy soldier disappeared into the night.

'One evening our crew had an unusual experience. We were called out of Laos to drop flares between Ubon and the Mekong River which constituted the border between Thailand and Laos. We were told to look for helicopters on the ground.

KC-130F of VMGR-152 landing at Đông Hà in 1967.

A 2nd Battalion, 503rd Regiment, 173rd Airborne Division paratrooper leaving a C-130 during Operation 'Junction City'.

Right: Dropping supplies during Operation 'Junction City'.

It turned out that North Viêtnamese aircraft had penetrated the area, evidently to deliver supplies to insurgents in the area or an enemy team. We did not see anything. Later we learned that an F-4 had been scrambled off of Ubon and had picked up the target on his radar, but in the rush to get him off the ground, the ordinance team had failed to pull the pins on his Sidewinders. The missiles failed to fire and the unidentified airplane - probably a helicopter - got away.

'Sometime in late 1966 a 'Blind Bat' crew from my squadron, the 35th TCS, tangled with a North Viêtnamese MiG and managed to live to tell about. They were working in northern Laos when 'Moonbeam' diverted them to a point just inside the Laotian border about 120 miles west of Hànôi to provide flare support for friendlies on the ground who were under attack. The crew was busy dropping flares when they were alerted by 'College Eye', an EC-121 radar ship orbiting over Thailand that a pair of MiGs had just taken off from Giá Lam Airport and were headed their way. It takes a MiG about ten minutes to cover 120 miles and it was not long before the crew had company. No American fighters were anywhere close to their position and the 'Blind Bat' flareship was not armed. The crew had only one weapon at their disposal and that was the manoeuvrability of their airplane, combined with rugged terrain beneath them. They dived toward the ground, knowing they were over mountains and had no maps of the terrain on board the airplane. But they had radar and a sharp navigator. Using the radar to keep from hitting a ridge, the C-130 crew wove their way through the valleys while the MiGs searched for them with their own radar. The enemy fighters were so close that the energy from their search radar caused waves on the C-130 crew's set. When they got back to Ubon later that evening, the fighter pilots in the officers club were disappointed that they had missed a chance at a MiG. The C-130 crew was just glad to be alive!

'Another crew that was glad to be alive was also from the 35th TCS. Major Frank's crew was working near the Communist stronghold of Tchepone in Laos when they took a hit from a large calibre anti-aircraft gun. This particular gun was a legend. The bad guys had it mounted on a railroad car and kept it hidden inside the mouth of either a tunnel or a large cave near the city. They would roll it inside where it was impervious to air strikes and then bring back out again to take a pot-shot at a 'Yankee Air Pirate.' The 'Blind Bat' crew thought their number was up. The round set fire to their left wing and was burning brightly fed by the hydraulic

fluid in the primary system. Major Frank had rung the 'prepare to bailout' bell and was just about to sound the 'bailout' signal when the loadmasters called that the fire had gone out. After consuming all the hydraulic fluid in the system, the fire burned itself out before reaching the fuel tanks that were on either side of the dry bay in which it was burning. Still, they had problems. The airplane would still fly, but all hydraulic pressure to the ailerons had been lost. Staff Sergeant Kenney, the engineer, went in back to help the loadmasters, Airmen Benstead, Taylor, Harris and Delaney, to put the fire out. Frank and the co-pilot, Lieutenant Nelson, used all of their strength on the controls while Kenney and the loadmasters provided additional muscle pulling on tie-down straps that they had attached to the aileron bell crank. (Kenney now says they didn't use a strap, but that was the story the crew told when they got back to Naha.) They managed to bring the airplane to a safe landing at Nakon Pha'm, Thailand where each of the crewmembers kissed the ground when they jumped out of the airplane.

'Getting hit on a 'Blind Bat' mission was almost a regular occurrence, but surprisingly, casualties were fairly low. Two 'Blind Bat' flare ships were lost during the course of the war, along with their crews. Some crewmembers were wounded by flak on other missions. There was some bitter humour with the mission as well. McNorton, a loadmaster in the 21st TCS, was called 'Combat McNorton' because of his thirst for

C-130 56-0471 'Surprise Package' 'Blind Bat'.

C-130 performing a LAPES drop to the US Army 1st Cavalry Division 'The Air Mobile Division' at An Khê in Gia Lai Province in the Central Highlands region of Viêtnam in 1965

adventure. Before Seventh Air Force put a stop to it, C-130 crews frequently fired their M-16s at the ground during strikes and sometimes used flares as bombs. I set up one bombing mission myself. We dropped a load of six after setting the fuses for a long interval over the Mu Giá Pass. McNorton threw out a flare and hit a B-57 with it. As I remember, it was McNorton who came up with the 'Blind Bat' black beret and patch that flare ship crewmembers wore at Ubon.

'A navigator had an experience of rather mixed blessing sometime in 1969. By this time 'Blind Bat' had received some new equipment, including the 'Black Crow' ignition detector and other equipment, including a system that required a navigator/operator to sit in a seat mounted on the outside of one of the paratroop doors. This particular navigator was coming inside the airplane when he accidentally caught the rip cord of his parachute and extracted himself from the airplane! He made it to the ground safely where he spent an uneasy night until the helicopters came for him at

dawn. He was picked up and returned to Ubon - where there was a message waiting for him that he had been passed over for promotion and was being RIF'ed out of the service!

'Bob Bartunek reminded me of an incident that happened one night when we were - literally! - upside down in a C-130! The navigator had drifted off and let us get a little bit too close to a flak trap. When the guns opened up, the pilots saw the tracers coming right at us. For years I thought Steve Taylor was flying, but Bartunek says that on this particular evening he was flying from the right seat and Taylor was in the left seat calling fighters. I know where I was - sitting on the door holding the flares in the chute with my feet. All of a sudden our A-model Herky bird was rolling all the way over onto its back! This is no shit, Sherlock! Bartunek rolled the airplane upside down and pulled through in a split-S - which probably kept us from getting shot out of the sky. And the whole thing was so smooth that not a single one of the flares came out the tray. The navigator, who was

USAF C-130 taxiing at Đông Hà.

still half asleep when we went through the aerobatic manoeuvre, said there was no way we could have gone upside down - because his coffee had not even spilled!

'There is an amazing footnote to the story of our crew's time at Ubon on the 'Blind Bat' mission. Although I never connected the dots, our crew played a role in one of the most amazing events of the Việtnam War, although we had no idea that we were a part at the time. In February 1966 US Navy Lieutenant (jg) Dieter Dengler was shot down over Laos in an A-1 Skyraider. After evading the enemy for several hours, he was finally captured by Pathet Lao troops and because he was captured by them, he remained in Pathet Lao custody. Dengler was kept in a decrepit Laotian camp along with two other Americans, an Air Force lieutenant who had been shot down in a helicopter the year before and a kicker from an Air America C-46 that was shot down in 1963 and four Asian Air America employees who were on the same airplane. Although no one at Ubon had an inkling of the role we were playing, our nightly missions passed over the camp where the PoWs were being held and our presence was a key element in the escape plans they made. In late June a few weeks before our crew finished our tour, the seven men escaped. Dengler and Air Force Lieutenant Duane Martin went off together while the others went in different groups. The rainy season had begun and they were unable to signal the nightly C-130 as they had planned. Finally, after they had been in the jungle for about five days, Dengler and Martin managed to signal a C-130, but no rescue mission came to save them. Apparently, it was our crew.

'After almost a week in the jungle, the two airmen were weak from fatigue and illness and were starving. Martin, who was already near death from malaria, convinced Dengler to go with him to try to steal some food from a nearby village. They were spotted by a young boy and a villager rushed out and attacked them with a machete. Martin was killed by the blow and Dengler, who was kneeling beside him, jumped up and rushed the village then fled into the forest and eventually returned to the abandoned guerrilla camp where they had been hiding. Demoralized and to the point he was ready to die, Dengler determined that he make a signal that the damned C-130 crew couldn't miss! He revived the small fire he had built a few days before and put torches aside to be ready to set the flimsy huts on fire. Later that night the C-130 did come over and he burned the village to the ground! The crew did, in fact, spot his fires - it was us - and when we got back to Ubon the debriefing officers were very excited about the account. Yet, for some reason, no rescue mission was sent out. Apparently the higher-ups in intelligence decided it must not be an American.

'When no rescue force appeared, Dengler was still demoralized and he wasn't sure if he had actually seen the C-130 or was hallucinating. He woke in another tropical thunderstorm but decided to try go find one of the parachutes from one of the flares. Just before daylight he found it and reading his account of how much that piece of cloth meant to him brought tears to my eyes when I read his account. He took the parachute and put it in his knapsack and used it a few days later to signal Air Force A-1 pilot Lieutenant Colonel Eugene

Dietrich when he was finally spotted and rescued. 'None of us had an inkling that the fires we had seen that night had been set by an escaped PoW and it wasn't until Bob Bartunek and Dieter Dengler got in contact through the Skyraider Association that the pieces were put together. (Bartunek commanded an Air Force A-1 squadron later in the war.) Although I knew about Dieter's book, I had never read it until after the movie about his ordeal was released in the summer of 2007. Had I read it sooner I would have known that Dengler owed his life to the parachute from the flare we dropped over him that night.'

In the period from February 1958 until 1965 about a dozen C-130s were lost worldwide. Then from 1965 to 1972 sixty-five Hercules (including gunships) were lost in South-East Asia alone. Moreover the airlift crewmen killed or MIA numbered 269. In 1966 seven Hercules were lost in South Việtnam. In 1967 thirteen were lost. In 1968 operations intensified and the heaviest losses among Hercules in South Việtnam were recorded, with a total of sixteen C-130s being lost.

At first the US Army and the USAF held opposite views on how best to deploy troops to the combat zones. The Army considered that air mobile operations using helicopters to deploy troops was a more efficient method than the paratroop landing method initially favoured by the Air Force; moreover the USAF were convinced that fixed-wing air-landed operations would deploy more troops to a given area than a paradrop ever would. From then on, airlift aircraft were used to deposit troops, cargo, equipment and supplies, except of course on a larger scale than the Army's air mobile helicopter force, which it complemented. In the assault role the Hercules was almost as versatile as the air mobile, since the one hundred rudimentary landing strips capable of accommodating C-l 30s rarely proved an obstacle to the aircraft's excellent short field performance.

PACAF was not designed for counter-insurgency (COIN) operations and so at the outset, the first aircraft to deploy to Việtnam were mostly provided by Tactical Air Command on a rotational basis. After April 1965 four Tactical Air Command squadrons, deployed from the US on ninety-day tours of temporary duty (TDY) backed up PACAF's own four C-130 squadrons; by the end of 1965 there were thirty-two Hercules operating in-

C-130B 60-0301 turns at the end of the short runway at Bam Bleh, Việtnam on 23 November 1966. The transport was one of several taking troops of the First Cavalry Division back to their base camp at Ăn Khê after an operation. Air Force aircraft made daily flights to fields like this one carrying troops and supplies to front line units. This aircraft was delivered to TAC in May 1961 and ended its days in 3 Squadron, Royal Jordanian Air Force from December 1973 to June 1979.

Supplies being dropped to ground troops during Operation 'Junction City' in Tây Ninh Province in February 1967.

country, positioned at four bases. All came under the unified control of the Common Service Airlift System (CSAS) and its Airlift Control Center (ALCC) which were subordinate to 834th Air Division, organized on 25 October 1966 at Tân Sơn Nhứt AB in the suburbs of Saïgon and responsible to the Seventh Air Force for tactical airlift within South Việtnam. ALCC functioned countrywide through local airlift control elements, liaison officers, field mission commanders and mobile combat control teams. ALCC also controlled the C-130s that were rotated into South Việtnam on one- and two-week cycles from the 315th Air Division in Japan.

In 1965 two US Army paratroop brigades were held in Việtnam as a central reserve force quickly available for offensive or reaction operations. In August the 173rd Airborne Brigade was airlifted from Biên Hòa to Pleiku in central Việtnam in 150 Hercules flights. During 'Operation New Life-65', which began on 21 November the 173rd made a helicopter assault into an improvised airstrip forty miles east of Biên Hòa; seventy-one C-130s arrived over the next thirty-six hours to resupply them, the first landing within an hour of the initial assault. Meanwhile, for twenty-nine days

beginning on 29 October the C-130s kept the 1st Cavalry Division supplied during operations against Piel Me, a small Special Forces camp about halfway between Buôn Ma Thuột (Ban Me Thout) and Pleiku.[6] The Việt Công had laid siege to the camp and the US, South Việtnamese and Montagnard native allies fought them in daily fire-fights with air support by helicopters and fighter bombers. Using a rough airstrip at Catecka Tea Plantation near the battle area the C-130s delivered on average 180 tons of supplies and munitions per day.[7]

On 20 November Captain John Dunn's crew in the 774th TAS, 463rd Tactical Airlift Wing made another in their series of flights, to Pleiku, Đà Nẵng and then Tân Sơn Nhứt. First Lieutenant (later Lieutenant Colonel) Bill Barry, a native of Scranton, Pennsylvania and a fully fledged Tactical Airlift navigator on his second tour[8] recalled:

'We were making our last airlift stop of the day. As we pulled into the cargo area at Đà Nẵng. ALCE (Airlift Control Element) told us we'd be going from there to Tan Son Nhut (Tân Sơn Nhứt) but there would be a longer than usual delay to reload because some higher priority missions were coming in just behind us.

'Captain John Dunn was an ex-fighter pilot (F-100s), new to airlift and having to look after a crew rather than just himself for the first time; but he was a good pilot and a nice guy. Married, he was in his thirties and had a wife and two boys. Hal Thorson, an ex-farm boy and college wrestler, was the co-pilot. Like me, he was a totally new trainee. Quiet and good natured, Hal was married and had a son. Hal was my age, mid-twenties. John, Hal and I were commissioned officers. Then there were the enlisted men (also known comically as the 'enlisted swine'). Ed Frame was our flight engineer. A sergeant with several years of experience as an aircraft mechanic, he was new to flying and being a crew member. His job was to monitor the cockpit instruments and watch for and correct, when possible, any mechanical problems, instrument errors, or engine fluxes which took place in flight. Finally, our loadmaster was a young airman, Carl Gross. He was about 20, big and lively and a novice like Hal, Ed and me. His job was to move the cargo, tie it down so it wouldn't move in flight, or roll on takeoff or landing. He also monitored the rear of the airplane in the air and threw the switches and locks that held the palletized cargo in place during airdrops. Most crews were a mix of new guys and veterans. Ours was less experienced than most of the others. Dunn's hands were going to be fuller than most. Though he was a good, experienced pilot, he had

no experience in TAC airlift and that was a big factor. The other four of us on the crew were all inexperienced in numerous ways, as we were soon to find out. There were a lot of young aviators mixed in with veteran flyers to make up the 24 crews the squadron had. Usually, all 24 were never present at any one time, someone always being TDY. The crews, together with a small number of personnel from Wing, flew all our assigned missions in the twelve aircraft the squadron had. The crews also performed all the planning, alert and administrative functions of the squadron. Everyone had one or more other tasks in addition to flying the line.

'Now we sat in the cockpit of our plane and watched another of our Wing's C-130s pull into the Đà Nẵng cargo area next to us. We recognized the call sign and even the co-pilot's voice as he asked the ALCE for offload instructions as the plane taxied in after landing. They parked off to our left and slightly behind us. From our cockpit windows we could see the unusual number of fire trucks and ambulances which were following them as they shut down their engines and prepared to offload. We weren't paying too much attention until Carl Gross came over our rear interphone system and said, 'Look at the crew scatter from that plane!' As soon as their propellers had stopped spinning and they were clear to come out of the cockpit, the entire crew ran from the stopped aircraft as if they

USAF C-130As and E's of the 817th TAS/374th TAW (YU) and 776th TAS/314th TAW (DL) and a C-123 on the line in Việtnam.

36

South Việtnamese civilians assist with construction of an airbase in South Việtnam.

were evading a cockpit fire. They then stood away from the plane at a distance of thirty yards. Now our interest was up.

'Since our on-load was going to be delayed, we had nothing better to do than walk over to see what the problem was with the other aircraft. We knew the entire crew, who were part of our temporary duty unit back at Clark and from another squadron in our Wing at Langley. We walked up to them and asked what the problem was that had caused their rapid and unorthodox departure from the cockpit. No one answered directly. They only told us to go take a look. They all appeared somewhat antagonized and hostile to our approach and questions.

'I mounted the steps leading to the cockpit and forward cargo area of the aircraft. The plane had been rigged for Personnel Air Evacuation. In this procedure, the C-130 had a series of metal stanchions which clipped into the floor and ceiling and created a U-shaped aisle formation inside the cargo compartment. Using the stanchions for support, a web of heavy nylon straps clipped into them and intermeshed into triple tiered levels of stretcher supports in the manner of the old Pullman railroad bunks. In the aircraft there were 50 or 60 individual stretchers, three levels high, in four aisles around the cargo compartment.

'Slowly and silently, together with the rest of our crew, I walked down the aisle on the right side of the cargo compartment between the two rows of three stretcher tiers. I took a left turn at the end of the aisle and walked forward to the flight station wall down the second aisle on the other side of the plane, also bounded on both sides by three high stretcher tiers. I noted that the plane was almost at the maximum number of stretchers that it could carry in this rigging assembly. Each stretcher contained one green body bag. In some of the bags the outline of a soldier could be traced horizontally from the feet to the head. In others, the occupant appeared contorted. Some were clearly less than a complete body. One, about the size of a basketball, sat alone on its stretcher, taking up little more than a quarter of the stretcher space. It was held in place by a seat strap. Most of the stretchers had a pair of boots and a dog tag fastened to them.

'They Were Dead. They Were All Dead! This Was an Airplane Full of Dead Men.'

'My walk through the darkened aircraft took less than five minutes. During that time I smelled the sickening sweet odour that permeated the entire craft. I noticed it as soon as I entered the cargo hold, but it wasn't initially overwhelming or disturbing. The longer I stayed in the compartment, the stronger a contaminated sweet portion of the overall odour came to the fore. This smell had driven the aircrew from the plane as soon as the doors were opened after their fifty minute flight. The build-up of this nauseous aroma within the sealed aircraft had made them all nearly airsick. In carrying only a very limited number of bodies in the past, such a smell had never before permeated an entire aircraft as this load did. It was a smell never to be forgotten, but one we would become increasingly familiar with.

'I exited the aircraft and exchanged words with the flight crew. The bodies were the results of the recent Ia Drang battle in the Central Highlands. All of the dead men were Americans. They had been loaded on the C-130 at Pleiku, the closest main airbase to the battle site and had been sent to Đà Nẵng since it held the only US mortuary in Việtnam at the time. There were two more similarly configured and loaded C-130s coming in to land behind this one. We returned to our airplane where a load of palletized cargo bound for Tân Sơn Nhứt was now ready to be put on. At the other C-130, the rear cargo door had been opened and the body laden stretchers were being put into waiting ambulances. As we took off for Saïgon, we heard the other two planes from Pleiku call in for landing and parking instructions.'[9]

'The C-130 was very accommodating to the Tactical Airlift role. It was ugly, slow and not jet propelled. Mounting four turboprop engines, it was capable of carrying 40,000lbs of cargo 2,500 miles. It had floor mounted cargo rails which allowed palletized cargo to be quickly slid in and out directly through the rear door and ramp. In an hour, the five man crew could pull up the cargo rails and put down seats or litter bearing straps. The plane could then take fifty paratroops on an airdrop or carry seventy passengers to a distant destination. In similar fashion, it could also carry fifty hospital patients, each in his litter. The C-130 was fully pressurized and cruised at 20,000 feet at 300 knots. It could take off in 1,500 feet or in 2,000 with a sizable load. It could land and come to a complete stop in less than 2,000 feet and operated easily from 3,500 and 5,000 foot airstrips. It was an all-weather, 24 hour a day machine with its own airborne radar and navigation equipment. Ugly, but practical and relatively cheap, the 130 was ahead of its time and a wonderful combination of '50s

Lieutenant Colonel Ron Dudley's C-130A transport crew when he (centre squatting with dark hair) was flying secret missions from Korat Royal Thai Air Force base in Thailand in 1967 during one of his three deployments to Việtnam.

technology suited to the Tactical Airlift mission. Normally it had a crew of five, including a pilot, co-pilot, navigator, flight engineer and loadmaster.' In March 1966 the 'Blind Bat' project relocated to Ubon, Thailand and that same year the 6315th Operations Group control was replaced by the 374th Troop Carrier Wing, later designated a Tactical Airlift Wing. Ronald Edward Dudley, born 28 January 1934, from Roanoke, Alabama flew the C-130A on three tours in Viêtnam. Much of the time, from 1966 to 1969, he served with the 41st Tactical Airlift Squadron, 345th Air Wing flying out of Okinawa in the Japanese home islands.

'Twenty-one days a month my five man crew and I would fly into Southeast Asia in my C-130A. It was the best airplane I ever flew; it was superb. Our general mission was to resupply and support our ground troops. We could handle 100 paratroopers combat loaded or 74 people if you put them in seats. Sometimes I'd fly in small tanks or armoured personnel carriers. I put one personnel carrier into a 1,900-foot strip and three months later I went back in and flew it out. I had some missions over North Viêtnam, but most of my missions were over Laos as a forward air controller. We flew in at night dropping flares at 1,500 feet so out bombers could see the targets. We took part in some secret missions in Laos flying out of the Royal Thai Air Base. At night we'd fly down Highway 1 in Laos and North Viêtnam looking for targets of opportunity to bomb. If we found a target we'd call in an air strike. On an average night you would take 100 rounds of 37mm anti-aircraft fire from VC gunners. On the worst night we took just short of 1,000 rounds. Our loadmaster, Sergeant Don Brant, came up with a name for our plane: *Super Dud and the Do-lighters*. This became our call sign until the VC caught on. The fighter planes we worked with would call in and I'd say *Good Evening. You're about to be entertained by Super Dud and the Do-lighters*. I had to stop using that call sign because the VC, the bad guys, would call on our frequency and say: *Super Dud, good to see you. We're gonna have fun tonight*.

During one secret mission over Laos one night the VC antiaircraft unit set up a flak trap. They were waiting specifically for Dudley and his C-130 to arrive. The enemy somehow already had the secret frequency he was given just before taking off from the base in Thailand.

'When we flew into the area the VC radio welcomed us by saying, *Super Dud you have just moved to the top of the money chart. There is now a $250,000 bounty on your heads. We have imported several Number-10 (top) gunners. Tonight is your last night. I'm gonna be rich tomorrow. We had a little problem at the original sight so we moved it eight clicks up the road.*

Dudley flew over the designated area and was beginning his decent to 1,500 feet where he would begin to patrol the area for the next six hours. 'All of a sudden there was a flicker on the ground. I realized immediately what had happened. The VC had lured me into a trap. They opened up on us with five 37mm guns. Lucky for me I was at 8,000 feet when they started shooting at us. If they had waited until I got down to 1,500 feet I would have been a dead duck. I only had to climb 5,000 to 6,000 feet to get out of the range of their guns. It

C-130s being loaded at Phan Rang Air Base in June 1967.

On 13 April 1968 C-130B 61-0967 of the 774th TAS, 463rd TAW with seven crew was landing at Khê Sanh when it suffered an engine failure and suddenly veered off the runway. The aircraft hit six recently dropped pallets, still containing cargo and then continued into a truck and a forklift vehicle before coming to a halt and bursting into flames. The aircraft was damaged beyond repair but all the crew were rescued, although a civilian who was on board later died of his injuries.

seemed like it took us twenty hours to get out of range. In reality it was only two or three minutes. But during those minutes we could hear stuff from what the enemy was firing at us hitting our plane. We finally made it back to base at 0300. I had just gotten to bed when an aide to Colonel Drummond, our squadron commander, knocked on my door and said he wanted to see me right away. I got dressed and the aide drove me out to the flight line where the commander was waiting.

'*What happened to you all tonight?*' the colonel inquired.

'I told him, *I got stuck in a flak trap and got shot up*.

'*You got 97 holes in the airplane*, the commander said incredulously.

'*Yea, but nobody got hurt*, I replied.

'The next night I was right back up their flying.

When I checked in on the radio the same oriental VC voice on the ground said to me, *Did you have fun last night?*

'I told him *You can take your radio and stick it where the sun won't hit it*.'

In 1967 Dudley and his C-130 was taking part in a test programme in Viêtnam to perfect a low altitude extraction system for equipment they were trying to drop off while under fire or in areas where there was insufficient landing space. 'I dropped the first extraction under fire at a little Army outpost along the Cambodian Border called Cam Duc. Another plane had flown into the base before me and got all shot up by quad .50 calibre machine guns the VC had at the end of the runway. I came down through a hole in the clouds too steep to escape the enemy machine-guns. Because I was too steep the balled up parachute that was suppose to pull the loaded pallet out the back of the airplane dropped back inside the plane. I had to come around a second time. On the second pass Sgt Brant, my loadmaster, went back behind the hot load that was ready to go, picked up the parachute and tossed it out. Then he stood in the wall of the plane when the pallet was dragged out after the chute opened. The skid went out the back of the plane that was flying 180 mph just above the ground and skidded to a stop within a few feet of the waiting soldiers.'[10]

The 41st TAS lost two more 'Blind Bat' C-130As to enemy action over Laos in 1968-1969. On 22 May 1968 C-130A 56-0477 with a crew of nine captained by Lieutenant Colonel William Henderson Mason was shot down on a flare mission to southern Laos near Muang Nong about twenty miles southwest of the A Shau Valley (thung lũng A Sầu) in Thừa Thiên-Huế Province west of the coastal city of Huế, where another aircraft had reported a large fire on the ground. On 24 November 1969 C-130A 56-0533 a 'Blind Bat'

A C-130E comes in for a landing in January 1968 at the airstrip at Đông Hà combat base, South Việtnam where men of US Naval Construction Battalion Maintenance Unit 301 are repairing the runway. (USN)

Forward air control aircraft flown by Captain Earl Carlyle Brown was orbiting at 9,000 feet in the Ban Bak area to the east of Saravan in southern Laos. The aircraft was above a 4,000 feet cloud base when it was hit by several rounds of 37mm flak and burst into flames, crashing about fifteen miles east of Bạn Talan. All eight men on board were killed. A third 'Blind Bat' - C-130A 56-0499 - crashed on an attempted three-engine take-off from the small airstrip at Bu Dop near the South Việtnamese border with Cambodia on 13 December 1969. The strip often suffered from enemy mortar attacks and three-engined departures were not uncommon as they were preferable to staying on the ground overnight until spares could be flown in. Three successful three-engined take offs had been made by C-130s from Bu Dop in recent months but the fourth attempt failed.[11] The flare-dropping missions continued until 15 June 1970 when AC-130 hunter-killer gunships took over: with electronic detection and image-intensifying night observation equipment and a 1.5 million candlepower searchlight. They were by now better equipped than the 'Blind Bat's for the task of identifying and destroying enemy troop and transport convoys using the Hồ Chi Minh Trail.

On 19 June 1966 after a week of not flying, Captain John Dunn's crew left Mactan at 9:00 in the morning on their return to the shuttle. 'We passed through Clark, as usual' wrote Bill Barry 'and picked up a load of cargo and passengers for Đà Nẵng and Tân Sơn Nhứt. We landed in Saïgon as the daily replacement aircraft at 6:30 in the evening. We left Tân Sơn Nhứt and checked into the Globe. Unfortunately, the hotel was all but full for the first time and since rooms were short, our crew checked into just two suites rather than three rooms. The two enlisted members stayed in one suite and we three officers checked into another. It was a time for real togetherness. The next day, we headed out to the base about noon but found that our aircraft was being worked on by maintenance. We drew a version of the passenger run as our first mission, but it was four in the afternoon before we got off the ground. We flew clockwise to An Khê, then Chu Lai, Đà Nẵng, then back to Chu Lai because there was a large marine influx in that area all of a sudden. Then we went to Đà Nẵng to pick up a cargo load, which we took back to Saïgon. It was fifteen minutes after midnight when we finally landed and shut down the engines.

'The next day, we left the hotel at noon and ate on base at the officers' club. We checked into 130 Ops and were scheduled for a cargo hauling mission with a 4:30 takeoff. Our first stop was the army base at An Khê, where we picked up cargo and passengers. We flew from An Khê in the Central Highlands due east to the coast and then south to a new army base which was being established at Tuy Hòa, a large plain on the coast. To the north of it was a river clearly identifiable on my radar. The base itself, however, was not a good radar target, as the runway blended into the coastal plain and, other than distance from the river, there was nothing to distinguish it from the plain itself. We quickly offloaded the cargo and troops through the back door and ramp with our engines running and were airborne again in five minutes. It was still daylight, but the sun was setting and the field had a low cloud cover over it which appeared to be decreasing in height. It was also lightly raining.

'It was only a twenty minute flight back to An Khê and we returned there to pick up another similar mixed load also bound for Tuy Hòa. It took forty minutes to get the new load onboard and we again set off for Tuy Hòa. When we got abeam Tuy Hòa this time, it was beginning to get dark due to a combination of the time of day and the steadily increasing cloud build-up and rain around the base. Again, we landed visually, offloaded quickly and got airborne in less than five minutes.

'Now, with an empty aircraft, we flew 25 minutes down the coast to Cam Ranh Bay, where we were supposed to pick up cargo and take it to Tân Sơn Nhứt. It took us nearly an hour to get offloaded and put a pallet on at Cam Ranh Bay. We then took off and proceeded east for a return to Saïgon. Just after we were airborne, the Cam Ranh Bay ALCE called and told us that things had taken a turn for the worst back at Tuy Hòa and we were to turn around and go back to An Khê for another

load to take into Tuy Hòa. As directed, we turned around and flew back to An Khê.

'It was now dark in the An Khê valley and the base's approach radar was again out of commission. There was a low cloud layer over the base just a hundred or so feet above our minimums. We first attempted a prescribed letdown, flying with the base radio antenna as our guidance; but when we hit our minimums the runway was not in sight. My radar was working, so we next attempted another radio approach with me giving final guidance and altitude levels using the radar as the primary aid. The base runway showed up well on the radar, but the valley was not all that big and had a 3,000 foot mountain less than ten miles south of the runway. Right next to the runway was a 500 foot high karst hill. We made our approach in a southerly direction, staying to the east of the hill just as we had earlier when I was flying with John Dunn and we evacuated a medical case. In the event of a missed approach, the pilot was to immediately climb to 1,500 feet, thus keeping us above the hill while circling counter-clockwise to avoid the mountain.

'On our second radar assisted approach, we

Quảng Trị US Marine Corps, US Army and ARVN Combat Base on Highway 1 about 8 kilometres southeast of Đông Hà in April 1967.

One of the RAAF C-130 Hercules in 1966 that beat a regular path to Việtnam, transporting troops and supplies and taking the wounded home. (Bert Lane)

broke out just in time to see the lighted runway, but we were not lined up with it so we climbed back into the clouds and circled for another attempt. The third attempt was successful. We were on the ground after an hour of shooting approaches to get down in the weather and black night. The flight would usually have taken 25 minutes. It took an hour for the army to load us up with pallets of ammunition and then we were off again for Tuy Hòa.

'We were inbound to Tuy Hòa in twenty minutes, but now it was also night over the South China Sea. It was still raining and the cloud layer had thickened. Just as at An Khê, we were just 100 or 200 feet above our minimum approach altitude. Tuy Hòa did not yet have radar or even an approach radio to use for a landing aid. We were cleared for an approach, again using the radar and me as our main aids. The radar, however, did not paint the field at Tuy Hòa; so the approach was planned as a turn so many seconds after we came abeam of the river, which sat a half mile to the north of the Base. The river did give a strong radar return. Tuy Hòa sat just inland from the coast and the nearest mountains were ten or fifteen miles east of the runway. Our missed approach plan was to climb straight ahead to 1,000 feet and then circle to the south and back out over the ocean for another attempt.

'On the first approach, we let down over the ocean in the dark and flew south, 90 degrees off the heading of the Tuy Hòa runway. At 1,000 feet, we couldn't see anything on shore because the rain and cloud layer had blocked out all light. Twenty-five seconds after the radar showed me that we were abeam the river we turned to the runway heading. I corrected the heading to make up for drift, which read out on the Doppler above my desk. We then descended at 150 feet per mile, hoping to break out of the clouds in time to see and line up with the runway. On the first attempt, we didn't break out by the time we hit our minimums at 500 feet. We began our go-around turn and suddenly, off to the right, we could see three lights or flare pots set up on the extremities of a barely visible runway. Two lights marked the approach end and the last light sat in the middle of the runway's far end.

'We climbed back up to 1,000 feet and proceeded out over the ocean and repeated our approach pattern. This time we turned twenty seconds after passing the river on radar. We hit 600 feet altitude and suddenly broke out of the clouds and rain. In front of us, in good visibility were the three lights perfectly aligned but as we moved in closer, the lights begin to shift. Suddenly the three evenly spaced lights were now bunched to the right. We weren't lined up and the light at the far end moved toward the light at the right front. We now initiated another missed approach. Three lights of approximately equal size and intensity can take on numerous designs and undergo rapid shifts if you are not lined up exactly with them. We all knew this from having practiced numerous night paradrops where the drop zone was marked by the same light pattern as the Tuy Hòa airbase. But we had just learned the lesson again in the rain and fog.

'Our next approach followed the same pattern, except we turned at 23 seconds past the river. Now we broke out again at 600 feet, but this time we could clearly see that we had lined up with the runway. Again we were on the ground after an hour in the air on what would normally have been a 20 minute flight. The army rapidly unloaded the ammunition pallets. Artillery was firing just off to the side of the parking area as we turned back on the runway and proceeded back to An Khê. It again took two tries to get on the runway at An Khê due to the low cloud base and the lack of any night-time approach aid except our own radar.

'At 1:15 in the morning, we took off with another load of ammunition. As we approached Tuy Hòa from over the ocean, we could see that the rain had stopped and the cloud layer had thinned out and lifted. We proceeded in and landed visually with no further problems, using the three marking lights as our landing reference. The army was still firing artillery off as we unloaded, but the pace was much reduced from the previous landing.

After fifteen minutes on the ground, we were unloaded and back in the air.

'An hour later we landed at Tân Sơn Nhứt and called it a night at 2:30 in the morning. The combination of the bad weather at both landing sites and the lack of any reliable approach aid other than our own radar made this an interesting and hairy night of flying. Each night-time approach was hazardous. We could have all used a drink before turning in; but the club was closed, so it was back to the Globe for an attempt at a night's sleep. 'That evening we were again airborne at 9:30 and shuttled with cargo between An Khê, Đà Nẵng and Chu Lai. We got back into Saïgon at 5:00 in the morning. On landing we were told that our crew had been submitted for a medal citation to each receive a DFC for the previous night's flights into An Khê and Tuy Hòa.

'That was the second DFC I was recommended for. I never got either one.'[12]

By the summer of 1966 PACAF's permanently assigned C-130 strength stood at twelve squadrons

KC-130F BuNo148892 of VMGR-152. This Hercules was delivered to the USMC in May 1961. In around 1975 it was transferred to VMGR-234 at NAS Glenview, Illinois. In January 1994 it was transferred to VMGRT-253 at MCAS Cherry Point, North Carolina. In October 1997 it was permanently withdrawn from use and in November it went to the Fort Worth Joint Reserve Base at Dallas-Fort Worth, Texas and used as a maintenance trainer.

and this reached a peak of fifteen units early in 1968 with three deployed TAC squadrons on TDY tours. Thus in February 1968 a total of ninety-six C-130s were stationed in Việtnam: the huge port complex at Cam Ranh Bay was home to fifty-one C-130As and -Es; Tân Sơn Nhứt accommodated twenty-seven C-130Bs; Tuy Hòa had ten C-130Es; and Nha Trang, eight C-130Es. By the end of 1971 only five C-130 squadrons remained in the Pacific, although the VNAF airlift force operated two squadrons. Two squadrons were equipped with C-130As just before the 1973 ceasefire.

During the spring and summer of 1966 the 1st Brigade, 101st 'Screaming Eagles' Airborne Division, was transported on five occasions by the C-130s; each deployment involved 200 Hercules lifts and each operation was mainly resupplied by air. Operation 'Birmingham' was a four-week air deployment into Tây Ninh province beginning on 24 April in which the C-130s flew fifty-six sorties into the 4,600 feet airstrip, delivering supplies and munitions around the clock. (At the same time they also supplier, the airborne brigade at Nhơn Co.) By

the time 'Birmingham' ended on 17 May, the C-130s and C-123s had flown almost 1,001 sorties and delivered nearly 10,000 tons of cargo for the 1st Cavalry Division.

The USMC also played a part in airlift operations. By July 1966 the road network north of Đà Nẵng was in a state of disrepair - though in any event, Communist activity had made transport by convoy extremely hazardous, while port facilities and ail fields near the DMZ were poor. Therefore the only way to resupply the marines in country was by air. USMC KC-130Fs backed up by USAF Hercules, flew more than 250 lifts into a red dirt strip at Đông Hà . Further C-130 flights to the area delivered large quantities of materials and PSP steel matting and the airstrip was later resurfaced; a second all-weather strip we opened at Quảng Tri.

In late June 1966 Captain John Dunn's crew were nearly halfway through their assigned thirteen month tour. 'On 27 June' wrote navigator Bill Barry 'we were up at 3:00 in the morning and again took the crew vehicle to the base. Same routine as

South Việtnamese troops leaving a battle zone after landing in C-130E 63-7883. This aircraft was delivered to MAC in June 1964.

South Viêtnamese troops milling around C-130A 56-0489. This Hercules was delivered in May 1957 and after service in TAC was allocated to the SVAF in November 1972. It was one of many aircraft captured by the NVA in April 1975.

the day before, but this time the airplane worked and we were off to the small runway at Sông Bé and another Army 'search-and-destroy' operation. Sông Bé is forty miles North of Saïgon. The bare runway with no parking area sat just adjacent to a 200 foot mountain in an otherwise flat plain. Lộc Ninh is fifteen miles due west of Sông Bé and both sit within ten miles of the Cambodian border.

'All day we made seven shuttles between the two sites, hauling army troops and equipment in rapid onload/offload operations where the troops and vehicles rolled on and off through the rear ramp and door while our engines were running. It was hot and dusty and the aircraft's broken air conditioner would not have been of any use on the short flights anyway. Halfway through the day we returned to Tân Sơn Nhứt for fuel and an hour on the ground. We finally landed back at Tân Sơn Nhứt for good at 10:30 that night. We logged five and a half hours of flying time in an eighteen and a half hour day with twelve separate individual sorties flown.

'The variety of loads that we were carrying was in some ways funny and in others amazing. Probably only the C-130 could safely accommodate them all and that is in spite of the many errors and miscalculations that kept them from having any kind of 'ordinary.' Largely for these reasons, the Tactical Airlift mission and its crews became known as 'trash hauls and trash haulers' since, like garbage men in the states, they would haul anyone and anything.

'When we picked up a load from the army, it was their responsibility to identify the load and correctly indicate its weight and contents. Many army loads included large metal Conex containers, which they used to store everything from ammunition to the personal belongings of units which were moving or going into the field. We were used to moving the containers to storage areas or to the deploying unit's next location.

'Many, many times the loading data for the containers gave an incorrect weight for them. On other occasions the weight was given for an empty container when in fact the container was loaded to the fullest with something or other. Sometimes it became apparent that the container was mislabelled when the forklift putting it on the aircraft had trouble lifting the listed weight. At other times, several palletized containers might be loaded and each of them would weigh more than listed, but not enough to, individually, indicate that something was wrong.

'The same could be said for many of the army trucks, jeeps and trailers that we loaded and carried. Our loadmaster planned each load according to the listed weights so that the airplane maintained the best centre of gravity for performing according to standards for both flying and takeoff and landing. When the actual load was widely off from what was listed, the aircraft would either tilt on its tail or give indications of sinking on its front nose wheel. Many times we had to raise our legs to get in the crew door on the steps which should have been resting comfortably on the ground. On occasion I've even had to physically climb up the steps to get in the door. Thank God the C-130 handled so well and was so forgiving.

'One load that we had was a five pallet shipment of army boots packed in large cardboard boxes. The boxes were oversize commercial moving containers about four feet square by five feet high. They were stacked two high and tied down so that twenty or so boxes were on each pallet. The pallets had been sitting in the Tân Sơn Nhứt cargo storage hangar for some time. Once we were in-flight carrying the boots to an army base, several of the boxes collapsed inward or caved in. Some were completely empty and others had half a load of boots in them. Between their original destination and our flight to their final one, they had been looted. I doubt if the whole load had more than one-quarter of the number of boots in it that we cited on the loading document.

'Another time, our load was the cannon barrels for 155mm or 175mm guns. Each of the guns sat on two wooden frames, which they fit into on each end of the gun. They were palletized on three interlocked pallets and secured to individual pallets by metal bands running over the wooden frames. Carl figured out the proper loading for them as far as the plane's centre of gravity was concerned. They were long and heavy and with the loading end larger than the firing end, an unusual load. When the loading crew pushed the triple palleted guns onto the aircraft, the metal band on the rear pallet of one of the guns broke when crossing the point where the rollers on the rear door of the plane met the body. The long narrow end of the gun pivoted upward, held in place only by the metal band on the opposite wooden frame, which was on the first pallet inside the aircraft. As the gun barrel swung upward, it stopped just short of going through the ceiling of the aircraft.

'Another load to be avoided was a plane full of Việtnamese troops when they were 'combat loaded' Usually when we carried troops or passengers of any sort, they were seated in nylon strap seats which folded down from the side walls of the C-130 or were secured by ceiling mounted stanchions and straps. But when we carried Việtnamese troops in combat gear, we usually put

John Steinbeck over Việtnam in a helicopter while reporting the war in 1967.

HC-130P refuelling a HH-53B over North Việtnam.

five pallets on the floor rollers and stretched nylon straps across them secured to the sidewalls. By doing this, we could get twice as many troops on board (more than 150 versus 92 seated) as we could by giving them individual seats. When this mass of humanity got onboard, however, if someone needed to go to the rear of the aircraft for any reason he had to wade through them in-flight. That was not a pleasant experience, since our allies, the Việtnamese, liked to goose, fondle and sexually stroke male flyers in that atmosphere. They also shared an Asian affinity for holding hands when there were two males together in close proximity. 'During the conflict the C-130 carried a variety of loads under all sorts of conditions, from normal operations as well as emergency introduction and extraction missions in the face of combat, poor weather and sometimes both. During 1965 and 1966 some of the passenger and troop carrying runs included chickens and little potbellied pigs.

Later in the war, when the Việtnamese organized a loading organization and the issuance of flight passes, creatures such as these were no longer seen. The all time champion animal load, however, has got to be the elephants. A small Việtnamese village somewhere in I Corps up near Đà Nẵng had a lumbering operation as their main industry and they used elephants to do their hauling. Somehow or other, deliberately by the Việt Công or as the accidental result of firing, all of the local elephants were killed and the village was left without a livelihood. Enter the US Civil Affairs folks, who saw restoring the village to prosperity as one means of winning the hearts and minds of the people. The elephants were slated to return and the C-130 was chosen to deliver them.'

John Steinbeck the famous novelist and WWII reporter had been asked in 1965 by President Lyndon Johnson to visit South Việtnam and report to him personally on US operations. (Steinbeck's

A C-130 making a LAPES drop in Việtnam.

third wife, Elaine and Lady Bird Johnson had been friends at college and the Steinbecks were frequent visitors to the White House.) Steinbeck was reluctant to go to Việtnam on behalf of the president, but when the Long Island daily *Newsday* suggested that he travel throughout Southeast Asia as a roving reporter, he accepted. By that time, his two sons were serving in the Army.[13] In January 1967 Steinbeck took a ride in a C-130 and wrote about it.

'Did you know that the airport at Saigon is the busiest in the world, that it has more traffic than O'Hare field in Chicago and much more than Kennedy in New York - Well it's true. We stood around - maybe ten thousand of us all looking like overdone biscuits until our plane was called. It was not a pretty ship this USAF C-130. Its rear end opens and it looks like an anopheles mosquito but into this huge anal orifice can be loaded anything smaller than a church and even that would go in if it had a folding steeple. For passengers, the C-130 lacks a hominess. Four rows of bucket seats extending lengthwise into infinity. You lean back against cargo slings and tangle your feet in a maze of cordage and cables.

'Before we took off a towering sergeant (I guess) whipped us with a loud speaker. First he told us the dismal things that could happen to our new home by ground fire, lightning or just bad luck. He said that if any of these things did happen he would tell us later what to do about it. Finally he came to the subject nearest his heart. He said there was dreadful weather ahead. He asked each of us to reach down the paper bag above and put it in our laps and if we felt queasy for God's sake not to miss the bag because he had to clean it up and the hundred plus of us could make him unhappy. After a few more intimations of disaster he signed off on the loud speaker and the monster ship took off in a series of leaps like a Calaveras County frog.

'Once airborne, I got invited to the cockpit where I had a fine view of the country and merciful cup of black scalding coffee. They gave me earphones so I could hear directions for avoiding ground fire and the even more dangerous hazard of our own artillery. The flight was as smooth as an unruffled pond. And when we landed at Pleiku I asked the God-like sergeant why he had talked about rough weather.

'Well, it's the Viets,' he said. 'They have delicate stomachs and some of them are first flights. If I tell them to expect the worst and it isn't, they're so relieved that they don't get sick. And you know I do have to clean up and sometimes it's just awful'.

On 3 February 1967 Captain John Dunn's crew hauled cargo to Pleiku, Đà Nẵng, Huế, Đà Nẵng again, Cam Ranh Bay and then back to Tân Sơn Nhứt. 'On the leg between Đà Nẵng and Cam Ranh Bay' wrote Bill Barry 'we experienced fluctuations on one of the engines. The load taken on at Đà Nẵng consisted of fifteen manifested army passengers, a large army truck and a small trailer which the truck towed behind. Both the truck and the trailer were filled with duffel bags and assorted other cargo.

'The army had filled out the cargo sheet for the flight and that included the weight of the load and the names and weight of all the passengers. Because we were going home to Saïgon from Cam Ranh we took the maximum gasoline load out of Đà Nẵng so we would not have to fill up again. The flight from Đà Nẵng to Cam Ranh usually ran about seventy minutes from takeoff to landing and the route was almost entirely over water.

'The day was bright and sunny and we were 30 minutes or so into the flight when we lost an engine. Accordingly, we lost some altitude and airspeed after shutting the engine down and feathering the propeller to reduce its wind drag. Almost as soon as that was done, another engine on the opposite side began to act up and looked as if it too would have to be shut down. That was when the engineer calculated that with the remainder of our fuel load and the weight of the truck and trailer in the rear, we could not stay airborne on two engines if we did shut the second one down.

'The plan immediately became to jettison the truck and trailer as soon as possible in the event the second engine was lost. By regulation, all of the manifested passengers sat forward of the truck. That is, they were seated right behind the crew cabin and fire wall in the rear of the cargo hold. The truck and its rear end full of cargo came next and then the trailer, which was chained down on the ramp. Together with the rear cargo door, this formed the sealed rear of the aircraft. The truck had been driven onto the aircraft and would exit backward out the rear end in the event of jettisoning. Both the truck and the trailer were chained down to the floor and ramp.

'Now the loadmaster undid any excess chains not likely to be needed in flight. This was in anticipation of jettisoning the load and would reduce the time necessary for undoing all of the remaining chains and then jettisoning first the trailer and then the truck. For 10 or 15 minutes, we monitored the sputtering engine and then, as suddenly as it had begun acting up, it stopped and everything was normal. By that time, we were much closer to final landing at Cam Ranh. Before long the loadmaster reconnected the chains to ensure both vehicles were secured prior to landing.

Quagmire conditions at a churned up landing strip in Việtnam after repeated rains and constant use by TAC C-130s.

Suddenly, over the interphone, Gross said, 'Hey, guess what just showed up in the back of that truck we were ready to jettison?'

'We couldn't imagine, so the reply was a simple, 'What?'

'There are six guys we didn't know about sleeping in it' he said.'

The only major US combat parachute assault of the war took place on 22 February 1967 at the start of Operation 'Junction City' when twenty-two US battalions and four ARVN battalions were airdropped in Tây Ninh and bordering provinces. Thirteen Hercules carried 846 paratroopers of the 173rd Airborne Brigade from Biên Hòa and dropped them in the drop zone at Katum near the border with Cambodia. Almost thirty minutes later, ten C-130s dropped the brigade's equipment, returning in the early afternoon to carry out further cargo drops; five C-130s were hit, but they suffered no serious damage. Next day 38 Hercules flew resupply sorties and these continued for the next five days, during which daily drops averaged 100 tons. By late March, during the final stages of the operation, the C-130s carried out airdrops to a 'floating brigade', using drop-zone locations which the ground unit provided by radio. By the time 'Junction City' finished, 1,700 tons of supplies and munitions had been airdropped by the Hercules.

On four other occasions during 1967-68 small teams of US advisers from the 5th Special Forces Group were parachuted in, along with 300 to 500 Viêtnamese paratroopers. Each C-130 could carry eighty fully-equipped paratroops that were dropped in two forty-man sticks. In November 1967 C-130s lifted the 173rd Airborne Brigade to Đắk Tô in 250 sorties; they also kept them supplied in the Central Highlands with more than 5,000 tons of cargo, deposited on the 4,200 feet asphalt strip during the three weeks of heavy fighting that ensued. After three weeks of heavy fighting the US 4th Infantry Division and the 173rd Airborne Brigade forced the NVA to retire, leaving many casualties on both sides. Having noted the pattern of early morning arrivals of C-130s at Đắk Tô, on 15 November the North Viêtnamese waited until three Hercules were sitting on the parking ramp before firing ten rockets into the area. Two C-130Es (62-1865 and 63-7827) of the 776th TAS were hit and soon engulfed in flames. A third aircraft was backed out of the way of the inferno by Captain Joseph K. Glenn and Sergeant Joseph F. Mack during a lull in the attack and a fourth aircraft, which had landed moments before the first rounds exploded, took off again rapidly. The attack also destroyed 17.000 gallons of fuel and over 1,300 tons of ordnance when the ammunition dump was hit by artillery. The airfield

Motorised US Army forces and their equipment await boarding of 345th TAS, 314th TAW C-130Es.

was closed for two days and when it re-opened only one C-130 was permitted on the ground at a time. Glenn and Mack were awarded the Silver Star and Distinguished Flying Cross for their actions.

For three months in 1968 transports were called upon to keep the remote outpost at Khê Sanh supplied and in fulfilling this requirement the Hercules made one of its most famous contributions in South-East Asia. Located ten miles from the Laotian border and sixteen miles south of the DMZ, Khê Sanh was to become one of the Viêtnam War's most controversial battles. Manned initially in 1962 by the US Army, it had become, in 1967, a major Marine Corps base from which search-and-destroy operations were mounted to control Communist infiltrations. The first C-130 to land at Khê Sanh, on 17 February 1966, was piloted by Captain John Dunn of the 463rd Tactical Airlift Wing, as was recalled by his navigator First Lieutenant Bill Barry:

'On this day, we were going to fly a base inspection mission with no load on the airplane. John Dunn got to be a spectator for the day as the in-country wing commander took over the piloting, accompanied by a flight examiner who was going to give him his semi-annual flight check during the day's flying. Our first stop was a new field in the North of Viêtnam called Khê Sanh. As we flew upcountry towards Khê Sanh we could see that there were many fires raging everywhere. At first we thought that they might have been the result of air strikes; but gradually it became clear that Viêtnamese farmers were clearing their fields by burning off the ground cover.

'It took us two hours to get in the vicinity of Khê Sanh. The weather was clear and we could easily make out this laterite strip that ran east to west on the top of a low plateau. To the east was a large valley that sat several hundred feet lower than the airstrip. To the west and quite close to the strip, was a forested mountain range that rose steeply.

'We had the coordinates of the strip and several radio frequencies that were supposed to allow us to talk to the people on the ground. But the frequencies were wrong or their radios were broken or turned off, because we couldn't talk to anyone. We could see people alongside the runway with a few vehicles and they waved to us as we flew by; but we couldn't talk to them.

'The purpose of our visit was to ascertain that this strip was suitable for C-130B operations and we couldn't do that without landing. Since we couldn't talk to anyone, we weren't sure of how long the runway was. The two pilots guessed about it and I tried to figure it out roughly by timing our passage down the runway in the air and then mathematically combining the time and our ground speed as indicated on our Doppler. At best, we were operating on a big estimate; but we all agreed the runway was between 3 and 4,000 feet long. Plenty of length for an empty C-130B. Still, we weren't quite sure.

'Colonel David Lewis, who was flying the plane, decided to minimize any errors in our calculations. When a C-130 lands, the pilot puts the turbo props into reverse shortly after the plane is solidly on the ground and the pilot is sure of being in control of the landing, thus slowing the aircraft in conjunction with the brakes. In this instance, Lewis reversed the props while we were still 3 to 5 feet off the ground. What followed was the hardest landing I ever sat through. We stopped flying and crashed into the ground vertically. All of us were slammed into our seats. We easily stopped within the length of the runway. We were the first C-130 into Khê Sanh; but we wouldn't be the last. (Others claim they had been in Khê Sanh earlier, but those claims may relate to C-130As or Marine C-130s, which might have conducted their own base inspection in a similar fashion.)

'We turned around on the runway and then taxied back to meet the base personnel who had been watching us. They hastened to tell us that they had been sure the runway was long enough, but had to wait for a verification flight (which was us) to prove it. While they and Colonel Lewis discussed the base's qualifications, I set off on a tour of the runway and the base. There wasn't much to the base. A single storey operations building adjoined the runway at about the midpoint and that was about it. The remainder of the plateau on which the runway sat had been cleared and stood out in the blazing red laterite and clay which marked much of Viêtnam. I walked to the eastern end of the runway and stood on the edge of the plateau. Several hundred feet below was nothing but dense green jungle. After a few minutes of looking at it and out into the vast valley beyond, I began to think about what kind of target I made to

52

anyone on the forest floor below. Standing on the brink of the steep bank and with the clear blue sky behind me, I could be a chip shot for someone like a Việt Công lurking below. With that in mind, I stepped back and retreated to the airplane.

'We stayed at Khê Sanh for 45 minutes. Colonel Lewis agreed with the base residents that it was suitable for C-130 ops, but he cautioned that they needed to add overruns to both ends of the runway and put taxi stripes down for the parking area. We took off to the west and proceeded to another new airstrip north of Biên Hòa. We only overflew the second place, however, as the runway was still being worked on, the approaches had to be cleared of trees and there were vehicles all over the strip and its parking area. At this location we did have contact with the ground personnel over an established radio frequency so that all these suggested changes were passed on verbally.'[14]

Late in 1967 a prolonged Hercules airdrop supported operations and airstrip construction at Khê Sanh. By January 1968 6,000 marines were holed up at Khê Sanh and they were entirely dependent on resupply by air. The situation bore comparison to the Việt Minh's three-month siege of Điện Biên Phủ in the war with France from 1946-54. Điện Biên Phủ had been defended by 16,000 troops, but the French had nowhere near the air support that was available to the defenders of

Khê Sanh and this had resulted in its loss. Furthermore, the loss of Điện Biên Phủ had led directly to total French defeat in Indo-China - so if, militarily, history was not to be repeated then the Marines had to be kept supplied. Operation 'Niagara' involved a series of air strikes, together with a planned succession of resupply flights and was put into effect to keep the beleaguered 'grunts' in business during the long siege.

The NVA first attacked in the pre-dawn hours of 21 January. Eight days later, a thirty-six hour ceasefire for the Tet religious holiday began - but NVA and Việt Công activity almost immediately brought it to an end. On the 31st, just two days before the Tet offensive, the Communists launched massive ground attacks throughout South Việtnam. Many cities were attacked, including Huế, which was overrun. NVA troops stormed the A Shau valley and renewed their attack on the American outpost at Khê Sanh.

First operating independently, marine combat aircraft, transports and helicopters, with effective support by Navy and Air Force aircraft (including B-52s), mounted a major effort to help repel the Communist assault; during 'Niagara' 100,000 tons of bombs were dropped by all US aircraft. VMGR-152 operated four KC-130Fs out of Đà Nẵng AB, together with a single aircraft detached from VMGR-352, primarily to refuel USN and USMC

'Grunts' on the move as a C-130 lands on the runway.

Clearing up the debris after a Việt
Công attack on an air base in Viêtnam.

combat aircraft and to fly flare-dropping sorties.
On 10 February 1968 the USMC lost the first C-
130 in the operation when KC-130F BuNo 149813
of VMGR-152, MAG-15 was hit in the cockpit and
fuselage several times by .50 calibre gunfire as it
approached the airfield. The aircraft was carrying
a load of flamethrowers and several large rubber
bladders full of jet fuel for the Marine's turbine-
engined helicopters. The No.3 engine caught fire
and a fuel bladder was ruptured and trailed burning
fuel. Despite extensive smoke and flames the
aircraft touched down normally but then burst into
flames as the fuel bladders exploded. The pilot and
co-pilot escaped through the cockpit windows after
they turned the aircraft off the runway and fire-
fighters rescued another occupant before fire
consumed the aircraft. Eight of the eleven men on
board the aircraft were killed and Lance Corporal
Ferren died of his injuries on 1 March. One of the
passengers who was killed was Colonel C. E.
Peterson from the 1st MAW headquarters. Two
days after this incident the Seventh Air Force

prohibited landings by C-130s at
Khê Sanh although the prohibition
was lifted briefly towards the end
of the month. Henry Wildfang was
awarded his fifth DFC for his skill
in landing the aircraft at Khê
Sanh.[15]

On 8 March all Marine aircraft
and their air control system came
under the command of General
William Wallace Momyer USAF.
For seventy-one during which the
weather was nearly a bad and the
fighting intensive, the ports and
helicopters flew in supplies from
Đà Nẵng - only thirty minutes'
flying time away - to Khê Sanh and
brought out casualties (when the
siege was lifted on 6 April
American losses included 200 dead
and 600 wounded). Between 21
January and 8 April the Air Force transports
delivered 2,400 tons of cargo to Khê Sanh. A
staggering 92 per cent of the total tonnage lifted
was carried by the Hercules in 496 drops and 67
extractions, delivering 3,558 tons of cargo and
depositing another 7,826 tons in 273 landings.

When the runway at Khê Sanh was weathered
in the C-130s, C-123s and C-7s made aerial drops
of cargo with the help of ground-controlled radar-
directed approaches to the drop zones. Potentially
the transports were an easy target for Communist
small-arms fire, Triple-A and shoulder-launched
missiles, so normal approach procedures were
often abandoned in favour of what became known
as the 'Khê Sanh approach'. In this, each in-bound
transport remained at height as long as it could,
then the pilot put the nose down into a near-vertical
dive and flared out to land on the runway at the last
possible moment. Thanks almost entirely to the
extensive airborne resupply and the huge volume
of tactical and strategic support, the garrison held
out. Flying 1,128 missions between 21 January and

8 April, the USAF C-130s (who flew 74 per cent of these), the C-123s (24 per cent) and the C-7s (1 per cent) delivered 12,430 tons of cargo to Khê Sanh.[16] The lifting of the Khê Sanh siege was a victory for the Americans and was due almost entirely to the massive air effort. In contrast, the Tet offensive was a tactical disaster for the Communists; Khê Sanh on its own cost the NVA and Việt Công an estimated 10,000 casualties. But the propaganda effect of the Khê Sanh siege was far greater than they could have ever imagined. The press and television reportage accorded the Communists a strength they did not have, fanning the flames of the anti-war lobby in the US and causing public opinion to turn against the continued prosecution of the war. It led in March 1968 to the cessation of all bombing north of the 20th Parallel, a move that was meant to be a sign of conciliation but one which was interpreted as weakness by the Communists. As a result only stalemate was achieved and the war dragged on.

Chapter 2 Endnotes

1   A national independence coalition formed at Pác Bó on 19 May 1941.

2   Kung Kuan Air Base was renamed Ching Chuan Kang Air Base on 20 March 1966 in memory of ROC Army General Qiu Qingquan and was thereafter known throughout the theatre by its initials, CCK.

3   The two C-130As lost (55-0039 and 55-0042) were from the 817th TCS during one of the first Communist successes against US airfields at the major port and jet-capable airfield at Đà Nẵng in Quảng Nam Province when the Việt Công (VC), equipped with mortars and light artillery, landed by sea and proceeded to destroy eight aircraft.

4   Samuel E. McGowan flew in the 93rd Bomb Group in the 8th Air Force out of Hardwick, England in WW2. Sam's uncle Delmar D. McGowan started out in the 492nd but went to another group when it was broken up.

5   Nùng (pronounced as noong) are an ethnic minority in Việtnam whose language belongs to the Central Tai branch of the Tai-Kadai language family.

6   The camp was established in October 1963 by the US Army Special Forces 25 miles south of Pleiku city and less than 20 miles from the Cambodia border in the Central Highlands of Việtnam. Plei Me was one of many Special Forces camps scattered around the Central Highlands and charged with gaining and maintaining the support of the Montagnards for the South Việtnamese war effort and gathering intelligence about the infiltration into South Việtnam of North Việtnamese soldiers along the Hồ Chi Minh trail. In 1965 the camp was manned by more than 400 CIDG soldiers - local Montagnard irregulars, mostly members of the Jarai ethnic group. Many of them had families living just outside the camp. Twelve American soldiers from the 5th Special Forces Group and 14th Army of the Republic of Việtnam Special Forces assisted and advised the Montagnards. At the time of the attack on Plei Me about 300 Montagnards, the fourteen Việtnamese and ten Americans were inside the camp, the others were on patrol or stationed at nearby listening posts. The camp itself was under the control and command of II Corps Command.

7   The Plei Mei siege was followed by a larger battle in the Ia Drang Valley further to the west near the Cambodian border.

8   *A Trash Hauler in Vietnam; Memoir of Four Tactical Airlift Tours, 1965-1968* by Bill Barry (McFarland & Company Inc 2008).

9   *A Trash Hauler in Vietnam; Memoir of Four Tactical Airlift Tours, 1965-1968.*

10   Dudley and Brant were both awarded the DFC. A short time later, Dudley's C-130 crew and a number of other transport pilots perfected this drop off method on numerous occasions while supplying the beleaguered Marines under siege by the North Việtnamese Army (NVA) and the VC at their base at Khê Sanh near the Demilitarized Zone. After returning from Việtnam in 1969, Dudley went to work at Holloman Air Force Base in New Mexico testing Maverick missiles.

11   *Vietnam Air Losses* by Chris Hobson.

12   *A Trash Hauler in Vietnam; Memoir of Four Tactical Airlift Tours, 1965-1968.*

13   Between December 1966 and May 1967, Steinbeck wrote 86 stories for the newspaper. Those columns - collected in a book by the University of Virginia Press titled *Steinbeck in Vietnam* - were the last work to be published during Steinbeck's lifetime.

14   Following a two month return to the States to finalize personal affairs and returning to the Philippines in February 1966 he spent a 13 month tour flying 10 to 14 day deployments in Việtnam from a remote home base at Mactan Island in the southern Philippines. Barry's primary base of operations in Việtnam during this period was at Tân Sơn Nhất Airport in Sàigòn. He completed this tour in February 1967 and he was promoted to captain a month later. *A Trash Hauler in Vietnam; Memoir of Four Tactical Airlift Tours, 1965-1968.*

15   *Vietnam Air Losses* by Chris Hobson (Midland Publishing 2001).

16   The only other recorded loss of a Hercules was just after the Khê Sanh operation, on 13 April, when 61-0967, a TAC C-130B in the 774th Tactical Airlift Squadron, 463rd TAW suffered an engine failure as it was landing at Khê Sanh and suddenly veered off the runway. The aircraft hit six recently dropped pallets, still containing cargo and then continued into a truck and a forklift vehicle before coming to a halt and bursting into flames. The aircraft was damaged beyond repair but all seven crew were rescued, although a civilian who was on board later died of his injuries. *Vietnam Air Losses* by Chris Hobson (Midland Publishing 2001).

Chapter Three

The Last Flight
of The 'Stray Goose'

Colonel John Gargus, USAF (Ret)

During the course of our lives we experience events whose vivid memories remain undiminished in spite of the passage of time. My unforgettable event is the loss of eleven fellow crewmembers who failed to return from their mission over North Việtnam on 29 December 1967. They flew in a 'Stray Goose' Combat Talon MC-130E that belonged to Detachment 1 of the 314th TAW based at Nha Trang Air Base in South Việtnam. I was one of the three mission planners who charted the route for this tragic flight. S-01 crew, commanded by Captain Edwin N. Osborne, was tasked to fly it. It was a challenging mission that consisted of two air drops. The first one was a high altitude leaflet drop over the Red River [Sông Hồng] west of Hànôi and the second one a low level resupply drop on the other side of the mountains east of Điện Biên Phủ.

Before 'Romeo Charlie' 64-0547 took off, I walked through its inside length touching the lined up cardboard boxes that were secured to the floor mounted skateboard rails. They were filled with millions of propaganda leaflets that would be freed from the boxes once they ripped open after rolling off the exit ramp. After them were two palletized resupply bundles. After I exited the crew door, loadmaster James Williams closed it giving me thumbs up. We witnessed an orderly engine start and watched them taxi out to the end of the runway. From our vantage point, we saw the aircraft take off and disappear into the darkness over the South China Sea.

Three hours later, we, the flight planners, returned to our Detachment's Operations Office to monitor the aircraft's flight progress. All went well. Leaflets were gone and Gene Clapper, radio operator, sent a two Morse Code letter message signifying that the drop was successfully completed. The aircraft was back in a terrain following configuration, flying at 230 knots, headed westwards through the mountains. Then they would turn south for a drop of two 'notional' resupply bundles before exiting from North Việtnam.

John Gargus was born on 18 June 1934 in Velka Poloma, Czechoslovakia and escaped at the age of fifteen with the assistance of his parents in 1949 when the Communists pulled the country behind the Iron Curtain, to join his grandmother in the United States. He served in the Military Airlift Command as a navigator, then as an instructor in AFROTC. He went to Việtnam as a member of Special Operations and served in that field of operations for seven years in various units at home and in Europe. He is the author of *The Son Tay Raid: American POWs in Vietnam Were Not Forgotten* (Texas A&M University Military History Series).

Our whole detachment celebrated Christmas 1967 in the courtyard of Nha Trang's Roman Catholic Cathedral with Christian Boy and Girl Scouts and their parents. Detachment 1 of the 314th Tactical Airlift Wing[1] was based at Nha Trang Air Base, bounded on the north by Ninh Hoà district, on the south by Cam Ranh town and on the west by Diên

Khánh District with six eleven-member crews and four MC-130E Combat Talon I aircraft. These were equipped with terrain following radar, Fulton Recovery System and an array of passive electronic countermeasures. They were painted with special dark green paint that significantly reduced their reflected radar energy and because of their overall appearance they were affectionately called the 'Blackbirds'. They provided Military Advisory Command-Studies and Observations Group (MAC-SOG) with dedicated airlift during daytime and conducted highly classified, clandestine missions at night. These night missions were called 'combat missions' even though we never intended to engage in what would certainly be a one sided battle with the enemy. The only arms we carried were our survival .38 calibre pistols. We relied on our low level terrain following capability, the element of surprise and experienced airmanship to fly wherever tasked over North Viêtnam.

'When we returned to our hotel after the festivities, Major Roy Thompson, a C-130 navigator, came by to tell me that First Flight Operations had a classified message tasking us with our next combat mission. He wanted to know if I was interested in going with him to review it. I was eager to see what it was all about, so we hopped into our jeep and drove to the Viêtnamese side of the base where we shared our secure mission planning and communications facilities with our sister unit designated 'First Flight'; another SOG air asset flying C-123s with some very interesting crewmembers. First Flight cargo specialists assembled all our airdrop packages, rigged all our parachutes and even loaded the cargo

for our combat missions. We were to trust their methods and procedures no matter how weird or foreign the resulting drop configurations looked to our loadmasters.

'Our 'combat missions' were generated at SOG headquarters in Sàigòn. They ranged from quite ordinary to some bizarre airdrop operations. Thus, we would drop teams of infiltrators behind enemy lines and then resupply them periodically with all their needs. At times we would drop specially rigged personnel parachutes without infiltrators and imaginatively assembled resupply loads to convince the enemy that we had teams operating in this or that area. Sometimes our air dropped loads were rigged to fall apart in the air or be booby trapped for the NVA soldiers on the ground. And, of course, there were psychological operations consisting of high altitude leaflet drops and low altitude çwas now busy in the kitchen making sure that everything was going on schedule for our big evening meal. We were hosting the American officers of First Flight and borrowed their gourmet cook to assist our own very capable Chinese kitchen staff. Captain Gerald Van Buren, our Officers Open Mess steward, had already done his job. He made sure that all needed kitchen supplies were either procured in the Sàigòn Commissary, or that they were obtained from his various contacts at Special Forces operating locations. We would

MC-130E 'Stray Goose' 'Combat Talon I' 64-0547 'Romeo Charlie' of the 314th TAW taking off on a mission. (John Gargus)

trade with the Special Forces outposts on almost every visit to their remote sites. We would trade San Miguel beer, obtained on our visits to Taiwan or to the Philippines, for crates of fresh vegetables grown in their neighbouring Montagnard villages. Charlie Claxton was aspiring to replace Gerald Van Buren as the mess steward when Gerry completed his one-year tour in Việtnam.

'That evening we had what must have been the best feast of our Việtnam tour. We all complimented our kitchen staff and Charlie Claxton and Gerald Van Buren for their superb performance. Our rooftop bar activity that night was somewhat subdued; Most of us retreated to our rooms early to make audiotapes for our families. We all owed special thanks to our wives for making our Việtnamese Christmas as good as it could have been. All the sweets, toys and clothing for the Cathedral party and gift dispensing visits to several local orphanages were sent to us by our well-organized wives. They enlisted support of their local Chambers of Commerce for donations of clothing, candy and gifts and arranged with the USAF for shipment of assembled goods by opportune C-130 airlift. We were proud of them for their contribution to this civic action effort. Sorting of donated clothing became a major undertaking which took us several days to complete. We sized and sorted the clothing in the hot unventilated upstairs storage rooms of our operations building. Sergeant Jim Williams spent countless hours helping me in my capacity as the unit's Civic Action Officer. He took charge in keeping the effort going when some other volunteers gave up because of uncomfortable heat and troublesome clothing lint and dust in our improvised Santa's work shop. It was he who recruited Staff Sergeant Ed Darcy to help us until the clothing was finally sorted, boxed and labelled for distribution. During the festivities in the cathedral courtyard, both of these young men displayed great enthusiasm in playing games with the Scouts. We all had a great time. Christmas spirit and joy overcame all language and age barriers.

'Early next morning Roy Thompson, John Lewis and I settled down in our secure planning room where we drew out the route and prepared master charts for the crew that was going to fly the mission. Our master charts would be used the next day by the mission crewmembers who would study

them and customize them for their own personal use.

'The entire flight would take about eight hours. It would follow our often-repeated high-level route from Nha Trang to the Skyline beacon in Laos. There the 'Blackbird' would descend to a terrain following altitude and fly a short zigzagging route toward the first leaflet drop area. Then, after a 'short look' (rapid climb to high altitude, quick drop and rapid descent), the aircraft would resume terrain following through the low level resupply drop and return to the Skyline beacon. From that point the aircraft would continue back home at normal cruising altitude.

'In planning our terrain following routes, we always tried to stay away from populated areas, selecting prominent radar return targets for turning points and navigational instrument updates. A unique feature of our terrain following flights was that we flew at controlled ground speeds rather than constant airspeeds. Our aircraft was equipped with the APQ-115 terrain following radar that used aircraft's speed over the ground in its computations for maintaining desired altitude above the ground. Typically, we flew at 500 feet above the ground during daytime and at 1,000 feet at night. Flights over uneven terrain required continuous throttle adjustments to maintain our standard 230-knot ground speed (265 mph). The pilots had a Doppler ground speed indicator that they monitored incessantly. The pilot (left seat) had an APQ-115 screen, which in one display mode traced the terrain directly ahead of the aircraft and in another, cross scan mode, painted the terrain 20 degrees left and right of the projected ground track. Radar navigator had a third mode option for map reading. This one gave him a 45-degree left and right view of the aircraft's projected track, but when the radar was in this mode, the terrain following input used by the pilot was disabled. Flying in the left seat was very strenuous. For all practical purposes it was like flying sustained instrument landing system (ILS). 'Blackbird' pilots had to fly the attitude director indicator's (ADI's) pitch bar which received commands based on radar terrain returns and Doppler ground speed. They had to monitor their radar scope for visual terrain signals and manipulate engine throttles to maintain the desired ground speed. During daytime, well-placed cockpit windows allowed the pilot to verify approaching terrain, but on a dark night, this was impossible. One could not fix his eyes to the outside through the ever-present glare of the cockpit's amber lights and not lose focus on the instruments by which he had to fly. For that reason it became our standard practice to have the First Pilot fly in the left seat and have the Aircraft Commander sit on the right. This was the only way he could command his eleven-member crew. He could not take time away from the instruments to focus on even a routine in-flight problem.

'Terrain following combined with special navigational and flying techniques would get us to where we needed to go, but our ultimate survivability over North Việtnam depended on the skills of our Electronic Warfare Officers (EWOs). At that time, North Việtnam had the most formidable air defence system in the history of air warfare. It is true that their radars were not of the latest state-of-the-art, but they were effectively used by operators who had gained considerable skills with them. The same could be said about the AAA and SAM crews. Their tours of duty were not limited to one year like ours. They were at home defending their families against the most advanced American war machines for as long as their war lasted. So these Soviet-made radars, which were first introduced in Eastern Europe, were now being combat tested. The US intelligence had appropriate nicknames for all of them. Thus we confronted 'Bar Locks' (Soviet P-35M acquisition radar for incoming aircraft) and 'Spoon Rests' (for long-range early warning), 'Fan Song' (for SA-2 surface to air missiles (SAMs) and 'Fire Cans' (SON-9 radar which controlled 57mm and 100m anti-aircraft artillery (AAA).[2] Our knowledge of the locations of these radars, combined with our low level tactics, would get us into most target areas without detection. Once detected, however, it became the EWO's job to analyze the threats these radars posed. If all radars were in the locations we plotted on our charts, we would be able to fly through their scanning ranges and stay away from the effective ranges of missiles or artillery they controlled. During mission planning, the EWO would prepare a scenario which would tell him at which point of flight and from which direction each radar scan would illuminate our aircraft. If he detected radars not plotted on his chart and the received signal strength was stronger, indicating a closer proximity to our flight track, he would have to direct the pilots to get us out of there.

'By monitoring his state of the art instruments, he could tell whether the enemy radars were in routine mode or were focused on his aircraft in sector scans with added height finders that would help them to acquire aircraft's track, speed and altitude. The missile and AAA crews needed all this information before they could zero in on our aircraft's position and fire. In addition, with SAM's 'Fan Song' radar, he could tell when the radar pulse recurrence frequency changed to forecast an imminent missile launch. All that required good eyes to monitor several visual displays and good hearing to discern distinct chirping audio signals radar propagated. In a concentrated radar signal area, such as our aircraft would enter upon its climb to drop altitude, the EWO would receive welcomed assistance from the crew radio operator

Leaflet dropping from the rear of the Hercules. (John Gargus)

The lost aircraft and the 'Stray Goose' insignia. (John Gargus)

who shared his instrument console and sat on his left. All our radio operators became very adept EWO assistants.

'Blackbird's EWOs also had the capability to detect and disrupt an attack by a MiG interceptor. Using passive electronic techniques, they could confuse a MiG long enough to enable their aircraft to escape into a hilly terrain where the interceptor's radar became ineffective and the pursuing pilot risked flying into the ground.

First, by monitoring aural and visual signals, they could tell that ground control intercept radar was tracking their 'Blackbird' and most likely vectoring a MiG for an attack from the rear. Once the EWO picked up the interceptor's radar, he could play with the target a pursuing pilot would see on his radarscope. By manipulating the radar echoes reflected from the 'Blackbird' to the interceptor's radar he could offset the pilot's target to the left or right. Then just as the MiG was ready to fire, he would call for a sharp break away from the established aircraft heading, causing the interceptor to miss his radar target. After the first missed pass the GCI site and the interceptor pilot would get smarter and come around for another

pass. In the meantime our 'Blackbird' would make a rapid descent to the treetop level and get lost in the ground clutter where the airborne radar could not find it. The interceptor would have to abort the chase or risk flying into the ground.

'In addition, 'Blackbird's EWOs could dispense highly reflective chaff, which would instantly paint a brighter and larger target than the aircraft. With all that equipment and our special training, we had what we needed to conduct gutsy, but safe operations in the hostile skies of North Viêtnam. No one expected a large, slow and unarmed transport aircraft to operate in the same North Viêtnamese air space, which proved to be so challenging to the most advanced high performance aircraft in the US inventory.

'Our success rate over the enemy territory was commendable. Many of our low level missions through the North Viêtnamese air space went undetected. Some were tracked during portions of their flight, but always succeeded in avoiding AAA fire. A few had to abort their high altitude leaflet drops when a missile control radar locked on to them and the EWO detected a frequency shift, which signalled an imminent SA-2 missile launch. They always managed to break their radar lock on during a rapid roller coaster dive down to the minimum safe altitude. Fewer still experienced a MiG chase with an airborne radar lock on. Our EWOs always saved the night for us. Consequently, it didn't take long for the 'Blackbird' crews to develop a due respect for the skills of their EWOs.

'Two months before, in mid October, our S-05 crew's EWO, John Lewis, defeated three passes of an interceptor that jumped upon us just off the coast near the Hảiphòng harbour. We were dropping pre-tuned radios to the local fishermen. Pursued, we flew as low and as fast as we could, shaking and bouncing on the air currents our aircraft stirred off the otherwise calm sea water. When John called 'Break Left', we had to pop up a few feet in order to avoid dipping the left wing into the water. Our Ops Officer, Lieutenant Colonel Tom Hines, flew with us that night. It was daylight when we landed at Nha Trang. The wings and the fuselage of our 'Blackbird' were white with salt. John Lewis may still hold the 'Combat Talon' record for besting a pursuing fighter pilot three times on a single 'combat mission'.

'Our first problem on the 29 December mission would be the early warning radar at Nà Sản in Sơn La Province. We had to stay as low and as far south of its range as possible in order to avoid detection while crossing into North Viêtnam. Once inside North Viêtnam we had to get to the east side of the central mountains and stay out of range of well-placed AAA and SAM sites along the Red River Valley. We tried to avoid getting picked up and tracked by the multitude of radars associated with those anti-aircraft weapons. These radars by themselves could not hurt us but would alert AAA and SAM crews for possible action if we came within range of their weapons. Our best scenario

was to have no radar track us until we began our rapid climb to 30,000+ feet for the leaflet drop. We knew that once our aircraft got to 9-10,000 feet, all available radars would come up and keep our EWO extremely busy. If the enemy did not respond with a launch of interceptors, the leaflet drop would be completed and the aircraft would resume low level terrain following and proceed westward just south of the China border along the 22nd parallel until reaching the Black River Valley. There a southbound turn would be made. Then staying in the mountains along the west side of the river, the second airdrop would be executed NW of the Na San early warning radar.

'Our avoidance of Nà Sản radar was not our concern at this point in the flight. By this time a warning would have been issued from the Hànôi side of the mountains that a leaflet dropping intruder was moving westward toward Điện Biên Phủ. Consequently this early warning radar would be scanning in a NW direction, expecting the emergence of our 'Blackbird'. Nà Sản's detection of our flight at this time could actually assist in the accomplishment of the second portion of our mission. Our resupply drop was what we called a 'notional' drop or a diversionary drop. There was no friendly team to receive the two resupply bundles. These bundles were carefully planned by imaginative minds at SOG to confuse the enemy and to have him expend considerable resources searching for infiltrators that did not exist. So the resupply bundles were meant to be captured by the enemy. Nà Sản's detection of our aircraft's slow down could assist the enemy in locating this bogus cargo.[3]

'By the time we finished with our planning, we learned that augmented S-01 crew would fly the mission. It was S-01's turn to take the next mission, but there were some questions about the possibility of having this crew skip its turn. Major Dick Day, its Aircraft Commander and one of the crew's loadmasters were on duty not involving flying (DNIF). His senior navigator, Lieutenant Colonel Don Fisher, was not yet back from his R&R (rest and recreation) in Hawaii. His earliest expected return was on that day, 26 December. Earlier on this day, the other crew load master departed with S-03 crew on that crew's flight to our parent 314th Wing in Taiwan. He had made arrangements with Staff Sergeant Ed Darcy from S-03 crew to switch places. Ed Darcy, a quiet, conscientious young man, planned to save some money by staying in Nha Trang. He did not want to spend it on a three to five day stay in Taiwan while the ferried 'Blackbird' went through its scheduled inspection and repair as necessary (IRAN) in a maintenance facility that was equipped to handle C130 aircraft. The crews looked forward to their turn to ferry a 'Blackbird' for an IRAN in Taiwan. It was a most welcomed vacation break from the wartime conditions in Việtnam. So, Ed Darcy became a volunteer replacement for one S-01 loadmaster. Sergeant James Williams agreed to take the place of the other load master who was also DNIF.

'This mission provided an opportunity for Captain Edwin Osborne to take command of the S-01 crew and for Captain Gerald Van Buren to move up to the first pilot's position. The second pilot's slot was filled by Major Charlie Claxton from my S-05 crew. He had missed an earlier combat mission when he was DNIF, so this would become a make-up mission for him. I made up my mind that I would take Lieutenant Colonel Don Fisher's place if he did not return in time from Hawaii. I would have been the logical replacement in any case because I already knew the route and mission details and could be used to step in to replace him up to the last minute. Later on that evening I heard that Don Fisher was back. I went to see him and found him in a most jovial mood. He had just returned from a memorable R&R in Hawaii with

his whole family. He had just had the greatest of Christmases and repeated to me and to others that he was 'in love with the whole world.' He was ready to fly combat.

'Edwin Osborne was also ready to fly as an aircraft commander of a combat mission. All our first pilots were highly experienced as C-130 airlift aircraft commanders before becoming qualified in the Combat Talon 'Blackbirds'. Many felt that to become a highly qualified co-pilot in the Combat Talon programme was somewhat of a career regression even though they understood the need for such demanding pilot qualification. As experienced pilots, they were simply outranked by others with more impressive pilot credentials that became Combat Talon Aircraft Commanders. Edwin Osborne was clearly a pilot who should not be taking a back seat to anyone. He was an excellent pilot qualified as an instructor pilot in the 'Blackbirds'.

'The next day John Lewis and I rode with the S-01 officer crew to the mission planning room. Van Buren drove the crew van. He normally drove whenever his crew went places. I was told that as our Commissary Officer he even drove through Sàigòn on his crew's periodic commissary runs when his crew's 'Blackbird' got extra ground time at Tân Sơn Nhứt to accommodate his grocery shopping. Since Charlie Claxton was destined to inherit that duty from him, it meant that my S-05 crew would get the long ground time on some

Lieutenant Colonel Tom Hines, Ops Officer and John Gargus at Nha Trang Air Base. (John Gargus)

future transits through Sàigòn.

'On the way to our secure mission planning room, I sat right across from Captain Frank Parker, a tall blond young man who was the crew's EWO. He was telling several of us how fortunate we were in having missions where we could sneak in and sneak out without stirring up a hornets' nest. He had recently returned from Thailand where he ran into several of his EWO classmates who were flying the RB-66s. Their mission was to deliberately challenge the enemy's electronic detection systems and deadly retaliation in their efforts to pinpoint locations of enemy radars. He used the term we sometimes applied to those situations when one would prefer to be on the ground rather than in the air. He said that his friends were 'eating their livers' on their RB-66 missions.

'Roy Thompson had everything ready for us when we arrived. All the charts we prepared the day before were either posted on easels or laid out on worktables. Fresh, unmarked charts, flight plan

logs and other necessary mission forms were placed on tables where the crewmembers would use them. Roy gave a brief overview of what the mission entailed. About the only unusual thing that he noted was that TOTs (times on targets) were not prescribed because neither drop zone had a reception team. The psy-ops (leaflet) drop had a fixed drop leg at altitude of 30,000 or more feet, depending on the wind velocity and direction. Weaker winds would require a higher altitude. The heart of Hànôi would be from 65 to 70 miles away and it was hoped that some of the leaflets would make it that far before the sunrise. Lack of TOTs also explained to them why their flight plan was not completed with time of arrival at turning points. They were to calculate these by themselves, planning on a 260-265 true air speed at high altitudes and a standard 230 ground speed at terrain following levels.

'Once Roy Thompson was finished with his mission introduction, I joined Don Fisher and Gordie Wenaas, the two crew navigators, to work

John Gargus at his navigator's position. (John Gargus)

on the flight planned route. John Lewis and Frank Parker got together to work on the enemy's defences. Roy joined the three pilots. Our enlisted crew members: two flight engineers, two load masters and one radio operator, normally did not participate in mission planning.

'Gordie Wenaas thought the mission would be a 'piece of cake.' He quickly noted that there were practically no threat circles anywhere near our track. Then he started crunching out flight plan times between turning points. Don and I went over each low level turning point, examining the terrain in its vicinity. Practically all were river bends or rivers that would show up well on radar. Some turning points had been used on previous missions and were reported to be good ones. Selected drop zone for the second drop was a location with good radar targets everywhere. He was satisfied with everything and began to prepare his own navigational chart. In this task, Gordie was way ahead of him. Gordie was a man who undertook every single task very seriously. I remember him going around our hotel taking care of chores whenever his S-01 crew was scheduled to be the hotel's duty crew. Each crew was regularly scheduled for hotel crew duty by the Ops Scheduling as if it were a flight assignment. These duties consisted of servicing our two electrical generators, bringing in fresh potable water from the Air Base, taking care of mail; stocking the rooftop bar and performing whatever maintenance chores were needed at the hotel. Gordie Wenaas was conspicuous by keeping himself occupied with these chores. He showed me how to start up and switch our two noisy generators.

'I was then drawn into a conversation with the pilots. Osborne liked the route and had only one concern. It was the time interval between the end of the first drop and the start of the second one. Would his two loadmasters have enough time to move the cargo to the ramp for this drop? How many bundles would there be? How much would they weigh? And, of course, 'What is this notional stuff?' The answer to this question could only be provided by our cargo rigger, a Warrant Officer from the First Flight. Van Buren was dispatched to go next door to get him. Van returned alone, but he had the information we needed. He also succeeded in making arrangements for the loadmasters and the flight engineers to be at the aircraft next morning to witness the cargo loading. He commented that the Warrant Officer reminded him that no one was to mess with the cargo and question its rigging. Everything would be set up by the First Flight crew just the way it should be dropped. Anything non-standard or out of place should be ignored. Our job was to fly it there and drop it just as it was configured.

'Ed Osborne showed much interest in the terrain following portion of flight. So the pilots gathered around Don Fisher who had already drawn his chart. He walked through every leg of flight and explained each turning point. Charlie Claxton had the weight of the aircraft calculated at the point of acceleration and climb to high altitude. There were questions about how much of the area west of Hànôi the crew would be able to see. Aircraft's track was over the eastern slopes of the central highlands. Numerous peaks with elevations of up to 9,000 feet were immediately to the left and the sprawling Red River Valley with level terrain west of Hànôi to the right. It was to be a dark night with new moon beginning on 30 December. There would be total darkness. Some lights would no doubt be lighted towards Hànôi. Our prior flights noted that North Viêtnam did not have a complete night-time blackout. The night would be perfect for the two map-readers - Gordie Wenaas on the right and Charlie Claxton on the left - to use the somewhat cumbersome starlight scope to monitor the terrain below. The scope was of little use at terrain following levels because it had excessive tunnel vision. This made the terrain whiz by so fast that it caused the images to blur. But at drop altitude, where the 'Blackbird' would seem to be at a standstill in relation to the ground below, the scope would give its user a fascinating view of terrain otherwise hidden in total darkness. Very little cloud coverage was predicted for that night.

'We pointed out the location of Yên Bái Air Base that would be at the aircraft's 1 to 2 o'clock position during the drop. If there were any MiGs on night alert, that base would pose their greatest threat. This would also be Frank Parker's greatest challenge that night. He would have to defend against a possible interceptor activity.

'Ed Osborne examined the terrain into which the aircraft would have to descend after the leaflet drop. He was concerned about the rapidly approaching ground during their maximum rate of descent when the radar stabilization was habitually, but only temporarily, lost and the Doppler limits were also exceeded. Here I pointed out that a rapid descent should not be executed unless the aircraft was in jeopardy due to SAM or interceptor attack. All crews seemed to have the same Pope AFB training mind set. During our training there, each short look was followed by a maximum rate descent, a manoeuvre which put a lot of stress on the aircraft. This needed to be practiced at every opportunity. Now in real life, if a threat to our aircraft did not materialize, there was no need to put it through such a stressful manoeuvre where the crew experienced weightlessness and everything not tied down started floating about. Then at the point of level off, the tremendous G load would force the standing crewmembers down to their knees. On this mission there would be additional cargo just behind the EWO and the radio operator compartment. We did not want any of it to break loose during such a stressful manoeuvre.

'Ed was concerned with the time remaining before the second drop. His loadmasters and the second flight engineer would have to move the cargo to the back of the aircraft and get it set for the drop. Normally, the cargo would be all set from the point of take off. But not this time. The back of the aircraft would have to be cleared of any remaining restraining straps from the leaflet drop. Then the resupply bundles would have to be moved into place. Normally this would not be that difficult because the palletized bundles were on rollers. But being on rollers in straight and level flight is one thing, being on rollers in an up and down terrain following flight is another. Great care was needed to avoid an injury or have a cargo slip off the rollers at an angle where the pallet would jam. This would no doubt be a new experience for these loadmasters. Ed noted with some satisfaction that the terrain following leg going westbound along the 22nd parallel was relatively level because we were taking advantage of the break between 10,000 feet high peaks on the right and 9,000 feet ones on the left.

'At a prominent turning point over the Black River the mission would turn south. The 'Blackbird' would fly almost due south hiding behind the high terrain west of the river. This would keep it west of the valley's populated areas. Ahead at the aircraft's 10 to 11 o'clock position

would be the Nà Sản early warning radar. This radar would be looking for the reappearance of the intruder that was sure to excite the radars on the Hànôi side of the mountains in the Red River valley. This radar was not capable of directing MiG interceptors and none were expected to come west out of the Red River valley.

'Our drop zone was in an isolated area just north of Highway 6. It was a logical place for a drop zone. This would no doubt add to the credibility to the nonexistent team's presence. Roy Thompson explained the deceptive nature of this drop. There would be no ground markings or signals. The drop would occur on Don Fisher's green light command when his Doppler distance to go ran out. After this drop the crew would continue terrain following into Laos where the high altitude route home would resume at the Skyline beacon. North Việtnam's western early warning radar at Nà Sản would have an unobstructed scan of our aircraft's pre drop slow down and the post drop acceleration on its escape heading. The enemy would have a good indication for where to look for whatever the intruding aircraft delivered. We planned it that way.

'At some point during this low-level route review we were joined by Frank Parker and John Lewis who had concluded their study of the enemy's electronic air order of battle. They pointed out correctly that once the aircraft crossed into the Black River region the enemy defences were such that a return home at any altitude would be safe. That was a good thought in case of any in-flight problems, such as navigational, mechanical, or outside visibility degradation due to weather.

'Then the whole group gathered around Frank Parker's chart. His chart differed from those of Don Fisher and the map-readers Charlie Claxton and Gordie Wenaas. Theirs had smaller threat circles along the flight-planned track. They represented lethal ranges of SAMs and AAA. Frank's chart had the mission flying through much larger circles that outlined scan ranges of various radars. His chart showed that the aircraft would be exposed to many types of radar throughout its northbound portion of flight along the Red River. He estimated that even before the aircraft would reach its drop altitude of 30,000+ feet, all available radars would be alerted to their presence and that he would be saturated with a tremendous amount of visual and aural signals. He acknowledged that he would have to rely on very able assistance from Gean Clapper, the crew radio operator, who would be sharing his console behind the cargo compartment curtain.

'Gean Clapper was a true professional in his field. He had many years of experience as a HAM radio operator. As such he had contacts with colleagues throughout the world. On flights over international waters, where it was permissible, he would raise his contacts and relay personal greetings and messages to families back home. He was also very good at electronic warfare. He could positively recognize the chirping sounds of various radars. This should be a great asset on a flight such as this one where sound-wise things would get extremely noisy for Frank. Frank concluded that with Gean's help he should be able to detect anything out of the ordinary and call for evasive action before any harm could come to the 'Blackbird'. It would be Don Fisher's task to find a safe evasive flight path through the mountains on the left.

'After that each crewmember went on his own, putting finishing touches on all paperwork he was producing. We three mission planners assisted them with anything they needed and insured that all mission documents they produced were properly stamped TOP SECRET. None of the documents could leave with the crew. They were collected by us and locked in First Flight's safe. They would not be released to the crew until the next night before the pre-departure mission briefing.

'The next day's mission briefing was a whole crew affair attended by our Commander, Lieutenant Colonel Dow Rogers and our Operations Officer, Lieutenant Colonel Tom Hines. This would be the first time the enlisted crewmembers learned about the target area. All five, the two engineers, two loadmasters and the radio operator, were present when the First Flight's cargo handlers loaded the aircraft. Flight engineer Tech Sergeant Jack McCrary gave us thumbs up on the condition of the aircraft. He was a very

John Gargus receiving the Bronze Star. (John Gargus)

Nha Trang air base. (John Gargus)

meticulous crewmember, well regarded, not just by Ed Osborne, but also by his flight engineer peers. I wondered how much sleep he had gotten during the day. His eyes looked red as if he had not slept at all. But we all knew that his nickname was 'Red Eye.' He had an eye condition that made them look red and blood shot all the time. His second, Staff Sergeant Wayne Eckley, was an engineer of lesser experience, but not short on enthusiasm. His nickname was 'Bones.' The jungle fatigue uniforms (designed as one size fits all) exaggerated his lean and bony body. There was so much more space left for him inside his fatigues.

'The mission briefing started with Roy Thompson who stood in front of several chart filled easels placed in the front of the briefing room. He briefed the weather. It was going to be favourable for this flight with very few clouds on the east side of the mountains in North Viêtnam and strong favourable WNW winds at drop altitude. A low level pressure was moving southeast from China, bringing some cloudiness into the target area in the Black River valley late in the morning.

'Then, the mission briefing was turned over to Don Fisher who briefed the route and the drop sequences. He was followed by Frank Parker, who covered the enemy order of battle. He presented the latest SOG intelligence that included known numbers of different MiG interceptors available to North Viêtnamese defences. As always, he mentioned the standard radio silence precautions. Minimum chatter on the intercom! He was going to run every one of his sophisticated tape recorders that registered all electronic signals generated by enemy radars and also captured crew's intercom transmissions. This was going to be a special night for him to gather electronic intelligence signals for our future use. We should end up with a sizable amount of signals from all types of radars. These tapes would then be used by other crew EWOs interested in sharpening their listening and signal interpretation skills.

'Frank's briefing was followed by the Aircraft Commander Osborne. He briefed the crew assignments that had been previously reviewed with Lieutenant Colonel Tom Hines. He would fly the entire mission in the right seat. Van Buren would be in the left seat from the take off through the low level terrain following part of the flight. Charlie Claxton would map read from behind Van

Buren during terrain following and then take the left seat at high altitude on the way home. Don Fisher would ride the radar navigator's seat with the curtain drawn during terrain following and the leaflet drop. Gordie Wenaas would stand behind Osborne's right seat and map read from there. Jack McCrary would fly the engineer's seat during terrain following. Wayne Eckley would spend his time in the back playing the safety observer role and provide assistance to the loadmasters. Frank Parker and Gean Clapper were to man their console behind the bulkhead curtain and the two substitute loadmasters, Jim Williams and Ed Darcy, were to make sure they kept their restraining harnesses on during the drops. All crewmembers were to go on demand regulator oxygen upon entering North Viêtnam and then on 100% oxygen during the leaflet drop.

'There were a few standard questions from Lieutenant Colonels Rogers and Hines about everyone's fitness and emphasis on safety. Finally, the crew was wished good luck.

'After this the crew was sanitized. All personal effects, identifications, family photographs and even jewellery were placed into plastic bags and saved for the crew's return. Each crewmember had only his dog tags and Geneva Convention card as identifying documents. That was the standard procedure for all combat missions.

'Because the mission planners had to secure all the classified mission documents and personal effects, the crewmembers were already in their assigned positions running their pre-departure checklists when we rejoined them at the aircraft. We witnessed an orderly engine start and watched the 'Blackbird' taxi out to the end of the runway. From our vantage point we saw them take off and disappear into the darkness over the South China Sea.

'About three hours later, I returned with Roy Thompson to our Operations Office to monitor the North Viêtnamese portion of the mission. We had one of our radio operators monitor a special HF radio frequency over which Gean Clapper transmitted coded mission progress reports every 30 to 40 minutes when the aircraft reached a significant in-flight turning point. A radio station in an unknown location would broadcast continuous one letter Morse code at regular intervals. Our airborne operator would monitor the same frequency and at proper moments would insert a two letter Morse code signal which would let us know which point of the route was reached and gave us the status of the mission's progress. This was such a short burst of transmitted energy that our enemy, who was sure to monitor the same

frequency, would not have enough time to zero in his direction finders to locate the position of our aircraft. These transmissions were the only breaks in radio silence allowed during our combat missions.

'Upon checking with our radio operator, we learned that the flight was already over North Việtnam and right on time. We did not have any mission documents with us other than the radio operator's log with numbered points and corresponding estimated times of arrival over them, but we had a good mental picture of what must have been happening in the cockpit. So as we sat there, sipping on some very strong coffee that the radio operator prepared, we made occasional comments on what the crew must have been going through.

'For the leaflet drop, all the lights were at their dimmest and the radar navigator and EWO/radio operator compartment curtains were drawn to prevent any outside light to affect the night vision of the rest of the crew. All were on oxygen and their intercom voices were muffled by the oxygen mask microphones that registered and exaggerated the sound of every breath they took. The aircraft began its acceleration prior to the rapid climb. Maximum aircraft acceleration to 932-degree turbine inlet temperature was attained in relatively short level flight with aircraft shaking as if its four turbojets were ready to tear loose and leave the bulky aircraft carcass behind.

'Then as the aircraft began its rapid climb, Frank Parker's console surely began to light up. At first he would pick up a number of AAA and SAM radars, which would routinely scan their assigned areas. As they detected the 'Blackbird', they would focus their scan on their just discovered target and activate their height finders to establish the aircraft's altitude. They would pass their acquired target data through their established notification channels. This would cause even more radars to come up and focus on this rapidly rising, but now slow moving target. The crew would hear Frank reporting the inevitable. Two or three AAA radars were tracking them, but from a safe distance. Of greater concern would be the SAM radars. These had longer reach, but were expected to be out of range. He would certainly be calling these to Osborne's attention. Then would come the level off and the start of drop. Each man could tell when

each cardboard box exited the aircraft. There was a whoosh sound to each exit as the departing load created an added vacuum in the rare atmosphere of the cargo compartment. The aircraft would seem to stand still, just hanging on in the thin air, being as high as it could climb on the thin cushion of available air. And as Frank watched for the emergence of a GCI radar and its tracking pattern in order to determine if there was an intent to launch a MiG, Gordie Wenaas must have struggled with the night vision scope looking for Yên Bái Air Base 30 miles away. This was the place from which the nearest MIGs could come. His night vision scope would certainly pick up the heat of an interceptor at take off. He would have to be pointed in the right direction. Others in the cockpit were getting the answer to whether they could see the lights of distant Hànôi now at their 3 o'clock position. Don Fisher must have had his face buried in the hood of his radar as he carefully traced every mile of ground covered by the aircraft. He had to know exactly where he was in case Frank reported radar or interceptor lock on which would demand an immediate descent to a safe terrain between the mountain peaks on the left.

'We did not hear any interruptions to the monotonous 'V' sound on the radio, so we assumed that all was okay. All the leaflets were delivered. The aircraft was on its way down and proceeding westward to its turning point over the Black River. The next report came just as expected. All was still okay. The aircraft was now southbound running its checklist for the bundle drop by Highway 6.

While we waited for the next report, that would come when the aircraft turned southward along the western side of the Black River valley, we talked about some of the peculiar missions which we called 'notional' resupply drops. These were drops of resupply bundles into drop zones where we did not have previously infiltrated South Việtnamese Special Forces teams. These bogus resupply bundles were designed to be discovered by the enemy who would then spend much time combing the area searching for non-existing infiltrators. Among the usual resupply items of food, ammunition, explosives and medicines would be false targeting plans and even points of contact with friendly supporters that would cast doubts on the loyalty of some local officials. Some bundles were booby trapped, designed explode during disassembly by those who discovered them. We knew that the two resupply bundles that were about to be delivered were not of this type.

At 0430 we received a coded letter signal that all was still normal. The aircraft was now headed southward and the crew was running the air drop checklist. The next report would be made after the drop when the aircraft headed for the Laotian border and from there, home at normal high altitude. We planned to return to the hotel right after the next report and get a couple of hours of sleep before coming back to greet the returning crew. But as we waited, nothing happened. There were no further reports from the aircraft. Our first assumption was that something went wrong with their radios. We would surely hear something once the aircraft emerged from radio silence over the Skyline TACAN in Laos. That is where the aircraft would report a small problem like that to our radar sites in Thailand. Once again, there was nothing.

The track taken by MC-130E 64-0547 'Romeo Charlie' on 29 December 1967. (John Gargus)

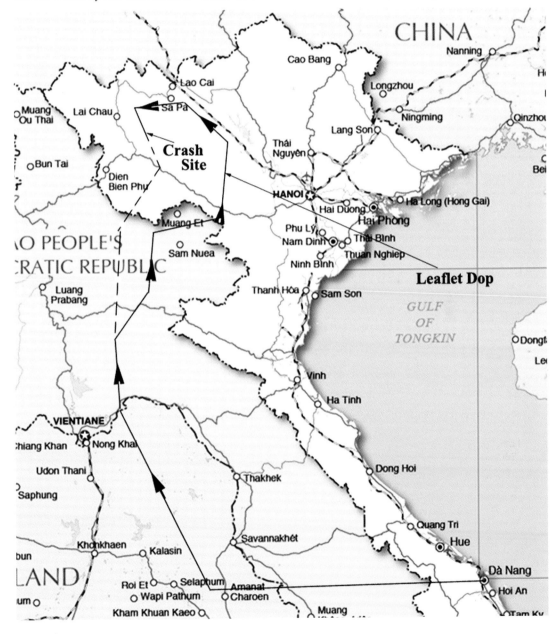

With that we returned to the hotel and reported our concerns to the Detachment's Commander and the Operations Officer.

'Roy and I planned to return to the hotel right after the next report and get a couple of hours of sleep before coming back to greet the returning crew. But as we waited, nothing happened. There were no further reports from the aircraft. Our first assumption was that something went wrong with Clapper's radio. We would surely hear something once the aircraft emerged from its radio silence over the Skyline beacon. That is when the aircraft would report a small problem like that to our radar sites in Thailand. Once again, there was nothing. With that we returned to the hotel and reported our concerns to Dow Rogers and Tom Hines.

'There were anxious moments as the aircraft's return time approached. Calls were made to find out if any landings were made in Thailand or at Đà Nẵng. Then the command at SOG was notified. The SOG took over all search and rescue efforts. Several F-4 Phantoms were launched to survey the area south of the last known reported position. The weather turned bad. The front moved in as expected and the F-4s could not see a thing on the ground. They monitored radios for signals from the aircraft's crash position indicator and from any crewmember survival radios. They heard nothing. After several attempts, the search was given up. The crew of eleven was declared as missing in action (MIA).

'At the time of the crash the crew was getting ready for the second drop. Eckley, Darcy and Williams were in the cargo compartment making sure that the load was properly positioned for the drop. They were moving about and did not yet have their restraining harnesses hooked on. Claxton and Wenaas were the other two crewmembers that were not fastened to any seats. Their map reading duties called for them to stand behind the pilots and peer outside through the side windows.

'The first person on the scene of the crash was a twelve-year-old boy. He reported that the aircraft was in many pieces and that it was still burning. He saw several bodies, many of them burnt. He did not find any survivors.

'After many years of silence, Major John Plaster authored a book, *SOG - The Secret Wars of America's Commandos in Vietnam*, in which he described exploits of commandos who lost their lives on missions that had not been brought to public attention for numerous security reasons. The loss of this aircraft fits into that mould. It was, according to Major Plaster, our largest single aircraft loss over North Việtnam.'

Chapter 3 Endnotes

1   Later, the 15th Air Commando Squadron and finally the 90th Special Operations Squadron.

2   'Fan Song' got its name from its horizontal and vertical fan scanning antennas and its distinctive sounding emissions, which could be picked up by the aircraft's warning equipment. The 'Spoon Rest' radar detected incoming aircraft as far as seventy miles, providing location data to the system computer. The 'Fan Song' guidance radar performed two functions: target acquisition and missile guidance. It acquired as many as four targets before firing. After launch, it guided up to three SA-2s against one target. The North Việtnamese sometimes placed the radars away from the missiles to make the site harder to destroy.

3   'Notional' resupply drops were drops of resupply bundles into drop zones where we did not have previously infiltrated South Việtnamese Special Forces teams. These bogus resupply bundles were designed to be discovered by the enemy who would then spend much time combing the area searching for non-existing infiltrators. Among the usual resupply items of food, ammunition, explosives and medicines would be false targeting plans and even points of contact with friendly supporters that would cast doubts on the loyalty of some local officials. Some bundles were booby trapped, designed explode during disassembly by those who discovered them. We knew that the two resupply bundles that were about to be delivered were not of this type.

Chapter Four

Haul On Call

We left for Ubon RTAB, Thailand on a C-130 transport. All of the pilots were on board, lined up on portable seats that were attached to each side of the aircraft. They were made of aluminium tubes and red nylon straps, kind of like lawn furniture and were very uncomfortable. The backrests were vertical, making it impossible to recline. Every time the aircraft would turn, accelerate, or decelerate, we would all be pushed forward or against each other, the last man in the row bearing the brunt of the weight.

'When we arrived, the C-130 pilot, who must have been a frustrated fighter pilot decided to pitch-out the Hercules and land like a fighter. He aligned the aircraft with the runway at fifteen hundred feet and when he reached the approach-end, made a fast 360 degree left turn, using about sixty degrees of bank, losing altitude during the turn. While still in a slight bank, the giant aircraft crunched down on one wheel and the pilot placed all four engines in reverse, stopping in about three thousand feet - less than the first half of the runway. He probably thought his manoeuvre would thrill the troops. It was a thrill all right. Most of us were thrown on the deck, completely out of our seatbelts and were probably lucky not to have been hurt. Welcome to Thailand. Our war had begun.

Memories Of Ubon Thailand: A Fighter Pilot's Journal by Richard E. Hamilton

Two airlift operations were notable in 1968; the first, in April, was Operation 'Delaware/Lam Son 216', the air invasion of the A Shau Valley, one of the main North Việtnamese infiltration routes into the South. The A Shau Valley, west of Đà Nẵng /Huế and south of Khê Sanh was an old supply route and arms depot for the Việt Cộng and the North Việtnamese Army which the US had gone into and cleared out several times before. In early 1968 reports started coming in to indicate that new roads were being constructed in the A Shau Valley. Operation 'Delaware' started on 19 April to contest

C-130E 64-0542 *Haul On Call* was delivered to the 314th TCW in February 1965 and served eight other units before being assigned to the 317th TAW at Pope AFB in 1978. It is now used by the Technical Training Centre, Sheppard AFB, Wichita Falls, Texas.

an enemy build-up in the A Shau Valley after preparatory B-52 and tactical bombings of PAVN anti-aircraft and troop positions. Troops of the 1st Cavalry Division were inserted into the north of A Shau Valley by helicopter, as the 1st Brigade, 101st Airborne Division; the 3rd Regiment, 1st ARVN Division; and the 3rd ARVN Airborne Task Force provided the blocking force on the southeast fringe of the valley on both sides of Route 547 that lead to Huế. Poor weather and anti-aircraft fire made flying very dangerous. On the 25th the 1st Cavalry landed at the abandoned airstrip at A Lưới. For nine days, beginning on the 26 April, the C-130s flew 165 sorties, dropping 2,300 tons, most of it ammunition. Despite bad weather and Communist ground fire, the Hercules flew daily airdrops to the 1st Cavalry Division (Airmobile), the 101st Airborne Division and ARVN units at A Lưới. Ground radar was unavailable so the Hercules' crews had to navigate up the cloud-filled valley using their radar and Doppler equipment, breaking out of the overcast just before visual release of their cargo.

Such was the urgency that the C-130s continued to fly during one period when the weather was so bad that it grounded even the helicopters. On 26 April C-130s from Cam Ranh Bay, Biên Hòa and Tân Sơn Nhứt dropped supplies to the troops on the A Lưới airstrip. The airdrops were made under a low overcast without the benefit of air strikes, which had been cancelled due to the low cloud. Seven C-130s were hit by ground fire during the first twenty airdrops but on the 21st mission as the C-130B 60-0298 in the 773rd TAS, 463rd TAW flown by Captain James J. McKinstry and Major John Lewis McDaniel from Tân Sơn Nhứt broke out through the cloud it was hit by .50 calibre and 37mm ground fire. The crew tried to jettison the load, which had caught fire in the cargo bay. The aircraft turned towards the airstrip to attempt a landing but it then hit some trees and crashed and exploded. All on board, including six crew and two USAF photographers were killed. No more airdrops were attempted at A Lưới on the 26th although they were resumed with more success the next day.

Captain John Dunn's crew went to the officers' club for dinner 'and' wrote Captain Bill Barry, who had deployed with members of the Wing to Tachikawa Air Base in February 1968, 'that's where we found out that the airdrop the next day was scheduled to be in the A Shau Valley. Supposedly, the VC in the valley were dug into spider holes on the approach to the runway/drop zone. The spider holes had hatched camouflaged covers so that they could not be seen from the air beforehand. The VC opened the holes up and emerged to fire at a plane as it came in for the drop

A M551 Sheridan battle tank being landed using LAPES.

C-130B 61-0967 in the 774th TAS, which suffered an engine failure upon landing at Khê Sanh on Saturday 13th April 1968 and veered off the runway, striking cargo pallets and several vehicles before coming to rest. A fire then erupted.

at slow speed and low altitude.

'We were up bright and early at 4:00 the next morning for the mission. In the briefing, we and seven other crews were told that we would be dropping CDS loads and heavy equipment in the morning and then return in the afternoon and drop again after C-123s had air landed other equipment. As a result of the damage done to the drop force the previous day, we would be escorted by fighters who were to provide ground attack capability to support us.

'There would be a radar beacon on the drop zone to help us locate it and drop. The air force had an all-weather drop capability using such a beacon, in which the drop was made with a combination of a distance check mark at two miles as indicated on our airborne radar and a forward and cross-check countdown using the airborne Doppler. The other crews in the formation, which were all Pacific Air Force (PACAF) units, were told to use the all-weather system if necessary to complete their drop. Because we were a TAC crew and not PACAF, we were told that we could only drop visually, even though we were also checked out in the all-weather procedures. We just hadn't been checked out in them by PACAF.

'As we were pre-flighting the aircraft and getting ready to take off, I paused to consider that

I was now, after four years in this war, going to be involved in a combat airdrop in the face of hostile fire that in the past week had shot down one C-130 and damaged over ten. How in the hell did I get myself in this predicament?

'Fortunately, there was not a long time within which one could contemplate such sentiments. We took off for the mission at 6:25 am and were the number two aircraft in a flight of eight. Each plane took off at fifteen minute increments from the one preceding it and flew north toward the drop zone. When we got close to the A Shau Valley, we made contact with the ALCE at Đà Nẵng. They told us that the valley was weathered in and that the radar beacon on the drop zone was not yet operational. All eight aircraft went into a holding pattern at 500-foot altitude intervals using a bearing and distance off the Đà Nẵng Tactical Air Navigation (TACAN) station.

'After an hour in the holding pattern, Đà Nẵng informed us that weather in the valley was a broken undercast at drop altitude but that the beacon was now working and the formation was cleared for drops at five minute intervals. The first airplane called back that it was leaving its drop altitude and proceeding to air drop. Five minutes later, we did the same. As we descended toward the valley and the much lower drop altitude, I could see the escorting F-4 fighters far above us and off to the side. They had problems staying with us and providing any kind of covering fire due to our slow (130K) drop airspeed. It was the only view of them that any of us had for the rest of the day.

'When we departed the orbit and began

The encirclement of Khê Sanh meant that there was no safe corridor for the transport aircraft to use for their approach. Any descent towards the airstrip attracted heavy fire from enemy weapons, ranging from infantry small arms up to 12.7mm heavy machine guns and larger calibre anti-aircraft cannon. In order to minimise the risks posed by these hazardous conditions, the transport crews perfected the manoeuvre that came to be known as the 'Khê Sanh Approach'. [you prob won't get the rest in] A standard landing approach towards a runway would consist of a constant, controlled descent at a shallow angle, but the surrounding hills and risk of enemy fire forced the crews to keep their large, comparatively unwieldy transports at a much higher level for longer in order to stay out of range of small-arms and present a smaller target to the larger-calibre weapons. Then, as the aircraft approached the end of the runway, the pilot would drop the nose and put the aircraft into a steep dive, levelling out only at the very last moment. From here, the pilot could either land or make a very low-level pass along the runway at an altitude of about five feet, dropping the supplies out of the open rear cargo doors along the way. The pilot would then pull up sharply at the far end of the runway and execute a steep climb out of the valley, helped by the fact that the plane was now much lighter, having deposited its load.

A near miss during Operation 'Niagara'.

descending to airdrop altitude, we lost contact with Đà Nẵng; but we switched to another frequency and immediately got contact with the drop zone. My radar was in good condition and I shortly picked up the beacon, which we then used to establish our distance from the drop zone and heading into it. We had descended toward our 400-foot drop altitude above the terrain when the drop zone notified the first aircraft that its drop was half a mile beyond the DZ. Something was evidently wrong, as a CDS drop should be much closer to the desired point of impact than that.

'At 400 feet above ground level (agl), we were in and out of sparse, wispy clouds. It was now after 8:00 am; but due to the mountains surrounding the A Shau, dawn was just breaking. The clouds were thicker below drop altitude and we had only intermittent views of the ground as we approached the drop zone. At two minutes out from drop time, we were level and at drop altitude. We were also on centreline of the radar beacon and moving toward the two mile marker. The CDS load in the back had been unlocked for airdrop and the rear ramp and door were open. So far, we hadn't seen

any visual signs that might assist us in finding or identifying the DZ. We were in the clear at drop altitude, but below us there were still dense, scattered clouds. A dirt road appeared on the ground; but it was gone again, obscured by the clouds.

'The marker beacon return appeared at the two mile distance on the radar. I turned the Doppler to the preset course and distance module for the airdrop and returned to looking out the window for the DZ. We were one minute from airdrop. I couldn't see anything on the ground but broken clouds. No DZ. No panel marked impact point. Nothing.

'The Doppler and the radar indicated that we had reached the desired drop position. I hacked my watch. We could still see nothing as the watch counted down in seconds. Just as the watch reached the point where I must call 'Red Light' to terminate the airdrop at the far end of the DZ, Ron Hardy called, 'Do you see that smoke?' I looked down and to the right of where he pointed. There was one wisp of coloured smoke among the broken wisps of cloud. 'Green Light,' I called. Out goes the load.

The airplane, relieved of the several thousand pounds of cargo, surged upward as Daly began to gain altitude and turn to the escape heading.

'I went back to my desk to record the values I had used to estimate the drop and looked in the radar to see where we were, generally. Except for a small hole and a few returns in the centre of the scope, everything else was black. We were on a collision course with something.

'I threw the radar range out from the five miles it had been set on for the drop to twenty. I turned the elevation of the radar up a degree or two. Normally, the elevation is set a degree or two below the nose of the aircraft. We were in a 100 degree turn from the drop heading, which was near 360 degrees north, to the planned escape heading of 260 degrees. When I reconfigured the radar, the first clear space that I saw on it was near 230 degrees. Everything else remained black, even though we were climbing as best we could. I immediately hit the interphone and said, 'Joe, climb as quick as you can and turn to a heading of 210 degrees.' It was evident from my voice tone that we were in deep kimshy, as the Koreans say.

'Slowly, as if every second were an eternity, we climbed and turned. At last, after what seemed like a millennium, the clear space on the radar began to expand. Now I called for a heading of 200. The clear area was growing greater by the minute as we turned toward it. Relieved, I pulled my head out of the rubber cover that surrounded the radar scope and looked up into the cockpit. Weiss was sitting, turned 90 degrees in his engineer's seat and looking at me with eyes as wide and white as giant sized dollars. Following his eyes, I looked out the cockpit window behind Ron Hardy's seat. The cloud layer was now below us and straight ahead and on all sides just below was nothing but dense treetops and forest. The right wing looked as if it was 50 feet or so above the top of the jungle and the lateral distance to the jungle also appeared to be 50 feet. Individual leaves and branches of trees could be seen as we turned away from and above a mountainside. We had just missed becoming a permanent navigation aid on the mountain.

'We flew back to Cam Ranh and landed at 10:35. They had questions about our drop and indicated that it landed long or far beyond, the drop zone. Joe and I testified to the weather conditions and what had happened from our point of view. Ron Hardy swore to everything that we said. Nothing was said as to what happened to the drops of the planes behind us. There had been no reports of aircraft damage or firing from the morning drops. Father Charley had moved out of his spider holes on the approach, or the morning weather had kept him from seeing us as much as it kept us from seeing the DZ.

'We got new information (weight and chutes) about the load that we were going to drop in the afternoon. Again it was a CDS load, but the weather forecast for the second drop was different from that expected for the morning. We went back to the airplane and got ready for our next sortie. For the afternoon drop, we were again number two in a drop formation of eight C-130s. But ahead of us in use of the A Shau DZ and runway were ten C-123s which were to land and offload palletized cargo. Once the runway was cleared of the C-123s and their loads, we would be cleared to airdrop our CDS.

'We left Cam Ranh at 25 minutes after noon and proceeded to the orbit point off Đà Nẵng. When we got there, we were directed by the Đà Nẵng ALCE to once again get into orbit with the remainder of the C-130 force and hold with 500-foot separation until cleared to begin dropping. The

weather in the valley had deteriorated, even from the broken conditions which had existed in the morning. The C-123s had not been able to land at the scheduled times. When they did begin to land, the third aircraft landed and blew a tyre on the runway. That put a stop to all further landing attempts while a ground crew tried to locate and put a new tyre on the damaged aircraft.

'We stayed in orbit for an hour. The damaged C-123 was still on the runway down in the valley. Whether they were having trouble getting the load off the aircraft and then changing the tyre or just changing the tyre, we had no idea. We could talk to the Đà Nẵng ALCE, but not to the army in the A Shau. The ALCE could relay anything we had to say to the army and vice-versa, but we could not all communicate with each other. The weather in orbit was broken. We were in and out of clouds 50 percent of the time. The other 50 percent, it was clear at our altitude and for a thousand or so feet below; but below that it was completely undercast.

'Suddenly, as we turned one corner of the orbit, out of the clouds came an army Flying Crane (CH-54) helicopter. He was exactly at our altitude and turned broadside to us. He was there five seconds

A C-130 drops supplies to US Marines at Khê Sanh in April 1968. (USAF)

78

and probably never saw us; then he disappeared into the clouds and was gone. Ron Hardy immediately contacted Đà Nẵng to tell them that our orbit had been penetrated by a giant helicopter. 'Roger' came the reply. 'Be advised we have no contact with them.' 'Roger,' Hardy shot back. 'Hope we don't either.'

'As our second hour in orbit arrived, several of the other C-130s began to call Đà Nẵng and we all could listen in on the conversations. Some of them had heavy equipment loads rather than CDS and thus had different weights and fuel loads than we did. One said that if we didn't get drop clearance

soon he would have to return to Cam Ranh or Đà Nẵng to refuel. The remainder of the C-123s vacated their orbit and returned home due to low fuel. Their part of the mission was over. The ALCE listened to all the comments and said little except that they would pass them on; they weren't in charge of the airdrop, they were merely its message relay. Although some officer in the C-130s may have outranked anyone else in the formation, neither he nor anyone else was designated in command of the formation.

'My radar was still working well and from our orbit I had a very good radar picture of the A Shau

On Tuesday 18 April 1968 C-130E 63-7775 of Detachment 1 in the 374th TAW at Tân Sơn Nhứt flown by Captain Donald B. 'Doc' Jensen was hit by automatic weapons fire west of An Lộc on approach to An Lộc at 200 feet as it climbed to commence the final run in to drop its load of ammunition to South Viêtnamese troops. The FAC was unaware of their mission and told them where to drop their load, by way of an unsecure radio transmission, which could have been picked up by the NVA. They were supposed to follow a B-52 bombing mission, which would have kept the NVA quiet, but they were not told whether that the mission had ever taken place and a two-fighter escort the plane should have had, to protect it from the inevitable heavy ground fire they would attract, failed to materialise. The C-130's starboard wing caught fire and the load had to be jettisoned. Jensen headed south in the hope of reaching Tân Sơn Nhứt but he had to crash-land the aircraft in a swamp near Lai Khê where all the crew were recovered by Army helicopters.

On 26 April 1968 C-130E 64-0548 commanded by Captain Joseph L. Hannah departed Đà Nẵng Air Base with 14,616 lbs of empty sandbags at 1245 hours for Khê Sanh to perform a free fall Container Delivery drop. Due to rapid fluctuations of the weather during the day, Hannah selected to remain under control of Huế Approach Control and Khê Sanh GCA until visual, then proceed with drop at west end of runway 28. After the arrival of the aircraft, the first GCA was broken off at 7 miles and 4,000 feet due to weather going below minimum. Hannah was cleared to hold at 6,000 feet. After holding approximately 30 minutes, he was advised the weather was improving and was asked if he wished to perform another GCA. Hannah accepted the GCA and was proceeding with a normal GCA until ½ mile from touchdown when asked if he had drop zone in sight. He replied negative. Hannah was told the course was straight ahead (he was slightly below glide path) and shortly thereafter advised he was over end of runway and was asked did he have the drop zone in sight. There was no reply. 64-0548 had impacted about 150 feet short of the approach end of the runway, bounced and slid 800 feet down the runway. The aircraft was completely destroyed by impact and fire. Six of the seven crew sustained fatal injuries and Hannah sustained minor injury.

Valley below. The north and west of the valley were bounded by steep and relatively high karst mountains that rose steeply from the valley floor. As the afternoon wore on, I could see clouds form behind those mountains and slowly build over them. By the third hour in orbit, it was becoming clear that the cloud formations were building and merging and slowly moving over the mountains and into the valley itself. Đà Nẵng ALCE was told of this impending weather, but again it could do nothing more than pass on the message.

'Shortly thereafter, ALCE called and said that the airdrop was cancelled and we should return to Cam Ranh. It had begun to rain in the valley. Nothing further was said of the C-123. As one C-130 left orbit for the return, he called into ALCE and let them know that the entire effort with regard to A Shau had been 'a Goddamned disaster.'

'Roger. Copy,' was the reply. We landed at Cam Ranh at 4:25 and went to dinner and back to our rooms. We hadn't been shot at or hit, but the day had been a long and unrewarding experience nonetheless.'

The 1st Cavalry Division commander during Operation 'Delaware/Lam Son 216' described the Hercules effort as 'one of the most magnificent displays of airmanship that I have ever seen.' A rebuilt A Lưới airstrip received its first transport aircraft on 2 May and before heavy rains turned it to mud on the 11th, USAF Caribous, C-123s and C-130s made 113 landings, more than half by the Hercules.

Members of the 101st Airborne Division being evacuated aboard a USAF C-130 at Pham Thiết Air Base, a coastal port city in Southeast Việtnam.

Equally spectacular was the evacuation of the extremely remote US Special Forces camp (designated A-105J) at Khâm Đức. This mountain post was situated on a narrow plain surrounded by dense forest and the Annamite Mountains, 55 miles west of Chu Lai. The camp had been occupied by US and ARVN Special Forces since September 1963. By the spring of 1968 it was the last remaining border camp in Military Region 1 still in American hands. The camp's only contact with the main operating bases was by air and had an airstrip that could take C-123s and C-130s. Five miles to the south was a small forward operating base at Ngoc Tavak defended by just over 100 men. In the early hours of 10 May the outpost was attacked by an NVA infantry battalion using mortars and rockets. Fierce fighting continued as night turned into day and two Marine Corps CH-46s were lost attempting to extract the survivors. The North Việtnamese also began a simultaneous

mortar attack on Khâm Đức. Reinforcements were brought in by helicopter throughout the 11th despite enemy fire and low-lying fog. The enemy assault intensified in the early-hours of the 12th and the perimeter defences were soon overrun. A massive enemy assault on the main compound started around noon but this was thwarted by accurate and devastating air strikes. However, it became obvious that the situation was hopeless and the decision was taken to evacuate the camp by helicopter and transport aircraft. At first General Westmoreland had decided to reinforce and hold Khâm Đức. Later in the day, it was decided to abandon the base and use tactical transport planes to land and take the forces there to safety. In the confusion caused by the surprise attack on the base and the complete change in the US Air Force mission to save and then evacuate the camp, chaos reigned. Air strikes went ahead as the first C-130 landed during the morning: it received heavy battle damage and left hurriedly, carrying only three soldiers, fuel streaming from holes and tyres ripped to shreds.

In the afternoon C-130A 65-0548 in the 21st TAS, 374th TAW from Naha Air Base on Okinawa, temporarily deployed to Cam Ranh Bay piloted by Lieutenant Colonel John R. Delmore was hit repeatedly by small arms fire as it was landing at Khan Duc. The linkage to the power levers on all four engines was damaged and the engines could not be throttled back for the landing so Delmore had to feather all four props so he could set the aircraft down on Khâm Đức's runway. With the brakes shot out the aircraft veered off to one side of the runway, struck the wreckage of the Chinook that had been shot down earlier and came to rest with its nose stuck in the earth. Twenty minutes later a Marine Corps CH-46 evacuated all five crew out of Khâm Đức. C-130B 60-0297 in the 773rd TAS, 463 TAW temporarily based at Tân Sơn Nhứt and flown by Major Bernard Ludwig Bucher with a crew of six was one of the last aircraft to fly out of Khâm Đức. The aircraft, which was crammed with an estimated 150 Viêtnamese irregular troops and their dependants, took several hits and a few minutes later an FAC pilot who was airborne in the vicinity reported that the Hercules had exploded in mid-air and crashed into a ravine about one mile from the camp. Although it was not possible to reach the wreckage the aircraft was completely burnt out and there was no chance of any survivors. Captain Warren Robert Orr, 5th Special Forces Group also died.[1]

Captain Bill Barry, whose C-130 had taken off from Cam Ranh and carried palletized cargo to Đà Nẵng and spent two hours waiting for directions as to where to go next was not especially looking forward to flying into Khâm Đức in the face of NVA troops, 'who clearly surrounded the place and would have been firing directly on us in any further evacuation flights at that point in the afternoon. Finally, at 11:20 in the morning, we were told to return to Cam Ranh and await further orders. We landed at Cam Ranh an hour and ten minutes later and were informed that we were now the number two alert crew for dispatch to Khâm Đức in support of the evacuation mission. We sat for about two hours and then were told to go into crew rest. One crew from our deployed squadron at Tachikawa was new to the theatre and was tasked to take a three-man combat control team (CCT) into Khâm Đức to coordinate the original reinforcement order. Their airplane required maintenance after they were tasked and it wasn't until later that they finally took off with the CCT aboard. By this time, the camp had been ordered to evacuate, but the C-130 crew did not know it. They landed at Khâm Đức and the CCT drove off the ramp of their plane in a jeep. For all intents and purposes, the CCT were now trapped on a base that everyone else thought had been evacuated. Once the situation became clear to aircraft in the area, a C-123 Provider flown by Lieutenant Colonel Joe Jackson landed in the face of intense enemy fire and took the CCT out again.'[2]

It was not until 1630 hours in the afternoon that three C-130s succeeded in evacuating the last of the garrison. Of 1,500 survivors at Khâm Đức, the

C-130E of the 50th TAS/314th TAW boarding troops at Đà Nẵng Air Base.

Air Force succeeded in bringing out more than 500, almost all of them just before the outpost was overrun.

'The evacuation of Khâm Đức was complete and no more crews were needed for that action' wrote Captain Bill Barry. 'After a day spent sitting in the cockpit in the heat of Đà Nẵng and Cam Ranh, once we were released from alert I literally skipped off the plane and made for the officers' club, an early dinner and a goodly number of drinks. Khâm Đức was a cardinal example of the 'fog of war' principle. It began with a surprise enemy action, went through two exactly opposite command decisions as to how to respond and, with messed up communications, resulted in both heroism and tragedy. By the time it was over, Khâm Đức cost losses of two C-130s, an A-1 Skyraider and five helicopters.'

That night US aircraft bombed and strafed the camp's new occupants. Despite the loss of the camp, the evacuation of Khâm Đức stands out as one the most heroic episodes in the history of the war in Việtnam.

On 18 May Captain Bill Barry left Tachikawa as the navigator on a rapidly configured crew, all of whom had previously spent a thirteen month tour in Southeast Asia. 'We proceeded across the Pacific in a somewhat random manner. We flew as a deadhead crew to Mactan where we picked up a C-130B that was going back to the US for major maintenance and inspection. Our route home was from Mactan to Clark to 'CCK' [Ching Chuang Kang Air Base] in Taiwan and then to Midway Island and McClellan AFB in California. From McClellan, I flew home on a commercial jet. My last tour in support of the Việtnam War was over.'[3]

In May 1966 Hercules aircraft were employed in an operation to destroy the giant Long Biên or Ham Rong ('Dragon's Jaw') road and rail bridge over the Sông Mã River, three miles north of Thanh Hòa, the capital of Annam Province, in North Việtnam's bloody 'Iron Triangle' (Hảiphòng, Hànôi and Thanh Hòa). The 540 feet long, 56 feet wide, Chinese-engineered cantilever bridge, which stood 50 feet above the river, was a replacement for the original French-built Bridge destroyed by the Việt Minh in 1945, blown up by simply loading two locomotives with explosives and running them together in the middle of the bridge. The new bridge, completed in 1964, had two steel through-truss spans which rested in the centre on a massive reinforced concrete pier sixteen feet in diameter and on concrete abutments at the other ends. Hills on both sides of the river provided solid bracing for the structure. Between 1965 and 1972 eight concrete piers were added near the approaches to give additional resistance to bomb damage. A one-metre gauge single railway track ran down the 12 foot wide centre and 22 foot wide concrete highways were cantilevered on each side. This giant would prove to be one of the single most challenging targets for American air power in Việtnam. It had first captured the attention of the US planners in March 1965 when the decision to interdict the North Việtnamese rail system south of the 20th Parallel led immediately to the 3 April strike against the bridge. This and the repeated strikes by USAF and USN fighter-bombers, ended in failure and with the loss of sixteen USAF pilots alone.

The Air Force decided to try mass-focusing the energy of certain high explosive weapons against the stubborn structure using two specially modified C-130E aircraft in the 314th Troop Carrier Wing to drop the weapon, a rather large, pancake-shaped bomb 8 feet in diameter, 2.5 feet thick and weighing 5,000lb. The USAF had undertaken a special project in late 1965 to develop a method of conducting a stand-off attack against bridges in North Việtnam, many of which were heavily protected by anti-aircraft artillery. The primary target of such an operation was the Thanh Hòa rail bridge about nine miles upstream from the mouth of the Sông Mã River in northern Việtnam, one of the longest of the region, rising in the northwest. It flows south-eastward through Laos for about fifty miles, cutting gorges through uplands to reach the plains region at which northern Việtnam begins to narrow. The river enters the Gulf of Tonkin, 65 miles south of Hànôi, after a course of 250 miles. Like the Red River to the north, it has an irregular regime with maximum flow toward the end of summer. The Ma River delta differs, however, from that of the Red River because of its narrowness and the presence of sandy soil.

In September 1965 the Air Force Armament Laboratory (AFATL) undertook development of a floating mine, that could be dropped in the river away from the bridge and detonate when it came into contact with it. As part of Project 1559, also

10 February 1968 - USMC KC-130F BuNo149813 of VMGR-152 piloted by CWO Henry Wilefang, which was delivering 115/145 avgas to Khê Sanh when it was riddled by .50-calibre machine gun fire during its final seconds in the air and skidded the length of the runway in a fireball when the fuel bladders on board were set alight and the airframe burned out on the runway, killing one crewman and five passengers. A bullet also struck the cockpit and one of the engines caught fire. Struggling to reach them - and to clear the runway - rescue teams fought the holocaust with foam. One rescuer had to be saved when overcome by smoke. Rescuers edged their fire trucks directly against the flaming plane, aiming high-pressure foam at the inferno's heart. They ignored the danger of the other fuel tanks bursting into geysers of burning aviation fuels. The fire chief without even a mask, had tried to enter the cabin, but its roof collapsed just ahead of him. It had been hopeless from the start. Finally, the rescue team chief, never having found time to put on his mask, stood exhausted by the hulk of the plane and helpless tears streaked down his face. (David Douglas Duncan)

known as 'Carolina Moon', AFATL's Technology Branch designed a mine with a 6-foot diameter and an approximate weight of 4,000lbs, of which half was explosive in a focused warhead. The weapon would be dropped from either a C-123 or C-130 aircraft and would feature two 64-foot parachutes to retard its fall. The mine would have two fuses. One of these was modified from that used on the CIM-10 Bomarc surface to air missile. The other was an infrared optical fuse. The radar fuse had a cone of 70 degrees, while the optical fuse had a cone of 3 degrees. Work began on fabricating the weapons in October 1965. The steel mine casings were fabricated at the Oak Ridge National Laboratory, an Atomic Energy Commission facility operated by Union Carbide. AFATL's Targets

Division designed and built the optical fuses and the safe-and-arm assembly with parts fabrication by a local contractor. The US Army's Picatinny Arsenal modified thirty BOMARC fuses and the Air Proving Ground Center assembled the weapons.

In the end, twenty live weapons and another ten inert items were produced at a cost of $600,000, in addition to wages for personnel working on the project. The final design had a weight of 3,750lbs, a maximum width of 96 inches and a maximum height of 31.5 inches. In November 1965 preparations were made for testing of the assembled weapons at Eglin Air Force Base. During the tests 75 drops were made into water to develop a working rigging design and dropping procedure. The mine's sensors were tested separately in dummy mines against a bridge and the boom of a floating crane. The safe-arm device was found to be successful. No full destruction test of the weapon was conducted at Eglin because of lack of suitable facilities. Test data theoretically estimated an equivalent 1 kiloton blast effect approximately 20-30 feet above the weapon.

Following the tests, an initial operation plan was developed on 28 February 1966. TAWC analyzed the proposed operation and concluded that the chances of success were small because the mines, when dropped far enough upstream to avoid effective anti-aircraft defences, would, run aground. Alternative proposals were said, however, to apparently offer a lesser chance of success and TAWC was directed by Headquarters, USAF to develop an operation plan to support the project. On 4 April TAWC published OPLAN 155, 'Carolina Moon' in which two crews (a primary and an alternate) would be trained to conduct the operation using two C-130E aircraft provided by TAC, including one equipped with the AN/APN-161 Ka-Band radar system. The aircraft (64-0513 and 64-0511; the first aircraft being equipped with the specialized radar) were provided by Ninth Air Force. Between 11 April and 15 May Major Richard T. Renners and crew and Major Thomas Franklin Case and crew in the 62nd Troop Carrier Squadron trained at Eglin for the operation. Training included three hours of mission orientation, forty hours of weapon system training, 24 hours of target study, 24 hours of mission planning, 25 hours of day mission training and lastly fifty hours of night mission training. The last two segments involved two and seven weapon drops respectively and the two crews completed a total of fourteen drops.

The two crews and their aircraft deployed to Đà Nẵng Air Base on or about 19 May where they received additional target information and participated in final selection of the mission profile. On 20 May Pacific Air Forces ordered the execution of Operation 'Carolina Moon' by

Cargo ground crew girls clowning at left side paratrooper door (aft of the wing) of the C-130 at Tân Sơn Nhứt AB, Saïgon in 1972. Note the four mounts at left side of photo for a JATO (Jet Assisted Takeoff) system. The jets would be ignited for a short time during takeoff, propelling the C-130 into the air supposedly and incredibly in as little as a few hundred feet. (Robert D.Young)

Seventh Air Force. The first mission was conducted on 29/30 May. Both aircraft were sortied, with the second acting as an airborne spare. The C-130s flew very low to evade radar along a 43-mile route - which meant they were vulnerable to enemy attack for about seventeen minutes - and dropped the bombs, which floated down the Sông Mã River until they passed under the 'Dragon's Jaw', where sensors in the bombs would detect the metal of the bridge structure and cause them to detonate.

After the first aircraft successfully reached the mouth of the Sông Mã River, the second aircraft was recalled. The first aircraft flew at 100 feet AGL toward the target, with the planned release point of 12,000 feet short of the Thanh Hòa Bridge. A proviso had been inserted into the frag order that said that if the anti-aircraft fire was light the aircraft could continue another 5,000 feet, releasing the weapon 7,000 feet short of the span. The aircraft received light fire and proceeded to the 7,000 foot release point, popping up to 400 feet AGL for thirty seconds prior to the release. After releasing five weapons, the aircraft returned to the previous altitude and departed the area. A flight of four F-4C aircraft were tasked to conduct a diversionary strike fifteen miles south of the bridge as well. Both the C-130E aircraft and the F-4C flight reported heavy anti-aircraft fire in the vicinity of the bridge during the operation. The crew of the C-130E reported that the mission had been a success, but subsequent bomb damage assessment showed no damage to the bridge.

Concerns about appropriate river flow rate and about compromising the objectives of the operation led to the decision to launch a second strike on the night immediately following, on 31 May/1 June. The ingress route was changed for the second mission, but the final run remained the same. Because the slow-moving C-130Es would need protection, F-4C Phantoms of the 8th Tactical Fighter Wing at Ubon would fly a diversionary attack to the south, using flares and bombs on the highway just before the C-130E was to drop its ordnance. The F-4Cs were to enter their target area at 300 feet attack at 50 feet and pull off the target back to 300 feet for subsequent attacks. Additionally, an EB-66 was tasked to jam the radar in the area during the attack period. The first C-130E was to be flown by Major Richard T. Renners

and the second by Major Thomas Franklin Case who had been deployed to Việtnam only two weeks before. Ten mass focus weapons were provided, allowing for a second mission should the first fail to accomplish the desired results. Last minute changes to coincide with up-to-late intelligence included one that would be very significant. Renners felt that the aircraft was tough enough to survive moderate AAA hits and gain enough altitude should hail-out be necessary. Case agreed that the aircraft could take hits, but considered that the low-level flight would preclude a controlled bail-out. In view of these conflicting philosophies and the fact that either parachutes or flak vests could be worn, but not both, Renners decided that his crew would wear parachutes and stack their flak vests on the floor of the aircraft, whereas Case decided that his crew would wear only flak vests and store the parachutes.

Renners and his crew, including navigators Captain Norman G. Clanton and 1st Lieutenant William 'Rocky' Edmondson, departed Đà Nẵng at 00.25 hours and headed north under radio silence. Although the Hercules met no resistance at the beginning of its approach, heavy - though fortunately, inaccurate - ground fire was encountered after it was too late to turn back. The five weapons were dropped successfully in the river and Renners made for the safety of the Gulf of Tonkin. The operation had gone flawlessly and the Hercules escaped unharmed thanks, in part, to the diversionary attack by the two Phantoms and jamming of North Việtnamese radar by the RB-66. Both F-4s returned to Thailand unscathed. Unfortunately the excitement of the C-130 crew was short-lived, because post-strike reconnaissance photos taken at dawn showed that there was no noticeable damage to the bridge, nor was any trace of the bombs found indicating either that the bombs had not detonated or they had not exploded in the right position. A second mission was therefore planned for the night of 31 May.

The plan for Major Case's crew was basically the same, with the exception of a minor time change and a slight modification to the flight route. A crew change was made when Case asked 1st Lieutenant 'Rocky' Edmondson, the navigator from the previous night's mission, to go along on this one because of his experience gained on the first 'pancake bomb' mission. C-130E 64-0511

AC-130E 69-6573 of the 16th SOS shows the results of a deadly new threat, the man-portable SA-7 surface-to-air missile, which on 13 May 1972 hit the tail just above the ramp on the port side and fragments punched large holes on the starboard side. Ken Felty was injured in this missile strike and the aircraft landed safely. It was repaired and returned to combat for the Easter Offensive in Viêtnam. [Ken Felty]

departed Đà Nẵng at 01.10 hours and the two F-4s again flew as a diversion for the Hercules strike. At 0850 Seventh Air Force reported that an F-4C had been lost south of the Thanh Hòa Bridge and that this was one of the aircraft involved in a second diversionary strike related to 'Carolina Moon'. One of the two F-4C's backseaters (63-76640) was 38-year old Major Dayton William Ragland, a top USAF fighter pilot during the Korean War and the veteran of many missions in 'MiG Alley'.[4] Having flown 97 combat missions in Viêtnam, Ragland was about ready to be rotated back to the US, but agreed to fly in the back seat of the 497th Tactical Fighter Squadron F-4C piloted by 25-year old 1st Lieutenant Ned Raymond Herrold from New Brunswick, New Jersey to give the younger man more combat flight time while he operated the sophisticated technical

navigational and bombing equipment. The two Phantoms left Thailand and headed for the area south of the 'Dragon', flying at times only 50 feet above the ground. At about two minutes prior to the scheduled C-130 drop time, the F-4Cs were in the midst of creating the diversion when crew members saw AA fire and a large ground flash in the vicinity of the bridge and it was assumed that the aircraft had either been shot down or had flown into the ground or the river. No trace of the aircraft or its crew was discovered despite several reconnaissance missions. During the F-4C attack, Herrold and Ragland's jet was hit: on its final pass the damaged Phantom did not pull up, but went out to sea, continuing nearly five miles off shore before exploding. The two crew may have ejected before the explosion because a search-and-rescue aircraft discovered a dinghy in the water the following day.

At 1103 Seventh Air Force reported that the 'Carolina Moon' C-130E (64-0511) was missing. The members of the diversionary strike (call sign 'Neon') reported that they had witnessed heavy anti-aircraft fire in the vicinity of the Thanh Hòa Bridge at around 0200 during their mission, followed by a large ground flash. The 'Carolina Moon' C-130E was never heard from again, but it was unofficially believed that it had arrived in the target area and had been shot down. The official time of loss was set at 1812 on 31 May. Seventh

Air Force reported that 'Carolina Moon' had concluded on 1 June following the loss of one of the aircraft and its crew. Interrogation of a North Viêtnam torpedo boat crewman some time later reportedly contained information about the first 'Carolina Moon' mission. The individual reportedly admitted to having seen a US aircraft drop five objects into the river near the Thanh Hòa Bridge and that four of the five devices had detonated. In April 1986 and February 1987 the remains of Case and two of his crew were returned to the US. Herrold and Ragland are among the 2,303 Americans still listed as 'unaccounted for' in South-East Asia.

By 1967 almost 700 sorties had been flown against the bridge, at a cost of 104 crewmen shot down over an area 75 square miles around the 'Dragon'. In March that year the US Navy attacked the charmed bridge with new 'Walleye' missiles but failed to knock out the structure despite three direct hits. The spans were finally brought down on 13 May 1972 by laser-guided 'smart' bombs dropped by F-4Ds of the 8th TFW. Unfortunately, by then the Communists had built several other back-up routes around the bridge and so the flow of supplies across the Ma River was not seriously affected.

From 1968, under Project 'Commando Vault', C-130s were used to drop 5-ton (10,000lb) M-121 and 7.5-ton (15,000lb) BLU-82 - Bomb Live Unit - weapons to blast out helicopter landing zones

about 260 feet in diameter in jungle areas. Air Force Systems Command and the US Army co-operated closely to develop a method whereby these large bombs could be dropped from both the C-130 and the US Army CH-54 Tarhe helicopter (after an 18th-century chief of the Wyandot Indian tribe whose nickname was 'The Crane'). The 'Big Blue' was first dropped operationally from a Hercules on 23 March using a delivery technique similar to that used to unleash the M-120, though a 'daisy cutter' fuse-extending rod ensured that the block-buster detonated at a height of 4 feet above the ground. The first tests involving both types of aircraft proved so successful that late in 1968 operational deployment in South-East Asia took place, the Hercules 'bomber' being assigned to the 463rd Tactical Airlift Wing. In Viêtnam, approach to the designated release point was made easier by using signals from the MSQ-77 ground radar sites.

The Hercules could carry two palletized weapons in the hold and given that a single M-121 bomb was capable of clearing an area about 200 feet in diameter, more than enough for a helicopter to land safely, the C-130A and C-130E therefore had the advantage over the C-54, being able to create two clearings per mission and over greater distances. Invariably, Hercules bomb delivery was made by the parachute extraction method described earlier, usually from about 7,000 feet; stabilizing parachutes were deployed to lower the weapons to the ground. After a lull in operations during the

C-130s often operated from rough and ready airstrips during the war in SE Asia.

88

winter months, the 463rd TAW resumed 'Commando Vault' operations in March.

A series of military operations were conducted in eastern Cambodia by the US and the Republic of Viêtnam from 29 April to 22 July 1970. Thirteen major operations were conducted during the Cambodian Campaign (also known as the Cambodian Incursion) by the ARVN and US forces between 1 May and 30 June. After the Incursion, in which 463rd Wing crews played a large role, President Richard Nixon began withdrawing troops from South Viêtnam as he had promised during the 1968 presidential campaign. Several C-130 units were slated for deactivation, including the 463rd. The 29th TAS was the first to go; it deactivated in August 1970 and its personnel transferred to the other squadrons. The 463rd Wing survived for another year. The wing inactivated on 31 December 1971. The 774th Tactical Airlift Squadron remained active at Clark until mid-1972.

By spring 1970 there were more than 450 American PoWs in North Viêtnam and another 970 American servicemen who were missing in action.

Some of the PoWs had been imprisoned over 2,000 days, longer than any serviceman had ever spent in captivity in any war in America's history. Furthermore, Intelligence reports told of appalling conditions, brutality, torture and even death. In May reconnaissance photographs revealed the existence of two prison camps west of Hànôi. At Son Tây, 23 miles from Hànôi, one photograph identified a large 'K' - a code for 'come get us; - drawn in the dirt. at the other camp at Âp Lò Vôi about thirty miles west of Hànôi another photo showed the letters 'SAR' (Search and Rescue), apparently spelled out by prisoners' laundry and an arrow with the number '8'. Reconnaissance photos taken by SR-71 aircraft revealed that Son Tây 'was active'. The camp itself was open and surrounded by rice paddies. In close proximity was the 12th NVA Regiment totalling about 12,000 troops. Also nearby was an artillery school, a supply depot and an air defence installation. Five hundred yards further south was another compound called the 'secondary school' which was an administration centre, housing 45 guards. To make matters worse,

A USAF C-130B in the 774th TAS, 463rd TAW offloading supplies in Viêtnam.

Phúc Yên AB in Vĩnh Phúc Province was only twenty miles northeast of Son Tây. The heavy monsoon downpours prohibited the raid until finally, November was selected because the moon would be high enough over the horizon for good visibility but low enough to obscure the enemy's vision.

Twenty-four primary and five backup crew personnel, all 'Stray Goose'/'Combat Spear' veterans detached from 7th SOS ('Combat Arrow') and 1st SOW ('Combat Knife') developed helicopter-fixed wing formation procedures for low level night missions and jointly trained with selected Special Forces volunteers at Eglin AFB. Between the end of August and 28 September 'Talon', helicopter and A-1 Skyraider crews supervised by 'Combat Talon' Programme Manager Lieutenant Colonel Benjamin N. Kraljev rehearsed the flight profile in terrain-following missions over southern Alabama, flying 368 sorties that totalled more than 1,000 hours. A month of intensive joint training with the Special Forces rescue force followed at a replica of the prison camp. In early November the task force deployed to Takhli RTAF Base, Thailand.

The 24 primary crew members, a 7th SOS MC-130 'Combat Talon' crew ('Cherry 01') under Major Irl L. 'Leon' Franklin and a 1st SOW crew ('Cherry 02') commanded by Lieutenant Colonel Albert P. 'Friday' Blosch, conducted the mission. John Gargus[5] participated in the air operations planning for the Son Tây raid and then flew as the lead navigator of 'Cherry 02' that led three 'Jolly Greens' on the mission ('Cherry 02' led another three - a total of one HH-3 'Banana' and five 'Apple' HH-53s). In total, 116 aircraft from seven airbases and three aircraft carriers comprised the total force under the command of Brigadier General LeRoy J. Manor. The air element (primary force) included five HH-53s, one HH-3, two MC-130 Combat Talons and five A-1Es.

Dr. Joe Cataldo issued sleeping pills. At 2200 hours the men boarded a C-130 and left Takhli for Udorn where helicopters were waiting. Upon landing at Udorn the men transferred to three of the helicopters, carefully rechecking all the equipment that had been deemed necessary for the mission that lay ahead. At 2318 hours the first helo launched; at 2325 hours the last helo launched. They were led by two HC-130 refuellers en-route to an air refuelling area over Northern Laos. Bill Kornitzer, Aircraft Commander of the lead HC-130, 'Lime One' recalls 'Our mission was to launch from Udorn, join up with the six helicopters and lead them to the North Việtnam border. After joining up we refuelled the five HH-53s and the

C-130A-45-LM 57-0460 of the South Việtnamese Air Force at Tân Sơn Nhứt near Sàigòn in 1972. The aircraft served with the VNAF from October 1972 to April 1975. During the fall of Sàigòn, it was flown from Tân Sơn Nhứt Air Base to Singapore, carrying about 350 Việtnamese. Returning to USAF service in August 1975 it was assigned to the 16th Special Operations Squadron (SOS) at Korat Royal Thai Air Force Base; then used by the USAF Air National Guard for many years before being retired in 1989. Today this aircraft is part of the National Air and Space Museum, given its historic past.

Final evacuation of the Khê Sanh base complex on 1 July 1968. North Viêtnamese gunners, who were controlled by always-moving ridge top observers, rarely missed hitting something or someone, with every salvo fired. So the 26th Marines lived like prairie dogs, in and out of their vast colony of bunkers. On tough days five or six 122mm rockets hurtled in every minute. It took a special sort of man to stand quietly during such an attack while guiding other men to cover.

HH-3. This was done in total silence without any incidents. The HH-3 stayed close behind our left wing in order to maintain the speed required by the rest of formation. After leaving the helicopters for their final assault, we immediately returned to Udorn for refuelling. We were to refuel as soon as possible and return to the Northern Laos area to provide air refuelling and search and rescue support as needed.'

On board 'Apple Two', Jay Stayer recalls: 'Just as we had practiced, the formation lead HC-130P refueller aircraft, 'Lime One', got off on time, as did the rest of us, the HH-3 'Banana' and five 'Apple' HH-53s. We routinely fell into the seven ship formation, three helicopters stacking high on each side of the leading HC-130 at about 1,500 feet AGL. There was a partial moon and some clouds that we climbed through, when suddenly the call came to 'break, 'break, 'break!', indicating that someone had lost sight of the formation lead and

we were to execute the formation break-up procedure. Each helicopter turned to a predetermined heading and climbed to a predetermined altitude for one minute and then returned to the original landing. The effect was a very widely separated formation, each helicopter 500 feet above the other and at varying distances away from the lead HC-130. I could see other members of the formation flying in and out of the clouds and I thought we had blown the mission we had hardly started. Apparently a strange plane had almost flown through the formation and someone had called the lost contact procedure to avoid a mid-air collision. As it turned out, planning for such possible events and the training for such resulted in a rather routine formation break and with a subsequent rejoin being completed successfully. In the meantime, we had all topped off our fuel tanks from the lead HC-130 and had quite deftly exchanged formation leads from him to the just-arrived, blacked-out C-130 with all the fancy electronic gear.'

Happily, the weather in the refuelling area was clear. All refuellings were accomplished without difficulty. All six helos then joined formation with an MC-130 Combat Talon for the low altitude flight toward North Việtnam. The area over Laos is a mountainous area requiring precise navigation by the MC-130 crew.

In the meantime the five A-1s had departed Nakhon Phanom and joined formation with the second MC-130 Combat Talon. This formation was in close proximity of the MC-130/helo flight. All were en-route at low altitude for Son Tay. Close air support was the job of the A-1s because they were ideally suited. They had long endurance capability, carried a big load of ordnance and their relatively low speed permitted small orbits which would keep them close by overhead should assistance be needed on short notice.

Ten F-4s had taken off from Ubon to provide a MiG air patrol and five F-105 Wild Weasels had launched from Korat to provide protection from the SAM sites. The F-4s and F-105s would be flying at a high altitude providing cover over the general area and would not interfere in any way with the primary force.

The Navy force launched on time with a total of 59 sorties. As the primary force reached the Laos/North Việtnam border, the enemy radar's became aware of the Navy force coming from over the Tonkin Gulf. The diversionary raid was having the desired effects. The presence of the Navy on enemy radar caused near panic conditions within the North Việtnamese defence centres. It became obvious that the North Việtnamese total concern was directed eastward. the raiding force, coming from the west, in effect had a free ride.

Meanwhile, in 'Apple Two', as Jay Strayer vividly remembers - 'Tension was building up by this time, as we neared the IP for the final approach to the camp. I had done most of the flying up to this point and Jack Allison took over the controls for the final phase. I in turn picked up the navigation duties during this critical phase of the mission. As we had rehearsed so many times, the lead C-130 led us over the last mountain range and down to 500 feet above the ground. At the IP they, along with 'Apple Four' and 'Five' popped up to 1,500 feet to fly directly for the camp. A single

radio transmission with the last vector heading to the camp was made by the C-130's navigator and we continued on, maintaining a disciplined radio silence. Now we were only four - 'Apple Three' in the lead with the HH-3, 'Apple's One' and 'Two' following in trail, with 45-second separations between.'

Upon reaching the IP (Initial Point) the MC-130 climbed to 1,500 feet. The 130's mission at this point was to drop flares over the prison. Helos 4 and 5 were to provide a backup and were to drop flares should the C-130 flares not be effective. The flares worked as intended. The helos made a left turn and proceeded to a pre-selected landing area which was on an island in a large lake. There they would wait, hopefully to be called to move to Son Tay to pick up some PoWs. The C-130 made a right turn and dropped fire fight simulators (deception) and napalm to create a fire as an anchor point for the A-1s. The C-130 then left the area for an orbit point over Northern Laos. Immediately after the flares illuminated the prison compound HH-53 'Apple Three', under the command of Marty Donohue, flew low over the prison firing at the guard towers with his Gatling machine guns. The plan called for neutralizing the guard towers to eliminate that potential source of enemy opposition. Immediately following Donohue's pass the HH-3, carrying a 14-man assault force, landed in a relatively small space inside the prison walls. So far all was going strictly according to plan and precisely on time.

The landing was a hard one, but successful. Simultaneous with the landing of the assault force, HH-53s 'Apple One' and 'Two' were landed opposite the south side and immediately fanned out and conducted a search of all the buildings in search of Americans and to prevent reinforcements from interfering in any way with the rescue effort. Warner Britton in 'Apple One' saw the flares dropped by the C-130 ignite and was impressed by the surrealistic appearance of the illuminated landscape. Jack Allison, in the holding area, recalls - 'Sitting in the holding area waiting to be recalled to pick up the PoWs and ground forces, 'Apple' flight was treated to a spectacular fireworks display. Fourteen to sixteen SAMs were fired at the F-105 'Wild Weasel' aircraft, although one was at such a low angle, one of the departing helicopters took evasive action. One SAM was observed to explode and spray fuel over 'Firebird Three'. The aircraft descended in a ball of fire and appeared to be a loss. However the fire blew out and the crew continued with the mission. Another SAM exploded near 'Firebird Five', inflicting damage to his flight controls and fuel system. The crew later bailed out over the Plaine des Jarres and were picked up at first light by 'Apple Four' and 'Five'.

While all the helicopters were engaged with the compound and A-1s, which had arrived with the second C-130, were 'doing their thing'. The entire camp was searched. All North Vietnamese forces were annihilated and the devastatingly disappointing discovery was made that there were no Americans at the camp. The coded message - 'Negative Items' - was transmitted to Brigadier General Manor's command post at Udorn. Manor met a dejected force of raiders. 'They were disappointed because our hopes of returning with POWs were dashed. We had failed. This thoroughly dedicated group expressed the belief we should return the next night and search for the POWs. For many reasons, this could not be done.'

Prior to the raid all 65 prisoners had been moved to another camp at Đồng Hới about fifteen miles east of Sơn Tây, apparently due to the proximity of the camp to a river thought likely to flood.[6]

In the spring of 1970 Alan Baker transitioned from C-141 co-pilot to C-130 aircraft commander and arrived at CCK's 776th Tactical Airlift Squadron in the summer. 'Việtnam lacked maintenance facilities so the C-130 airplanes and crews were officially stationed in Taiwan at Ching Chuang Kang Air Base [formerly Kung Kuan Air Base] or CCK as it was more popularly known; and

Clark AB in the Philippines. I was 24 years old and I'd just been promoted to captain. I was eager to start flying in Việtnam and was simultaneously scared shitless. At boondock airfields C-130s were considered 'mortar magnets' because they made such a nice target for bad guys with mortars outside the perimeter fence. GI's liked getting mail and supplies, but did not like the mortar rounds we attracted.

He wrote hundreds of letters to his then-girlfriend Gloria. 'On 5 August I flew on the last leg of the day; a pax (passenger) run from Đà Nẵng to Tân Sơn Nhứt. As I was starting the #4 engine, the starter button didn't pop out at 70% like it was supposed to. So I pulled it out at 72% to make sure that the starter disengaged. (If the starter remained engaged until the engine reached full speed it would probably fly apart - don't want that.) So we shut the other engines down, deplaned our pax and the engineer spent about an hour removing the starter shaft. We buttoned everything up, cranked the three good engines and taxied out for a 'windmill' taxi start. Using those three good engines I accelerated down the runway to 100 knots then crammed on the brakes (fortunately Đà Nẵng had a nice long runway). The 100-knot airflow got the prop of the dead engine turning enough for the engine to sustain itself - sort of an air start on the runway. I taxied back in, picked up our pax with all four engines running, got a crew duty day extension and leaped off for TSN. Piece of cake. I wonder what the pax thought of all this - it was probably not a confidence-builder.

'To get checked out as an aircraft commander I needed short field landings. On 15 August I rode along with a 50th Squadron crew as an auxiliary crew member on a 'bladder bird' to deliver

C-130A A97-206 (57-0499) of 36 Squadron RAAF on arrival at Sàigòn (Tân Sòn Nhứt) in 1969.

Australian MPs on the line at Tân Sòn Nhứt in May 1968. (Stan Middleton).

30,000lb of JP4 for helicopters flying out of Sông Bé. In May 1965 the fortified capital of Phước Long Province had seen a major action between the Việt Công and Army of the Republic of Việtnam (ARVN) which had resulted in the city being re-taken by the end of the second day of combat. 'The trip meant no stick time but there are always things to learn. When we got overhead Sông Bé there was a solid overcast and no instrument approaches available, so we returned to Biên Hỏa to wait it out. After a rain storm the weather at Sông Bé improved, but its 3,400 foot aluminium runway was now too wet to land at this heavy weight. So we offloaded 15,000lbs of JP4 at Biên Hỏa and then pressed on to Sông Bé. After some diligent searching we found a hole in the overcast and then made a normal 'firm' landing. We offloaded the JP4 and cranked up, but the starter button for the #4 engine didn't pop out (just like a week earlier at Đà Nẵng) so the engineer pulled the starter out while the rest of the crew sampled army chow. Sông Bé's runway was too short for a windmill taxi start (which involves charging down the runway on three engines until you're going fast enough that the airflow starts turning the dead prop) so we waited until another C-130 landed and requested a 'buddy start' (also called a 'blow job'). We pulled up behind him on the runway with about 5 feet tail-to-nose clearance. He set his power to max on all four engines and his propwash caused us to rock and roll. It took three attempts to get our #4 prop turning fast enough for the engine to sustain itself, then it took two minutes to accelerate to normal speed.'

'On 13 October I was finally scheduled for an instrument check flight on a round-trip to Việtnam - we called such a trip an 'out-and-back'. Our orders were to fly to Biên Hỏa and return. In addition to being a check ride, it was my first trip as the aircraft commander and my first flight with my own crew, so I was pumped! The flight engineer was also getting a check ride and after our previous mechanical problems we were paying especially close attention to the airplane's condition. The airplane checked out just fine so we cranked it up.

'We taxied out and the engineer brought the outboard engines up to normal ground idle, which sped up the airplane a bit. I applied the brakes to slow us down and nothing happened! I tried the brakes a second time and still got no braking. So I told the co-pilot to turn on the auxiliary hydraulic pump and select emergency brakes. Those worked! (If this had happened while we were landing on a short field we would have been in trouble.) We tried normal brakes again and they worked very erratically, so we switched back to emergency brakes and taxied back in. We picked up some maintenance guys and did a taxi check. This time the brakes worked just fine! We never found out what went wrong, but since everything was working again we pressed on out to the runway.

'At CCK the military there was on a high state of alert, ready to go to war at any moment. Before we reached the runway, the Chinese scrambled their F-104s and in a rush to take off, one taxied under our right wing!

'We were carrying 21 tons of fresh vegetables for the troops in Việtnam. To avoid refuelling in Việtnam we also carried enough fuel for the round-trip; 18 tons. At this heavy weight we made a very slow climb out and could only reach 18,000 feet - below the preferred altitude for this route. But the trip to Biên Hỏa was uneventful and I made a really good GCA (ground-controlled radar approach) and a grease job landing. I hoped this impressed the check pilot.

'After a Biên Hỏa 'heartburn hamburger' I returned to the airplane to return to CCK. But meanwhile the plane had been loaded with two passengers and five pallets of cargo whose destination was Cam Ranh Bay! Strange. So I called up 'Herman Billy' (call sign for the CCK command post) and asked what was going on. They told me that while in Việtnam I was under the control of the Việtnam command post (call sign 'Hilda' - the airlift control centre at Tân Sơn Nhứt). Apparently someone at 'Hilda' had decided we could make a little stop at Cam Ranh Bay on our way back to Taiwan! OK, whatever...

'So we flew TAC VFR (visual flight rules in the clouds with radar flight-following) to Cam Ranh Bay, where I flew a very good VFR approach and landing. I filed a new flight plan to CCK because the original one was only good for returning directly from Biên Hỏa. I made a disappointing ILS (instrument landing system) approach and landing at CCK. So after doing well all day long I ended my check ride on a down note. But at my check ride debriefing the flight examiner had only praise for my flying and my crew management. Hurray!

'En route the monsoon season in Việtnam made flying tough. Every day there was rain, overcast and low visibility, which made it nearly impossible to get from airport to airport using Visual Flight Rules (VFR). So we used other means. In Việtnam the civil en route air traffic controllers didn't have radar. Instead, Instrument Flight Rules (IFR) was done the pre-radar way based on aircraft reporting

During 'Lam Son 719' in 1971 when eleven C-130Bs were temporarily stationed at Đà Nẵng to fly loads into Khê Sanh, C-130B 61-2642 was destroyed on the ground in an early morning rocket attack on Sunday 21st February by a 122 mm rocket which went into the fuselage, which also damaged others nearby. Đà Nẵng was nicknamed 'Rocket City' because it was subject to such frequent rocket attacks. The only salvageable part of 642 was its tail, which was reused on an AC-130. The quick action of the men of the 15th Aerial Port Squadron kept this attack from becoming a disaster. Luckily, 642 was the only bird on the ramp that was not loaded with Class A explosives bound for Khê Sanh next morning and it had no flight or ground personnel inside.

KC-130F Bu150688 of VMGR-152 at Đông Hà combat base in Việtnam in 1969.

over various navigation aids. This meant that very few aircraft could fly IFR in the same airspace at the same time, so IFR departure delays of up to four hours were typical. But the Air Force didn't wait for civil aviation rules in Việtnam. Instead, we used 'Tactical' Visual Flight Rules using visual flight rules in instrument meteorological conditions. If this sounds like an oxymoron, it was!

The Air Force GCI (Ground Control Interception) guys had radar. In good weather they used radar to direct air attacks on specific locations. In bad weather they did advisory radar flight following for guys like us flying TAC VFR. There were GCI sites in Sàigòn (call sign 'Paris'), Buôn Ma Thuột (call sign 'Pyramid'), Nha Trang (call sign 'Port Call'), Đà Nẵng (call sign 'Panama'), Bình Thủy (call sign 'Paddy') and others. The good news was that the GCI controllers' radar could see aircraft quite effectively in the weather. The bad news was that the controllers didn't have information about all flights. And their radar had no information about what altitude the traffic was using. 'Panama' might call us and advise, 'Fast mover northbound at your 12 o'clock, two miles, non-beacon.' This meant that there was an unknown jet directly ahead of us with no transponder information. It may have been thousands of feet above or below us, but we couldn't tell, so we had to take immediate evasive action.

'Theoretically, IFR-assigned altitudes provided vertical separation between IFR and VFR (and TAC VFR) traffic so long as you were in level flight. Aircraft flying IFR were assigned altitudes at thousands of feet, e.g. 4,000 feet (flight level 40). VFR and TAC VFR rules said to fly at thousands of feet plus 500, e.g. 4,500 feet. (In the weather Army helicopters made up their own convention, flying at altitudes of thousands of feet plus 250 feet, e.g. 4,250 feet, which they called flight level 42.5.) When flying TAC VFR, I tried to find a cruise altitude above 10,000 feet, which was above most helicopters, unpressurized aircraft and piston-engine aircraft. All in all TAC VFR was an effective but risky method of getting from place to place in the weather.

'Approach and landing at the destination was a whole different ball game. Most airports had published instrument approaches that gave us a path to descend safely in the clouds to a specified minimum altitude. If at minimums we had the runway in sight, we could land. If we couldn't land safely, we followed the published missed approach procedure and climbed out again. Large airfields had precision approaches that allowed us to fly down to 200 feet or even 100 feet in the clouds. At medium-sized airfields we could use radio navigation aids to descend to about 500 feet above the ground. Small fields typically had no navigation aids.

'On 6 November the weather was lousy that day and as soon as we departed Tân Sơn Nhứt, departure control told us that the field was now closed because the ceiling was below landing minimums (100 feet). At nearby Biên Hòa we picked up eighty Marines who had arrived in Việtnam just the day before. They were replacement troops for one organization, so this was considered a 'unit move'. That meant that they didn't get to enjoy our luxurious bucket seats. Instead they were 'combat-loaded' onto pallets with tie-down straps for seat belts. I believe

96

this was to welcome them to the combat zone and help them make their brand-new jungle fatigues look less brand new.

'We flew TAC VFR to Chu Lai, where approach control eventually picked us up on radar. They gave us a GCA (radar ground-controlled approach) so we had precision radar guidance all the way down. We broke out of the cloud layer at about 250 feet, but unfortunately they hadn't aligned us with the runway and we couldn't make a safe landing from that position. So we followed the missed approach procedure and climbed back into the clouds. This down-and-back-up stuff was probably pretty disconcerting to our green-bean passengers, who had probably never done a go-around or missed approach before. But we'd done it hundreds of times and it was pretty routine.

'We told approach control how they had aligned us so they could adjust on the next try. The weather had apparently gotten worse, because this time we descended in the overcast all the way to minimums - 200 feet above the ground. We couldn't see anything but clouds, so we went missed approach again. We gave up on landing at Chu Lai so we called up our Airlift Control Center

and asked where we they wanted us to take our passengers. They told us to go to Cam Ranh Bay. So that day our passengers flew with us 300 miles up to Chu Lai, endured two missed approaches, then flew 200 miles back down to Cam Ranh Bay. Maybe you could call that 100 miles of progress - welcome to Việtnam, guys!

'And this brings me to a related issue: optimistic weather observations. We could not make an instrument approach if the weather was below minimums for that approach. For example, if the cloud ceiling was at 200 feet, it wouldn't make sense to start an approach that had a minimum descent altitude of 300 feet. But when the weather was really bad and approach controllers were really busy, they had a temptation to fudge the numbers a little. For example...That day we returned from Cam Ranh Bay to Tân Sơn Nhứt and the weather was still bad there. Approach control called it a 300-feet-overcast so they gave us a non-precision approach, which allowed us to descend to 300 feet above the ground and didn't require a radar controller. At 300 feet we were still in the clouds so we had to go missed approach. Obviously the ceiling was well below

C-130 crew moments before take-off for an airdrop at An Lộc.

300 feet. Next they revised the weather observation down to 200 feet overcast and gave us a precision GCA down to 100 feet. At 100 feet above the ground we still didn't see any runway so we went missed approach again. Obviously the ceiling was well below 200 feet. On the third try we broke out of the weather at 100 feet above the ground and landed OK. Whew! Can you imagine an airline doing this?

'Whatever else, it's the GI's inalienable right to complain. On 4 December it was the last day of my in-country shuttle and my airplane had been given the 67/2 configuration - 67 passenger seats and two baggage pallets. It was a bad configuration for Việtnam because passengers brought little baggage and really only one baggage pallet was needed. 67/2 also packed the passengers more tightly together, eliminated rear ladders for passenger entry, moved the centre of gravity too far forward and reduced our capacity to 67 pax. Departing Tân Sơn Nhứt our pax were Việtnamese and it took a half hour to explain that we were going to take only sixty-seven of their seventy troops to Cam Ranh Bay.

'At Cam Ranh Bay passenger service couldn't find our scheduled passengers for Biên Hỏa (!) so they gave us some space-available pax whose destination was Tân Sơn Nhứt. Our onboard radar died as we taxied out, so we taxied back in to get it fixed. While the radar man began his work, pax service found our scheduled troops! They were packed in like sardines and it was so uncomfortable that after an hour two passengers got off. Our radar wasn't fixable, so I checked the weather closely and decided to press on. Departing Cam Ranh Bay IFR in the soup, departure control told us we had traffic at 12 o'clock, two miles and converging. Then he said he couldn't vector us clear because we had not yet reached his minimum vectoring altitude! We were on course for a mid-air collision, needed a little advice on which way to turn and his rule book said not to give any! So I made a sharp 45-degree-bank turn and hoped for the best. I evaded the traffic, the controller and the artillery and climbed up to 14,000 feet to be above the weather. Then the air conditioning crapped out, so we swam in our sweat for a while.

'Descending into Biên Hỏa there was more artillery to avoid and more bad weather. The co-pilot saw some perimeter lights and told approach control that we had the field in sight. To approach control that meant we were in visual conditions and didn't need their services anymore, so they handed us off to the tower. Unfortunately the lights he saw were not Biên Hỏa's so we didn't really have the field in sight. I spiralled down, spotted Biên Hỏa through a hole in the clouds and sneaked in underneath them. But on base leg the overcast was too low to fly under. To stay out of the clouds I had to turn onto final approach prematurely. I cut the power to idle, but we still crossed the runway threshold hot and high. Since Biên Hỏa had a 10,000 foot runway, I landed 5,000 feet long with plenty of runway left over. I think 5,000 feet long was my personal record.)

'In January 1971 the war was in the wind down stage, but the 834th was still hauling supplies to various areas in-country. Most missions were the 'bladder bird' variety, but we also flew a few 'Daisy Cutter' and med-evac missions. On 23 January we loaded up our pax for Huế and Đà Nẵng. Meanwhile the loadmaster found hydraulic fluid leaking from the aux system pressure transmitter behind the right side seats. There's also a direct-reading gauge so we just capped off the line for the remote gauge. It probably did not instill confidence as the passengers watched the hydraulics man working on our leaky plumbing. But with that taken care of, we started engines and taxied out. Before the first takeoff of the day I ran up the engines to full speed to verify that all was well in that department. Unfortunately the tachometer showed that the #4 prop was fluctuating badly. Uh oh. C-130 engines are supposed to run at a constant speed - only the angle of the propeller blades should vary. We called maintenance and taxied back in. The passengers remained onboard while the prop man worked on #4. He said it was all fixed so I taxied out and ran it up again. The fluctuation was better, but still out of limits so we taxied back in again. Sigh. Again they tweaked #4 and again we taxied out. When I ran it up again, the prop was still fluctuating, but within limits. I still had a hinky feeling about #4 but not liking the airplane wasn't a good enough reason not to fly it. So I took off. On climb out #4 confirmed my hinky feeling. The fluctuation got much worse - now three times the max allowable. If a prop fluctuates too wildly, it can decouple from the engine. And if the prop goes out of control it can leave its usual position on the wing and crash into the fuselage or another prop. Would not want that. So we climbed up to traffic pattern altitude, ran the engine shutdown checklist and feathered #4. That stopped the engine from turning and set the prop to its maximum blade angle so it had the least wind resistance.

'This was my first 'opportunity' to feather an engine and make a three-engine landing, but I'd practiced it many times so I wasn't worried. But when our passengers saw our #4 prop come to a stop, it probably did not add to their confidence in air travel. I declared an emergency, flew the Tân Sơn Nhứt traffic pattern and returned for a smooth landing. 'It is better to be on the ground wishing you were in the air than in the air wishing you were on the ground.' I told maintenance that they needed to really fix that airplane and that we had flown it all we were going to that day. There were no more flyable airplanes available so we were done for the day. After three trips to the runway and one trip around the traffic pattern our passengers were a bit tired and cranky. We couldn't give them complimentary drinks so we sent them back to the aerial port where they had started hours earlier.

'Our destination on 30 January was classified: Phnom Penh, Cambodia. The airfield had been attacked a week earlier - here's a newspaper article about it. But the runway was apparently OK again so we loaded up ten tons of 'Class A' (explosives) and took to the skies. As the crow flies, it was just 110 miles from Sàigòn to Phnom Penh, but between the two were restricted areas where bombs fell. To avoid ground fire, traffic and artillery we frequently flew 'feet wet'- parallel to the coastline. So from Sàigòn we flew south across the Mekong Delta until we reached the South China Sea, then around the southern tip of Việtnam and up the Gulf of Thailand into Cambodia, about an hour's flying time. I mentioned that this day's flying might be interesting and indeed it was. We flew less than two hours but when I landed and turned off the runway I was amazed at what a scene of destruction the place was - collapsed hangars, burned out buildings, burned out passenger terminal, burned out control tower. Spooky and deserted. The only thing moving was a T-28 taxiing down the runway with its crew chiefs taking a ride.

'There was no aerial port to talk to, but eventually a guy with a forklift came out and offloaded our five pallets of 'Class A'. So far so good and we started engines to leave this godforsaken place. Unfortunately, when we tried to start our #1 engine, its starter shaft sheared off. Bad. There were no maintenance facilities so we shut down the other engines so our flight engineer, Bruno Fronzaglio could climb up and remove the broken starter. There were no maintenance stands, so he found an empty pallet and got the forklift driver to lift him and the pallet up to the #1 engine. He still couldn't reach the starter so he found a ladder and extended it up from the pallet. From this rickety perch he removed the offending starter, buttoned up the engine and climbed back down.

'So now what? One of our four engines would not start and we were on our own, but C-130s were uniquely designed to work around such problems in remote locations. We still had some good options available: 1, 'Buddy start': Pull up very close behind another C-130; allow their propwash to turn the dead prop until it could run on its own. I did this for another C-130 a few weeks earlier and it worked fine. But we had no buddy here. 2. Windmill taxi start. This involves charging down the runway on three engines until you're going fast enough that the airflow starts turning the dead prop. Cram on the brakes and allow the engine to come up to speed. Be sure to do this before reaching the end of the runway. 2. 3-engine takeoff: Too often this is followed by a crash so it is not recommended.

'A windmill taxi start was the best option available to us and I'd done one a few months ago at Đà Nẵng, so I felt ready. We started up our three good engines, but before we reached the runway another C-130 unexpectedly arrived! This was especially good news because he could give us a buddy start. So we called him up on the radio and he agreed to give us a 'buddy start' before offloading his 'Class A'.

'Getting a 'buddy start' is a very sensory experience; full of sight, sound and movement. First you pull up close behind the other C-130 - really close - so close that their ramp and duckbutt fills your field of vision. The flight deck of your bird needs to be under the tail of the other bird if you want it to work the first time. As the other pilot advances his throttles to max, the noise and the turbulence increases until you're bouncing

Engine maintenance at Phú Cat Air Base. (Robert D. Young)

around like you were in a thunderstorm. Now you're watching that dead #1 prop waiting for it to turn. Come on, turn! Now it begins to slowly rotate - not even enough to register on the tach, but it is moving. Slowly turning and... WHUMPWHUMP! I could feel the concussion more than hear it - mortar rounds!

'Talk about a sitting duck - not a good time to be sitting under the tail of another C-130 carrying ten tons of 'Class A'. The prop was accelerating imperceptibly - it takes over a minute to come up to speed this way. Then the tower called telling us to clear the runway. I was wondering when the next round would hit, but I was staying put until the engine was running. So were our buddies.

'The prop was slowly accelerating now. Tower called again for us to clear the runway so they could launch a T-28 to hose down the bad guys. Eventually the engine was turning fast enough that it was time to add fuel. Now the tower was calling frantically - clear for takeoff, clear for takeoff. Finally the engine was accelerating on its own power, so we thanked our buddies and said we were on our own. As they released the brakes I expected them to take off, but instead they turned

off at the taxiway! I was pretty surprised - I didn't think it was a good idea to hang around while the field was under attack. But there was no time for questions or contemplation so I called for the before-takeoff checklist. Even before they cleared the runway the tower was calling clear to take off, clear to take off. I released the brakes, put the power to max and began rolling for a downwind takeoff. Longest minute of my life. We flew feet wet back to Tân Sơn Nhứt expecting to get the starter replaced and take another load to Phnom Penh. Anticlimax: no starter was available so we terminated early.

'On 29 January things were picking up at Det One. No scheduled pax runs - all combat essential frags. Fourteen (!) additional crews rotated in from CCK the day before. A week earlier we were mostly flying scheduled passenger runs between large airfields in Việtnam - crews couldn't even get enough short-field missions to complete needed check rides. Suddenly there were many more crews and everyone was flying combat essential (high priority) missions into small airfields. In this round-the-clock push we carried Việtnamese troops and equipment north for 'Lam Son 719'. GI's and routine cargo still needed to move between large airfields like Đà Nẵng, Cam Ranh Bay, Tân Sơn Nhứt and Biên Hỏa so Military Airlift Command brought in C-141s to help. Khê Sanh was the staging area for the 'Lam Son 719' invasion because it was just ten miles from Laos. Its 3,200 feet runway was ready for use February 15th. For some reason the USAF always called it Ham Ngai. There was a continuous stream of C-130s flying in and out, so artillery-free corridors were arranged with the army to avoid friendly-fire accidents. These corridors also helped smooth out the air traffic. The inbound corridor was from Huế to the southeast and the outbound corridor was to Quảng Tri to the northeast.

'This day I flew two combat essential missions up to Quảng Tri, thirteen miles from the DMZ. We delivered trucks and jeeps and trailers and Việtnamese troops who didn't even know their destination. C-130 operations were all about bringing passengers and cargo into small airfields like Quảng Tri and that's when aircraft commanders were tested. A few weeks earlier two C-130 instructor pilots from CCK went off the end of its 3,500 feet runway. My first approach was in daylight but the weather was bad. Radar was unavailable so I shot an ADF non-precision approach. We broke through the overcast and got the field in sight about 30 seconds before touchdown. Piece of cake.

'The second time we arrived at night - more challenging because there are fewer visual cues for a short-field landing. And this time the Det One safety officer was riding along, looking over my shoulder. We had to hold for 40 minutes over the Quảng Trị ADF because the weather was still bad - low ceiling, low visibility and drizzle. At least the radar was back up, so I shot a ground controlled approach. We broke out of the overcast at about 600 feet and I planted the airplane firmly onto the runway. Night-time, lousy weather, combat essential, short field, near the DMZ. That's when AC's earn their pay.

'I arose at 0200 on the morning of 1 February after attempting to sleep several hours. We showed at 02:30 and finally blocked out at 0600 due to some maintenance and loading delays. We combat-loaded a Viêtnamese battle unit (130 troops with all their gear). Our destination was Đông Hà, a newly-activated airfield eleven miles from the DMZ. Flying that close to North Viêtnam was not

comfortable. Speaking of comfort, our C-130E could carry up to 92 passengers in bucket seats attached to the airplane's sides and to stanchions down the centre of the cargo compartment, so passengers travelled sideways. This helped passengers get to know each other better because they sit knee-to knee and during takeoffs and landings they lean against each other. But combat loading did not offer such luxuries as seats. The loadmaster rolled in five empty 463L pallets, covering the whole cargo floor. Next he stretched cargo tie-down straps across the pallets, acting as 7 foot-wide seat belts. Theoretically everyone would sit in rows facing forward and slip their legs under the straps so they have lap belts - uncomfortable but organized. In an actual combat environment it was both uncomfortable and disorganized. Commercial air travel is more comfortable for passengers on a bad day than it is for C-130 passengers on a good day. And this was a bad day. The loadmaster opened the rear cargo door and lowered the ramp so the troops could enter carrying all their weapons and equipment. They were instructed to walk forward as far as they could and keep standing. As the airplane filled up they were told to move farther forward and pack

C-130s on the ramp at Nakhon Phanom AFB, Thailand in 1972. (Robert D. Young)

in. When no more troops could stand on the five pallets the loadmaster closed the ramp, the troops sat down and we took off for Đông Hà.

'There was a traffic overload at Đông Hà so I ended up holding for over an hour. When I finally got my turn, I shot a GCA approach and the landing went well. But with all that holding we didn't have enough gas to make it back to Tân Sơn Nhứt. All the C-130s were in the same situation and most stopped at Đà Nẵng for fuel, resulting in extensive delays there. Phù Cát [17.7 miles northwest of Qui Nhơn in Bình Định Province] was another 120 miles beyond Đà Nẵng so I opted to go there and avoid the delays. We had just enough fuel for one approach and I was watching the fuel gauges closely. When we landed I shut down the outboards immediately - I didn't want to run out of fuel before we were parked. Close. All this messing around put us ten hours into our crew day, so I told mother there was no way we could make it up and back again in four more hours, so they terminated us. I'm just as glad. I was pretty tired.

'Next day we had a 0945 show - quite civilized - but we had some problems with brakes and anti-skid, but got it resolved. So I leaped off for Đông Hà and this time there was no holding. I even made a pretty good max effort landing. The antiskid circuit breaker on one wheel popped out so we planned to get that fixed at Tân Sơn Nhứt. As I later learned at Khê Sanh, it's unwise to land at short fields without antiskid. We couldn't get it fixed.

'On 4 February the Marilyn Monroe foldout at the nav station had been replaced by the latest *Playboy* 'playmate' and the frag called for two round trips to Biên Hòa and Đông Hà. We were flying the *Red Rabbit,* which was the best aircraft in the fleet and easy to spot on the ramp - on its crew door steps was a red silhouette of the *Playboy* bunny. The navigator's station had the centrefold of the *Playboy* 'playmate' of the month under a sheet of plexiglas. But the best thing about that airplane was that everything worked! I think its tail number was 64-17680. When I flew the *Red Rabbit* I could expect to finish all the legs of my frag and bring everyone home without breaking down somewhere. The crew chief did an amazing job. (While I was at CCK he was promoted to staff sergeant - well deserved). We actually completed our whole frag!

'On 17 February we flew several trips to Katum. It was pretty remote - in the fish hook area about four miles from Cambodia. The VC operated freely back and forth across the border bringing weapons large and small to shoot at big targets like C-130s. To make the VC easier to spot, the USAF defoliated the nearby jungle with 'Agent Orange'. Katum was known as a hot spot for hostile fire. A couple of years earlier the VC hit a C-130 on departure there and they crash landed at nearby Tay Ninh. Katum's runway was shorter than most - 3,000 feet of red dirt treated with Peneprime to keep the dust down. The soil there is called laterite and it is red because of the high concentration of iron. Army helicopters operating out of there needed fuel and it was too hazardous to send tank trucks through 'Indian Country' so we brought it to them. These flights were called 'bladder birds'. Sometimes we brought the fuel in 2 foot diameter round bladders called 'elephant balls', which could be rolled if necessary. But usually we carried the fuel in two 18 foot lozenge-shaped bladders and pumped the fuel out to trucks at the destination.

'The airplane's landing weight determined the length of its landing roll, which was quite limited at small fields like Katum. Based on the field length we calculated our maximum rollout and from that we determined how many tons of fuel we could bring in. 'Normal' short field landing criteria are different from 'combat essential' landing criteria. If your mission was high priority (combat essential), thinner safety margins were acceptable. Max gross weight for normal short field landings was calculated assuming two props in reverse and two in ground idle. For combat essential missions we calculated the landing rollout assuming all four in reverse. This increased the allowable gross weight (and the possibility of going off the far end of the runway if something went wrong).

'Our last sortie to Katum, on 22 February, turned out to be kind of interesting. On the first two sorties John Roohms was giving another pilot an initial SEA check. Stace rode along on both to log some time to put him closer to upgrading from co-pilot to AC. I rode out on the first shuttle just to scope out the situation. After sitting out the second one I flew the third mission.

'We dealt with friendly fire and hostile fire daily. As we approached the field on that third flight we monitored the radio frequency for 'Tailpipe Alpha'. 'Tailpipe' was the call sign for the combat control team - the first USAF guys into a remote airfield like Katum. They coordinated airlift operations at the field, acting as control tower where there was no tower and aerial port where there was no aerial port. 'Tailpipe Alpha' reported that there were incoming rounds but no damage yet so we orbited nearby and talked with 'Alpha' and 'Hilda'. They told us that it was all clear and the runway was OK. Meanwhile the good guys at several nearby Fire Support Bases had cranked up their artillery and begun shooting back. One of these FSBs was located at the approach end of the runway.

'These artillery bases had no radio communication on VHF or UHF aviation frequencies; instead they had their own FM frequencies. C-130s had been retrofitted with an FM radio at the navigator's station so we could communicate with them and stay clear of their fire. This day as usual the navigator talked with them to ensure that they held their fire while we landed right over them. And as usual they said they would. I was concentrating on my short final approach when I saw puffs of white smoke coming up from the FSB! They were firing their Howitzers again and we were flying right into their fire! I immediately dodged to the right and broke off the approach. I climbed back up and orbited nearby while the nav chewed them out for not passing the

word to the guys firing the guns. Once they had really halted their fire we landed uneventfully and firmly. We pumped out our fuel, flew on to Bình Thúy, then back to Tân Sơn Nhứt. In a similar situation three years earlier, a Caribou was shot down by friendly artillery on short final to Đức Phổ.[7]

'In early February, we were told of a campaign that was to start soon up north and we would be sending aircraft and support personnel to Đà Nẵng, which was to be the staging area for the Laos incursion - 'Lam Son 719/Operation Dewey Canyon II'. After some delays, we finally made it to Đà Nẵng in mid February and set up our support shop area in a corner of the Aerial Port squadron facilities. The support personnel contingent numbered between seventy and ninety men split up working twelve hour shifts. We brought two spare engines and two spare props with us, along with tyres, avionics equipment, tools, etc. Finding room for us to bed down was a problem and we were scattered around in different barracks on the opposite side of the airfield from 'Gunfighter Village'. We were trash hauler types and the jet jocks didn't want anything to do with us.

'Flying was continuous from pre-dawn to the late evening, most missions consisting of troop transport, fuel, munitions and medevac. We had a policy to have all line maintenance accomplished by 0200 hours. The reasoning was that most rocket and mortar attacks occurred between 0200 and

C-130E baking in midday sun on the ramp at Phú Cat located along the South China Sea in Central Việtnam in 1971 with coastal hills and blossoming thunderstorms in the background. One crewmember is seated on the ground in the shade of the wing; while parked on the ramp the inside of the aircraft was like an oven with temperatures well over 100 degrees. Same heat was true during taxi and takeoff as the air conditioning was ineffective until after lift-off when engines really got going to provide the AC energy. To the rear of the plane a tractor fork lift is moving a large pallet of cargo into position for loading. (Robert D. Young)

0400 hours. The demand on the support troops to keep the aircraft mission ready was unbelievable. Spare parts became a concern and there were times we 'bartered' with the Marine Corps C-130 wing for starters and instruments.

'About a week after we arrived in Đà Nẵng, on 24 February, the first stop on my frag schedule was Khê Sanh. After reading the airfield folder and being briefed on the corridor procedures and talking with other crew members I expected it to be pretty hairy. We first blocked out with a load of ARVN troops, cases of vegetables, coops of chickens and two pigs - when I got on the airplane I thought that smell was familiar! However, as we taxied out 'Sàigòn Tea' (TSN ALCE) told us to return and take over another mission of a higher (Combat Essential) priority. So we and our troops and chickens and pigs taxied back in and parked. We flew an empty airplane down to Vũng Tàu and picked up a fire engine. Because of our destination I had the loadmaster put additional chains on it, which he didn't appreciate (sorry, Steve). Khê Sanh was actually a piece of cake. The aluminium matting runway was quite good, the corridors in and out went smoothly, the GCA went smoothly and I even made a good landing. I was glad to be able to take Colonel Rogers his mail from Det One too - I sure know how much receiving or not receiving those letters can mean.

'We rarely had our courage tested. Others did. During 'Lam Son 719', eleven C-130Bs were temporarily stationed at Đà Nẵng. Their mission was to fly loads into Khê Sanh. Đà Nẵng was nicknamed 'Rocket City' because it was subject to such frequent rocket attacks. On 24 February the workload was heavier than normal. Aircraft 61-2642 was parked on the ramp about 75 yards from the Aerial Port squadron facilities. It was already loaded with munitions for the first mission in the morning. Repairs to number one and two engines were delayed while waiting for parts. The decision was made to off load 2642 and move the load to another aircraft. This gave us more time for repairs and engine maintenance run checks, while still trying to clear the line maintenance by 0200. We overshot that by 40 minutes, but all write-ups on all aircraft were cleared and we settled down in our shop area for some serious card playing and warm Cokes. Roughly ten minutes into the game a thunderous explosion threw us all to the floor;

followed in quick succession by at least a dozen more explosions. We were under a rocket attack! The air raid sirens were blaring and all power and lights were shut off. The floor rumbled from the impact of incoming rounds and none of us had our flak jackets or helmets. In fact, they were still locked up in a conex container behind the Aerial Port.

Captain James Theis, a young enlisted air freighter at the 15th Aerial Port working seven nights a week recalled that night.

'I was one of a few guys on break in the line shack about 150 feet from that unfortunate bird. We heard the rocket's whish a split second before it hit the plane on the top part of the left wing. Needless to say we hit the floor first then hit the road briefly before running back at full tilt. Despite the inferno, I personally can attest to the sheer and unrecognized bravery of many Air Freighters that night. One guy grabbed the fuel line next to the plane to make sure the fire didn't spread to the fuel system, one moved the fuel pumper away, one grabbed the large extinguisher and started trying to control the fire and one went around back to check for personnel. Others grabbed forklifts and yanked the ammo from the adjacent planes as we did not know if the burning plane was loaded or not and, as far as we knew, it could blow at any moment. The fire was awfully hot but it didn't blow up as can be seen in the pictures. None of us were trained to do any of those things yet it all seemed a perfectly choreographed play, well rehearsed and acted. Yes, it was a tough night. The rocket on the C-130 was only one of several that landed near the 15th APS that night. We were lucky that no one was injured and that the damage wasn't worse. Most men cannot remember or they do not have an event that changes them from being a boy to a man. I do.'

'It was over as fast as it started' says Alan Baker. 'We scrambled outside and found the fire department already on scene spraying foam on aircraft 2642. It sustained a direct hit in the APU compartment, forward of the left main gear, by a 122mm rocket. The explosion ripped off all of the port wing outboard of number two engine. The resulting fire was so intense that half the length of the prop blades on number two, were melted off. The centre section of the aircraft buckled in the main spar area and the weight of the aircraft caused it to tilt and lean to the right. Four other aircraft were damaged along with some ground power equipment, one of which was a power cart that also received a direct hit and left a crater in the ramp seven feet wide and three feet deep. Luckily, there were no injuries to anyone in our detachment and only minor injuries elsewhere on base. Our 'off the line by 0200' policy worked that night. Given the trajectory of the rocket that impacted the aircraft, had it fallen short there would have been many casualties. Also, if the munitions had still been loaded, damage would have been much more extensive.

'The only salvageable part of 642 was its tail, which was reused on an AC-130. The quick action of the men of the 15th Aerial Port Squadron kept this attack from becoming a disaster. Luckily, 642 was the only bird on the ramp that was not loaded with 'Class A' explosives bound for Khê Sanh next morning and it had no flight or ground personnel inside.

'During the next week our 'off duty time' was spent trying to salvage as much as possible from the other engines. We needed the spare parts. Eventually, a crane was brought in and the aircraft was dismantled in sections, loaded on a flatbed truck and hauled away.

'On 25 February we were s'pozed to carry a 35,000lb forklift to Khê Sanh but decided not to because it was just too heavy. Loadmaster Steve Hank reported that this two-axle 35,000lb forklift was way over the 13,000lb single axle weight limitation on the floor. So after considerable hassle with various colonels, majors and captains we took drums of Peneprime instead. Landing at Huế a warning light told us that the antiskid system was inoperative on one main wheel but I decided to

"Spare 617"

Capt. Bill Caldwell
Lt. John Hering
Lt. Richard Lentz

TSgt. Jon Sanders (KIA)
SSgt. Charlie Shaub
A1C Dave McAleece

15 April 1972

Captain William Caldwell (born 20 August 1943 in Illinois) whose crew on Saturday 15th April 1972 of Lieutenant John Hering, co-pilot; Lieutenant Richard A. Lenz, navigator; T/Sgt Jon Sanders, flight engineer and loadmasters T/Sgt Charlie Shaub and A1C Dave McAleece attempted to airdrop ammunition to surrounded SVN troops at An Lôc. While approaching the drop zone 'Spare 617' received heavy enemy ground fire that killed Sanders and wounded Hering and Lenz, damaged two engines, ruptured a bleed air duct in the cargo compartment and set the ammunition on fire. Shaub jettisoned the cargo pallets, which exploded in midair. Despite receiving severe burns from the hot air escaping the damaged air bleed duct he extinguished a fire in the cargo compartment. Caldwell decided to head for Tân Sơn Nhứt AB, which had the best medical facilities. His engineer dead and his co-pilot wounded, Caldwell closed the damaged bleed air duct and he shut down the two damaged engines. The landing gear would not come down and the wounded and badly burned Shaub directed McAleece as he hand-cranked the landing gear down using the emergency extension system. Though a third engine lost power Caldwell landed safely. He received the AFC. Charlie Shaub was nominated for the MoH for his role in saving the aircraft, but the recommendation was downgraded to an AFC. Shaub also received the William H. Pitsenbarger award for heroism from the AF Sergeants Association. Colonel Caldwell retired from the Air Force on 1 October 1993. C-130E 62-1787 eventually returned to the US to the 314th Tactical Airlift Wing at Little Rock, Arkansas and then served with several ANG squadrons before being added to the Smithsonian's collection on 18 August 2011.

press on to Khê Sanh anyway. At Khê Sanh one wheel locked up and scrubbed a big bald spot into the tyre as it dragged its way down the runway (we can at least say we've left our mark at Khê Sanh!) We could have flown it out that way, but there was a spare available, so flight engineer Bruno Fronzaglio changed the tyre. (Sorry, Bruno.)

'As we taxied out to the runway the air was filled with choppers and the tower frequency was filled with instructions. Tower cleared us to take off, so I put the power to max and released the brakes. As we started to roll, a helicopter from the right flew across the runway directly in front of us - idiot. I crammed on the brakes and aborted the takeoff. I put the props into reverse pitch and started backing the airplane up toward the beginning of the runway. Meanwhile loadmaster Steve Hank opened the ramp and told me when we reached the beginning again. With a wary eye out for helicopters we leaped off for Đà Nẵng for fuel. Our troublesome wheel was now leaking brake fluid, but fortunately we had no more short-field landings ahead. So we just capped off the brake line (leaving three good wheel brakes) and leaped off for Tân Sơn Nhứt feet wet. En route near Phú Cát we listened to an F-4 jock with a crippled airplane punch out near a beach and get picked up by a helicopter.[8] All this was getting too much like war for my taste. A rather disquieting day.

Late in 1971 the 374th Tactical Airlift Wing at Tân Sơn Nhứt had assumed direction of 'Commando Vault' operations and not surprisingly perhaps, they were extended to include attacks with BLU-82B 'Big Blues' on troop and vehicle concentrations in South-East Asia. These accounted for many of the 600 weapons dropped (about two-thirds of which were 'Big Blues') in Việtnam, Laos and Cambodia, before the Việtnamese ceasefire in 1973. In the last days of the Việtnam War from 9 to 21 April 1975 South Việtnamese VNAF aircraft dropped BLU-82B bombs on NVA positions in desperation to support ARVN troops in the Battle of Xuân Lộc when the town was captured by the PAVN 4th Army Corps.[9] During the Mayaguez[10] incident 12-15 May 1975 a MC-130 dropped a single BLU-82B to assist US Marine forces attempting to extract themselves from Koh Tang Island.[11]

After the C-7 Caribou and C-123 Provider were phased out of service by the USAF, the Hercules units remained the only Air Force tactical transports in southeast Asia and these operated from Thailand during the final months of the war. During 1969-71 massive air transport activity supported US and ARVN incursions into Cambodia and southern Laos. C-130s made ammunition drops to US forces near Ô Rang and Operation 'Lam Son 719' was preceded by 250 C-130 sorties lifting an ARVN airborne division and other Việtnamese forces from Saïgon to Đông Hà the capital of Quảng Trị Province and Quảng Trị. Over a seven-week period the Hercules lifted more than 14,000 tons of cargo to a reconstructed logistics base at Khê Sanh (which had been abandoned on 23 June 1968).[12]

In April and May 1972 the Communist spring offensive resulted in more Air Force supply operations being mounted during to isolated pockets at Kontum in the Central Highlands region which shares borders with Laos and Cambodia and An Lộc, a small provincial capital sixty miles northwest of Saïgon which lies on a plateau surrounded by plantations with tall rubber trees. Major Edward N. Brya (later Brigadier General Brya) designed and tested both the low- and high-level airdrop tactics that relieved the siege of An Lộc. After completing pilot training at Williams AFB, Arizona in May 1962 Brya, who was born in Los Angeles in 1938, was assigned to Dyess AFB, Texas as a C-130 pilot. In January 1965 he transferred to the 35th Troop Carrier Squadron at Naha AB, Okinawa. While there he spent two years flying as an instructor pilot on missions to Southeast Asia, including leaflet drops in North Việtnam. He transitioned to B-52s with an assignment to Carswell AFB, Texas in August 1967. During 1969 and 1970 he rotated with his crew to Guam and the 'Arc Light' mission (as the B-52 operations were known) in Southeast Asia. Brya returned to tactical airlift and C-130s in May 1970. He was assigned to Pope AFB, North Carolina, where he served as an instructor, flight commander and wing plans officer. In January 1972 he transferred to Ching Chuan Kang AB, Taiwan, as the wing standardization pilot.

'In April 1972 as the war in Southeast Asia was winding down the North Việtnamese Army (NVA) launched their spring offensive. This caused a major build up and reinforcement of Air Force,

Navy and Marine Air from both the cones and Pacific Theatre. In late 1971 and '72 we had been withdrawing forces from Southeast Asia. The C-130 wings at Clark, Mactan and Naha had been deactivated and the airplanes returned to the states. The 374th TAW at CCK in Taiwan, with its four squadrons, was the only PACAF asset for C-130 airlift in sea. At the start of the spring offensive the wing had 27 aircraft, 43 crews and 260 maintenance personnel deployed to Việtnam, or in-country as we called it. During April we surged to 44 aircraft, sixty crews and 370 maintenance personnel. In response to the NVA spring offensive our short-field operations increased from the occasional landing at an out of the way field to major operations on a 24 hour basis. Early in April we brought ARVN troops from the 3,000-foot strips in the delta to Biên Hòa for defence of the Saïgon area. Other aircraft went to long-forgotten places to pull out men, land and equipment. We operated in the DMZ and Quảng Tri until the enemy forced us out. The major areas of operation were at Kontum, in the highlands and in the south surrounding Biên Hòa and Saïgon. During April we made 358 short field landings including 51 at night. In the south the centrepiece battle of the spring offensive was fought in Biên Long province. The communists boasted that An Lôc would become the seat of government for the liberated provinces. Colonel Ray Bowers in his excellent air force history of tactical airlift describes the battle for An Lôc as 'the most trying time of the war for the C-130 crews.'

'In early April the area was cut off and

Left: Sam McGowan 'The TAC-Trained Killer' at Recife, Brazil on 1 August 1965.

Below: Supplies ready for shipment by the 'Trash Haulers'.

surrounded by the NVA. The northern half of the town was captured... The Raven[13] and their American advisors were forced into a small area in the southeast corner of town. The command element was inside a bunker, which was located by a soccer field 200 metres square. The VNAF had tried without much success to resupply the beleaguered troops; during this time, a C-119 was lost to ground fire. On Saturday, 15th April three C-130s were sent in.[14] They used the then approved method of a descending slow down into the DZ. They were briefed by 7th Air Force to approach up the road from the south, as all the VNAF drops had been flown and drop on the soccer field. The first aircraft [commanded by Major Robert Wallace of the 776th TAS, 374th TAW at Ching Chuang Kang AB, Taiwan] made a successful run taking only a couple of hits from ground fire [but released their load]. The second aircraft [62-1787, operating under the call sign 'Spare 617' and flown by Captain William Caldwell] came in approximately fifteen minutes later and was under constant fire. One 51 calibre round came through the right hand circuit breaker panel, killed the engineer and went on to shatter the windows on the left side of the cockpit. Other shells ripped the cargo compartment and ignited part of the ammo load. The loadmasters jettisoned the load, which landed on the DZ. Number one and two engines were shut down. The navigator and co-pilot were both wounded and incapacitated. With the loadmasters fighting the fire and manually cranking down the landing gear, the pilot, Captain Bill Caldwell managed to get the aircraft back to Tân Sơn Nhứt. [The third C-130 was unable to drop because of problems with its ramp and door. Though both Wallace and Caldwell dropped in the vicinity of the DZ, none of the cargo from either Hercules was recovered by friendly forces].

'Around 10 April I had gone in-county with our wing commander Colonel Andy Iosue. That day we had been out flying a leaflet drop. We returned to Saïgon shortly after Captain Caldwell landed. Colonel Iosue directed me to get with our chief navigator, Major Bob Highly and plan a better way and that the three of us would fly it the next day [16 April]. That night we got together with the airborne FACS and devised some ways, which would hopefully get us through with minimum damage. [The plan called for the C-130s to approach the drop zone at tree-top level at 250 knots, then pop-up to the 600 foot release altitude when about two minutes out]. The FAC would serve as our combat controller. To avoid the appearance of the C-130 from the same heading, we drew a circle around An Lôc and laid out six different inbound tracks into the DZ. The FAC would assess the situation and choose the track which would be the safest for us to enter. He also gave us a recommended outbound track to escape on. We proceeded to an orbit point approximately ten minutes from the Drop Zone. In this orbit at a safe altitude of 5 to 10,000 feet we completed the twenty, ten and six minute checklists. After depressurizing, the bleed valves were closed - this item was not mentioned anywhere in our manuals except for assault landings and takeoffs. We were having a problem with the aft cargo door. The up lock did not always work and thus the door would not stay up. While still in the orbit we opened the door from the back of the airplane and left the aux pump on after the loadmaster completed his checklist. The load was hot, all restraint had been removed and it was being held in only by the CDS gate but if the aircraft were hit and the load needed to be jettisoned. The ramp could be opened and the gate cut.

'Another new checklist item we instituted was for the pilot and co-pilot to lock their shoulder harness to prevent one of them from falling on the yoke if he was hit. When the FAC cleared the crew into the DZ they would start a Low level dash at approximately 100 feet and 250 knots. Inside two minutes, the slowdown was started. While maintaining the low altitude, the power was reduced to idle. Flaps were lowered on Air speed to the proper CDS setting. At approximately 170 knots the engineer started down the ramp; thirty seconds out, the pilot attained his 600 foot altitude and airspeed in order to identify the drop area. The navigator drew three circles around the DZ, a slowdown, a one minute warning and a release line. The pilot and co-pilot were too busy flying the aircraft to be looking for the DZ. The engineer was watching his panel so the navigator was the only one who could make the drop. Of course during all of this time from two minutes in, the aircraft was under attack from ground fire. As soon as the load was clear the pilot increased airspeed, descended and turned to his escape heading. During the escape manoeuvre, the FAC, who was flying up behind the 130 during the run in, gave directions to help the escape. He would tell you to break left or right as required; then clear you to pop up when out of the threat area. Once out of the area, the crew reviewed the checklist and turned off the green light, which was invariably left on. Unfortunately, we were required to return again and again to the same DZ, at roughly the same altitude and airspeed. Even though we made the drops that day, they had us in their sights and the aircraft were hit.'[15]

Beginning on Tuesday 18 April the first four C-130s successfully parachuted supplies but each received battle damage. A fifth, C-130E 63-7775 of Detachment 1 in the 374th TAW from Tân Sơn Nhứt flown by Captain Donald B. 'Doc' Jensen, which was being used to drop ammunition to South Việtnamese troops was hit west of An Lôc and crash-landed into a swamp near Lai Khê. For several days the detachment at Tân Sơn Nhứt had been trying to drop ammunition and supplies to the defenders of An Lôc, which came under heavy attack from 12 April following the loss of Lộc Ninh seven days earlier. Several attempts were made but most of the loads fell into enemy hands and anti-aircraft fire was becoming more ferocious so a change of tactics to low level CDS drops was required. The CDS drops started with a high-speed, low-level approach (250 knots and below 200 feet) until the aircraft climbed rapidly to about 600 feet and slowed to 130 knots for the actual drop. On the 18th as Captain Jensen approached An Lôc at 200 feet to drop its load his C-130 was hit by automatic weapons fire and damaged as it climbed to commence the final run in. The starboard wing caught fire and the load had to be jettisoned but Jensen headed south in the hope of reaching Tân Sơn Nhứt. However, Jensen had to crash-land the aircraft in a swamp near Lai Khê and all the crew were recovered by Army helicopters. (CDS drops were suspended after this incident but later attempted again during the resupply of An Lôc)[16]

Major Robert W. Kirkpatrick the navigator recalled: 'As we prepared for the drop, we started taking some sporadic ground fire; nothing very intense at this point, but soon I noticed an orange flash on the horizon, about three miles out. In a voice about 2-3 octaves higher than normal I made the announcement on interphone to the crew:

'We're taking fire at 1230 - three miles', about that time the aircraft made a significant jump with the sound of metal to metal contact, ground fire intensity started to increase drastically at the same time. On the right side of the aircraft we had a big hole, about the size of a basketball and on the right wing the engines spewed fuel and the fire, going well past the tail of the aircraft. About the same time I looked out the left cockpit window and noticed an NVA tank on the ground, with the hatch open, pennants on the antennae and an NVA tank commander standing in the hatch with his pith helmet on looking up at us; I waved at him and he returned the wave. I knew we were on track to the drop zone as the tank's tube was visually parallel to our track, pointing at An Lôc. After we had dropped our cargo things really started to accelerate for us and the ground fire was extremely intense.

'We were losing oil from an engine. Then we began losing oil pressure. The pilot tried to shut down the engine and an effort was made to climb and accelerate with the idea of blowing the fire out, none of which worked. The intense ground fire we encountered sounded like a shooting gallery at a carnival; it gradually subsided and the situation with the fire and controlling the aircraft brought up the subject of us bailing out. I knew we were by then over an area where there was a significant concentration of NVA, so my immediate verbal response to the bail-out idea was 'let's hold on as long as possible due to the NVA in the area' (I didn't feel we would be very welcome guest of the NVA and even if we were, I was not particularly interested in being a guest at the 'Hànôi Hilton'). Sergeant Bemis continued to scan and report the situation with the fire and condition of the wing from his vantage point in the cargo bay, when all of a sudden he announced in a very calm voice, 'There goes the wing flap on the right side,' just very matter of fact, no obvious excitement noted in his voice. When we were getting one problem under control another would come up and we started losing hydraulic pressure, causing the pilots to increasingly focus on the latest problems, which in all likelihood would soon increase in intensity. For the first time the realization that we possibly wouldn't get out of this came to my mind, however in about the same instant I was able to rationalize that if this was the way it was to be, it would be, but I wasn't going to give up or just quit trying, so I maintained a can-do attitude and tried to keep the Grim Reaper at a respectable distance.

'Sergeant Bemis made another announcement, this time that the right aileron was leaving the right wing; the fire seemed to be spreading and globs of metal were rolling off the wing. This must have been about the time an Army helicopter recon team saw our plane and thought we could use some help, as they noticed the fire going past the tail and parts of the aircraft shedding off the wing. We were not aware of their sighting us until later in the day; we were not in any way involved with each other's activities and they just happened to be in the area and saw us go by.

'An oxygen bottle exploded, leaving a gaping hole on the right side of the aircraft. Sergeant Bemis reported that white smoke was visible (white smoke in an aircraft fire is not a good thing, it indicates a magnesium fire that won't go out till it is all consumed) and I was convinced it was time to find a place to set the bird down and quickly.

'I noticed the pilots were both very busy trying to maintain altitude and directional control. I looked around for a clearing and dead ahead of us was a clearing that appeared level and free of trees. I announced on interphone it was time to land 'ASAP' and that we had a clearing just in front of us and I turned and started to strap in my seat, facing forward. Just then, our South Viêtnamese Sergeant Kiem came up on the flight deck with a bandage in his hand. He wanted me to help him put it on a neat bullet hole midway between his knee and ankle on his left leg. Since we were about to touch down I said 'NO' and motioned for him to get back down the steps to the cargo area.

'The pilots were beginning to really have some serious control problems since the right wing was melting off as we flew, including the right aileron and flap being gone; flight control hydraulics were also gone, making holding the wings level and aircraft directional control a real challenge.

'The last thing I remember about the pilots before touchdown was of them expending a lot of effort trying to hold the wings level. The significant aspect of the entire thing was just prior to touch down the right wing started to drop significantly, if the landing aircraft has a wing tip touch down before the rest of the plane, disastrous results can be expected (like a cartwheel and aircraft disintegration). However just prior to touch down, the right wing came level almost simultaneous as we crashed and we were going straight ahead.

'With rice paddy dykes and craters from artillery or B-52 bombing, the crash landing was

C-130E (63-7811 or 63-9811) gets airborne on a hot sunny day at Đà Nẵng Air Base in Viêtnam in 1972. The main landing gear is already almost fully retracted and the nose gear in transit with the nose gear doors still open ... co-pilot hot on the landing gear lever. Getting the landing gear retracted quickly was important on takeoff with heavy loads in order to reduce drag and allow for much improved climb performance. (Robert D. Young)

not very smooth. As it turned out, we had landed downwind instead of the preferred into the wind but even that turned out to be rather fortunate for us since the aircraft made a180 degree turn with the nose of the aircraft facing into the wind and all the smoke from the aircraft fire was blowing back toward the tail section.

'Again we were lucky because the wind was light and kept the smoke away from where everyone was located in or near the aircraft after the crash landing without fanning the flames, making recovery so much easier.

'I was strapped in with the seat facing forward. During this short span of time which seemed to be an eternity, I was hanging on to the navigator's desk with all my might; things were flying all around the cockpit and I was just about to give up trying to hang on when all the motion and noise stopped and a deadly silence settled over the airplane.

'The airplane was burning, a lot of smoke was in the vicinity but the cockpit appeared to be fairly clear of smoke. I was attempting to untangle myself from radio cables that had wrapped around me and the seat during the crash landing and there was an eerie cry for help coming from the cargo area, 'Don't Leave Me' - it was Sergeant Ralph Bemis, with all sorts of debris on top of him.

'I was having difficulties with the seatbelt release, it wouldn't release in the normal fashion, so I got my knife from the pocket on my flight suit and I started cutting seat belt and the radio cords . Just after the crash, I must have been rendered unconscious for a short while as I don't have any recollection of the pilots departing the flight deck.

'Fortunately for Sergeant Kiem, the South Viêtnamese soldier, he was able to hang on throughout the crash landing about mid way down a 3½ foot ladder that goes between the flight deck and cargo floor level. When the aircraft came to a halt, the nose gear was collapsed and under the aircraft, the crew entrance door had been torn off and all he had to do was step out onto the ground that was level with the lower floor.

'Captain Jensen, once outside the aircraft, noticed Sergeant Kiem was unable to walk, so he picked him up and carried him away from the aircraft and eventually to one of the rescue Hueys that would pull up in front of the aircraft nose. Captain Jensen later relayed to me his thought was

one of the Cobra helicopters may have mistaken Sergeant Kiem for an unfriendly and done him in, so picking him up would take care of that potential problem.

'During the crash landing, with the wheels hitting soft ground, rice paddy dykes and craters, the aircraft slowed down much faster than it was designed to do; therefore a considerable amount of debris from the back of the cargo bay had come loose, pinning Sergeant Bemis to the floor with a broken arm and ankle. Airman Armstead was free and relatively unhurt and he attempted to dig Sergeant Bemis out of his predicament with no success and found it necessary to exit the cargo area through a large hole in the right side of the aircraft for some fresh air, due to the smoke in the cargo area. He exited and re-entered several times, not wanting to leave his fellow loadmaster. I went down the ladder and immediately saw a pile of twisted metal and an assortment of other aircraft parts all on top of Sergeant Bemis. I made an attempt to clear them, but it seemed to be an impossible task as I couldn't move anything and started bleeding rather vigorously from cuts on my forearms and hands from the jagged, sharp edges of the various pieces of metal I was trying to remove.

'After some time in my attempt I decided we would need some outside help in extracting him from his position so I went out of the crew door opening and walked a few steps to about the nose of the aircraft and promptly found myself up to my chin in water. I had stepped into one of the bomb craters that had filled with water and which was covered with thick elephant grass on top. I figured it would be best to just stay there and try to call for help on my SAR (Search and Rescue) radio from that position, keeping a low silhouette in case someone was looking for a large upright target to shoot at.

'I pulled out my radio to make a 'Mayday' call and the antenna fell off and went 'Plop' into the water - a bad thing. Next I heard a helicopter approaching from the front of the aircraft - a good thing and I started to climb out of the watery hole. I had just got clear of that when I heard this very loud swishing sound. At first I felt the aircraft was exploding from the fuel fire but it was a rocket being fired by a Cobra gunship overhead. I eventually made it to the Huey that had pulled up near the plane and all the C-130 crew had by now been rescued from the burning aircraft. We had just lifted off when both door gunners started firing their .30 calibre machine guns. Someone had seen fire coming from the tree line, which the door gunners were trying to suppress.

'Upon arrival at the 3rd Field Hospital in Saïgon we all scrambled out of the Hueys and walked, limped or were carried into the emergency room. Since only Sergeant's Bemis, Airman Armstead and Sergeant Kiem had wounds requiring immediate attention and hospitalization, the rest of us wandered out of the hospital and found a ride over to Tân Sơn Nhứt. Two days later, my entire body became black and blue from the banging around I received during the crash landing. I still had not had contact with any medical personnel. That was a big mistake.'[17]

The crash of 'Doc' Jensen's aircraft when the only serious injuries were the loadmasters who were hurt by flying debris in the cargo compartment led to changes, as Edward Brya recalled: 'We learned to take the unnecessary equipment out: all the seats, stanchions, chains, devices, tool boxes, etc. while we were flying around the country our resourceful crews were acquiring, some defensive equipment. Later on the

supply system finally authorized us ballistic helmets, flak vests and some armour-plated vests. However in the early stages of the battle, we were scrounging for equipment anyway we could. Let me tell you about the way the loadmaster went to war. He would put that armoured vest on, take a flak vest apart, tape it around his legs, lay chains on the floor, put the garbage can on the chains, get in and from that position activate the static line retriever as back up for the drop. Next we tried the MLRADS or the mid level radar air drop system, which used 'Charlie Brown' reef cutters on the parachutes. We felt we could increase the accuracy of the deliveries by employing the SAC MSQ radar bomb procedures, which the B-52s used for the 'Arc Light' mission and the C-130 for the 'Commando Vault' mission our BLU 82 10,000lb bomb. The navigator would give a time and ground speed and drift angle to the MSQ site and they in turn could place you within 50 feet of a requested point by means of a GCA. However we still had to compute an accurate carp for use by The MSQ site. The problem as always was the wind so we took readings each thousand feet on the way up. We made the drops from 8,000 feet using the 40 second cutters. A few of the bundles hit the DZ but a majority fell long. We found out later the chutes

South Viêtnamese refugees at U-Tapao, Thailand.

were opening early due to improper rigging of the cutters.

'After two days MACV stopped the high drops and directed us to go back low. Down we went. But this time we went at night and we had gunships to help us. The gunship was much better for our purposes than a fighter. He could loiter in the area and deliver continuous fire on a target while we made our run-in. A side note on how we got the gunships - I was over at 7th AF one morning and saw a friend from Pope, Howard Rowland. He was pulling a 30 day TDY from Ubon as the gunship liaison. The rest is history because the crews couldn't see the obstacles at night. We flew 500 feet above the terrain. We hoped that at night they wouldn't see us until we were at the target. But of course with a bright moonlit night, they saw you anyway. We had pretty good success putting the bundles on the DZ from low altitude. But once we got in 2 or 3 per night they wanted more. A requirement for ten sorties a night was laid on.

'During this time Kampong Trach in Cambodia[18] came under attack and was surrounded. We ran a drop to the DZ in the daytime and the aircraft sustained 86 hits. The next night we took in three successful sorties. But this same night we lost our second plane at An Lôc. He was hit and downed approximately two clicks southwest of town. The following night the FACS would not clear any more 130s into the An Lôc area. They considered the fire to be murderous. 23

and 37 mm were active; .51-calibre was everywhere. Meanwhile at Kampong Trach the first aircraft in was hit by .51-calibre from a four-sided box pattern. The next two airplanes were sent back by the FAC. We had lost any element of surprise. New ground rules were laid down by 7th Air Force. We would have either gunships or fighters for all night drops and fighters for all day drops. Then 7th Air Force directed planning for a ten ship daylight standard level - one minute in trail airdrop to be supported by fire power from A-37s. Colonel Iosue considered this plan suicide [a view shared by the forward air controllers who were working targets around the city] and when he was unable to get MACV to shut it off, somehow he got word to the C-in-C at PACAF and General Clay turned it off. Again the drops were renewed using night low level procedures. However, some day drops were scheduled to make up for those we could not complete at night.

'In a few more days we lost the third airplane, this time just east of the town. By now the higher echelons of command were convinced of the danger inherent in our mission and we were allowed to go back to high altitude. But due to defences of the enemy such as 37 mm and the new SA-7 Strela-2 missile [Soviet: 'arrow'; NATO reporting name SA-7 'Grail'],[19] we were being forced to go to higher altitudes. The SA-7 downed AC-119 gunships over An Lôc and hit a C-130 gunship at 7,500 feet. By this time help was on its

KC-130F BuNo150687 VMGR-152 possibly at MCAS Futema, Okinawa in 1973.

way from the States. TAC deployed two 130 squadrons, the 61st from Little Rock and the 36th from Langley. The 61st was an AWADS [All Weather Air Delivery System] squadron, which along with a newly developed high velocity airdrop. Using 1,000lb bundles fitted to 15-foot slotted parachutes provided the needed airdrop accuracy. The successful airdrops turned the tide and by mid-May the NVA had ceased ground attacks on An Lôc. However, Highway 13 from Saïgon remained closed until late June. From mid-April to mid-May C-130 crews made 57 low-level and ninety mid- or high-level drops at An Lôc. During that time at least 56 airplanes were hit plus the five we lost. Seventeen crew members were killed or MIA and another ten wounded. At night, planes who knew they were hit would come back to Saïgon, shut down and discover fuel streaming out of all four main tanks.'

Linking Pleiku with the port cities of the coast was Route 19; ninety miles of winding roadway capable of supporting heavy truck traffic but vulnerable to sabotage or ambush. During early April, clashes along Highway 19 raised concern for security of the important highlands lifeline. On 11 April North Viêtnamese elements succeeded in blocking the road at the An Khê Pass near the old American cavalry base. Despite heavy Allied airstrikes the Communists held the roadway closed for sixteen days, requiring that all resupply and reinforcement into the interior by air. On 16 April stocks of fuel in the highlands were down to three days and there simply was not yet enough transport available to sustain the necessary military effort.

The next day three C-130s each fitted with large rubber fuel bladders in the cargo compartment began special POL deliveries into Pleiku. The bladders permitted delivery of 4,500 gallons of fuel per sortie (standard C-130s later delivered POL in cylindrical containers, allowing faster off loading than with the bladder-birds). The dark approaches into the high airhead by the heavily loaded C-130s called for peak flying precision. To avoid ground fire from sectors of Kontum city, crews used overhead circling approaches down to 3,000 feet, avoiding use of landing lights until the last possible moment. Portable lights outlined the location of the runway and fuel could be emptied by pumps carried in the aircraft in fifteen minutes. Three such 'bladder-

bird' aircraft made twelve trips to Pleiku from Tân Sơn Nhứt and Cam Ranh Bay on the 17th. The effort continued the next day and on the 19th a fourth ship joined the effort - three planes hauled JP-4 and one carried aviation gasoline for reciprocating engines. Other C-130s arrived regularly with hard cargo, interspersed with C-141s temporarily tasked to perform missions inside Viêtnam. After offloading at Pleiku, many of the cargo-carriers took aboard passengers - refugees from the battered region headed for safer places. Many were dependents of Viêtnamese military men; few carried more than scant possessions. One C-141, flown by Captain Richard Semingson and crew, took off with 394 passengers - the most ever lifted by a Starlifter and more than four times the normal load. Observers on the ground at Tân Sơn Nhứt were amazed at the endless file of humanity streaming from the ship's tail doors.

The reopening of Highway 19 in late April ended the critical dependence on airlift for transport to Pleiku, but the closure of Highway 14 north of Pleiku on 24 April left the defenders of Kontum wholly isolated except by air during more than two months of heavy and close fighting. Bladder-bird deliveries into Kontum commenced on 23 April, expanding to 24,000 gallons the next day, rebuilding reserves against daily consumption of 15,600. Meanwhile other aircraft landed with hard cargo, departing with the last of the airborne brigade ordered out earlier. Enemy shells periodically interrupted flight-line activity and ground-to-air fire harassed arriving and departing planes. USAF control and aerial port teams worked on the ground at Kontum to speed the flow, as the volume of shelling increased daily.

Hair-raising episodes became commonplace. A bladder-bird received major damage on the 26th. The pilot, Lieutenant Colonel Reed Mulkey of the 50th Tactical Airlift Squadron and a veteran of the 1968 campaign, was attempting departure when a rocket detonated immediately in front of his aircraft, flattening the landing gear, silencing one of the engines and causing major fuel leaks. A three man repair party arrived to inspect the damage and begin repairs. While they worked, more rockets began detonating - one ventilated a C-130 which had just landed and another made a direct hit on a VNAF C-123 parked nearby. US Army and USAF bystanders fought the fire with hand extinguishers, courageously climbing inside and atop the burning hulk. An eleven-man repair team arrived to complete repairs shortly before dusk on 30 April. Working with flashlights and into the morning, the team finished at midday. Rockets continued to detonate, nearly destroying a VNAF C-123 taking off loaded with refugees. Mulkey's repaired craft and a relief C-130 barely managed take-offs in early afternoon, as both received additional shrapnel holes. Mulkey, with fresh fuel leaks and a lost engine on the previously undamaged side - made a three- engine emergency landing at Pleiku. In a separate episode, Staff Sergeant Floyd J. Monville, a fuels NCO, received acclaim for successfully offloading a damaged C-130 and transferring its bladder system to another C-130, all under fire, using the only vehicle available - a small warehouse type forklift. Monville was later nominated for the Jaycee's award, 'America's Ten Outstanding Young Men of 1972,' both for his exploits at Kontum and for his role as volunteer director of the Gò Vấp Orphanage in Viêtnam.

Altitudes were swiftly increased to above 6,000 feet dropping with ground-radar guidance (GRADS). The drop crews worked with AC-130 gunship crews who provided winds aloft information to the C-130 navigators from their gunsight computers. The results were considerably improved over those attained previously, but 'high altitude, low-opening' parachute techniques proved unsuccessful because numerous chutes failed - in part because they had been incorrectly packed by Viêtnamese packers. The C-130 crews had no option but to resume the more deadly low-level conventional airdrops; and inevitably the aircraft received hits. Finally, Air Force switched to resupply at night. On the first two nights, the blacked-out C-130 crews enjoyed the element of surprise and managed to get their loads close enough to the target that the South Viêtnamese managed to recover most of them. AC-130 gunships provided covering fire. Many if not most of the AC-130 pilots had come from tactical airlift units and were familiar with the airdrop techniques. Light signals used on the ground failed to guide the 130s and many bundles of supplies missed their mark, some falling into Communist hands. Colonel Andrew Iosue felt that the night landings at Kontum were 'a dicey operation' and that the absence of accidents under the conditions was remarkable. Landings ended shortly before dawn on the 25th, with Communist troops lodged at the east end of the runway and delivering small arms fire from three directions at the last C-130 lifting off with the USAF ground teams. Fighting continued throughout the city, with resupply by American and VNAF Chinook helicopters, while the USAF prepared to start C-130 paradrops.

On the third night, 25/26 April, C-130E 64-0508 of Detachment 1, 374th TAW at CCK AB, Taiwan was flown by Major Harry Arlo Amesbury. This crew had dropped supplies to ARVN forces on the 24th at Kompo Trach and their aircraft had been hit by ground fire no less 86 times on that mission. The aircraft approached the drop zone at An Lôc at 500 feet and 170 knots when it entered 'a wall of fire' and was hit and crashed shortly afterwards about five miles south of An Lôc. All the crew were killed. Two other Hercules had already been hit by ground fire during the night's operation and when Major Amesbury's aircraft was lost the airdrop was brought to a halt for the night.[20]

On 29 April an SA-7 surface-to-air missile was fired in Quảng Trị, confirming for the first time that the NVA were now equipped with the deadly shoulder-fired missiles. With SA-7s in South Viêtnam, low-altitude airdrop missions were almost unthinkable. Fortunately, the Air Force riggers at CCK had come up with a solution to the problem. In World War II and Korea supplies were often dropped without a parachute attached and the USAF riggers discovered that with the proper amount of packing material, bundles containing even ammunition could be safely dropped using slotted extraction parachutes to stabilize, but not retard the descent of the load. The loads descended four times faster than a similar load suspended beneath a G-12 parachute and were thus less susceptible to the winds at altitude. As it turned out the high-velocity drops using the GRADS technique not only allowed the C-130 crews to drop from altitudes above the range of the antiaircraft guns at An Lôc and even the SA-7s (which are effective only to about 4,000 feet), they also allowed unprecedented accuracy. Some supplies such as medical materials and fuel proved unsuitable for the high velocity method and had to be dropped using the HALO parachutes, but most items could be delivered without restraining parachutes. Fortunately, the defenders at An Lôc

Operation 'Homecoming' at Gia Lam Airport in Hànôi in 1973.

had discovered a source of fresh water so ammunition and rations were the primary commodities that had to be airdropped to the defenders.

The USAF resumed high altitude GRADS daylight drops at An Lôc on 5 May having solved some of the earlier problems with the system and achieved a 90 per cent success rate using this radar-directed drop procedure. Loads were attached to parachutes rigged properly and only one of the twenty-four bundles dropped fell into enemy hands.

The high-velocity method was developed just in time, for on 11 May the first SA-7 firings were reported at An Lôc. The drop planes were able to operate without fear of the Strela missiles, but the AC-130 gunships were considerably affected. Their guns lost their effectiveness at the 10,000 foot altitudes that were necessary to avoid the SA-7s. Tactics were worked out for the AC-130 and C-130 crews to fire decoy flares when an SA-7 firing was observed. The heat-seeking missiles would home on the more intense heat of the flares instead of the C-130's exhaust. Four C-130 crews reported SA-7 firings in South Viêtnam in May/June but none were hit. The AC-130s did not fare as well; one was badly damaged on 12 May

and another was shot down near Huê in June.

Because only a portion of the C-130 crews at CCK were drop qualified, the missions over An Lôc meant that the same people were bearing the brunt of the burden. The crews were well aware that each mission might be their last. They wore flak suits and helmets while the loadmasters filled the airplane garbage can with tie-down chains and climbed inside it while over the drop zone. For a week the night drops continued, with the C-130 crews encountering heavy fire on each mission and only about 10% of the loads were positively recovered. More than half of the drop planes took hits and several crewmembers were wounded. Two daylight supply operations and one night drop to 20,000 defenders and refugees at An Lôc had cost three C-130s by 3 May and on the night of 2/3 May the C-130s failed to make a single successful delivery. The following night, C-130E 62-1797 of Detachment 1in the 374th TAW from Tân Sơn Nhứt was shot down. Captain Donald Lee Unger had made his low level CDS drop and was pulling up from 500 feet to return to Tân Sơn Nhứt when his aircraft was hit by automatic weapons fire. The Hercules crashed a few miles from An Lôc and all the crew were killed. After this incident no more low level drops were made at An Lôc.

As from 8 May, when the An Lôc garrison recovered 65 of the 88 tons dropped, things improved and by the end of the siege, on 18 June, 7,600 tons had been dropped by the C-130s in more than 600 sorties.

Meanwhile, Kontum had been cut off when the NVA captured Đắk Tô on 24 April and cut the road from Pleiku. From then on the only method of resupply of fuel, food, ammunition and other supplies was by air. During the eight days prior to 3 May, the C-130s made approximately fifteen landings daily at Kontum - a typical day's work was seven loads of munitions, five of POL and three of rice. During the same eight days VNAF transports made fifteen deliveries. On 2 May, a C-130 lost several feet of wingtip in a collision with a helicopter at the crowded airhead, but managed an emergency landing at Pleiku. Rocket damage to another C-130 the next day brought a decision to

Stretcher cases being airlifted from Việtnam in a RAAF C-130. (Australian War Memorial)

shift to night operations. Meanwhile, rocket attacks were beginning at Pleiku, threatening both C-130s on the ground there. Day operations to Kontum ceased abruptly on 17 May after enemy fire damaged several C-130s, burned two VNAF C-123s and destroyed a C-130E (63-7798) in the 776th TAS 374th TAW; the latter was hit in one of its engines by a mortar or a rocket while taking off. Captain Richard Harold Hagman and three other crewmen were killed. The lone survivor was rescued by an American helicopter. Hercules operations resumed exclusively at night on 18/19 May, with seventeen C-130s running the gauntlet of enemy fire to carry out successful deliveries and fifteen more on the 20th sustained the flow of supplies. Resupply continued nightly under cover of allied gunships. On the night of 22/23 May two C-130s received shrapnel damage, one managing an emergency landing at Đà Nẵng. C-130E 62-1854 *Quan Loi Queen* of 'E' Flight, 21st Tactical Airlift Squadron, damaged after midnight on 22 May, was further damaged and the next day when it delayed its departure past dawn and was destroyed by a missile on the ground. Two days later the Communists seized a part of the Kontum runway, closing the airfield to landings except by helicopters and it was not until the 28th that the Hercules could resume airdrops overhead. More than 2,000 tons were dropped in 130 C-130 sorties before the Hercules could resume night landings on 8 June.

An important forerunner of the Kontum airdrops were the drops begun in mid-May at several isolated and hard-pressed camps farther north and west. Dak Pek, Mang Buk and Ben Het received a total of 19 C-130 drops during May using techniques developed recently for release from altitudes above the level of anti-aircraft effectiveness. Drops began at Kontum with a single mission on the afternoon of 27 May. During the next four days, 19 C-130 loads were parachuted to a drop zone near the city's south-west corner (the Communists held much of the east half of the city). With some success in pushing the Communists from their sectors, the drop zone was shifted to the more convenient north-west sector; 68 C-130 drop sorties took place during the first seven days of June. Although retrieval parties on the ground had trouble keeping up with the volume of deliveries, the II Corps G-4 reported that the drops 'have been

Australian troops leaving Việtnam in C-130E A97-189 (65-12906).

very accurate and nearly all parachute bundles are impacting in the recovery area.' Much of this success reflected the painful evolution of effective methods experienced earlier at An Lôc. C-130 landings resumed on the night of 8/9 June. Six 130s made blacked-out GCA approaches and landings that night. During C-130 approaches, friendly artillery fire was directed into the likely danger area to discourage enemy shelling and flare shells were detonated near the runway in hopes of distracting any surface-to-air missile. The daytime drops continued, ending on 14 June after another 48 sorties since the 7th. Through the nineteen days of drops, not a single C-130 received battle damage.

A further aspect gave added significance to the Kontum resupply. Sixteen of the drops were performed using the All Weather Air Delivery System (AWADS) by aircraft and crews recently deployed under 'Constant Guard IV' from the United States. A preliminary mission on 1 June attained moderate success at Svay Rieng in Cambodia. Two days later, two aircraft released at Kontum, aiming with the aid of a ground radar beacon transponder. Accuracy appeared satisfactory, but half the bundles could not be recovered because of enemy fire on the drop zone. During 7-14 June C-130 crews made another fifteen AWADS drops at Kontum. Navigators aimed using the self-contained radar and computer system, now using reflected radar returns. A bridge

south of the town served for late computer update; a river bend at the city served as the final offset aiming point. The largest recorded impact error was 300 metres; all drops were from 10,000 feet. One drop, on 12 June, was performed in two-ship formation using the electronic station-keeping equipment (SKE), the trail ship dropping 5.4 seconds behind the AWADS-equipped leader. The result was spectacular; the second ship's load landed atop the leader's. The only significant problems in SKE appeared to be the trail ship's difficulty in flying in the leader's turbulent wake while heavy and slow.

From July 1965-November 1972 the Hercules flew no fewer than 708,087 sorties in Việtnam, with peak monthly operations being recorded in May 1968 when in-country Hercules flew 14,392 sorties.

US bombing of North Việtnam had resumed with a vengeance on 10 May 1972 with 'Linebacker I' raids aimed at the enemy's road and rail system to prevent supplies reaching the Communists operating in South Việtnam. 'Linebacker II' operations began on 18 December 1972 and lasted until the 29th. These were the most effective strikes against enemy defences in the whole war and they ultimately persuaded the Hànôi government to seek an end to hostilities and to conclude a peace treaty. Negotiations in Paris ended with the signing of a peace agreement on 23 January 1973 and all air operations ceased four

'Grunts' of the US 3rd Marine Division embarking on KC-130F transport/tanker BuNo150687 of VMGR-152 at MCAS Futema, Okinawa en route home to the US late in 1974. (S/Sgt Mennillo USMC).

days later; this brought to an end one of the most horrific wars in history. In its course 58,022 Americans died and it brought America it worldwide condemnation for its role in South-East Asia. A total of 126 tactical airlift aircraft were lost during the war, fifty-five of them Hercules.

Although all US ground forces were withdrawn from South Việtnam, air-raids into neighbouring Cambodia and Laos continued until August 1973. In the spring of 1973 the C-130s switched their full attention to the airlift of supplies to Cambodia, with the last war-related sorties being undertaken in 1975 by an aircraft flown by civilian crews of Birdair Inc., a contract operator to which the USAF gave equipment and technical assistance. Then both Cambodia and Laos fell to the Communists and early in 1975 the North turned its attentions to the final take-over of South Việtnam. Inevitably the South, now without US military support, collapsed under the full might of the Communists' spring offensive. Indeed the onslaught was so rapid and so intensive that by March, the original 'Talon Vise' contingency plan to evacuate US dependents and non-essential personnel was abandoned and beginning on 1 April 'Frequent Wind' began the wholesale evacuation of all US forces left in Việtnam.

C-130s of Tactical Airlift Command joined C-141As and C-5A Galaxies of the Military Airlift Command (MAC) in a mass exodus of US and Việtnamese military and civilians fleeing South

Việtnam before the country was completely overwhelmed. (C-5 flights were withdrawn following a tragic crash of a Galaxy on 4 April, which claimed 155 lives.) After 20 April the situation became even more critical and safe operating loads were ignored so that transports could take off from Saïgon, now completely surrounded by Communist troops, in grossly overloaded condition. C-130s departed carrying between 180 and even 260 evacuees on board, while a VNAF C-130 is reported to have fled loaded with 452 people. By 27 April the danger from Communist small arms, Triple-A and shoulder- fired ground-to-air missiles had become too great for most aircraft and all C-141A flights were suspended. The Hercules, however, carried on, flying right around the clock until the early

Việtnamese refugees being evacuated in April 1973.

hours of 29 April when heavy and accurate Communist rocket fire at Tân Sơn Nhứt forced even these to cease operations.

From 1-29 April 1975 a total of 50,493 people had been airlifted during the course of 375 C-130, C-141 and other aircraft sorties. On 12 April the US Embassy in Saïgon was evacuated and 287 staff were flown to US carriers offshore. The last US military C-130 loss was the 314th Tactical Airlift Wing C-130E 72-1297, hit by advancing NVA rocket fire on 28 April, forcing Tân Sơn Nhứt Air Base to close to fixed wing evacuation of the collapsing South Việtnamese capital of Saïgon. On 29 April 900 Americans were airlifted by the US Navy to five carriers. Next day, Saïgon was in Communist hands and the South was under control of North Việtnam. Six C-130s were among the ninety aircraft flown out of the country to Thailand by VNAF personnel, but about 1,100 aircraft, including twenty-three C-130As in the 435th and 437th Squadrons, fell into Communist hands before the ink was dry on the surrender document issued to the Republic of Việtnam's President Dương Văn Minh.

Chapter 4 Endnotes

1   This incident was undoubtedly the worst air disaster of the war until the loss of a C-5A near Saigon on 4 April 1975. *Vietnam Air Losses* by Chris Hobson (Midland Publishing 2001).

2   Joe M Jackson and Major Jesse W. Campbell of the 311th ACS landed the Provider which was fired at continuously until it took off with the three men safely on board. Lieutenant Colonel Jackson received the Medal of Honor for this feat of skill and courage under fire.

3   *A Trash Hauler in Vietnam; Memoir of Four Tactical Airlift Tours, 1965-1968.*

4   1st Lieutenant Ragland had been shot down over Korea in November 1951by a Soviet Ace pilot, Colonel Yevgeny Pepelyayev in his MiG-15, forcing Ragland to bail out of his F-86E. Prior to his shoot down, Ragland had shot down a Soviet MiG flown by Lieutenant Alfey Dostoievsky and he and Lieutenant Kenneth Chandler had performed an audacious strike against North Korean airbase of Uiju ten days earlier, on 18 November, destroying four MiGs on the ground). He was a PoW in the Pyok-Dong prison camp for two years.

5   John Gargus was awarded the Silver Star. In part, his citation said: 'In the face of heavy enemy anti-aircraft artillery and surface-to-air missile fire, Major Gargus skilfully managed all navigational systems and equipment to insure precise navigation

and accurate timing on target which were essential for completion of this dangerous mission. As a result of Major Gargus' heroic efforts, the force arrived at Sơn Tây without incident, the enemy ground forces were completely surprised and the mission was successfully completed.'

6   US intelligence may have identified this the day before the raid, but the raid was sent anyway. Three commando teams landed at the camp: The first team intentionally crash landed a helicopter right in the middle of the camp to get into position as quickly as possible. The second landed 400 metres away by accident, at what turned out to be a base for Russian and Chinese military advisers. The team attacked the headquarters and killed an estimated more than 100 people at the base. The third team landed outside the main complex and assisted in securing the facility. The raid succeeded completely at its technical objective of seizing control of the camp. There were no prisoners present to rescue, though 26 minutes after the first helicopter intentionally crash landed all US commandoes were recovered and flying home. One US soldier was wounded in the leg and one broke his ankle in the intentional crash landing. An unknown number of North Việtnamese soldiers were killed in the raid. The unsuccessful mission did bring an ironic success for Simons and his troops. The attempt to rescue prisoners brought the world's attention to the inhumane treatment of the American PoWs. The raid on Sơn Tây altered how the North Việtnamese housed, treated and interacted with the foreign prisoners. Some have questioned whether the real intention of the raid was dual purpose and in addition to the attempted rescues of PoWs was designed to send a message to the Russians and the Chinese assisting the Việtnamese.

7   Caribou C-7B 62-4161 of the 459 TAS, 483 TAW at Phú Cat was approaching the Đức Phổ Special Forces camp, about 20 miles south of Quảng Ngai on 3 August 1967 when it was hit by a shell from a US Army 155mm howitzer. The aircraft had flown into the line of fire and the shell blew off its entire rear fuselage and tail section. Captains Alan Eugene Hendrickson and John Dudley Wiley and Tech Sergeant Zane Aubry Carter were killed.

8   F-4D 65-0637 in the 12th TFW at Phù Cát crewed by Captain Hedditch and 1st Lieutenant T. McLaughlin was taking part in a 'Steel Tiger' night mission in southern Laos. Hedditch was making his third pass on a target near Ban Tampanko [in Savannakhet Province, Laos] when his aircraft was struck by ground fire. Both crew ejected successfully and were rescued by a USAF helicopter. *Vietnam Air Losses* by Chris Hobson (Midland Publishing 2001).

9   Once Xuân Lộc fell on 21 April 1975, the PVN battled with the last remaining elements of III Corp Armoured Task Force, remnants of the 18th Infantry Division and depleted ARVN Marine, Airborne and Ranger Battalions in a fighting retreat that lasted nine days, until they reached Sàigòn and PVN armoured columns crashed throughout the gates of South Việtnam's Presidential Palace on 30 April 1975, effectively ending the war.

10   The merchant ship's crew, whose seizure at sea had prompted the US attack, had been released in good health, unknown to the US Marines or the US command of the operation before they attacked. Nevertheless, the Marines boarded and recaptured the ship anchored offshore a Cambodian island, finding it empty. It was the only known engagement between US ground forces and the Khmer Rouge.

11   The incident took place between the Kingdom of Cambodia and the US less than a month after the Khmer Rouge took control of the capital Phnom Penh ousting the US backed Khmer Republic. It was the last official battle of the Việtnam War. The names of the Americans killed, as well as those of three US Marines who were left behind on the island of Koh Tang after the battle and were subsequently executed by the Khmer Rouge, are the last names on the Việtnam Veterans Memorial.

12   On 19 June 1968 Operation 'Charlie', the final evacuation and destruction of the Khê Sanh Combat Base began. The Marines withdrew all salvageable material and destroyed everything else. The NVA continued shelling the base and on 1 July launched a company-sized infantry attack against its perimeter. On 9 July the flag of the Việt Công was set up at Ta Con (Khê Sanh) airfield. On 13 July Hồ Chi Minh sent a message to the soldiers of the Route 9 - Khê Sanh Front affirming their victory at Khê Sanh. It was the first time in the war that the Americans abandoned a major combat base because of enemy pressure.

13   The 'Raven' Forward Air Controllers, also known as 'The Ravens', were fighter pilots used for forward air control in a covert operation in conjunction with the Central Intelligence Agency in Laos. The Ravens provided direction for most of the air strikes against communist Pathet Lao targets and People's Army of Việtnam's infiltrators in support of the Laotian Hmong guerrilla army.

14   On the night of 14 April three 374th crews were briefed for airdrop missions over An Lôc the next morning. After an initial mission delay, the three C-130Es took off from Tân Sơn Nhất for the short flight to An Lôc. The first crew over the DZ, took hits. The second crew elected to approach the drop zone from a different direction.

15   Although the two C-130 crews, including one with Iosue, Brya and Highley, thought they identified the drop zone, it turned out that they had been given the wrong coordinates and the loads were not recovered.

16   *Vietnam Air Losses* by Chris Hobson (Midland Publishing 2001).

17   'Sp4 Shearer was the Huey crew member that had the job of getting out of the Huey to make a close up visual of the wreckage. I found out much later that he was positive he would find a group of mangled bodies in the wreckage and not knowing the fate of the survivors was something that was to haunt him for 32 years, which is when we met at the coffee shop of Luke Air Force Base, Arizona, in 2004.'

18   One of the eight districts of the Kampot Province, at the eastern part bordering Việtnam to the east, Banteay Meas District to the north, Kep Province to the west and the Gulf of Thailand to the south.

19   The Strela-2 system along with the more advanced Strela-2M it achieved 204 hits out of 589 firings against US aircraft between 1972 and 1975 according to Russian sources.

20   See *Vietnam Air Losses* by Chris Hobson (Midland Publishing 2001).

Chapter Five

Operation 'Dragon Rouge'

In mid-November 1964 the C-130Es and crews of the Tactical Air Command rotational squadron from Pope AFB, North Carolina were called back to their temporary duty base at Évreux-Fauville AB, France. The crews were told simply to go to their barracks and get some rest, because something big was brewing. On Tuesday evening, 17 November the crews were told to report to the operations room on the Margarite where the planes were deployed. The crews were told to rig seats and take-off. Just before take-off, each navigator was given a Manila envelope and instructed not to open it until their airplane had reached 2,000 feet and there were no mechanical problems to make them turn back. When the crews opened the envelopes, they learned they were going to Kleine Brogel Air Base in the municipality Peer outside Brussels. When they got to Kleine Brogel each plane loaded with paratroopers wearing red berets and then took off again after being handed another envelope. This time it told them to head south for Morón Air Base in southern Spain, 35 miles southeast of the city of Seville. At Morón the navigators went into Base Operations where they were given maps and instructions for the next leg of their flight, to Ascension Island in the South Atlantic, where they arrived eighteen hours after leaving France. By this time everyone knew they were on their way to Africa, but first there was a time of 'hurry up and wait' on secluded Ascension, where the rescue force was out of sight of the prying eyes of the world. While they waited, the American airmen and Belgian paras got to know each other and began working out procedures to drop the Belgians.

On Sunday before Thanksgiving the force left Ascension and flew across the Atlantic and much of Africa to Kamina, an airfield in the southern Congo. There the crews and paratroopers waited again. By this time all hopes of negotiation had vanished and that evening the American and Belgian commanders were told to launch Operation 'Dragon Rouge'.

'Red Dragon' was one of the most dramatic military missions undertaken during the Cold War. It involved a flight of more than 4,000 miles by USAF C-130s carrying paratroopers of the crack Belgian 1st ParaCommando to rescue hostages who had been held for more than three months in the Congolese city of Stanleyville. The former Belgian Colony of Congo (now Zaire) was granted independence in 1960 and almost immediately became the site of chaos. When the crisis ended in early 1964, a new one broke out as Congolese rebels calling themselves 'Simba' rebelled against the government. The Congolese government turned to the US for help. In response, the US Strike Command sent JTF LEO, a task force made up of a detachment of C-130s, communications personnel and 82nd Airborne security team to Leopoldville. By early August 1964 the Congolese, with the help of the LEO force and a group of white mercenaries led by Major Mike Hoare was making headway against the 'Simbas'. In retaliation, the 'Simbas' began taking hostages of the whites in areas under their control. They took them to Stanleyville and placed them under guard in the Victoria Hotel. In Washington and Brussels the United States and Belgium were hard at work trying to come up with a rescue plan. Several ideas were considered and discarded, while attempts at negotiating with the Simbas failed - no one could be found to negotiate with!

Sam McGowan, who flew C-130s as a loadmaster with the USAF in Việtnam and authored *The C-130 Hercules Tactical Aircraft Missions, 1956-1975.*

In the early hours of 23 November 1964 five C-130Es took off from Kamina, each with 64 Belgian Red Berets in full combat gear seated on the red nylon troop seats in its cargo compartment. Behind the assault force came seven more Herks, with 'Chalk 12' configured as a hospital ship. The C-130Es flew north at high altitude and then dropped down to treetop altitudes to follow the Congo River as they neared the city of Stanleyville. At exactly 0600 hours on the morning of 24 November, as the sun was breaking over the horizon out of the African Veldt in the former Belgian colony of Congo, the five Hercules transports appeared only 700 feet above the Sabena Simi-Simi airport on the outskirts of the city of Stanleyville. A CIA A-26 Invader flown by a Cuban mercenary pilot made a strafing pass over the airport. Right behind the A-26 the first C-130 roared low over the runway. As the first Hercules, with 'US Air Force' stencilled in large block letters along the fuselage, approached a narrow swath of grass

alongside the airport's main runway, navigator First Lieutenant John Coble called out 'Green Light' over the aircraft's intercom. Immediately, the co-pilot, Captain Robert Kitchen, reached down to the panel by his right armrest and flipped

C-130E 62-1816, one of fourteen Hercules were used to fly one of the fourteen C-130 crews that flew part of the 500 Belgian paratroopers to the Belgian Congo to quell a native uprising. Sergeant Norman Page, mechanic and flight engineer (front row, left, squatting) recalled: 'We dropped the paratroopers at 500 feet. Their chutes popped open as their feet hit the ground. The Belgian commander told me, 'We're down here to fight. Drop them low so they hit the ground fast. Two days later the troopers won their little skirmish and we flew back in and picked them up. We flew them back to Leopoldville. When we landed we found our airplane was full of bullet holes; one through a wing tank. One of our guys stuffed a big rag in the hole and plugged it with a piece of broom stick. We flew home with it like that. When you're in a war zone you do funny things.' A few days later Page and his crew were ordered to fly to Stanleyville and rescue Dr. Paul Carlson, a California physician (pictured on the front covers of *Time* and *Life* magazines) who worked his wonders treating Congo natives. 'We found out Dr. Carlson and 28 of his nurses had been murdered two days earlier and their remains wrapped up in blankets lying on the ground'. The C-130s flew the corpses out.

the paratrooper jump lights from red to green. As the lights in the cargo compartment changed from the red 'Prepare to jump' signal to green for 'Go,' 50-year old Colonel Pierre Charles Laurent, commander of Belgium's crack Régiment Para-Commando, leaped out into the cool, moist dawn air, followed by 64 other troopers spilling from the doors on either side of the airplane into the African skies. Within seconds, 310 paratroopers were in the air and then landing on the strip of grass alongside the runway. The five jump planes came around for another pass to drop the jumpmasters and bundles of equipment. As the planes came off the drop zone, they began taking fire from a .50-calibre machinegun. After dropping the troops, 'Chalks Two' to 'Five' left the area for Leopoldville, where they were to refuel and stand-by. 'Chalk One', carrying the C-130 mission commander, Colonel Burgess Gradwell and flown by Captain Huey Long of the 777th TCS, orbited over the airfield until they were hit by several heavy shells that knocked out hydraulics. Long pointed the battle-damaged airplane toward Leopoldville.

Events of Thanksgiving week of 1964 in Africa were the direct results of years of political unrest in the Congo, which began within days of Belgium's declaration of Congolese independence in 1960. An outbreak of fighting in the newly independent country led to United Nations intervention as USAF transports under the control of the 322nd Air Division, US Air Force Europe (USAFE), airlifted a peacekeeping team made up of military personnel from several nations to Leopoldville. For three years, the UN peacekeeping force remained in the Congo, supported by C-130E and Fairchild C-124 cargo planes. Within weeks of the withdrawal of the UN force in the summer of 1964, fighting again broke out in the Congo. Christophe Gbenye, a Marxist who declared himself 'President of the Congo,' led a rebellion of fierce tribesmen calling themselves Simbas - 'lions' in Swahili. The rebels soon captured large sections of the northern half of the country, leading foreign governments, including those of the United States and Belgium, to urge their citizens to flee the threatened areas.

To combat the rebellion, 45-year old Congolese President Moïse Kapenda Tshombe recruited 44-year old Major Michael Hoare. a fiery Irish mercenary leader known for military activities in Africa (and his failed attempt to conduct a coup d'état in the Seychelles in 1978) and gave him authority to raise a mercenary army of white Africans to assist the black Congolese army. Hoare would become a legend in the world of the professional soldier; during World War II he had fought in Burma with Brigadier General Orde Wingate and then became a professional soldier after that conflict. With his reputation already made from leading an earlier band during the Katangan secessionist revolt - in which Tshombe had been a participant - Hoare had no trouble training a 300-man unit of mostly South African 'mercs' that he dubbed 5 Commando. Hoare, often called 'Mad Mike' by those who knew him, enforced only two rules among his men - that they shaved and refrained from drinking before battle. Aside from that, he 'cared not a whit' what they did.

Tshombe also turned to the United States for assistance. Lessons from World War II, Korea and the French Indochina War indicated that air support and air transportation were crucial for combating a large rebel force. President Lyndon Johnson responded to Tshombe's request for aid by sending Joint Task Force (JTF) Leo, a United States Strike Command task force consisting primarily of three Tactical Air Command C-130s and support personnel, to Leopoldville. The transports were from the 464th Troop Carrier Wing, based at tiny Pope Air Force Base (AFB), adjacent to Fort Bragg, North Carolina. A platoon of paratroopers from the 82nd Airborne Division provided protection for the C-130s while they were on the ground at remote African airstrips. A fourth C-130 was part of Leo, a 'Talking Bird' communications package that allowed long-range radio communications between the task force and Strike Command headquarters at McDill AFB as well as the Pentagon, the State Department and the White House.

Another aspect of US aid was a mercenary air force made up of North American T-28 Trojans and Douglas B-26 Intruders flown by Cuban expatriate pilots in the employ of a civilian corporation under contract to the Central Intelligence Agency. The Congolese air force consisted primarily of World War II-vintage

North American T-6 trainers, which, like the Cuban-flown T-28s, had been converted into attack planes.

In August the Simbas captured the city of Stanleyville with its large concentration of Europeans and Americans. For a time the whites were treated relatively well. But later, with additional American-supplied firepower and airlift support, the Congolese army made steady gains against the rebel forces. As the Simbas saw the tide begin to turn against them, their radio station in Stanleyville began denouncing the United States, accusing it of sending combat troops to aid the government forces. Rebel hostility caused fear for the safety of whites in rebel-held territory, especially after news of atrocities performed by the revels against their own people reached the outside world.

While the whites were under a semblance of protection by the rebels, Stanleyville's black residents were not and a reign of terror began as the Simbas systematically tortured and killed prominent Congolese. Then, evidently realizing that the whites in their territory could serve as bargaining chips, the rebels began taking hostages. On 5 September US Consul Michael Hoyt was taken into custody, along with other members of the consulate staff and thrown into the city's Central Prison. Other whites were seized. Some were thrown into the prison with the Americans, while others were held in the Victoria Hotel. Over the next two months the Simbas arrested foreigners from as many as twenty countries, placing them under custody in hotels, prisons and military bases. The rebels began making threats that the hostages would be killed if the United States did not withdraw its support for the Congolese government.

In late October the rebels accused an American medical missionary, Dr. Paul Carlson of being a US Army major on assignment for the CIA. Carlson, with the Protestant Relief Agency, was a medical doctor who first went to the Congo on a special six-month mission, then returned in 1963 with his family. Less than a year later, after having sent his wife and four children to safety in the Central African Republic, Carlson was seized by the Simbas because he owned a radio, was an American and the rebels wanted hostages. Over the next few weeks, Dr. Paul Carlson's

name would be featured in the world's headlines.

With the fate of the white hostages in doubt, the United States and Belgium tried to negotiate with the rebels. At the same time, they began planning various means of military intervention, even as the Congolese government forces launched a major offensive toward Stanleyville. Several possible schemes were put forth, including a large paratrooper assault by members of the 82nd Airborne Division, supported by heavy tactical air strikes. While military forces in the United States worked on the larger plan, the US military command in Europe came up with a less involved one, calling for the use of a small force of paratroopers begin airlifted to Africa for the rescue. That plan, formulated jointly by the United States and Belgium, was given the French code name 'Dragon Rouge' ('Red Dragon').

On 15 November Brigadier General Robert D. Forman, commander of the 322nd Air Division, was given word to begin preparations to airlift a force of Belgium paratroopers to the Congo for a possible rescue attempt. Forman's command had supported the UN peacekeeping forces in the Congo from 1960 until early 1964. During those years, however, the 322nd had undergone some changes. Previously, the division had been directly under the commander of USAFE, but a reorganization of American forces in Europe led to the transfer of the division's transfer to Military Air Transport Service a few months earlier.

Permanently assigned C-130s had been replaced by temporary duty aircraft and crews from Tactical Air Command units in the United States. In 1964 two TAC wings were supporting rotational squadrons at Évreux-Fauville Air Base, France the 317th and 464th Troop Carrier wings from Lockbourne AFB, Ohio and Pope AFB. Rotational Squadron 'A', or 'Rote Alpha,' was made up of Pope personnel who flew the newest version of the already proven Hercules, the C-130E, while 'Rote Bravo' was manned by Lockbourne crews and equipped with the older C-130A.

General Forman called Colonel Burgess Gradwell to Châteauroux to brief him on the upcoming mission. Gradwell, commander of Detachment One, 332nd Air Division at Évreux-

Fauville, would have command. 'Dragon Rouge' would involve a fourteen-plane airlift of 600 Belgian paratroopers to Africa. Since the E-model of the Hercules featured special long-range fuel tanks, 'Rote Alpha' would provide the planes and crews. When Gradwell got back to Évreux that night, he called in 'Rote Alpha' commander Lieutenant Colonel Robert A. Lindsay and the TAC liaison officer with the division, Colonel Gene Adams. Wheels were set in motion for the mission.

Before 'Dragon Rouge' could be launched, the aircraft and crews had to be recalled from their normal missions throughout Europe. By the evening of 16 November, all fifteen Hercules were back at Évreux and the crews were on 'crew rest' for an 'important' mission. At 1740 Greenwich Mean Time-'Zulu time-on 17 November, the first C-130 took off from Évreux, bound for Kleine Brogel, Belgium. Aboard the first plane were Colonel Gradwell, Captain Donald R. Strobaugh, commander of the 5th

Aerial Port Squadron (APRON) combat control team and Sergeant Robert J. Dias, a radio repairman with the 5th APRON. Like the C-130 crews, Strobaugh had been called back to Évreux from duties elsewhere in Europe. Other than certain key officers, no one aboard the airplanes knew where they were going until after they were airborne with no problems requiring them to turn back. Each navigator had been given a sealed envelope, with instructions not to open it until the airplane's altitude exceeded 2,000 feet.

At Kleine Brogel, elements of the Belgian 1st Para-Commando Regiment, including the 1st Para-Commando Battalion, a company from the 2nd Battalion and a detachment from the 3rd, were loaded aboard the C-130s, along with their equipment. At 2240Z, the first Hercules departed Kleine Brogel for a fuel stop at Móron Air Base on the southern coast of Spain, then on to Ascension Island in the South Atlantic. The first plane arrived at Ascension at 1310Z on 18 November. At Ascension Captain Strobaugh

Belgian paratroopers spring into action during Operation 'Dragon Rouge'.

instructed the Belgians on the use of the PRC-41 and PRC-47 radio sets he had brought for Évreux for communication between the men on the ground and the planes overhead. He also instructed 21 Belgian jumpmasters on C-130 jump techniques - few of the Belgian paras had ever jumped from the Hercules - then supervised as they trained the remainder of the force.

For the next three days, the joint rescue force waited while communications were passed back and force between there and Washington by a TAC C-130 'Talking Bird' that joined the mission at Ascension. On 20 November a special briefing

of the various commanders was held to determine exactly how the assault was to be performed. Once it was firmed, Captain Strobaugh transmitted the plan to Washington. At 1800Z, the force was put on alert; 30 minutes later, the launch order came over the teletype. An hour later, at 1935Z, 'Chalk One' (tactical airlift missions are designated by 'chalk' numbers, after the practice of numbering loads with chalk) departed Ascension bound for Kamina, an airfield in the southern Congo, with the other thirteen C-130s right behind.

At daybreak, the first Hercules arrived at

Belgian paratroopers in one of the USAF C-130s en route to Stanleyville during Operation 'Dragon Rouge'.

Kamina after a nine-hour flight across part of the Atlantic and halfway across Africa. The field was obscured by fog, but English-speaking air traffic controllers directed each plane to the airport in turn. Once the force was on the ground more briefings were held, including an update on the mission's status by Colonel Clayton Issacson, commander of JTF Leo and now in overall command of 'Dragon Rouge' and other activities in the Congo. Then the 'Dragon Rouge' force went into another waiting period while Belgium and the United States continued their efforts to win the hostages' freedom through negotiations.

On Monday evening, 23 November, the rescue force relaxed at Kamina while watching what one critic in the crowd described as a 'terrible movie' in one of the hangars. At 2230Z (2030 local time), the teletype machines in the 'Talking Bird' began clattering as messages came in from Washington and Brussels. 'Dragon Rouge' was on, with takeoff scheduled for 0045Z, so as to arrive over the Stanleyville airport at dawn. The first C-130E, flown by Captain Huey Long's Standardizations and Evacuation crew from the 777th Troop Carrier Squadron, lifted off from Kamina's long runway right on time, followed at 20-second intervals by the other eleven planes of the assault force. 'Chalk Six' flown by Captain William 'Mack' Secord's crew had lost a life raft from a wing storage compartment after takeoff from Kamina and had to return for the spare plane. Secord was told to land and wait with 'Chalk Twelve', the hospital plane, until the Belgians returned to the airport with the hostages in the formation. The rest of the 'Dragon Rouge' formation proceeded northbound at high altitude, following the Congo River, descending to treetop altitudes as the planes neared revel territory.

Nearing Stanleyville, lead navigator John Coble led the formation south of the city, still at low altitude, so as to approach from the west. As the formation reached the one-minute warning point, two B-26s made a low pass over the airport. Laurent and 299 of his men jumped over Stanleyville airport exactly at dawn.

The jump plane crews were briefed to expect only small-arms fire over the airport. Instead, they were greeted by tracers from Chinese-made 12.7mm antiaircraft machine guns. In spite of the

unexpected fire, the American pilots held their course as they dropped their troopers right on the narrow drop zone beside the runway, then came back around for another pass to allow the 20 jumpmasters to exit, along with the bundles of extra equipment. Only the first five airplanes in the formation dropped at that time: 'Dragons Six' and 'Seven' were rigged to either drop or land with equipment (Secord's 'Dragon Six' had gone back to Kamina and was still en route), while 'Dragons 'Eight', 'Nine' and 'Eleven' orbited nearly, their troops at the ready to jump in if needed, or land when the field was secure.

Once on the ground, the Para-Commandos began rushing to secure the field so rescue force aircraft could land. Within thirty minutes the Belgians managed to eliminate all resistance at the airport and within 10 minutes had cleared away about 300 water-filled 55-gallon drums and eleven wheel-less vehicles that had been placed on the runway as obstacles. To Captain Strobaugh, who was serving aboard 'Dragon Nine' as jumpmaster, the Belgians' efforts were 'nothing short of miraculous.' At 0450Z, the first C-130E landed at Stanleyville and discharged a load of equipment and troops, then took off again to fly to Leopoldville-where the drop planes had already gone-for refuelling and to await word to return to Stanleyville and evacuate refugees. 'Dragon One' remained overhead, serving as a command ship for Colonel Gradwell. Colonel Issacson also made an appearance over Stanleyville in one of the JTF Leo aircraft, using the call sign 'Dragon Chief.'

After 'Dragon Seven' landed and took off again, 'Dragons 'Eight', 'Nine', 'Eleven' and 'Ten' followed in that order. Each crew offloaded their troopers and then took off again for Leopoldville; no more than three airplanes were to be on the ground at one time. The last two planes, 'Six' and 'Twelve', flown respectively by Secord and Captain B. J. Nunnally, were told to remain on the ground to bring out the first hostages when they were brought out of town. 'Dragon One' continued orbiting over the airport at 2,000 feet. Navigator Coble was uncomfortable about being so low over a combat zone; he had served four temporary duty tours in South Viêtnam flying C-123s. The rest of the crew laughed, calling him 'combat happy'- until they suddenly felt and heard the sound of bullets striking the airplane. Seven rounds hit the Hercules, knocking out hydraulics and leaving two large holes in the wing fuel tanks. With Gradwell's approval, Long headed his C-130 for Leopoldville for repairs.

Once the airport was secure, the Belgian rescue force headed for downtown Stanleyville, where the hostages were known to be held. The hostages themselves were awakened by the wounds of the battle at the airport and the alarmed Simbas who came after them shouting: 'Your brothers have come from the sky! Now you will be killed!' Dressed in manes of monkey fur and feathers, the Simbas bashed down the doors of the Victoria Hotel with spears and gun butts and then roughly hustled their white hostages out into the streets. For more than an hour, the hostages had been hearing sounds of airplanes engines and gunfire while others not in captivity saw parachutes falling from the sky over the airport. Knowing that the Simbas had threatened to kill everyone under their control in the event of a rescue attempt, they were fearful.

Now the Simbas ordered the 250 whites from the Victoria out into the broad streets of the city and began marching them toward the city park and toward the Patrice Lumumba 'monument'-a large photograph of the late prime minister-where the rebels had already slain more than 100 Congolese during recent weeks. The hostages still entertained some hope; they were being marched in the direction of the airport, leading some to believe that the rebel commander intended to turn them over to the rescue force unharmed. Then, rebel-operated Radio Stanleyville shrilled out a message: '*Ciyuga! Ciyuga! Kill! Kill! Kill them all*! Have no scruples! Men, women, children - kill them all!'

Colonel Joseph Opepe, who had befriended some of the hostages, tried in vain to stop the Simbas from carrying out the orders screamed over the radios. Many of the Simbas were drunk from a mixture of alcohol and hemp. According to some survivors, the signal to fire came from a deaf-mute ex-boxer known as 'Major Bubu' who served as a personal bodyguard to rebel defence minister Gaston Soumialot. Whoever gave the word, the rebels suddenly started firing into the assembled hostages with rifles and automatic weapons. The firing was not random - the rebels deliberately chose women and children as their first targets. One of those who fell was Dr. Paul Carlson, shot as he tried to run to safety. After an initial volley, the rebels temporarily ceased firing. Marcel Debuisson, a Belgian engineer, heard them say, 'Now we'll turn them over and finish off the ones left alive.' Debuisson prayed for a miracle and his prayers were answered. 'To my amazement,' he told news reporters afterward 'it happened. Round the corner of the square walked a single Belgian paratrooper, submachine gun on his hip.' The rebels saw the Belgian red beret as well; immediately they turned and fled. What the Belgians found in Sergeant Kitele Avenue was not a pretty sight. About thirty whites had been killed, while dozens of others were wounded. The sight of the bloodshed left the Belgians angered, as would be the white mercenaries who came into the city a few hours later, spearheading a ground assault from the east. For the remainder of the afternoon, it was open season on Simbas in Stanleyville as the rebels paid in blood for their folly.

Back at the airport, the situation was still far from calm. More than 300 rebels occupied positions near the runway. As many hostages were freed, they were returned to the airport for evacuation. The first group arrived at the airport around 0945 and was loaded aboard the two waiting C-130s. The most badly wounded were loaded on 'Dragon Twelve', the hospital plane. Many of the hostages were wounded, while all were terrified and in a state of shock. After more than an hour on the ground at Stanleyville, Captain Mack Secord's crew finally saw the first hostages coming toward them. As they were the most badly injured, they had been driven to the airport. Seeing the engines running and thinking the C-130 was about to take-off, the frightened whites rushed aboard the plane through the open rear ramp. Secord reckoned he had 'around a hundred' hostages aboard. Secord's two loadmasters got some of the most seriously injured people over to the other Hercules where a doctor waited to tend their wounds. Finally, Secord's crew closed up their C-130 and began taxiing for the runway. As he taxied for takeoff, the plane passed by a clump of elephant grass. A pair of Simbas leapt out from the grass and one ran alongside the plane, trying to force a way inside, although nobody aboard it was aware of it at the time, while the other sprayed the underside of the wing with a submachine gun. Secord took off with fuel streaming from the wing and headed for Leopoldville, where he landed with no flaps, no prop-reverse and on only three engines. When he got there, he had to be bodily lifted from the airplane and taken to the hospital where he was treated for a brain concussion he had received the night before when he bumped his head getting into the airplane.

Although the Belgians spoke English, they were not used to speaking with rapid-talking Americans, many of whom were Southerners with distinct accents. To eliminate possible confusion, Colonel Laurent asked Captain Strobaugh and Sergeant Dias to take charge of communications with the American aircrewmen and radio operators.

Forty-five minutes after he jumped, Colonel Laurent reported that the airfield was secure and the freed hostages beginning to make their way there. Strobaugh requested an airlift to take them out, along with air support for the strike forces. In addition to the American C-130s, Belgian Douglas DC-6s joined the airlift. Several airplanes landed with bullet holes received while on landing approach. Periodically throughout the day, Strobaugh had to direct aircraft to orbit nearby while the Belgians repulsed attacks on the airport. As the last C-130 of the day landed at 1545Z, impacting mortar rounds signalled the start of a 150-man rebel assault on the west end of the airport. The Belgians repulsed five separate attacks as the airplane landed on the east end of the runway. Thirty minutes later, a Belgian DC-6 came in with a damaged engine that forced it to remain on the ground overnight.

Belgian paratroops boarding a C-130 during 'Dragon Rouge'. Permanently assigned C-130s had been replaced by temporary duty aircraft and crews from Tactical Air Command units in the US. Rotational Squadron 'A', or 'Rote Alpha' was made up of Pope personnel who flew the C-130E while 'Rote Bravo' was manned by Lockbourne crews and equipped with the older C-130A. Since the C-130E featured special long-range fuel tanks, 'Rote Alpha' provided the planes and crews.

Rebel opposition continued in the vicinity of the Stanleyville airport on November 25 as snipers took pot-shots at Belgian and Congolese national troops. A Belgian mechanic working on a DC-4 was killed by sniper fire. Several times during the day the field was mortared and every aircraft was hit by ground fire during their landings and takeoffs. One was hit in a wing fuel tank. The crew chief whittled a plug from a broom handle and wrapped it with a rag and used it to plug the leak. Early that morning, sniper fire killed one of the Belgian officers from the stranded DC-6. Less than an hour later, a sniper's bullets hit the control tower.

On the 26th, the evacuation of whites and some Congolese from the city resumed. Over the two-day period 41 sorties by the C-130Es and Belgian DC-6s brought out more than 1,800 American and European whites, as well as 300 Congolese. Late in the evening, seven C-130Es flew into Stanleyville to pick up troops for another rescue mission to the town of Paulis, a town 225 miles northwest of Stanleyville. Early on the morning of Thanksgiving Day the seven-plane flight took off on Operation 'Dragon Noir', a repeat of Tuesday's mission. Arriving over Paulis at daybreak, the crews found their objective enshrouded in fog. The Belgians jumped anyway, making their descent into mist that obscured the ground. Every trooper landed on the designated drop zone. As soon as the fog lifted, the C-130s began landing on the dirt runway, their propellers stirring up a thick red cloud of dust as the pilots brought them into reverse after touchdown. The scene was one that would be repeated by many of those some crews in the same planes in Việtnam, where American involvement was starting to escalate. One pilot, Major Joe Hildebrand, reversed his prop while the plane was still airborne; the resulting hard landing flamed out all four engines of his Hercules.

A hive of activity during 'Dragon Rouge'.

At Paulis the paratroopers found the condition of the hostages to be as bad as - or worse than - at Stanleyville. Phyliss Rine, an American missionary from Ohio had been systematically tortured and beaten until death mercifully brought relief. Meanwhile, back at Stanleyville, the Belgians and mercenaries who made their way into the city shortly after the parachute assault found more white victims. A missionary family from New Zealand was brought to the airport. The father had been slain, the mother cut with machetes, while the two young daughters had scalp wounds inflicted by the Simbas. Only the two sons were spared injury. Such senseless carnage caused the mercenaries and even the well-disciplined Belgian paratroopers to lose their restraint. Most rebels they encountered were slain on the spot. Congolese government soldiers frequently exhibited the same lack of concern for human life as their brothers on the other side, in one case kicking to death a Simba 'priest'

captured near the airport.

After leaving the airport, the Belgian rescue team made haste to reach the Victoria Hotel before the Simbas carried out their threats to kill the hostages if a rescue was attempted. Several blocks from the hotel a paratrooper rounded a corner just in time to prevent the Simbas from firing a second volley of shots into the assembled hostages, who had evidently been walking toward the airport. Some of the hostages later said they thought the Simba officers intended to turn them over to the Belgians unharmed, but some of the Simbas, who had been drinking and smoking Hemp all night the night before, decided to take matters in their own hands. They shot their own officers and then turned their guns on the hostages. They had fired one volley, picking women and children as their targets and were preparing to fire another when the Red Berets showed up on the scene. At the sight of the Belgians, the Simbas lost their courage and ran!

Cheerful National Congolese troops gathered around one of the USAF C-130s on Operation 'Dragon Rouge'.

On the evening of the 27th the last Belgian troopers were withdrawn from Stanleyville and flown to Kamina to begin the first leg of their journey home. Their departure was somewhat premature, largely due to a huge outcry of discontent in the Third World over Belgian and American intervention in Africa, as demonstrators made their feelings known. Sometimes the demonstrations got out of hand, as in Cairo, Egypt, where the new John F. Kennedy library was burned to the ground in protest over the white presence in Africa. A well-organized propaganda effort in Communist and Third World nations placed the blame for the atrocities in Stanleyville on American and Belgian shoulders. Some nations, including China, pledged aid to the Congo rebels.

But even though the fighting in the Congo would continue for several months, with many white still to be slain by the rebels, Operation 'Dragon Rouge' was over. On the morning of 29 November the rescue force departed Africa for Ascension. From there, it flew to the Canary Islands, then on to Melsbroek airfield, outside of Brussels. There the rescuers were welcomed home by several hundred high-ranking officers, news reporters, television camera crews and relatives. King Baudouin received the Belgian paratroopers and American aircrews at a review on the flight line and presented Colonels Laurent and Gradwell with the Order of Leopold II. After the ceremony, the Americans were taken on a tour of the city.

For the American and Belgian military personnel involved in 'Dragon Rouge', the operation was one that all would remember with pride. Even thought the rescue was not without cost to the Belgians, the mission had been an overall success, resulting in the release of hundreds of hostages who doubtless would have been killed had it not occurred.

'After 'Dragon Noir' the rescue force retired to Kamina to await further orders' concludes Sam McGowan. 'While they were waiting, an African thunderstorm prompted one C-130 crewmember - none of whom had had a bath in days - to grab soap and go out into the rain for an impromptu shower. The rest of the force followed his lead as the airmen and paratroopers ran around naked in the rain! A few days later, in response to political pressure from the Third World, President Lyndon Johnson ordered the force out of Africa. For their role in 'Dragon Rouge', the C-130 crewmembers received the 1964 MacKay Trophy for the most meritorious flight of the year by USAF aircraft. All of the crewmembers were decorated with the Air Medal, while Captain Mack Secord received the Distinguished Flying Cross.'

Chapter Six

Operation 'Thunderbolt'

My biggest fear was not being shot at from the ground, but making a mistake as a pilot. All I could think the entire time was 'Don't screw this up!' True, the risks to my life were real, but I was more worried about botching the landing and endangering the success of the entire operation. Think about it - how many people would have died at Entebbe if I had made a mistake? In case something did go wrong, though, I was prepared for the worst. I was wearing a helmet, a bullet-proof vest and I had an Uzi. I was also given a thick wad of cash in case I needed to use it to escape Uganda. Luckily, I never had to use it. I returned the cash after returning to Israel.'

Lieutenant Colonel (later Brigadier General) Joshua Shani.

In June 1976 Lieutenant Colonel Joshua Shani was at a wedding when Aluf (Major General) Benny Peled who had become commander of the Israel Air Force (IAF) in 1973 when he was 45 years old, approached him and began asking questions about the capabilities of the C-130H. Peled, born Benjamin Weidenfeld in Tel Aviv in 1928, started as a mechanic in the beginnings of the Israeli Air Force. During the 1948 Arab-Israeli War he had assembled the first Messerschmitt Bf 109 which had arrived in Israel dismantled. He then became a pilot and fought in the Independence war. After the war he commanded the first Meteor, Ouragan and Mystère squadrons and was the first Israeli pilot to use an ejection seat when he was shot down near Sharm el-Sheikh in the Sinai Campaign in 1956 during Operation 'Kadesh' when he was the victim of Egyptian anti-aircraft. He was later rescued by an IAF Piper. Peled was a base commander during the Six-Day War. During the Yom Kippur War his son Yoram, flying a Phantom, was also shot down and rescued. 'It was a strange situation' recalled Colonel Shani 'the commander of the IAF asking a lieutenant colonel questions about an aircraft. But the C-130 was new and the IAF 'top brass' were always focused on fighter jets, not transport planes. Peled asked me if it was possible to fly almost 2,500 miles to Entebbe Airport, Uganda; how long it would take and what it could carry.'

Joshua Shani's parents lived in what is now Ukraine. Their small town was part of Poland at the time. They escaped the Nazis and ended up in Siberia, where Joshua was born in 1945. They were refugees, wherever they were. Soon after the war ended, Joshua's family lived in the Bergen-Belsen displaced persons camp in Germany, which was run by the British. They were there for almost a year. And then they made their way from Germany to Israel, via France and Egypt. His parents were lifelong Zionists and fluent in Hebrew, which they spoke to him as a baby. They were thrilled to arrive in Israel and begin a new life, never again to be refugees. 'I wasn't interested in airplanes as a teenager' recalled Shani. 'I wanted to be an electrical engineer. On my draft day I was sitting on the grass with other new recruits at the Bakum (the Israeli Defence Force induction base) and a major with wings on his uniform approached us. He said, 'You are all fit for flight school. Who here doesn't want to volunteer?' I started to raise my hand, but when it was about halfway up I realized that nobody else around me was raising his hand. So I put my hand down.

'The rest is history. I was drafted in 1963. I received my pilot's wings in 1965 from Ezer Weizmann, who was then the commander of the Israel Air Force. The first plane I flew was the Nord Noratlas, a transport plane. I was also a Fuga instructor for two years. The Air Force then sent

Yonatan 'Yoni' Netanyahu, born 13 March 1946, who commanded the elite commando unit Sayeret Matkal during Operation 'Entebbe'. He was awarded the Medal of Distinguished Service for his conduct in the Yom Kippur War of 1973. In June 1975 Netanyahu left the Armoured Corps and returned to Sayeret Matkal as unit commander. He was killed in action on 4 July 1976 while commanding an assault unit in Operation 'Entebbe'. Netanyahu was the only Israeli soldier killed during the raid (along with three hostages, all of the PLO members and dozens of Ugandan soldiers). Netanyahu was shot outside the building being stormed and soon died in the arms of Efraim Sneh, commander of the mission's medical unit. The operation itself was considered a success by Israel and was renamed as 'Mivtsa Yonatan' (Operation 'Yonatan') in honour of Netanyahu. (IDF Spokesman's Office photo)

me to the United States to learn how to fly the C-130 Hercules cargo plane. First I was in Little Rock, Arkansas and later in Pope, North Carolina. It was my first time in the United States. In 1967, during the Six-Day War, I supplied fuel and ammunition to IDF soldiers fighting in the Sinai Peninsula. In 1973, during the Yom Kippur War, I was a squadron commander. I was involved in fueling and reconnaissance missions with the C-97 Stratofreighter. I also flew the C-130 across the Suez Canal, deep into Egyptian territory in order to supply fuel and ammunition to the ground forces that were holding territory west of the Canal. Those forces, by the way, were led by Ariel Sharon.'

On Sunday 27 June 1976 what was supposed to be a routine flight for the 246 mainly Jewish and Israeli passengers on Air France flight 139 from Tel Aviv to Paris (via Athens) spiralled into a nightmare seven minutes after the jet rose into the sky from Athens. At that moment Air France Airbus F-BVGG found itself the latest target in the Palestine Liberation organization's endless war

against Israel when it was hijacked by four terrorists. Two of them were German members of the Baader-Meinhof guerrilla organisation and the others Arab members of the Popular Front for the Liberation of Palestine. The hijackers instructed the pilot to fly the airliner first to Casablanca, where it spent the night and then to Khartoum and Entebbe airport near Kampala, the capital of Uganda, 2,500 miles from Israel. The Israeli and Jewish hostages were confined in an old unused terminal building, and the hijackers demanded that Israel's government release 53 Palestinian prisoners, forty held in Israel and thirteen held in France, Kenya Switzerland and West Germany. If the prisoners were not released at a specified time, they would execute the 94 Jewish passengers in retaliation. With a new captain, the A300B4-203 set course for Benghazi, Libya. Upon arriving, the

The old terminal building at Entebbe at the time of the raid on 4 July 1976. Inset right: Lieutenant Colonel (later Brigadier General) Joshua Shani, who accumulated 13,000 flight hours in his Israeli Air Force career.

jet rolled to a stop and refueling began. During this time a pregnant passenger feigned a miscarriage and managed to get released. In all seven hours passed on the blistering tarmac before the A300 began taxiing into takeoff position for departure to its unknown final destination. As the airliner began descending in the darkness, the broad expanse of a freshwater lake appeared to grow before it disappeared into land and the passengers felt the gentle touchdown at a small airport deep in the African jungle, where it parked on the tarmac at 3:15 am at Entebbe.

Spotlights glared through the windows as soldiers in camouflaged uniforms surrounded the jet. There were no orders to prepare for debarking, just silence and casual talk among the hijackers. Another nine hours passed before the plane taxied towards an old terminal building where an airstair bumped against the fuselage and a hatchway opened. The hijackers screamed at the passengers to hurry off and into the terminal building where they were herded together in a dilapidated departure lounge. Here the hijackers met up with four other Palestinians and quickly complimented their pistols, with AK47s and hand grenades. The terrorists relaxed, not yet issuing demands and waited for another arrival. A few hours later it came in the sound of an approaching helicopter, which set down close to the terminal. Stepping down from it in a camouflaged uniform was the rotund leader of Uganda, Idi Amin and his eight-year-old son in similar dress. He entered the lounge exulting: 'Shalom! Shalom!' And began a speech to the captives berating and reassuring them the only way they could be saved was if Israel agreed to the hijackers' demands. As he walked out, the prisoners were under no illusion that Amin was going to do nothing to free them and in fact, was likely involved in the plot itself.

Throughout the next day news trickled all over the globe that the hijackers had set down at Entebbe and the press stood by awaiting word of their demands. But the anticipated radio transmissions never materialized, leaving the world wondering what demands the terrorists were going to make and what would be the response, especially from Israel. Israel maintained a simple policy in negotiating with terrorists. There would be no negotiations, for to do so simply emboldened future enemies of the Jewish state to commit more

terrorism. Such enemies whose only goal from the beginning was Israel's destruction. For them, that too, was non-negotiable. And Israel learned early on that groups of this nature understood and respected one thing. Force.

And so it began with that silent day in Entebbe, that Colonel Ehud Barak, Israel's Assistant Chief of Military Intelligence and commander of Special Operations Forces, convened an informal session of Israel's leading Counter-Terrorism experts. In it, he asked for an assessment of the Ugandan military and the necessary forces that might be mobilized for a rescue mission should negotiations, if they started, were to fail. Additionally, the Air Force began a feasibility inquiry into sending a rescue force the 2,200 miles to Uganda. On 28 June a PFLP-EO hijacker issued a declaration and formulated their demands: In addition to a ransom of $5 million for the release of the A300, they demanded the release of 53 Palestinian and Pro-Palestinian militants, forty of whom were prisoners in Israel. They threatened that if these demands were not met, they would begin to kill hostages on 1 July. At 3:30 pm on 29 June the terrorists released their demands over Radio Uganda. All the designated prisoners were to be released and flown to Entebbe by their captive nations. There, the hijackers would join them and fly to a safe haven in the Middle East. A sum of five million dollars was added for the safe return of the A300. All this must be achieved by 2:00 pm Israeli time on 1 July or the hostages would be executed.

In the sweltering insect ridden terminal the hostages settled in for a future of uncertainty when a short while later the German terrorists began a process that harkened back to the days of the holocaust and fueled further the urgency of someone to act. Amin made another visit that afternoon and gave a speech. A short time after he left, Ugandan soldiers pounded a partition wall with sledgehammers until a jagged entrance was completed. The female German terrorist began ordering those with Jewish passports through the opening into the other room, eerily reminiscent of the selections by Nazis of who would go to the gas chambers and who would be allowed to live as slaves. In fact, some of the very people transferring to the room were Holocaust survivors, terrified and incredulous that the same thing seemed to be happening again in 1976 and at the hands of a

German at that. Thereafter, this became known as the 'Room of Separation.'

In Israel, 30 June began with a number of rescue options presented to Prime Minister Yitzak Rabin. None were deemed satisfactory. Lieutenant Colonel Joshua Shani, later said that the Israelis had initially conceived of a rescue plan that involved dropping naval commandos into Lake Victoria. The commandos would have ridden rubber boats to the airport located on the edge of the lake. They planned to kill the hijackers and after freeing the hostages, ask Amin for passage home. The Israelis abandoned this plan because they lacked the time necessary and also received word that Lake Victoria was infested with crocodiles. Planning sessions continued onward while the country contacted Amin and tried to convince him to arrest the terrorists before realizing he was colluding with them. As the day drew to a close, 47 Gentile hostages were released and flown to Paris, supposedly secured by their self-confessed 'saviour', Idi Amin. At the airport they were greeted by their families and French officials then later debriefed by members of French Secret Service and the Israeli Embassy. The intelligence the former captives, particularly a former military officer gave proved invaluable; chief among them was the exact location of the hostages, guard routines and the hijacker's expectation that Israel would not respond, leading to an almost casual nature of security about the place.

On the morning of 1 July the remaining 101 Gentiles boarded another flight from Entebbe. This left 94 Jews and the twelve Air France crew. In Israel, with the 2 pm deadline looming, the public was greeted by the word Selektzia (Selection) as a banner headline on newspapers across the country. Family members besieged the Israeli government pleading for them to give in to the hijackers' demands. Inside a closed room heated arguments raged among Rabin's cabinet over the proper course of action. With great reluctance they agreed to negotiations and asked for an extension of the deadline, which was granted until 4 July. But back at Entebbe such news brought little comfort and they them remained unsure if the reprieve of three days was just delaying the inevitable. Now was the time to act.

With some time bought, reviews of different rescue proposals began. Four were presented only to have three vetoed as too large or too risky. The final one, involving a smaller force was approved, but still needed a final authorization. Shimon Peres, then Defence Minister in Yitzhak Rabin's (first) government, asked for the military options. As Benny Peled later remembered: 'I presented Shimon Peres with the plan to fly commandos to Uganda to rescue the people.' With the government determined not to give in to the hijackers' demands, Peled's idea was eventually adopted.

Brigadier General Dan Shomron (later to become the IDF's Chief of Staff), presented the rescue plan to Lieutenant General Mordechai Gur the Chief of Staff, Shimon Peres the Defence Minister and Prime Minister Yitzhak Rabin for final authorization to complete the highly secretive rescue mission. The incredible was deemed possible, as the IDF's plan was based on a few advantages that Israel held over the terrorists. The Entebbe airport terminal at which the hostages were being held was, coincidentally, built by an Israeli construction firm. This company provided blueprints allowing the IDF to erect a partial replica of the airport terminal to assist in planning the rescue. Additionally, the captors had released the non-Jewish prisoners, who were able to describe the terrorists, their arms, their positioning and the amount of help provided by the Ugandan military forces. As a result of this information, the IDF decided to send in an overwhelmingly powerful force: over 200 of its best soldiers. Finally, the element of surprise was probably the biggest edge that Israel held. According to Shomron: 'You had more than a hundred people sitting in a small room, surrounded by terrorists with their fingers on the trigger. They could fire in a fraction of a second. We had to fly seven hours, land safely, drive to the terminal area where the hostages were being held, get inside and eliminate all the terrorists before any of them could fire.'

With this, designated forces quickly organized in preparation, bringing together pilots, paratroopers and a special operations detachment known as 'The Unit.' Led by 30-year old Lieutenant Colonel Yonatan 'Yoni' Netanyahu (the older brother of Benjamin (Binyamin) 'Bibi' Netanyahu, the Prime Minister of Israel 1996-1999 and again, from 31 March 2009) its official name was Sayeret Matkal (Israeli special forces).

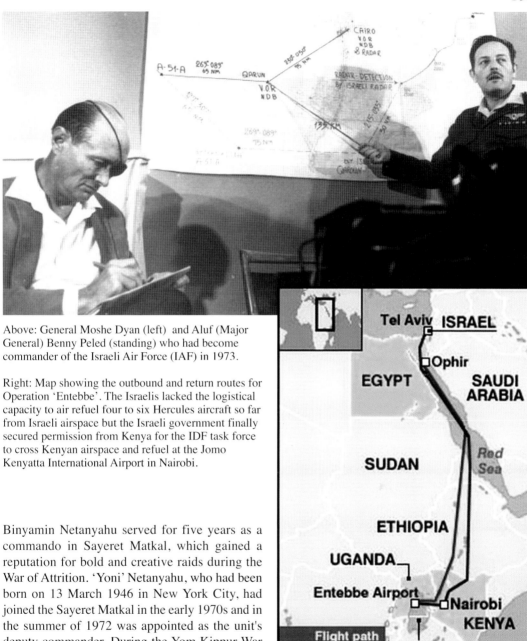

Above: General Moshe Dyan (left) and Aluf (Major General) Benny Peled (standing) who had become commander of the Israeli Air Force (IAF) in 1973.

Right: Map showing the outbound and return routes for Operation 'Entebbe'. The Israelis lacked the logistical capacity to air refuel four to six Hercules aircraft so far from Israeli airspace but the Israeli government finally secured permission from Kenya for the IDF task force to cross Kenyan airspace and refuel at the Jomo Kenyatta International Airport in Nairobi.

Binyamin Netanyahu served for five years as a commando in Sayeret Matkal, which gained a reputation for bold and creative raids during the War of Attrition. 'Yoni' Netanyahu, who had been born on 13 March 1946 in New York City, had joined the Sayeret Matkal in the early 1970s and in the summer of 1972 was appointed as the unit's deputy commander. During the Yom Kippur War in October 1973, Netanyahu commanded a Sayeret Matkal force in the Golan Heights that killed more than forty Syrian commandos in a battle which thwarted the Syrian commandos' raid in the Golan's heartland. For the raid on Entebbe 'The Unit' would don French 'lizard' camo uniforms - the same kind worn by Ugandan soldiers - and blackened their faces and hands. They would also carry similar weapons such as Chinese made AK-47s. Some of the guns had a crude mount with a small flashlight positioned atop the receiver. The rest of the force would don standard Israeli Defence Force clothing and equipment. The Sayeret Matkal was chosen to lead Operation 'Thunderbolt', undergoing final polishing at that very moment.[1]

Once he received the plan Netanyahu put his men immediately to work over the next two days, practicing breaching and entering mock ups like the building in Entebbe. They ran each rehearsal as many times as possible, tweaking how they would commence the rescue with the fewest minutes between start and finish. When the time came for the men to be briefed on the operation, they listened as the officer muttered one word amidst his others which formed the crux of 'Thunderbolt'.[2]

While planning the raid the Israeli forces had to figure out how to refuel the C-130 aircraft they intended to use while en route to Entebbe. The Israelis lacked the logistical capacity to aerially refuel four to six aircraft so far from Israeli airspace. While several East African nations, including the logistically preferred choice Kenya, were sympathetic, none wished to incur the wrath of Amin or the Palestinians by allowing the Israelis to land their aircraft within their borders. The raid could not proceed without assistance from at least one East African government. The Jewish owner of the Block hotels chain in Kenya, along with other members of the Jewish and Israeli community in Nairobi, may have used their political and economic influence to help persuade Kenya's President Mzee Jomo Kenyatta to help Israel. The Israeli government finally secured permission from Kenya for the IDF task force to cross Kenyan airspace and refuel at the Jomo

Kenyatta International Airport.[3]

Four C-130Hs would depart Israel, the first carrying 29 men of Sayeret Matkal and 52 paratroops. It also carried a black Mercedes limousine configured to look like Amin's personal vehicle and two Land Rover escorts to accompany the car to the terminal. There the Unit members would assault the building as the paratroops secured the airport. Hercules No.2 would carry seventeen more paratroops, two armed jeeps and a communications jeep. These were to occupy a newer terminal building and fuel depot along with the entrances to ward off Ugandan counterattacks. Shaul Mofaz, who years later would become Israel's vice prime minister, was in charge of the group who would destroy the small contingent of Soviet-built MiG-17s and MiG-21s at the airport. Hercules No.3 would depart thirty men of another Special Forces unit, the Sayeret Golani to provide security and another vehicle. The Golani were to help escort the hostages. Hercules No.4 would be the last to land carrying a medical team, two vehicles to transport hostages and wounded, along with a seventeen-man security element. It was this aircraft the hostages would leave on. Two Boeing 707 jets would follow the C-130s. The first contained medical facilities and General Peled and the Head of the Operations Branch of the IDF. Major General Yekutiel 'Kuti' Adam the

C-130H 4X-FBQ-420 (75-0534), one of four Israeli C-130Hs used on the highly successful Entebbe raid lands in Israel following the operation. The other three C-130Hs used on Operation 'Thunderbolt' were 4X-FBB/106 (71-1375); 4X-FBT/435 (75-0536) and C-130H 4X-FBA/102 (71-1374).

commander of the operation was on board the second Boeing.

Captain (later Lieutenant Colonel) Avi Mor's talent for navigation was about to be put to the test. In the middle of the night on the Wednesday before the mission he had received a house visit from a friend and fellow soldier in the Israel Air Force. 'My wife answered the door. My friend told her 'Norit, I suggest you go to your room and close the door.' By 6 the following morning, I was at an exercise with Sayeret Matkal. From that moment on, every single person who was in some way relevant to the mission was in a period of intensive brainstorming for the best possible rescue scenario to present to Israel's governing officials. By pinpointing these advantages, the IDF was able to use the element of surprise in its favour. Keep in mind it was the Sabbath, during which the IAF does not hold exercises or routine operations - making the rescue aircraft more likely to stand out. We had to fly slowly and in very low altitudes to remain unnoticeable. We had 103 Jewish hostages in Entebbe and over 200 IDF soldiers heading to rescue them. It was essential for us not to blow our cover: It is enough for the terrorists to have any sort of suspicion and not only would there have been no rescue mission, but there would have been a tragedy.'

Mor too knew what it meant to fight for freedom. Born in Poland he had escaped to Israel with his parents and seven siblings during the Nazi regime. He had enlisted in the Israeli Air Force and passed the rigorous Flight Academy course. 'The process by which the terrorists selected their hostages, it hurts me to say it - it was a similar selection process 'the Nazis administered when selecting who would go work and who would be sent to the gas chambers. One of the biggest problems we had was that we were operating with minimal clarity throughout the entire mission, as we had no reliable source of information. And, when faced with an ultimatum, time is of the essence.'

Peled had left Joshua Shani with the impression that a rescue at Entebbe would be possible. 'I had the great honour of being the leading navigator for aircraft two, three and four. I was in the second aircraft and, whether the first was successful or not, we had to land at the airport precisely six minutes after them. The rest of us had no details about the

first aircraft and what was going on down there. The second and third Israeli planes were to arrive six minutes later, carrying reinforcements and troops assigned to help fight the Ugandan forces surrounding the airport. The fourth aircraft - the only aircraft with enough fuel to fly to Entebbe and back to Israel - would arrive empty, ready to evacuate the hostages and take them home.'

With the operation receiving its final review and approval, the force transferred and began boarding the aircraft at 2:20 pm on 3 July, Israeli time. 'We began our journey from Sharm el-Sheikh, Egypt, which at the time was under Israeli control' says Joshua Shani. 'Matan Vilnai was in the cockpit with me. Ephraim Sneh was on the plane as a doctor. The takeoff from Sharm was one of the heaviest ever in the history of this aircraft. I didn't have a clue what would happen. I gave the plane maximum power and it was just taxiing, not accelerating. At the very end of the runway, I was probably two knots over the stall speed and I had to lift off. I took off to the north, but had to turn south where our destination was. I couldn't make the turn until I gained more speed. Just making that turn, I was struggling to keep control, but aircraft have feelings and all turned out well.

'We had to fly very close to Saudi Arabia and Egypt, over the Gulf of Suez. We weren't afraid of violating anyone's air space - it's an international air route. The problem was that they might pick us up on radar. We flew really low - 100 feet above the water, a formation of four planes. The main element was surprise. All it takes is one truck to block a runway and that's all. The operation would be over. Therefore, secrecy was critical. At some places that were particularly dangerous, we flew at an altitude of 35 feet. I recall the altimeter reading. Trust me, this is scary! In this situation, you cannot fly close formation. As flight leader, I didn't know if I still had planes 2, 3 and 4 behind me because there was total radio silence. You can't see behind you in a C-130. Luckily, they were smart, so from time to time they would show themselves to me and then go back to their place in the formation, so I still knew I had my formation with me.'

'Night stretched out over the darkened African continent as the C-130s maintained their designated intervals. Mostly they flew at a height of no more than 100 feet to avoid radar detection by Egyptian, Sudanese and Saudi Arabian forces.

No.1 crew on the Entebbe mission with Joshua Shani centre, front row.

Near the south outlet of the Red Sea the C-130s turned south and passed south of Djibouti. From there, they went to a point northeast of Nairobi, likely across Somalia and the Ogaden area of Ethiopia. Hours passed by and a monotonous hush pervaded the force until they received word Entebbe was minutes away. They turned west, passing through the African Rift Valley and weapons and equipment were rechecked and soon the planes vectored over Lake Victoria for the trail of lights which shone over the wet, grey sheen of the runway.

At 23:00 IST wheels bounced as Joshua Shani began braking and throttling back as he landed the first C-130 at Entebbe with cargo bay doors already open, dovetailing behind a British cargo flight and followed by the other C-130s without arousing suspicion in the control tower. 'I stopped in the middle of the runway and a group of paratroopers jumped out from the side doors and marked the runway with electric lights, so that the other planes behind me could have an easier time landing. The

paratroopers went on to take the control tower. The Mercedes [Ugandan flags fluttering from the front bumpers] and Land Rovers drove out from the back cargo door of my aircraft and the commandos stormed the old terminal building where the hostages were.'

'The Unit's' weapon selectors were set to single shot. Netanyahu and his men began a steady pace of 25 mph along the approach road to the old terminal. 250 metres from the building a Ugandan soldier appeared on either side of the road. Netanyahu sitting in the front passenger seat raised a silenced .22 pistol and began firing along with a comrade at the two men. One of them collapsed to his knees while the other bolted into the darkness. The wounded man rose back to his feet and fired a shot from his AK, the crack echoing into the night. A stutter from a machine gun on a Land Rover tore into him felling him by the road. Surprise was lost.

The motorcade revved into a high speed dash toward the building. Tyres slid to a stop on the wet pavement as the element jumped out of the limousine and Land Rovers. Netanyahu shouted for his men to assault the building. As they approached the terminal, two Ugandan sentries, aware that Idi Amin had recently purchased a white Mercedes, ordered the vehicles to stop. The commandos shot the sentries using silenced pistols, but did not kill them. As they pulled away, however, an Israeli commando in one of the following Land Rovers killed them with an unsuppressed rifle. Fearing the hijackers would be alerted prematurely, the assault team quickly approached the terminal. The Israelis sprang from their vehicles and burst towards the terminal. The hostages were in the main hall of the airport building, directly adjacent to the runway. Entering the terminal, the commandoes shouted through a megaphone, 'Stay down! Stay down! We are Israeli soldiers,' in both Hebrew and English. Jean-Jacques Maimoni, a 19-year-old French immigrant to Israel, stood up and was killed when Israeli company commander Muki Betzer and another soldier mistook him for a hijacker and fired at him.

Another hostage, Pasco Cohen, 52, the manager of an Israeli medical insurance fund, was also fatally wounded by gunfire from the commandos. A third hostage, 56-year-old Ida Borochovitch, a Russian Jew who had emigrated to Israel, was killed in the crossfire. According to hostage Ilan Hartuv, Wilfried Böse was the only hijacker who, after the operation began, entered the hall housing the hostages. At first he pointed his Kalashnikov rifle at hostages, but 'immediately came to his senses' and ordered them to find shelter in the restroom, before being killed by the commandos. According to Hartuv, Böse fired only at Israeli soldiers and not at hostages. One of the German terrorists screamed 'the Ugandan's have gone crazy. They are shooting at us!' He fired a burst through a glass window pane before a fusillade of bullets ripped into Yonatan Netanyahu's chest and would soon die in the arms of Ephraim Sneh, commander of the mission's medical unit.. Doors flew open and the team stormed into the terminal, shooting well aimed shots into the seven terrorists before making their way through the building, killing Ugandans trying to hide and fire back. In the hostage room megaphones barked, 'Everybody lie down! We are the Israeli Army!' At one point, an Israeli commando called out in Hebrew, 'Where are the rest of them?' referring to the hijackers. The hostages pointed to a connecting door of the airport's main hall, into which the commandos threw several hand grenades. Then, they entered

The black Mercedes limousine configured to look like Idi Amin's personal vehicle which was carried in one of the Hercules on the Entebbe mission.

The Hercules crews were mobbed on return to Tel Aviv by the joyful hostages rescued from Entebbe Airport.

the room and shot dead the three remaining hijackers, ending the assault. Muki Betser the second in command, radioed from the terminal. 'Hostages secure. Team intact. No casualties.'

'Yoni's down,' came the reply.

They retrieved Netanyahu's body and began filing the living hostages and bodies of four killed in the shootout out toward Hercules No .4, where Sayeret Golani formed a funnel to guide them in.

Meanwhile, the other three C-130s had landed and unloaded armoured personnel carriers to provide defence during the anticipated hour of refuelling. The Israeli paratroopers then destroyed Ugandan MiGs to prevent them from pursuing and conducted a sweep of the airfield for intelligence-gathering. Across the rest of the airport, the paratroopers occupied the new terminal without firing a shot. Hercules No.4 roared down the runway and lifted off before the remaining forces began returning to board the final three aircraft. The entire operation lasted 53 minutes - of which the assault lasted only thirty minutes. In all, 99 minutes had been spent on the ground before the

last C-130 left. The cost of Entebbe was as follows: One commando killed and at least five other commandos were wounded; four hostages killed; ten hostages wounded; seven terrorists killed; Approximately 45 Ugandan soldiers killed; Unknown number of Ugandan soldiers wounded; eleven MiG fighters destroyed.

After about fifty minutes on the ground in Entebbe Joshua Shani gave the order: 'Whoever is ready, take off. I remember the satisfaction of seeing plane number 4, with the hostages on board, taking off from Entebbe - the sight of its silhouette in the night. It was then that I knew. That's it. We did it. The mission succeeded.

'Now we had a little problem. We needed fuel to fly back home. We came on a one-way ticket! We had planned for a number of options for refuelling and I learned from the command-and-control aircraft flying above us that the option to refuel in Nairobi was open. I saw the freed passengers during the refuelling stop. I looked inside their plane and I saw all the expressions in the world, from total hysteria and crying to singing.

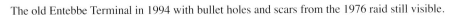

The old Entebbe Terminal in 1994 with bullet holes and scars from the 1976 raid still visible.

'The plane with the hostages landed at Ben-Gurion Airport, where they were reunited with their families. The three other planes remained for a debrief.'

'Our mission was accomplished the instant the hostages had left Entebbe' Captain Mor recalled. 'I did not register it then, as we were still in mission mode but we landed at Ben Gurion to a sea of Israelis swarming with pride, elated to welcome us home. It marked one of the best times in Israel's history in terms of international recognition and respect.'

Yitzhak Rabin, Prime Minister of Israel, walked up to Joshua Shani, who recalled: 'I had been in my flight suit for 24 hours straight, in temperatures over 100 degrees in the airplane, sweating and smelly and here walks the Prime Minister with big open arms. I'm thinking - please don't hug me - he may die from this! He hugged me for what felt like a full minute and said only 'Thanks.'

'My father hosted a party for me. Family and friends were all there to celebrate the success of my mission. My father was in a great mood. I know what he was thinking, a Holocaust survivor. His son at the time was a lieutenant colonel in the Israel Air Force and had just flown thousands of miles in order to save Jews. It probably added ten years to his life. After my father's death, I found his letters from Bergen-Belsen that he sent to Kibbutz Mishmar Haemek. The letters describe his experiences during the Holocaust, what happened to his family, etc. One of his letters said, *My only comfort is Joshua. He gives me reason to continue.*[4]

Chapter 6 Endnotes

1   The Israeli ground task force numbered approximately 100 personnel. The small ground command and control element comprised the operation and overall ground commander, Brigadier General Shomron, the air force representative Colonel Ami Ayalon and the communications and support personnel. The 29-man assault element was led by Yonatan Netanyahu, this force was composed entirely of commandos from Sayeret Matkal and was given the primary task of assaulting the old terminal and rescuing the hostages. The Paratroopers force - the securing element - led by Colonel Matan Vilnai was tasked with securing the airport, clearing and securing the runways, protection and fuelling of the Israeli aircraft in Entebbe. The Golani force led by Colonel Uri Sagi was tasked with securing the C-130 for the hostages' evacuation, getting it as close as possible to the terminal and boarding the hostages. They were also general reserves. The Sayeret Matkal force led by Major Shaul Mofaz was tasked with clearing the military airstrip, destroying the squadron of MiGs on the ground to prevent any possible interceptions by the Ugandan Air Force and holding off hostile ground forces from the city of Entebbe.

2   According to senior unit members, the first problem was that Netanyahu missed much of the planning stage. He only returned from a training exercise in the Sinai on Thursday, two days before the mission began.

3   Kenyan Minister of Agriculture Bruce MacKenzie persuaded Kenyan President Kenyatta to permit Israeli Mossad agents to gather information before the hostage rescue operation in Uganda and to allow Israeli Air Force aircraft to land and refuel at a Nairobi airport after the rescue. In retaliation, Ugandan President Idi Amin ordered Ugandan agents to assassinate MacKenzie, who was killed on 24 May 1978, when a time bomb attached to his plane exploded as it flew above Ngong Hills, Kenya in a flight from Entebbe.

4   Joshua Shani stayed in the IAF for a while - more than 30 years, in fact. He accumulated 13,000 flight hours, including nearly 7,000 in C-130s. Over the years, he commanded three squadrons and a mixed base of four squadrons and eight ground units. From 1985 to 1988 he was the Air Force attaché in the Embassy of Israel in Washington, DC. He retired from active duty in 1989 as a Brigadier General. For ten years after that he was in the reserves. He became the vice president of Israel operations for Lockheed Martin. 'And to think, as a new recruit in the IDF, I was not interested in being in the Air Force - and airplanes became my life. You never know how things will turn out.'

Chapter Seven

Operation 'Eagle Claw'

DC, 11 April 1980, Washington Noon.
The meeting began with Jimmy Carter's announcement: 'Gentlemen, I want you to know that I am seriously considering an attempt to rescue the hostages.'

Hamilton Jordan, the White House chief of staff, knew immediately that the president had made a decision. Planning and practice for a rescue mission had been going on in secret for five months, but it had always been regarded as the last resort and ever since the 4 November embassy takeover, the White House had made every effort to avoid it. As the president launched into a list of detailed questions about how it was to be done, his aides knew he had mentally crossed a line.

Carter had met the takeover in Iran with tremendous restraint, equating the national interest with the well-being of the fifty-three hostages and his measured response had elicited a great deal of admiration, both at home and abroad. His approval ratings had doubled in the first month of the crisis. But in the following months, restraint had begun to smell like weakness and indecision. Three times in the past five months, carefully negotiated secret settlements had been ditched by the inscrutable Iranian mullahs and the administration had been made to look more foolish each time. Approval ratings had nose-dived and even stalwart friends of the administration were demanding action.

Mark Bowden The Atlantic May 2006. Iran had been a US ally until the Shah was ousted from power by the Revolutionary Guard. Student militants stormed the US Embassy in Tehran in 1979 taking the Marine guards and embassy staff as hostages. After releasing some of the hostages, 53 remained. It is not usually militarily expedient for a commander in the field to have all his eggs in one basket. However, all the USAF, USN and USMC forces trained in air rescue and special operations are combined into one force and are therefore an exception to this rule. Nor is it militarily expedient to mount an operation using available USAF transports, Navy helicopters and USMC tanker aircraft - despite political attempts to the contrary, often using financial savings as a justification. This was proved at huge cost during the final days of the Carter administration when Operation 'Eagle Claw', a joint USAF/USMC attempt to rescue 52 diplomats held captive at the US embassy in Tehran on 24 April 1980 using Hercules aircraft and US Navy RH-53D Sea Stallion helicopters flown by marine pilots, ended in disaster at 'Desert One', Posht-i-Badam, a remote location in Iran. The operation encountered many obstacles and was eventually aborted. Its failure and the humiliating public debacle that ensued damaged US prestige worldwide.

'Colonel Charlie Beckwith, the creator of Delta Force, the Army's new, top-secret counter-terrorism unit, was summoned to the White House. He and President Jimmy Carter, both proud Georgians, swapped stories about their neighbouring home counties. Beckwith, a brave and commanding soldier, was a big, gruff man whose energy filled a room and he had flaws as outsized as his virtues. He was a difficult man, proud, tough and at times arrogant and capricious; these traits were aggravated when he drank, which was often. But at the White House he was on his best behaviour, impressing the president with his aura of blunt certainty as he presented the proposed mission in ever greater detail.

'The colonel was an accomplished salesman.

He had spent a career selling the idea of his elite unit and now that it existed, he was eager to show what miracles it could perform. His enthusiasm was infectious. He and his men had been rehearsing the mission for so long that they could have done it in their sleep and they were going to make history - not just cut this particular Gordian knot but write their names in the annals of military glory. In a sense, Beckwith's long crusade to create Delta Force had been a rebellion against the mechanization and bureaucratization of modern warfare. He held to an old and visceral conviction: that war was the business of brave men. He loved soldiers and soldiering and his vision was of a company of men like himself: impatient with rank, rules and politics, focused entirely on mission. He had created such a force, choosing the best of the best and training them to perfection. They were not just good, they were magnificent. And now he would lead them into battle.

'Technically, Carter had not yet given the go-ahead, but when Beckwith left the White House, he was certain he had sold the mission. He flew to Delta's stockade at Fort Bragg, North Carolina and immediately assembled his top men. 'You can't tell the people; you can't tell anybody,' he said. 'Don't talk about this to anyone. But the president has approved the mission and we're going to go on April 24.'

The operation was designed as a complex two-night mission. On the first night three EC-130Es (Call signs: 'Republic 4 to 6') would carry the Delta Force and other protection elements and three MC-130E Combat Talons ('Dragon 1 to 3') would carry the logistical supplies. They would enter Iran in a remote coastal area sixty miles west of Chabahar and fly to 'Desert One' via the Dasht-e Lut or Great Salt Desert, a 500-mile-long and 200-mile-wide expanse of sand and salt in the high plateau region of north central Iran. It is both desolate and unpopulated. Large tracts of it are broad, flat and hard packed. Its western edge is roughly a hundred miles southeast of Tehran. 'Desert One' would be secured and established with a protection force and approximately 6,000 gallons of jet fuel would be brought to the area in collapsible fuel bladders carried in each 'fuel bird'. Next, eight USN RH-53D Sea Stallion helicopters ('Bluebeard 1 to 8') of HM-16 with USMC crews would arrive from the USS *Nimitz* under way in the

Arabian Sea.[1] Marine pilots, who ended up flying almost all of the helicopters, had little experience in long distance flying over land with night vision goggles. They were not special operations personnel and had no experience with sand storm conditions but the helicopters would refuel and fly the Delta Force soldiers 260 miles further to 'Desert Two', 52 miles short of Tehran. The second night would involve the rescue operation. AC-130 gunships would be deployed over Tehran to provide any necessary supporting fire.

Logan Fitch, a tall Texan and one of Delta's squadron leaders recalled that: 'When we briefed General David Jones, the chairman of the Joint Chiefs of Staff it was just dusk. I can picture him today wearing a brown suede bomber jacket, a Madras shirt and blue trousers. And he put his arm around me and said, 'Logan, looks like y'all got at least the rudiments here. Now we have to get the other services involved. Think about that. What that means is, oh, gosh, there might be some glory here and since I'm in charge of all the military I've got to make sure that the Air Force gets its part, the Marines, Navy, blah, blah. Well, the bottom line was that we had people flying those helicopters who really didn't want to be there. Not that they were cowards or anything. I often use the analogy that, if you take a Greyhound bus driver who's been driving a bus for forty years and you put him behind the wheel of an Indy 500 race car, he'd kill himself and a bunch of other people, probably. So I think that the people that piloted the helicopters were not the right people; Not bad people, not cowardly people, just not the right people.'[2]

'Just after dark, the Hercules moved in over the coast of Iran at 250 feet, well below Iranian radar and began a gradual ascent to 5,000 feet. It was still flying dangerously low even at that altitude, because the land rose up abruptly in row after row of jagged ridges - the Zagros Mountains, which looked jet black in the grey-green tints of the pilots' night-vision goggles. Its terrain-hugging radar was so sensitive that even though the plane was safely above the peaks, the highest ridges triggered the loud, disconcerting horn of its warning system. The co-pilot kept one finger over the override button, poised to silence it.

'The decision had been made to fly into Iran on fixed-wing transports rather than helicopters and since then Beckwith had added still more men to

'Eagle Claw,' as the rescue mission was now code-named. Most notable among them were a group of soldiers from the 75th Ranger Regiment, out of Fort Benning, Georgia, who would block off both ends of the dirt road that angled through Desert One and man Redeye missile launchers to protect the force on the first night in the event it was discovered and attacked from the air. A separate thirteen-man Army Special Forces team would assault the foreign ministry to free the three diplomats being held there. Also on Beckwith's lead plane was John Carney, an Air Force major from the team that had slipped into Iran weeks earlier to scout the desert landing strip and bury infrared lights to mark a runway. He would command a small Air Force combat-control team that would orchestrate the complex manoeuvres at the impromptu airfield.

'Some of these men sat on and around the Jeep.

The mood was relaxed. If there was one trait these men shared, it was professional calm. They had taken off at dusk from the tiny island of Masirah near Oman. An hour behind them would come five more C-130s - one of them carrying most of the remainder of Beckwith's assault force, which now numbered 132 men; three serving as 'bladder planes' and a back-up fuel plane carrying the last Deltas and sophisticated telecommunications-monitoring equipment.

'Delta was made up of men who would have felt crushed to be excluded from this mission. They were ambitious for glory. They had volunteered to serve with Beckwith and had undergone the trials of a gruelling selection process precisely to serve in improbable exploits like this... They were a motley, deliberately unmilitary-looking bunch of young men. In fact, they looked a lot like the students who had seized the embassy. Most were

Delta Force 'B' Squadron shortly before Operation 'Eagle Claw'. Those ringed, including, far left, Major Richard L. Bakke, were killed during the operation when their EC-130E (62-1809) was destroyed in a collision with US Navy RH-53D 158761 Sea Stallion.

Map showing the routes
taken to and from 'Desert
One' on 24 April 1980
when Operation 'Eagle
Claw', a joint USAF/
USMC attempt to rescue 52
diplomats held captive at
the US embassy in Tehran
using Hercules aircraft and
US Navy RH-53D Sea
Stallion helicopters flown
by marine pilots, ended in
disaster at Posht-i-Badam, a
remote location in Iran.

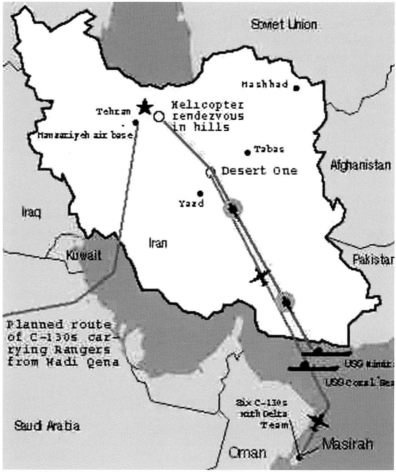

just a few years older than the hostage-takers. They had long hair and had grown moustaches and beards, or at least gone unshaven. Many of those with fair hair had dyed it dark brown or black, figuring that might nudge the odds at least slightly in their favour if they were forced to fight their way out of Iran. The loose-fitting, many-pocketed field jackets they wore, also dyed black were just like the ones favoured by young men in Iran. Under the Geneva Conventions, soldiers (as opposed to spies) must enter combat in uniform, so for the occasion the men all wore matching black knit caps and on their jacket sleeves had American flags that could be covered by small black Velcro patches... Beckwith had insisted on a Ranger tradition: each man carried clips and a length of rope wrapped around his waist, in case the need arose to rappel. With his white stubble, dangling cigarette or cigar and wild eyes under thick dark eyebrows, Beckwith himself looked like a dangerous vagrant.

Before leaving Masirah, the men had joked about which actors would portray them in the movie version of the raid and they decided that the hillbilly actor Slim Pickens, who in Stanley Kubrick's *Dr. Strangelove* had ridden a nuclear weapon down into doomsday waving his cowboy hat and hallooing, would be the perfect choice for the colonel.

'On the morning of the mission, the men had assembled in a warehouse, where Major Jerry Boykin had offered a prayer. Tall and lean, with a long, dark beard, Boykin stood at a podium before a plug box where electrical wires intersected and formed a big cross on the wall. Behind him was a poster-sized sheet displaying photographs of the Americans held hostage. Boykin chose a passage from the first Book of Samuel: *And David put his hand in his bag and took thence a stone and slang it and smote the Philistine in the forehead; that the stone sunk into his forehead and he fell on his face to the earth. So David prevailed over the Philistine with a sling and with a stone …*

'They had flown from Wadi Kena to Masirah, where they had hunkered in tents through a bright and broiling afternoon, fighting off large stinging flies and waiting impatiently for dusk. They would make a four-hour flight over the Gulf of Oman and across Iran to 'Desert One'. The route had been calculated to exploit gaps in Iran's coastal defences and to avoid passing over military bases and populated areas. Major Wayne Long, Delta's intelligence officer, was at a console in the telecommunications plane with a National Security Agency linguist, who was monitoring Iranian telecommunications for any sign that the aircraft had been discovered and the mission compromised. None came.'

Not long after the lead Hercules departed Masirah, eight Sea Stallions left the *Nimitz* nearly sixty miles off the coast of Iran and moved out over the Gulf in order to make landfall shortly after sunset. They had been preceded by the EC-130 refuellers and the MC-130 Combat Talons carrying Delta Force, from Masirah.

'Word of the successful helicopter launch - 'Eight off the deck' - reached those in the lead plane as especially welcome news, because they had expected only seven. Earlier reports had indicated that the eighth was having mechanical problems. Eight widened the margin of error.

'As the lead plane pushed on into Iran, Major Bucky Burruss, Beckwith's deputy, was on the second C-130, sprawled on a mattress near the front of the plane. Burruss was still somewhat startled to find himself on the actual mission; although there was still no telling if they were really going to go through with it. One thing President Carter had insisted on was the option of calling off the raid right up to the last minute: right before they were to storm the embassy walls. To make sure they could get real-time instructions from Washington, a satellite radio and relay system had been put in place at Wadi Kena.

'As the lead plane closed in on the landing site, its pilots noted curious milky patches in the night sky. They flew through one that appeared to be just haze, not even substantial enough to interfere with the downward-looking radar. They approached a second one as they got closer to the landing site. John Carney, who had come into the cockpit to be

ready to activate the landing lights he had buried on his trip weeks earlier, was asked, 'What do you make of that stuff out there?'

'He looked through the co-pilot's window and answered, 'You're in a haboob.'

'The men in the cockpit laughed at the word.

'No, we're flying through suspended dust,' Carney explained. 'The Iranians call it a haboob.'

'He had learned this from the CIA pilots who had flown him in earlier. Shifting air pressure sometimes forced especially fine desert sand straight up thousands of feet, where it hung like a vertical cloud for hours. It was just a desert curiosity, nothing that could cause a problem for the planes. But Air Force Colonel James H. Kyle, whose responsibility included all airborne aspects of the mission, knew that the haboob would be trouble for a helicopter. He had noticed that the temperature inside the plane went up significantly when they passed through the first haboob. He conferred with the plane's crew and suggested they break radio silence and call 'Red Barn,' the command centre at Wadi Kena, to warn the helicopter formation behind them. The chopper pilots might want to break formation or fly higher to avoid the stuff. It took the lead plane about thirty minutes to fly through this second patch, indicating that it extended about a hundred miles.

'As the MC-130 approached the landing area, Carney activated his runway lights, but just then the newfangled FLIR (forward-looking infrared radar) detected something moving, which proved to be a truck hurtling along the dirt road that ran through the landing site. The pilots passed over the spot and then circled back around. On the second pass the stretch of desert was clear. They circled around for the third time and touched down - Logan Fitch was amazed by how smoothly. The plane coasted to a stop and when the back ramp was lowered, the Rangers roared off in the Jeep and on a motorcycle to give chase to the truck. Word that an American plane had landed in the desert, relayed promptly to the right people, could defeat the whole effort.

'The hard-packed surface of three weeks prior was now coated with a layer of sand the consistency of baby powder - ankle-deep in some places - that accounted for the extraordinary softness of their landing. This fine sand made it more difficult to taxi the plane and the backwash from the propellers kicked up a serious dust storm.'

The landing however, resulted in substantial wing damage to the heavily loaded MC-130 but no one was hurt and it remained flyable. 'Dragon 1' 64-0565 captained by Lieutenant Colonel Robert L. Brenci of the 8th SOS in off-loaded a USAF Combat Control Team (CCT) consisting of 120 Delta operators, twelve Rangers forming the roadblock team and fifteen Iranian and American Persian-speakers, most of whom would act as truck drivers.

'Fitch followed with his men, walking down the ramp and stepping into a cauldron of noise and dust. His team had nothing to do at 'Desert One' except wait to offload camouflage netting and other equipment from the second C-130 when it arrived, then board helicopters for the short trip to the hiding places. The big plane's propellers were still roaring and kicking up sand. Shielding his eyes with an upraised arm, Fitch turned to his right and was shocked to see, coming straight toward him, a bus! Literally out of nowhere. The odds that the plane would encounter one vehicle at midnight on such an isolated desert road were vanishingly small, but there it was, honouring an absolute law of military operations: the inevitability of the unexpected. This second vehicle was a big Mercedes passenger bus, piled high with luggage, lit up like midday inside and filled with more than forty astonished Iranian passengers.

'Suddenly the night desert flashed as bright as daylight and shook with an explosion. In the near distance, a giant ball of flame rose high into the darkness. One of the Rangers had fired an anti-tank weapon at the fleeing truck, which turned out to have been loaded with fuel. It burned like a miniature sun.'

Shortly after midnight things grew louder and busier as the second and third MC-130s, using both runways roared in for a landing, right on schedule and discharged the remainder of the Delta operators.

'As Burruss and his men came down the lowered ramp of their plane, they gaped at the ball of flame, the bus and the passengers sitting on the sand.

Welcome to World War Three!' Fitch greeted them.

'Desert One' was now looking more like an airport and Carney's men were busy directing traffic, preparing for the arrival of the helicopters. Within the hour, all three C-130 bladder planes were positioned and parked, along with the [EC-130E ABCCC Airborne Battlefield Command and Control Centre) aircraft] communications plane.'

'Dragon 1' and '2' took off at 23:15 for Masirah to make room for the EC-130s and the RH-53Ds and to return to base to allow the crews to prepare for the second night operations.

'The unloading had gone pretty much as planned, with one exception: the second MC-130 had landed a few thousand feet farther away from the landing zone than expected, so the job of transferring the camouflage netting from it to the choppers was correspondingly bigger. The netting would be draped over the helicopters at their hiding places at daylight. It was not an especially warm night in the desert, but all the men were overdressed in layers of clothing and they were sweating heavily with exertion. Moving through the loose sand made the task even more difficult. The Air Force crews struggled to unfurl hundreds of pounds of hoses from the parked tankers, for fuelling the choppers.

'What is the status of the choppers?' Beckwith asked over a secure satellite radio.

The helicopter pilots had been told to fly at or below 200 feet to avoid radar. This limitation caused them to run into a haboob that they could not fly over without breaking the 200 foot limit. They had never even been briefed on the existence of haboob conditions, or their effects on low-flying formations. Two helicopters lost sight of the task force and landed, out of action. Another had landed earlier when a warning light had come on. Their crew had been picked up but 'Bluebeard 8' the helicopter that had stopped to retrieve them was now twenty minutes behind the rest of the formation. Battling dust storms and heavy winds, the RH-53s continued to make their way to 'Desert One'. After receiving word that the EC-130s and fuel had arrived, two of the Sea Stallions that had landed started up again and resumed their flight to the rendezvous. But then another helicopter had a malfunction and the pilot and Marine commander decided to turn back, halfway to the site. The task force was down to six helicopters, the bare minimum needed to pull off the rescue. However, less than two hours into the mission, 'Bluebeard 2' had an indicator light warn of a main rotor blade spar crack. This was often a false reading on RH-53Ds, but when the crew landed at 'Desert One' they decided to abandon the helicopter after inspecting the rotor blades. Six Sea Stallions had been deemed as the minimum number of helicopters needed for the mission and they were now down to five.

When Logan Fitch returned from rounding up the rest of his men, he was surprised to find that his second-in-command, Captain E. K. Smith, was still waiting with his squadron in the dust. Fitch told Smith to get the men on the helicopters.

'The mission is an abort,' Smith said.

'The abort scenario, which they had rehearsed, called for Fitch and his men to board not the helicopters but one of the tankers. The choppers would fly back to the carrier and the planes would return to Masirah. Fitch told Smith to prepare the men to board the plane, but said they should wait until he returned.

'When the decision to abort was relayed to Wadi Kena and to Washington, Zbigniew Brzezinski, the national-security adviser broke the news to Carter. Standing in a corridor between the Oval Office and the president's study, Carter muttered, 'Damn. Damn.'

'He and Brzezinski were soon joined by a larger group of advisers, including Walter Mondale, Hamilton Jordan, Warren Christopher and Jody Powell. Standing behind his desk, his sleeves rolled up and hands on his hips, the president told them, 'I've got some bad news … I had to abort the rescue mission … Two of our helicopters never reached 'Desert One'. That left us six. The Delta team was boarding the six helicopters when they found out that one of them had a mechanical problem and couldn't go on.'

'At least there were no American casualties and no innocent Iranians hurt,' Carter said.'

At 'Desert One' there was no time to dwell on the abort decision. Fuel consumption calculations had showed that the extra ninety minutes idling on the ground had made fuel critical for 'Republic 4'. When it became clear that only six helicopters would arrive at 'Desert One' authorization was given for the EC-130Es to transfer 1,000 US gallons from the bladders to their own main fuel tanks, but 'Republic 4' had already expended all of its bladder fuel refuelling three of the helicopters and had none to transfer. To make it to the tanker refuelling track without running out of fuel, it had to leave immediately. Logan Fitch directed his men to board. They piled in on top of the nearly emptied fuel bladders, which rippled like a giant black water bed. Everyone was weary and disappointed. Delta officer Eric Haney stripped off his gear and his black field jacket, balling it up behind him to form a cushion against the hard metal angles of the plane's inner wall. He and some of the other men wedged their weapons snugly between the bladder and the wall of the plane to keep them secure and out of the way. Some of the men immediately fell asleep.

'We're all set - let's go,' Fitch told the plane's crew chief.

A RH-53D - 'Bluebeard 3' - that needed additional fuel required it to be moved to the opposite side of the road. To accomplish both actions, 'Bluebeard 5' had to be moved from directly behind EC-130E (ABCCC) 62-1809. The aircraft could not be moved by ground taxi and had to be moved by hover taxi (flying a short distance at low speed and altitude). Just behind their tanker, a USAF Combat Controller in goggles, one of Carney's crew, appeared outside the cockpit of the RH-53 and informed Major Jim Schaefer, 'Bluebeard 3's pilot that he had to move his helicopter out of the way. Schaefer had refuelled behind that tanker and he now had enough fuel to fly back to the *Nimitz,* but first the C-130s needed to get off the ground. Schaefer lifted the front end of his Sea Stallion. His crew chief hopped out to straighten the nose wheels, which had been bent sideways when they landed. Straightened, they could be retracted so that they wouldn't cause drag in flight. The crew chief climbed back in.

'How much power do we have, Les?' Schaefer asked Petty his co-pilot, performing his usual checklist.

'Ninety-four percent,' Petty said.

Schaefer lifted the helicopter to a hover at about fifteen feet and held it, kicking up an intense storm of dust that whipped around the Combat Controller on the ground. He was the only thing Schaefer could see below, a hazy black image in a cloud of brown, so Schaefer fixed on him as a point of reference. The Combat Controller attempted to direct the manoeuvre from in front of the helicopter, but was blasted by desert sand churned up by the rotor. To escape the cloud created by

Schaefer's rotors, the Combat Controller retreated toward the wing of the parked EC-130E. Concentrating on his own aircraft, Schaefer did not notice that his blurry reference point on the ground had moved. He kept the nose of his blinded helicopter pointed at the man below and as the combat controller moved, the Sea Stallion turned in the same direction, drifting to a point almost directly above the Hercules. Schaefer perceived that he was drifting backward and thus attempted to 'correct' this situation by applying forward stick in order to maintain the same distance from the rearward moving marshaller. Then Schaefer heard and felt a loud, strong, metallic whack! It sounded like someone had hit the side of his aircraft with a large aluminium bat. Others heard a cracking sound as loud as an explosion, but somehow sharper-edged, more piercing and particular, like the shearing impact of giant industrial tools. The Marine pilot's main rotor had clipped the EC-130E's vertical stabilizer and crashed into the wing root, metal violently smashing into metal in a wild spray of sparks. Instantly the helicopter lost all aerodynamics, was wrenched forward by the collision, its cushion of air whipped out from beneath and it fell with a grinding bang into the EC-130E's cockpit, an impact so stunning that Schaefer briefly blacked out. Schaefer had just filled his tanks and the EC-130E still had fuel in the bladder in its rear and the sparks from the collision immediately ignited both of them with a powerful, lung-emptying thump that seemed to suck all the air out of the desert. A huge blue ball of fire formed around the front of the C-130 and a pillar of white flame rocketed 300 feet or more into the sky, turning the scene once more from night into day.

'Charlie Beckwith pivoted the moment he felt and heard the crash and started running toward it. He pulled up short, a football field away, stopped by the intense heat and thought with despair of his men: Fitch's entire troop, trapped.

'Inside the EC-130, Fitch had felt the plane begin to shudder, as though the pilots were revving the engines for takeoff. The hold had no windows and he couldn't tell if they were moving yet. Then he heard two loud, dull thunks. He thought maybe the nose gear or the landing gear had hit a rock, but when he looked toward the front of the aircraft he saw flames and sparks. He thought they were under attack. He had removed his rucksack and leaning against it was his weapon, an M203 grenade launcher. He grabbed it and stood, in a single motion. Beside him the plane's load master, responding wordlessly to the same sight, pulled open the troop door on the port side of the plane. It revealed a solid wall of flame. Fitch helped the load master slam the door down and push the handle in to lock it. He and the men were perched on a thousand gallons of fuel and they appeared to be caught in an inferno.

'Open the ramp!' Fitch shouted, but lowering it revealed more flames. The plane was going to explode. It was an enormous bomb on a short fuse and the fuse was lit. The only other way out was the starboard troop door, which had been calmly opened by three of the plane's crewmen. That way proved blessedly free of flames. Men started piling out of it before it was completely open.

'Still inside, Sergeant Major Dave Cheney, a bull of a man with a big deep voice, kept shouting, 'Don't panic! Don't panic!' as the men crowded toward the only escape. Flames were spreading fast along the roof, wrapping down the walls on both sides and igniting in each man a primitive flight instinct that none of them could control. One of the junior Air Force crewmen fell and was being trampled by fleeing Deltas when Technical Sergeant Ken Bancroft fought his way to the man, picked him up and carried him to the doorway and out. Cheney's natural authority and clarity helped prevent an utterly mad scramble and kept the men in a steady flow out the door. They were used to filing out this way on parachute jumps, so the line moved fast. Still, it was torture for the men at the rear.

'Ray Doyle, a load master on one of the other tankers, more than a hundred feet away, was knocked over by the force of the initial explosion. Jessie Rowe, a crewman on another tanker, felt his plane shake and the temperature of the air suddenly shoot up. Burruss saw the plane erupt as he stepped off the back of his C-130. He was carrying incendiary explosives down the ramp, to destroy the disabled Sea Stallion and the sight buckled him. He sat down and watched the tower of flame engulfing the plane, the downed chopper perched on top of it like a giant metal dragonfly, thinking, 'Man, Fitch and his whole squadron gone, those poor bastards.' But then he saw men running from the fireball. Pilots of the other craft quickly spread the word to their crews that they had not been attacked.

'Haney was still inside the burning plane, near the end of the line of men trying to get out. He and those around him had been jarred alert by the noise and impact of the crash and Haney had seen blue sparks overhead toward the front. Then the galley door at the front of the plane blew in and flames blasted in behind it. 'Haul ass!' shouted the man next to him, leaping to his feet.

'Captain E. K. Smith, who had dozed off right after boarding the plane, woke up to see men trying to gain their footing on the shifting surface of the fuel bladder and thought it was amusing - until he saw the flames. He and the men around him scrambled toward the door as best they could, fearing they would never outrace the flames. Ahead, men were jammed in the doorway. When Haney finally reached the door, he threw himself out, dropping down hard on the man who had jumped before him. They picked themselves up

and ran until they were about fifty yards away. Then they turned to watch with horror.

'Fitch felt it was his duty to stay in the plane until all the men were off, but it was hard. As the flames rapidly advanced, he realized that not everyone was going to make it. Instinct finally won out and both he and Cheney leaped out the door, falling when they hit the ground. Other men crashed on top of them. They helped one another up and over to where the others were now watching, brightly illuminated by the growing fire.

'Fitch ran to what seemed a safe distance and then turned around, still assuming they were under attack and lifted his weapon. He looked for the enemy and saw instead the awesome and ugly sight: the chopper, its rotors still turning, had clearly crashed down on the front of the plane. It wasn't an attack; it was an accident.

'He saw two more men jump out - one of them Staff Sergeant Joe Beyers, the radio operator, whose flight suit was burning. Other men rushed to put out the flames and drag him clear. Then

The eight USAF and USMC crewmembers killed on the failed attempt to release the Iranian hostages on 24 April 1980.

ammunition started 'cooking off,' all the grenades, missiles, explosives and rifle rounds on both aircraft, causing loud, cracking explosions and throwing flames and light. The Redeye missiles went off, drawing smoke trails high into the sky. Finally the fuel bladders ignited, sending a huge pillar of flame skyward in a loud explosion that buckled the fuselage. All four propellers dropped straight down into the sand and stuck there, as if somebody had planted them.

'In the chopper, Schaefer at last came to. He was sitting crooked in his seat, the chopper was listing to one side and flames engulfed the cockpit.

'What's wrong, Les, what's wrong?' he asked, turning to his co-pilot. But Petty was already gone. He had jumped out the window on his side.

'Schaefer shut down the engines and sat for a moment, certain he was about to die. Then, for some reason, an image came into his mind of his fiancée's father - who had never seemed much impressed by his future son-in-law - commenting

a few days hence on how the poor sap had been found roasted like a holiday turkey in the front seat of his aircraft. Something about that horrifying image motivated him. His body would not be found like a blackened Butterball; he had to at least try to escape. He ejected the window on his side and as fire closed over him, badly burning his face, he dropped hard to the ground and then ran from the erupting wreckage.

'The exploding aircraft and ammo sent flaming bits of hot metal and debris spraying across the makeshift airport, riddling the four remaining working helicopters, whose crews jumped out and moved to a safe distance. Most of the men had no idea what was going on; they knew only that a plane and a chopper had been destroyed. The air over the scene was heavy with the door of fuel, so it wasn't hard to imagine that all the other aircraft might burst into flames as well. The remaining C-130s began taxiing in different directions away from the conflagration.

MC-130E 64-0564 and 'Dragon 2' crew just before departing for Desert One.

'Word of the calamity reached the command centre in Wadi Kena in a hurried report: 'We have a crash. A helo crashed into one of the C-130s. We have some dead, some wounded and some trapped. The crash site is ablaze; ammunition is cooking off.'

'The only course now was to clear out and fast. Some thought was given to retrieving the bodies of the dead, but the fire was raging and there wasn't time... As Burruss headed back to his C-130, he took one last look at the flaming ruins of the plane and the chopper and felt a stab of remorse over leaving the dead behind. But nothing could be done about it.

'America's elite rescue force had lost eight servicemen - five of fourteen USAF aircrew in the EC-130 and three of the five USMC aircrew in the RH-53, with only the helicopter's pilot and co-pilot (both badly burned) surviving as well as seven helicopters and a C-130 and had not even made contact with the enemy. It was a debacle. It defined the word 'debacle.'[3]

During the frantic evacuation to the EC-130s by the helicopter crews, attempts were made to retrieve their classified mission documents and destroy the aircraft. The helicopter crews boarded the EC-130s. Five RH-53 aircraft were left behind mostly intact, some damaged by shrapnel. The EC-130s carried the remaining forces back to the intermediate airfield at Masirah Island, where two C-141 medical evacuation aircraft from the staging base at Wadi Abu Shihat, Egypt picked up the injured personnel, helicopter crews, Rangers and Delta Force members. The injured were then transported to Ramstein Air Base in Germany. The White House announced the failed rescue operation at 1:00 am the following day. On 20 January 1981, minutes after Carter's term ended, the 52 US captives held in Iran were released, ending the 444-day Iran hostage crisis.

Former 'Heavy Chain' and 'Desert One' veteran 64-0564 crashed into the ocean shortly after a pre-dawn takeoff from NAS Cubi Point, Philippines on 26 February 1981, killing fifteen passengers and eight of nine crewmen. The Talon was taking part in Special Warfare Exercise 81 and had flown twelve missions in the preceding sixteen days. Following an administrative flight the day before, the crew was scheduled for its last mission, a night exercise that was set back from 0100 local

time to 0430. The flight profile consisted of a normal takeoff, a tactical landing a half hour later to onload fifteen Navy SEALs, followed by a tactical takeoff. The Talon reported normal flight conditions six minutes after the tactical takeoff, but crashed nine minutes later. No cause was determined, but investigators found that the likely causes were either crew fatigue from operations tempo, or failure of the terrain following radar to enter 'override' mode while over water.

Within two weeks of the failure of Operation 'Eagle Claw' the Pentagon began planning for a second mission. A new organization, the Joint Test Directorate (JTD), was established to assist and support the Office of Secretary of Defense Directorate (OSD) joint planning staff. Under the name 'Honey Badger', the JTD conducted a series of large-scale joint-force exercises and projects to develop and validate a variety of capabilities that would be available to OSD when mission requirements were identified. JTD trained a large and diverse force of US Army and USAF special operations and aviation units, but the critical factor remained extracting the rescue team and freed hostages from Tehran. The 'Credible Sport' project, a joint undertaking of the USAF, US Navy and Lockheed-Georgia was created within 'Honey Badger' to develop a reliable extraction capability. 'Credible Sport' was tasked to create a large 'Super STOL' fixed-wing aircraft to extract the rescue team and hostages and overcome the 'weak link' in the previous plan, the heavy lift helicopter.

'Credible Sport' called for a modified C-130 to land in the Amjadien Stadium across the street from the US Embassy in Tehran and airlift out Delta Force operators and the rescued hostages. The aircraft would then be flown to and landed on an aircraft carrier for immediate medical treatment of an expected fifty wounded.

'Armi' Armitage the Lockheed test pilot said: 'The hostages were daily marched around the soccer field near the American Embassy and we were given advance notice of when the hostages would be at the field on a given day by one of the many Iranians who were still friendly to the US. The planes were equipped with flares, a radar altimeter and even a laser altimeter that looked ahead at the landing aim point to give a precise slant altitude above the touchdown point. A computer was to control the firing of the rockets.

If the retrorockets fired before they were on the ground, they were dead. A test was scheduled for three days before the planned mission date in October. If the test were successful, the mission would be a GO.'

Three MC-130 Combat Talon crews (all 'Eagle Claw' veterans) were assigned to fly the three aircraft, drawn from the 463rd Tactical Airlift Wing, with the concept plan calling for the mission of two aircraft (one primary and one spare) to originate in the US reaching Iran by five in flight refuellings and penetrate at low altitude in the dark to evade Iranian air defences. Three C-130s were modified under a top secret project at Eglin Air Force Base Auxiliary Field #1 (Wagner Field), Florida. The contract called for two to be modified to the proposed XFC-130H configuration within 90 days and the third to be used as a test bed for various rocket packages blistered onto the forward and aft fuselage, which theoretically enabled the aircraft to land and take off within the sports arena's confines. (A fourth aircraft, an EC-130 ABCCC, was used as the interior mock-up airframe for simulator training.)

After Lockheed was requested on 27 June 1980 to begin preliminary engineering studies on an STOL Hercules, the use of JATO units was explored, since these had previously been used to power takeoffs. Lockheed reported on 16 July that 58 JATO bottles (more than seven times greater than normal) would be required and that arresting gear would be insufficient to stop the C-130 in the required space. The US Navy's Naval Air Weapons Station China Lake organization was then brought into the project to provide expertise on existing rocket motor power. Lockheed proceeded with work to structurally reinforce the C-130 airframe to withstand rocket forces and to develop a passenger restraint system for 150 persons.

The resulting XFC-130H aircraft were modified by the installation of thirty rockets in multiple sets: eight forward-pointed ASROC rocket motors mounted around the forward fuselage to stop the aircraft, eight downward-pointed Shrike rockets fuselage-mounted above the wheel wells to brake its descent, eight rearward-pointed MK-56 rockets (from the RIM-66 Standard missile) mounted on the lower rear fuselage for takeoff assist, two Shrikes mounted in pairs on wing pylons to correct yaw during takeoff

transition and two ASROCs mounted at the rear of the tail to prevent it from striking the ground from over-rotation.

Other STOL features included a dorsal and two ventral fins on the rear fuselage, double-slotted flaps and extended ailerons, a new radome, a tail hook for landing aboard an aircraft carrier and Combat Talon avionics, including a Terrain Following/Terrain Avoidance radar, a defensive countermeasures suite and a Doppler radar/GPS tie-in to the aircraft's inertial navigation system.

The test bed aircraft (74-2065) was ready for its first test flight on 18 September 1980, just three weeks after the project's initiation. The first fully modified aircraft (74-1683) was delivered on 17 October to TAB 1 (Wagner Field/Eglin AF No. 1), a disused auxiliary airfield at Eglin Air Force Base, Florida. Between 19 October and 28 October, numerous flights were made testing various aspects, including the double-slotted flaps system, which enabled the C-130 to fly at 85 knots on final approach at a very steep eight-degree glide slope. All aspects worked flawlessly and a full profile test was scheduled for 29 October.

The test's takeoff phase was executed flawlessly, setting a number of short takeoff records. 'Armi' Armitage and the Lockheed test crew then assessed that the computer used to command the firing of the rockets during the landing sequence needed further calibration and elected to manually input commands. The reverse-mounted (forward-facing) eight ASROC rockets for decelerating the aircraft's forward speed were situated in pairs on the fuselage's upper curvature behind the cockpit and at the midpoint of each side of the fuselage beneath the uppers. Testing had determined that the upper pairs, fired sequentially, could be ignited while still airborne (specifically, at 20 feet), but that the lower pairs could only be fired after the aircraft was on the ground, with the descent-braking rockets also firing during the sequence.

The flight engineer, blinded by the firing of the upper deceleration rockets, thought the aircraft was on the runway and fired the lower set early. The descent-braking rockets didn't fire at all. Later unofficial disclaimers allegedly made by some of the Lockheed test crew's members asserted that the lower rockets fired themselves through an undetermined computer or electrical malfunction, which at the same time failed to fire the descent-braking rockets. As a result, the aircraft's forward flight was immediately reduced to nearly zero, dropping it hard to the runway and breaking the starboard wing between the third and fourth engines. During rollout, the trailing wing ignited a fire, but a medical evacuation helicopter dispersed the flame and crash response teams extinguished the fire within eight seconds of the aircraft stopping, enabling the crew to safely exit the aircraft. 74-1683 was dismantled and buried on-site for security reasons, but most of its unique systems were salvaged.

74-1686 was nearly ready for delivery, but when on 2 November 1980 the Iranian parliament accepted an Algerian plan for release of the hostages, followed two days later by Ronald Reagan's election as the US President, the rescue mission plan was cancelled. The hostages were subsequently released concurrent with Reagan's inauguration in January 1981.

The remaining airframes were stripped of their rocket modifications and 74-2065 returned to regular airlift duties. 74-1686, however, retained its other 'Credible Sport' STOL modifications and was sent to Robins Air Force Base, Georgia. There, in July 1981 it was designated YMC-130H as the test bed for the MC-130 Combat Talon II's development, under Project 'Credible Sport II'. Phase I was conducted between 24 August-11 November 1981 to test minor modifications to improve aerodynamics, satisfy 'Combat Talon II' prototype requirements on STOL performance, handling characteristics and avionics and to establish safety margins. It also identified design deficiencies in the airframe and determined that the 'Credible Sport' configuration was suitable only for its specific mission and didn't have the safety margins necessary for peacetime operations. Phase II testing which began on 15 June 1982 and continued until October determined that the final configuration resulted in significant improvements in design, avionics and equipment and that the 'Combat Talon II' design was ready for production.

The forlorn wreckage of EC-130E (ABCCC) 62-1809 which was destroyed in the collision with US Navy RH-53D 158761 Sea Stallion at 'Desert One'.

The 1st Special Operations Wing attempted to have the test bed transferred to operational duty as an interim 'Combat Talon II' until production models became available, but Headquarters, Tactical Airlift Command disagreed. The cost of returning the YMC-130H to stock airlift configuration was more than its value and it never flew again.[4]

The 1990 invasion of Kuwait by Iraq resulted in the deployment of four Combat Talons and six crews of the 8th SOS in August 1990 to King Fahd International Airport in Saudi Arabia as a component of Operation 'Desert Shield'. During Operation 'Desert Storm', the combat phase of the Gulf War in January and February 1991, the Combat Talon performed one-third of all airdrops during the campaign and participated in psychological operations, flying 15 leaflet-drop missions before and throughout the war. Combat Talon crews also conducted five BLU-82B 'Daisy Cutter' missions during the two weeks preceding the onset of the ground campaign, dropping eleven bombs on Iraqi positions at night from altitudes between 16,000 feet and 21,000 feet, once in concert with a bombardment by the battleship USS *Wisconsin*.

Two 7th SOS Talons deployed to Incirlik Air Base, Turkey, as part of Operation 'Proven Force'. They supported the first Joint Search and Rescue mission over Iraq, attempting to recover the crew of 'Corvette 03', a downed F-15E Strike Eagle. However permission from the Turkish government to fly the mission was delayed for 24 hours and the crew was not recovered.

Three MC-130H Combat Talon IIs of the 7th SOS were deployed in December 1995 to deliver peacekeeping forces to Tuzla and Sarajevo, Bosnia and Herzegovina, as part of Operation Joint Endeavour, during which one Talon was hit by ground fire. The first combat deployment of a Combat Talon II was on April 8, 1996, during Operation 'Assured Response'. Special operations forces were deployed to Liberia to assist in the evacuation of 2000 civilians from the American embassy when the country broke down into civil war. However orders to combat drop an eighteen-man SEAL team off Monrovia were rescinded and the mission landed in Sierra Leone. Similar circumstances brought the Combat Talon II to Zaire in 1997. Talon II deployments for joint exercises in 1997 included Australia, Guam, Indonesia, South Korea and Thailand. In July 1997 three Talon IIs deployed to Thailand as part of

The wreckage of EC-130E (ABCCC) 62-1809 with one of the abandoned RH-53D helicopters behind in the aftermath of Operation 'Eagle Claw' at Posht-i-Bada.

Operation 'Bevel Edge', a proposed rescue of 1000 American citizens trapped in Phnom Penh, Cambodia, by a possible civil war, but the crisis ended when the Cambodian government allowed all non-citizens who desired so to leave by commercial air. A 7th SOS Combat Talon II aircrew, Whiskey 05, earned the Mackay Trophy for an embassy evacuation mission in the Republic of the Congo in June 1997. The crew rescued thirty Americans and twenty-six foreign nationals and logged twenty-one hours of flight time.

Full operational capability for the 'Talon II' was reached in February 2000. At that time 24 MC-130Hs were deployed to four squadrons: 15th Special Operations Squadron, eleven at Hurlburt Field, Florida; 1st Special Operations Squadron, five at Kadena AB, Okinawa; 7th Special Operations Squadron, five at RAF Mildenhall; and 550th Special Operations Squadron, three at Kirtland AFB, New Mexico.

On the night of 19/20 October 2001 four Combat Talon IIs infiltrated a task force of 199 Rangers of the 3rd Battalion 75th Ranger Regiment and tactical PSYOP teams 658 miles inside Taliban-held Afghanistan. The force dropped onto Objective 'Rhino', an unused airfield in Kandahar Province 110 mi southwest of Kandahar, to secure a landing zone as a temporary operating base for Special Forces units conducting raids in the vicinity. A month later, two MC-130Hs, flying from Masirah Island, inserted a platoon of US ' Navy SEAL Team Three and four Humvee vehicles to within ten miles of the same airfield on the night of 20/21 November. The SEAL platoon was inserted to establish an observation post at the airstrip and then assist two USAF combat controllers inserted by military free fall in preparing a landing zone for the 15th Marine Expeditionary Unit. The 15th MEU landed in CH-53 helicopters on 25 November 2001 and established Camp 'Rhino', the first forward operating base in Afghanistan for US forces.

Combat Talon IIs of the 7th SOS, augmented by crews from the 15th and 550th SOSs, flew 13- to 15-hour airdrop and airlanding night resupply missions from Incirlik Air Base, Turkey to Special Forces Operational Detachments - Alpha (ODAs) in Afghanistan during the opening phase of Operation 'Enduring Freedom' in December 2001. Operating in mountainous terrain they innovated an airdrop tactic by replicating maximum-effort landing techniques to rapidly descend from 10,000 feet to 500 feet AGL to ensure accurate gravity drops after clearing high ridgelines into deep valleys.

Combat Shadow 66-0213 was lost when it flew into a mountain side in eastern Afghanistan on 13 February 2002. Assigned to the 9th SOS, the aircraft was called to perform on call refuelling for CSAR assets. The aircraft was forced to make an emergency climb in poor visibility to escape a box canyon in the mountainous terrain, ran out of climb performance and crash landed wheels up in deep snow. The aircraft was a total loss but the crew of eight survived. Combat Talon II 84-0475, assigned to the 15th SOS, was lost in a takeoff crash on 12 June 2002, near Gardez, Afghanistan. During a night exfiltration mission of two Special Forces soldiers from a landing strip at the Sardeh Band dam, the Talon crashed less than three miles from the airstrip shortly after takeoff. Conflicting reports point to overweight cargo and windshear as possible causes. The Talon's two loadmasters and a passenger were killed.

Combat Talon II 90-0161of the 15th SOS crashed into Monte Perucho, south of Caguas, Puerto Rico, during a training mission on 7 August 2002, killing all ten aboard. The Talon was flying a terrain following night mission in blowing rain and fog, along a low level route commonly used by the Puerto Rico Air National Guard. The crew misinterpreted and disregarded terrain obstacle warnings.

A Combat Talon II of the 7th SOS (87-0127 'Wrath 11') crashed during a terrain-following-and-avoidance night training exercise on 31 March 2005, near Rovie, in the Drizez Mountains in southeast Albania, 60 miles southeast of Tirana. The Talon had taken off from Tirana-Rinas Airport 20 minutes before and was one of two flying at 300 feet AGL at a reduced power setting. The aircraft was lost when it stalled attempting to clear terrain, killing all nine crew members.

The 7th SOS, commanded by Lieutenant Colonel Mark B. Alsid and part of the 352nd Special Operations Group, received the Gallant Unit Citation in 2006 for operations conducted during Operation 'Iraqi Freedom' between 12 February and 12 May 2003. The 7th SOS was tasked to Joint Special Operations Task Force -

162

North, known as Task Force 'Viking', whose objective was to hold 13 Iraqi Army divisions along the 'Green Line' in north-eastern Iraq to prevent those divisions from reinforcing other Iraqi operations against United States forces invading from Kuwait. Forward-based at Constanţa, Romania its primary mission was to infiltrate the 2nd and 3rd Battalions of the Army's 10th Special Forces Group and the 3rd Battalion of the 3rd Special Forces Group into Kurdish-held territory in preparation for Operation Northern Delay. Denied permission by Turkey to fly into Iraq from its airspace, the 7th SOS flew the first 280 troops on a circuitous path around Turkey to a base in Jordan on March 20–21, 2003. On March 22, six Combat Talon IIs (four from the 7th SOS) infiltrated 16 ODAs, four ODBs, battalion command elements and Air Force Combat Control Teams to complete the fifteen-hour mission, the longest in US ' Special Operations history. The insertion profile consisted of a four and one-half hour low level flight at night through western and northern Iraq to Bashur and Sulaymaniyah airfields, often taking heavy ground fire from the integrated air defences. The Talon IIs, at

emergency gross weight limits, operated blacked-out, employed chaff and electronic countermeasures, flew as low as 100 feet AGL and carried their troops tethered to the floor of the cargo holds. Three of the Talons were battle-damaged, with one forced to seek permission to land at Incirlik Air Base. The operation became known informally as 'Operation Ugly Baby'. Major Jason L. Hanover was individually honoured for commanding a mission that seized two austere airstrips during the operation. After airlanding their troops, the Talon IIs then had to fly back through the alerted defences to recover to their launching point.

Overflight permission was granted by Turkey on 23 March and the Combat Talon IIs delivered fifty ODAs into Iraq. The Talon IIs then resupplied Task Force Viking, assisted in operations to capture Kirkuk and Mosul, airlanded supplies at remote outposts using Internal Airlift Slingable Container Units (ISUs) and acted as pathfinders for conventional C-130 airlift missions.

The MC-130W 'Combat Spear' or 'Combat Wombat' to give its unofficial name, performs clandestine or low visibility missions into denied

EC-130E 62-1818 which was one of the Hercules used on the ill-fated 'Eagle Claw' operation on 24 April 1980, pictured here on its return to Hurlburt Field.

areas to provide aerial refuelling to SOF helicopters or to air drop small SOF teams and supply bundles. The first of twelve MC-130Ws (87-9286) was presented to Air Force Special Operations Command on 28 June 2006. The aircraft was developed to supplement the MC-130 Combat Talon and Combat Shadow forces as an interim measure after several training accidents and contingency losses in supporting the Global War on Terrorism. The programme modified C-130H-2 airframes from the 1987-1990 production run, acquired from airlift units in the AFRes Command and Air National Guard. Use of the H-2 airframe allowed installation of SOF systems already configured for Combat Talons without expensive and time-consuming development that would be required of new production C-130J aircraft, reducing the flyaway cost of the Spear to $60 million per aircraft. The Combat Spears, however, do not have a Terrain Following/Terrain Avoidance capability.

A standard system of special forces avionics equips the MC-130W: a fully integrated Global Positioning System and Inertial Navigation System, an AN/APN-241 Low Power Colour weather/navigation radar; interior and exterior NVG-compatible lighting; advanced threat detection and automated countermeasures, including active infrared countermeasures as well as chaff and flares; upgraded communication suites, including dual satellite communications using data burst transmission to make trackback difficult; aerial refuelling capability; and the ability to act as an aerial tanker for helicopters and CV-22 Osprey aircraft using Mk 32B-902E refuelling pods.

The MC-130Ws are assigned to the 73rd Special Operations Squadron at Cannon Air Force Base, New Mexico, with all twelve to be operational by 2010. Initially nicknamed the 'Whiskey' (NATO phonetic for the 'W' modifier), the MC-130W was officially dubbed the 'Combat Spear' in May 2007 to honour the historical legacy of the Combat Talons in Việtnam.

Beginning in 1997 studies of the vulnerability of the non-stealthy MC-130 force reflected concerns about its viability in modern high-threat environments, including the prevalence of man-portable air-defence systems ('MANPADs') in asymmetric conflicts. At least two studies were conducted or proposed to explore the prospect of a replacement aircraft (known variously as 'MC-X' or 'M-X'), with USAF at that time hoping for an Initial Operating Capability date of 2018. One analyst questioned the survivability of slow non-stealthy platforms such as the MC-130 in future threat environments in a 2007 presentation to the Centre for Strategic and International Studies and stated his opinion that development of a stealthy replacement for the MC-130 is a 'strategic priority'. The US ' Department of Defence's 2006 Quadrennial Defence Review Report also recognized the concern, asserting DoD's intention to 'enhance capabilities to support SOF insertion and extraction into denied areas from strategic distances.'

Despite these concerns, the USAF decided to proceed with modernization of the current force. The Air Force has stated it desires 37 MC-130Js to replace its MC-130Es and MC-130Ps, which are forty or more years old. Based on the KC-130J tanker operated by the USMC, the new MC-130J has added features for both combat search and rescue and special operations missions. The HC-130J and MC-130J both use the KC-130J tanker as a baseline, but with major modifications to the Block 6.5 KC-130J. The MC-130J adds an Enhanced Service Life Wing, an Enhanced Cargo Handling System, a Universal Aerial Refuelling Receptacle Slipway Installation (UARRSI) boom refuelling receptacle, more powerful electrical generators, an electro-optical/infrared sensor, a combat systems operator station on the flight deck, provisions for the Large Aircraft Infrared Countermeasures System and armour.

Production of the first MC-130J aircraft was started at Lockheed Martin's facility in Marietta, Georgia on 5 October 2009. Lockheed Martin will build an MC-130J tanker version for Air Force Special Operations Command on its standard C-130J production line. The MC-130J is the first C-130 specifically built for special operations, making it lighter and more efficient. Most special operations aircraft are modified after production to accommodate special operations missions. The MC-130J was initially dubbed the 'Combat Shadow II' in honour of the aging MC-130P platform that it was expected to replace but has now officially been named the Commando II.

The Air Force Special Operations Training

Within two weeks of the failure of Operation 'Eagle Claw' 'Credible Sport' was tasked to create a large 'Super STOL' fixed-wing aircraft fitted with ASROC units to extract the rescue team and hostages but when on 2 November 1980 the Iranian parliament accepted an Algerian plan for release of the hostages, followed two days later by Ronald Reagan's election as the US President, the rescue mission plan was cancelled.

Centre has begun the MC-130J training programme in conjunction with the 193rd Special Operations Wing, using any of the unit's four EC-130J 'Commando Solo' aircraft to form what will become the training regimen for MC-130J aircrew members. The MC-130J has a five-member crew, a major reduction in size from the standard eight-member MC-130P 'Combat Shadow' crew, thus requiring additional coordination among crew members. The MC-130J will begin replacing aging MC-130E Combat Talon I and MC-130P Combat Shadow aircraft after a period of testing and evaluation. The Commando II will fly clandestine, low-level aerial refuelling missions as well as infiltration, exfiltration and resupply missions.

Eventually the 415th Special Operations Squadron, a unit of the 58th Operations Group, will become the main training unit for both MC-130J and HC-130J operations.

The 522nd Special Operations Squadron is the first to operate the MC-130J Commando II. It is expected to achieve Initial Operational Capability in 2012. The first MC-130J (09-6207) undertook its first test flight on 22 April 2011. The 522nd Special Operations Squadron received its first MC-130J in late September 2011. A total of 37 MC-130J aircraft are planned, which will eventually replace all other MC-130 variants.

In 2013 the 7th SOS transitioned from the MC-130H to the Bell Boeing V-22 Osprey.

Chapter 7 Endnotes

1   The eight RH-53D Sea Stallion helicopters had been stowed on the hangar deck of the *Nimitz* to keep them away from the prying eyes of Iranian patrol aircraft as well as Soviet reconnaissance satellites. The helicopters had accidentally been sprayed with corrosive flame retardant (which had been quickly washed off), then seawater when a small fire broke out in the hangar and maintenance had been delayed until the last minute.

2   In a 24 June 2012 talk.

3   Mark Bowden is an *Atlantic* national correspondent. His most recent book is *The Finish: The Killing of Osama bin Laden*.

4   In 1988 74-1686 was placed on display at the Museum of Aviation at Robins Air Force Base in Warner Robins, Georgia. As of February 2008, the other surviving Credible Sport aircraft, 74-2065, was assigned to the 317th Airlift Group, 15th Expeditionary Mobility Task Force, at Dyess Air Force Base, Texas in grey scheme with blue tail band.

Chapter Eight

The Quiet Professionals

When the 105 goes off it gives a pretty good jolt to the ship, but probably worse is a continuous burst from the 20 mils. This leaves a lot of smoke floating around, even in the cockpit, but as we have so many open spaces on board it soon dissipates!'

An AC-130 pilot's perspective of flying the 'Spectre'

Largely because of the loss of the EC-130 ABCCC on 'Eagle Claw' and the subsequent acts of terrorism and hostage-taking, it was decided that all forces trained in air rescue and special operations should operate under a specialized, unified USAF command with its own helicopters and fixed-wing aircraft. And so on 1 March 1983 the 23rd Air Force was activated at Scott AFB, Illinois. The precursors of this organization's units, the air commando squadrons (from 1968, special operations squadrons), had played an essential covert role during the war in South-east Asia.

The first test for the new air force came on 25 October 1983 when the 23rd Air Force took part in Operation 'Urgent Fury', the rescue of US citizens from Grenada. During the invasion, AC-130 gunships and MC-130 and HC-130 tankers played their part very effectively. The operation even had the services of special EC-130E aircraft to broadcast recorded radio programmes to the

The rear deck of an AC-130A gunship at Ubon airfield with the 105mm trainable gun to provide air to ground firing capabilities in the left paratroop door. Each round of ammunition must be loaded by hand. Ammunition storage is provided by racks located on the right-hand side of the Gunship between the operator's compartment and the right paratroop door. The 105mm mount is capable of being moved manually within an elevation range of 0-20 degrees.

162

AC-130A gunship in the 16th SOS in flight over Việtnam. Note the ALQ-87 ECM pods fitted beneath the outer wings.

residents of Spice Island. Five Combat Talons of the 8th Special Operations Squadron took part. Unlike previous operations that involved months of planning, training and reconnaissance, the 8th SOS prepared in less than 72 hours after being alerted. Its assignment was to insert Rangers of the 1st and 2nd Ranger Battalions at night to capture Point Salines International Airport, defended by both Cuban and Grenadian troops, in the opening moments of the operation. The five Talons divided into three elements, two of them leading formations of Special Operations Low Level-equipped (SOLL) C-130 transports.

In clouds at 500 feet above the sea and twenty miles west of its objective, the lead Talon (64-0562) experienced a complete failure of its APQ-122 radar. Reorganization of the mission formations delayed the operation for 30 minutes, during which US Marines made their amphibious landing. To compound the lack of surprise, the US Department of State, apparently in a good faith but inept diplomatic gesture, contacted Cuban authorities and compromised the mission, further alerting the defences, including a dozen ZU-23-2 antiaircraft guns. An AC-130 Spectre gunship, directed to observe the main runway for obstructions, reported

it blocked by construction equipment and barricades. Loadmasters aboard the inbound Combat Talons reconfigured them for a parachute drop in less than thirty minutes.

Talon 64-0568, flown as Foxtrot 35 by 8th SOS commander Lieutenant Colonel (later Major General) James L. Hobson and with the commander of the Twenty-Third Air Force, Major Gen William J. Mall, Jr., aboard as a passenger, combat-dropped runway clearing teams from the Ranger Battalions on the airport, despite being targeted by a searchlight and under heavy AAA fire. Two Spectre gunships suppressed the AAA so that the other Combat Talons and the SOLL C-130s could complete the parachute drop of the Rangers, with the only damage to the Talons being three hits by small arms fire to 64-0572. For his actions, Hobson was awarded the MacKay Trophy in 1984.

In December 1989 and January 1990, 'Volant Solo II' EC-130Es - 'Coronet Solo' - were used during Operation 'Just Cause', the US invasion of Panama, to broadcast misinformation to Panamanian forces. Three MC-130E 'Combat Talons' from the 8th SOS, whose motto is 'With the Guts to Try', part of the 1st Special Operations Wing, deployed to Hunter Army Air Field, Georgia

AC-130A 56-0490 *Thor* on the ramp at Ubon, Thailand. This gunship was shot down near Pakse, Laos on 21 December 1972. In the nose is the AN/APN-59B navigation and moving target indicator. Behind the AN/ASQ-24A stabilized tracking set are twin 20mm M-61 cannon finally two 40mm Bofors cannon and the Motorola AN/APQ-133 beacon tracking radar which replaced the original NASARR F-151-A fire-control radar adapted from the F-104 Starfighter.

within 48 hours of being alerted and then airlanded Rangers of the 2nd Battalion 75th Ranger Regiment into Rio Hato Military airfield on 18 December with two HC-130 refuelling tankers from the 55th SOS supporting them. The operation was conducted under total blackout conditions, using night vision goggles, 35 minutes after the opening parachute assault. One of the MC-130s had an engine disabled by a ground obstruction while taxiing, then made an NVG takeoff on three engines under intense ground fire, earning its pilot the DFC. The lead Talon, the only MC-130E equipped with the Benson tank refuelling system, remained on the airfield as a Forward Area Refuelling and Rearming Point (FARRP) for US Army OH-6 helicopters.

In all, 21 aircraft of the 1st Special Operations

A closer view of the left hand side of AC-130 56-0490 *Thor* showing the ASN/ASD-5 'Black Crow' truck ignition sensor dome. Six AC-130A/E gunships were lost to enemy action in SE Asia, 1969-1972. Five were downed while truck hunting along the Hồ Chi Minh Trail by 57mm and 37 mm Triple A and a SA-2 SAM and one by a SA-7 shoulder fired SAM which struck the #3 engine and blew off the wing. The opening to the right contains the AN/ASQ-24A stabilized tracking set (Korad AN/AVQ-18 laser designator and bomb damage assessment camera).

Wing, plus the 1720th Special Tactics Group (STGP) and elements of the 9th and 55th Special Operations Squadrons, flew over 400 missions during the operation. Seven of the aircraft were AC-130 gunships from the 16th SOS which were among the first in action early on the morning of 20 December, destroying the Panamanian Defence Force's Comandancia HQ with devastating fusillades of cannon and machine-gun fire. MC-130E 'Combat Talons' and MH-53E helicopters were used to infiltrate US Navy SEALS (Sea-Air-Land) into Panamanian positions. When Panamanian General Manuel Noriega surrendered on 3 January he was immediately flown to Homestead AFB, Florida, by a Combat Talon.

'Just Cause' was the 23rd Air Force's final operation before its deactivation. On 22 May 1990 the 23rd Air Force became the USAF component of the Air Force Special Operations Command (AFSOC), when Special Forces of each branch of the armed forces came under its central operational control. Headquarters were established at Hurlburt Field, Florida, where special operations personnel have trained since 1942, when they prepared for the Doolittle raid on Tokyo. The new command's directive was to organize, train, equip and educate Air Force special operations forces. AFSOC is the air component of the unified US Special Operations Command. The 720th Special Tactics Group, with its headquarters at Hurlburt Field, has units in the US, Europe and the Pacific. The group has special operations combat control teams and para-rescue forces. AFSOC missions include air traffic control for establishing air-assault landing zones; close air support for strike aircraft and AC-130 'Spectre' gunship missions; establishing casualty collection stations; and providing trauma care for injured personnel.

The 16th Special Operations Wing at Hurlburt Field and Eglin AFB, Florida, is the oldest and most seasoned unit in AFSOC. It has no less than six special operations squadrons, three of which operate MC-130E 'Combat Talon P and MC-130P (formerly HC-130N/P) 'Combat Shadow' tankers: the 8th SOS (MC-130E), the 9th SOS (11 MC-130P tankers at Eglin) and the 15th SOS (MC-130H 'Combat Talon IP) - while the 4th SOS and 16th SOS operate AC-130H/U gunships and the 19th SOS operates AC-130s for training . The 7th SOS and the 67th SOS in the 352nd SOG at RAF Mildenhall, Suffolk, operate MC-130H and MC-130P tankers, respectively (alongside the 21st SOS, equipped with the MH-53J 'Pave Low'). In Japan, at Kadena AB, Okinawa, the 1st SOS and the 17th SOS in the 353rd SOG operate MC-130H and five MC-130P tanker aircraft, respectively.

The AC-130' wrote one 'Spectre' pilot 'has been developed as a highly sophisticated side-firing weapons platform, designed to orbit a target, firing downward on to it, the idea being that the ordnance

AC-130A *Azreal Angel of Death* Spectre gunship (Azrael in the Koran is the angel of death who severs the soul from the body). The crew of this AC-130A displayed courage and heroism during the closing hours of Operation 'Desert Storm'. On 26 February 1991, Coalition ground forces were driving the Iraqi army out of Kuwait. *Azrael* was sent to the Al Jahra highway between Kuwait City and Basrah, Iraq, to intercept the convoys of tanks, trucks, buses and cars fleeing the battle. Facing numerous enemy batteries of SA-6 and SA-8 surface-to-air missiles and 37mm and 57mm radar-guided anti-aircraft artillery, the crew inflicted significant damage on the convoys which left much of the enemy's equipment destroyed or unserviceable, contributing to the defeat of the Iraqi forces. The aircraft was assigned to the 919th Special Operations Wing and was retired to the National Museum of the Air Force at Dayton, Ohio in October 1995.

Head on view taken in March 1981 of AC-130H Spectre 69-6569 *Excalibur, Fatal Attraction* flown by the 4th SOS near Hurlburt Field, Florida. The AC-130H has a 40 mm L/60 Bofors cannon and a 105 mm M102 howitzer (USAF T/Sgt. Lee Schading)

hits the centre of the circle, the target and to complete its tasks the AC-130H is fitted with an impressive array of weaponry and sensors. These include two 20mm rotary 'Gatling' guns, each capable of delivering 2,500 rounds per minute (which can be geared down to 2,000 rounds per minute) and primarily used for' soft' targets. A single 40mm Bofors gun is also fitted, firing 100 rounds per minute and is used against targets such as vehicles. The most potent weapon on board is a single 105mm Army howitzer capable of dispatching between six and nine rounds per minute and this is used to strike 'hard' targets such as buildings. These guns are all fitted on trainable hydraulic mounts and 'tied in' to the ship's sensors.

'This 'trainable mode' allows us to attack targets in close proximity, without the pilot having to adjust the aircraft's position, but we are also able to operate them in a 'fixed mode', which allows the pilot to acquire the target visually in an F-16 style HUD which is fitted to the left-hand window of his cockpit. The gun crews strive for a particular proficiency with their hand-loaded 105mms: they aim to have a shell in the breech, one on the way down and one hitting the target at any given time -

'driving nails', in gunship parlance. Because the howitzer points downward, the shell cases have to be specially crimped to stop them sliding down the barrel. Like the 105mm, which uses single rounds, the 40mm is also hand-loaded using four-round clips and such is the appetite of the 20mm guns that one of the most important pieces of equipment aboard the Spectre is a 'snow shovel' to keep the spent cases from jamming up the breeches!

'The 'brains' of the Spectre is the fire control system. It has two INS's, two fire control computers and a GPS and these are tied into the Total Sensor Suite. This allows us to accurately navigate into an area and deliver our firepower (FCO, pronounced 'Foco'). Two gunners normally man the 20mms in the back and a third serves as a 'right scanner' sitting just forward of 'the booth', which is gunship slang for the sensor suite compartment. Inside 'the booth' is the infrared operator, a dedicated electronic warfare officer (EWO) and the LLLTV operator. In the aft cargo compartment are two more gunners who man the 40 and 105mm 'big guns' and finally, with his 'bubble' at the rear, is the loadmaster, whose duties in a combat situation include looking outside and below the aircraft for any threats.

MC-130P-66-0215, the last MC-130P to depart RAF Mildenhall to the 9th SOS.

'Before any combat mission there is an intensive briefing, where we look in as much detail as we can at our intended target or area of operations. The EWO is the recognised expert on all of the types of threat we could expect and he will, together with the navigator, plot our best route. We take an Intel update and during our tasking evaluation we try to get a tight set of co-ordinates for our target so that we can be on station in the minimum time possible. We are performance-limited because we carry a lot of high-drag devices, either sticking out or hung under the wings, all of which make it heavier and more difficult to fly than a 'slick' C-130. Also we must be the only attack aircraft in the world that goes into combat without ejector seats! However, we do have on board our own parachutes and we all wear a parachute harness, lifejacket, survival vest and flying helmets, with NVG attachments. The gunners wear Kevlar helmets that offer greater protection against blast problems.

'Once airborne, we need to do a sensor alignment, so we orbit the field at a nominal altitude, say 6,000 feet, picking a single point on the ground and tracking it with the visual sensors. We carry two basic types of sensor, 'visual' and 'electronic'. On the 'visual' side is the AN/AAD-7 FLIR, which is housed in a ball turret beneath the undercarriage bay. This gives a 360-degree view and is primarily used to locate targets en route and we are able to slave it to the INS to get a really tight position. Once we have found the target and established our orbit, we switch to our other visual sensor, the AN/ASQ-145V low light level television (LLLTV), which is mounted on an AN/AJQ-24 stabilized tracking set and fitted with an AN/AVQ-19 laser target designator and rangefinder. This equipment is located in the crew entrance door.' The electronic' sensors comprise an AN/APQ150 beacon tracking sensor, which is

AC-130H 69-6577 Spectre *Death Angel*, which was built in 1969 as a C-130E and was modified to AC-130E standard and to AC-130H in 1973.

AC-130H 69-6573 *Heavy Metal* in the 16th SOW, US Special Operations Command at Cannon AFB, New Mexico. On 13 May 1972 this gunship (see page 86) was hit by a SA-7 in the tail just above the ramp on the port side and fragments punched large holes on the starboard side. Ken Felty was injured in this missile strike and the aircraft landed safely. The aircraft was in combat for the Easter Offensive in Viêtnam and was repaired. During the twenty-year corrosion inspection the beer can patches from the ramp cargo compartment were removed!

essentially a SLAB (sideways-looking airborne radar) that searches for and acquires radar beacons from friendly forces. Once located, the signal from the beacon allows us to accurately fly to its location. It is also able to transmit data to us, updating our target information. Second is the AN/ASD-5 'Black Crow' sensor, which can be tuned to frequencies such as those transmitted by truck ignition systems. Also fitted is an AN/APN-59B search radar system (AGMTIP) in the nose, complete with moving target indicator (MTI) and external illumination is provided by a 2kW AN/AVQ-17 searchlight mounted in the aft cargo area and this is capable of 'normal' or infra-red operation. For self-defence we carry AN/ALE-20 chaff and flare dispensers fitted to the aft sections of the wheel bays and wing-mounted SUU/42A pods which can each fire chaff and flares. Additionally we can carry externally hung AN/ALQ-87 ECM pods if necessary.

'The 'Foco' then aligns all of the ship's sensors to that point. He also checks that the pilot's HUD is correct for AGL, airspeed and bank angle. Our next move is to 'tweak' the guns, which is a check to ensure the round will impact where the sensors are looking. What we do is find a remote place and then fire off a flare, to give us a fixed position to work with. A 'tweak' is one burst from each gun at 120-degree intervals, shooting three bursts from each gun in one orbit. On approach to the target area, we go to NVGs as the FLIR operator keeps a firm look-out to try and get an early target ID. Crew

co-operation is a big part of Spectre operations and primary conversations are on two separate networks, plus the main interphone to which everyone has access.

'About eight miles from the target we switch from 'En-Route Guidance' to 'Orbit Guidance', which will give us a tangent to the target as we roll in for our left-handed orbit around the area, using the attack mode segment of our orbit guidance system: this gives us a 'circle' of flight and shows us left or right, fore or aft of the target. Once those are centred up and we are close to the nominal bank angle for the orbit, I look through the HUD and get a 'diamond' superimposed over the target, which has now been acquired by the LLLTV operator, slewing his sensor around by using a 'thumbwheel' on his control panel. He 'sparkles' the target with laser energy, allowing us to get an accurate track and that allows the fire control computer to calculate the exact range. With all of the sensors now looking at the same point on the ground, the guns are set to 'trainable mode' and these come up on their hydraulic mounts. The sensor operator then keeps the target firmly fixed in the cross-hairs on his TV screen.

'The 'Foco' now works in concert with the two sensor operators, known simply as 'IR' or 'TV; and he will have predetermined with them what he wants to look for. The 'Foco' then 'calls' the target once he is sure and has already planned to use our No.6 gun (the 105mm). I call 'Pilot in the HUD, arm the gun!' The 'Foco' will have the No.6 gun

KC-130Ts of VMGR-152 refuelling F-18Cs of VFA-97 in 2006.

selected on his panel, so he flips all his switches and sets the correct ballistics into the computer. In conjunction with the navigator he again confirms the target and the flight engineer sets the master arm to 'Live'. In my HUD I get a CCIP (Constantly Computed Impact Point) and I have to keep that CCIP in the trainable box, which ensures that the target remains in the gun's correctable parameters, so even in high winds I can still adjust the orbit to enable us to fire all the way.

'When ready to shoot, I squeeze the trigger and in 'trainable mode' this is the last electronic link to the sensor operator. When I have my finger on the trigger and all the constraints are met, he gets a 'Ready to fire' light on his panel. He pushes a button, which is a momentary consent switch and this passes the firing pulse to the guns, with the computer constantly checking the rate and coincidence. As soon as the round is out, I come off the trigger and the gunners 'sling out the brass' and reload. They close the breech and call 'Gun ready'. I squeeze the trigger again. Meanwhile the sensor operators are looking at where the first round hits and making any adjustments for the next shell. When the 105 goes off it gives a pretty good jolt to the ship, but probably worse is a continuous burst from the 20 mils. This leaves a lot of smoke floating around, even in the cockpit, but as we have so many open spaces on board it soon dissipates!'[1]

AFSOC has seven SOS squadrons operating MC-130E, MC-130H and MC-130P tankers. AETC (Air Education and Training Command, activated

1 July 1993) and AFRes operate MC-130E, MC-130H and MC-130P Hercules. AETC has one SOS squadron -the 550th SOS/58th SQW (19th Air Force), at Kirtland AFB, New Mexico, which operates MC-130H and MC-130Ps and is also the operational base for 'Combat Talon II' training.

The AFRes (activated on 17 February 1997) has two SOS squadrons: the 5th SOS/919th SOW, with MC-130P tankers and the 711th SOS/919th SOW with MC-130E-Y 'Combat Talon P' and C-130E. Both units are based at Duke Field, Eglin AFB, Florida and come under AFSOC command when the organizations are mobilized, as does ANG's 193rd SOS/193rd SOW and its EC-130E 'Coronet Solo' aircraft at Harrisburg IAP, Pennsylvania: still the only weapon system within the USAF whose mission is to support Psychological Operations (PYSOP) with airborne broadcasting.

Fourteen C-130Es were modified to MC-130E 'Combat Talon I' configuration and equipped for use in low-level, deep-penetration tactical missions by the 1st and 8th Special Operations Squadrons based respectively in the Pacific and North America. ('Combat Talons' led the raid on the Son Tay prison camp, 20 miles northwest of Hànôi on 21 November 1970.) Deliveries of 24 MC-130H 'Combat Talon' IF aircraft (the first of which flew in 1988), began in mid-1991. They are fitted with an in-flight refuelling receptacle, have explosion-suppressive fuel tanks, a modified cargo ramp area for the high-speed, low-level aerial delivery system, Emerson Electric AN/APQ-170 precision terrain-following and terrain-avoidance radar, dual radar altimeters, dual INS and finally provision for a GPS receiver. Twenty-eight MC-130P 'Combat Shadow'/tanker aircraft are in service with AFSOC for single-ship or formation in-flight refuelling of its 'Pave Low' special operations' helicopters working in a no- to low-threat environment.

AC-130 gunships used by the Command have evolved since November 1965 when the 4th Air Commando Squadron in Việtnam became the first operational unit to use AC-47 gunships. Call-sign 'Spooky' AC-47s and those of the 14th ACS demonstrated such highly effective convoy escort and armed reconnaissance over the Hồ Chi Minh Trail that the US forces looked to another converted transport for its next generation, fixed-wing gunship. At the Wright-Patterson AFB, the Aeronautical Systems Division tested a Convair C-131B transport fitted with a 7.62mm General Electric SUU-11A minigun, while at Eglin AFB, Florida, experiments were conducted with a C-130 and a C-47. AC-47s flew their first sortie on 15 December 1964 - *'Puff the Magic Dragon'* was retired from the Special Operations Squadrons in 1969.

On 6 June 1967 the 4950th Test Wing had begun flight-testing a JC-130A (54-1626) modified by Aeronautical Systems Division, Air Force System Command at Wright-Patterson AFB, Ohio to 'Gunship II'/'Plain Jane' configuration. 54-1626 was fitted with four port-side-firing General Electric MXU-470 7.62mm GAU-2 miniguns and four port-side-firing General Electric M-61 20mm Vulcan cannon, to fire obliquely downward. *Vulcan Express*, as the AC-130A Gunship II was named, was equipped also with the 'Starlight Image-Intensifying Night-Observation Scope', AN/AAD-4 SLIR side-looking radar, computerized NASARR F-1551 fire-control system (adapted from the F-104 Starfighter), beacon tracker, DF homing instrumentation, FM radio transceiver and an inert tank system, while a semi-automatic flare dispenser and a steerable 1.5 million candlepower AN/AVQ-8 searchlight containing two Xenon arc lights (infra-red and ultra-violet), were mounted on the aft ramp.

Vulcan Express was despatched to the 711th SOS at Nha Trang, South Việtnam in September 1967 for combat evaluation. As might be expected, the complexity of its sophisticated equipment was responsible for many scrubbed missions, but nevertheless, it acquitted itself well between 24 September and December 1967. The aircraft was later refurbished in the US and was then sent to Ubon RTAFB (Royal Thai Air Force Base) in February 1968 for additional evaluation along the Hồ Chi Minh Trail until early June that year. In mid-June it was transferred to Tân Sơn Nhất near Saïgon, where it took part in operations in the so-called 'in-country' war against Việt Công insurgents.

An AC-130H gunship from the 16th Special Operations Squadron, Hurlburt Field, Florida, jettisons flares as an infrared countermeasure during multi-gunship formation egress training on 24 August 2007. (USAF photo/Senior Airman Julianne Showalter).

It returned to the US in November 1968.[2]

Meanwhile 'Project Gunboat', as it was code-named, went so well that the Pentagon awarded a contract to LTV Electrosystems of Greenville, Texas, for the modification of seven more JC-130As to AC-130A configuration. Delivered from August to December 1968, they differed from the prototype in being fitted with improved systems, including the AN/AAD-4 SLIR (side-looking infra-red) and AN/APQ-136 moving target indicator (MTI) sensors and AN/AWG-13 analogue computer.

53-3129, the first production C-130A made its maiden flight at Marietta, Georgia on 7 April 1955. Its career was almost cut short on 14 May 1955 when a fuel leak resulted in half the port wing being burned off during its third flight, but the aircraft was repaired and flew again in February 1956. In September 1957 53-3129 was modified as a JC-130A and completed tours of duty at the Cambridge Air Research Center, the Air Force Research Center, the Air Force Missile Center and Temco Division at Major Field in Texas. In December 1961

53-3129 was attached to the 6550th Support Wing (Range). On 31 October 1968 the 16th SOS based at Ubon - call-sign 'Spectre' - was activated and the aircraft became its inaugural AC-130A gunship. Christened *The First Lady* in November 1970 she was first used for night interdiction and armed reconnaissance missions during 'Barrel Roll' operations in Laos. Ubon became the home of the AC-130 gunships for the rest of the war, being used to mount operations in Cambodia until shortly before the ceasefire came into effect on 15 August 1973.

From Ubon *The First Lady* and her heir-apparents were used at night, mainly on 'out-country' operations in South-east Asia and in particular on the Hô Chi Minh Trail, on 'Commando Hunt' interdiction missions. *The First Lady* was hit in March 1971 by a 37mm shell. Again she was repaired and she went on to serve the 415th SOTS and, from November 1976 to 1994, the 711th Special Operations Squadron. *The First Lady* was almost certainly the oldest aircraft to take part in Operation 'Desert Storm' in 1991. She was

AC-130U 89-0509 *Total Carnage*. AC-130U Spooky gunship's primary missions are close air support, air interdiction and armed reconnaissance. Other missions include perimeter and point defence, escort, landing, drop and extraction zone support, forward air control, limited command and control, and combat search and rescue. The U-model gunship incorporates the latest sensor technology, along with an entirely new fire-control system, to substantially increase the gunship's combat effectiveness. The fire control system offers a dual-target attack capability, whereby two targets up to one kilometer apart can be simultaneously engaged by two different sensors, using two different guns. All light-level television, infrared sensors and the Hughes APQ-180 radar (also found on the F-15E Strike Eagle) provide night and adverse weather capability. To enhance survivability, emphasis has been placed on increasing the stand-off range of the gunship's weapons system and improving first-shot accuracy. In addition, a set of ECM has been installed to help defend the AC-130U against modern threats.

presented to the USAF Armament Museum at Eglin AFB in November 1995.

The other six AC-130A gunships of the 16th SOS also had colourful careers. From January to March 1969 three were used in South-east Asia and on average destroyed 2.7 enemy vehicles per sortie. Mainly up to twelve crew were carried, including three to five gunners. 54-1623 became better known as Ghost Rider and was retired in April 1997 to Dobbins AFB, Georgia before eventually being put on display at the Lockheed Museum at Marietta, Georgia.

In the early hours of 22 April 1970 54-1625 *War Lord* (call sign 'Adlib 1') in the 8th TFW captained by Major William Leslie Brooks took off from Ubon on a 'Commando Hunt' mission over the Hồ Chi Minh Trail in southern Laos and was later joined by two fighters to form a truck hunter-killer team. 'Adlib 1' started work over Route 96A about 25 miles east of the town of Saravan. As the attack proceeded the AC-130 was hit by 37mm AAA and the port wing caught fire near the wing root. Some of the eleven man crew attempted to fight the blaze but the fire was too intense. Staff Sergeant Eugene Fields groped his way forward through darkness and smoke but found the gunner's position vacant and a hatch open. Fields strapped on a parachute and abandoned the aircraft. 'Killer 2', one of the accompanying fighters, made voice contact with one of the crew who identified himself as 'Adlib 12', which was Major Donald Garth Fisher's call sign. Fields had suffered burns on his face and hands and his parachute snagged on a tree. He eventually climbed down and hid until morning when he was rescued by a SAR task force. He was the only survivor.[3]

54-1627 *Gomer Grimier* went on to serve the 415th SOTS and the 711th SOS before retirement in 1976; while 54-1628 *The Exterminator*, finished its career in 1994 with the 711th SOS. On 24 May 1969 AC-130A 54-1629 in the 8th TFW, which had been the first C-130 with rear-opening nose-gear doors, was on a night armed reconnaissance mission over southern Laos checking Routes 914 and 920 for truck traffic and was hit when the aircraft was about to attack a truck convoy on a road near the village of Ban Tanbok about twenty miles southwest of the A Shau Valley. It took two rounds of 37mm AAA in the tail and fuselage as it orbited at 6,500 feet. The hydraulic system failed and the

aircraft started climbing uncontrollably until the pilot and co-pilot wrestled the control columns to full forward and brought all the crewmembers to the flight deck to make the aircraft nose-heavy. It was then discovered that the elevator trim, rudder control and autopilot were no longer functioning but Lieutenant Colonel William H. Schwehm and Major Gerald H. Piehl regained partial control by the use of aileron trim and differential engine power. Staff Sergeant Jack Wayne Troglen the illuminator operator had been mortally wounded and died before the aircraft landed. Lieutenant Colonel Schwehm and Major Piehl nursed the damaged aircraft back to Ubon and ordered most of the crew to bail out near the airfield before attempting a landing. As the aircraft touched down the starboard undercarriage collapsed and the AC-130 veered off the runway shearing off the starboard wing when it hit the barrier cable housing causing the aircraft to catch fire. Staff Sergeant Cecil Taylor, the flight engineer, was unable to escape and died in the incident. This was the first AC-130 gunship to be lost during the Việtnam War.[4]

54-1630, which went by the equally colourful name of *Mors de Coelis* was later re-named *Azrael* (for the angel of death in Islam who severs the soul from the body) and figured prominently in the closing hours of Operation 'Desert Storm'. On 26 February 1991 Coalition ground forces were driving the Iraqi Army out of Kuwait. With an Air Force Reserve crew called to active duty, *Azrael* was sent to the Al Jahra highway (Highway 80) between Kuwait City and Basra, Iraq, to intercept the convoys of tanks, trucks, buses and cars fleeing the battle. Facing SA-6 and SA-8 surface-to-air missiles and 37 mm and 57 mm radar-guided anti-aircraft artillery the crew attacked and destroyed or disabled most of the convoys. *Azrael* was retired to the Cold War Gallery at the United States Air Force at Wright-Patterson AFB, Ohio in October 1995.

Used in the fighting in South-east Asia, the AC-130As proved very effective, especially against vehicles along the Hồ Chi Minh Trail at night. Operations continued until the summer of 1970, by which time it was clear that aircraft with improved all-weather operation and larger-calibre guns were needed. The surviving AC-130As were therefore withdrawn for refurbishment and a C-130A (55-0011) was modified to 'Pave Pronto' configuration under the 'Super Chicken' or 'Surprise Package'

176

The AC-130U 'Spooky II' has a General Dynamics 25 mm GAU-12/U Equalizer 5-barreled Gatling cannon (capable of firing 1,800 rounds per minute); a single-barrel, rapid-fire 40 mm L/60 Bofors cannon and a 105 mm M102 howitzer.

AC-130U aerial gunners of the 4th Special Operations Squadron conduct a live-fire mission in an AC-130U Gunship during 'Emerald Warrior' at Hurlburt Field, Florida in May 2016. 'Emerald Warrior' is the Department of Defense's only irregular warfare exercise, allowing joint and combined partners to train together and prepare for real world contingency operations.

programme to meet the requirement for improved all-weather capability. It was armed with two 20mm M-61 Vulcan cannon and two 7.62mm miniguns forward and two M-l Bofors clip-fed 40mm cannon aft of the wheel fairing. Uprated avionics included AN/ASD-5 'Black Crow' truck ignition sensor, Motorola AN/APQ-133 beacon-tracking radar, an AN/AVQ-18 laser designator/rangefinder and AN/ASQ-24A stabilized tracking set containing ASQ-145 LLLTV (low-light-level television). Tests were conducted in October 1969 and in November, 55-0011, better known as Night Stalker, was despatched to South-east Asia. (The aircraft remained on the active USAF inventory until 1995). 'Surprise Package' lived up to its name, with expectations proving higher than anticipated and subsequently nine more C-130As were modified to the AC-130A 'Pave Pronto' configuration, with AN/ASQ-24A stabilized tracking set, AN/AVQ-18 laser designator and bomb-damage assessment camera, SUU-42 flare ejection pods, dual AN/ALQ-87 ECM pods under the wings and some other improvements. The AN/ASD-5 'Black Crow' truck ignition sensor which was not originally included was reinstated.

In Southeast Asia the 'Pave Pronto' AC-130As of the 16th SOS wreaked havoc among enemy convoys at night and used their AN/AVQ-18 laser designator/rangefinder to mark targets for F-4D Phantoms carrying laser-guided bombs (LGBs). In December 1971 55-0044 Prometheus was damaged by a 37mm shell and lost Nos. 3 and 4 propellers, but survived, only to be shot down south-east of Tchepone, Laos on 28 March 1972. It set off with a fourteen man crew captained by Major Irving Burns Ramsower from Ubon on a truck hunting mission over the Hồ Chi Minh Trail in southern Laos. As the aircraft approached the town of Muang Phine, about 35 miles west of Khê Sanh. It was seen to be hit by an SA-2 missile fired from one of the newly-established SAM sites in Laos. The aircraft burst into flames, crashed and exploded. No parachutes were seen but an emergency beeper signal was picked up briefly. A SAR task force found no sign of any survivors although the search of the area was limited due to intense ground fire. The Pathet Lao ('Lao Nation') subsequently issued a news release claiming that they had shot down the aircraft.

The first half of May 1972 brought continuing heavy application of air-power, as the North Viêtnamese forces pressed toward Kontum. Numerous pitched battles took place in nearby villages, camps and fire support bases. One such engagement occurred at the compound of Polei Kleng (also known as Camp Le Vanh, Firebase Base, Landing Zone Base) Special Forces Camp about fifteen miles west of Kontum.[5] An AC-130 Spectre was already airborne in the highlands region, learning by radio that Polei Kleng was under attack by a Communist regiment with tanks. The situation was so serious that American personnel had already been evacuated. The AC-130 crew talked directly with the South Viêtnamese commander on the ground and placed fire all around the embattled post. The gunship expended a full load of ammunition, including 96 rounds of 105mm fire, aiming at enemy muzzle flashes and a bridge. The aircrew's mission report noted, 'Situation quiet upon departure.' Later reports revealed that Spectre 03, assisted by fighter-bombers, had killed over 350 enemy troops, destroyed the bridge and repulsed a full-scale attack by a North Viêtnamese regiment.

The emergency at An Lôc dictated diversion of the gunship effort away from the trails. On 15 April six AC-119 Stingers moved from Nakhon Phanom, one of the north-eastern provinces of Thailand, to Biên Hỏa, establishing a forward operating location for support of the battle at An Lôc. The AC-130s also shifted effort to An Lôc, but continued to operate from Ubon, landing once or twice at Tân Sơn Nhât during each mission day to replenish fuel and ammunition. The arrangement greatly lengthened a crew's time over target at An Lôc. Sometimes, crews remained on duty 24 hours or more without rest, fighting fatigue but appreciating the urgency of the situation on the ground. At least one gunship remained on station over An Lôc around-the-clock. Besides an important night detection and strike capability, the gunships could deliver ordnance far more accurately than the fighter-bombers.

The earliest AC-130 missions over Lôc Ninh and An Lôc were disappointing. FAC's were generally inclined to give priority to fighter-bombers and often held off gunships from targets to permit strikes by the jets. Lieutenant Colonel George F. Hall, a 'Pave Aegis' Fire Control Officer described his crew's disappointment on their first mission to An Lôc. 'Over the city the crew received a target assignment, an old French mansion south of the town. Confident in the precision of their 105, the crew promised to hit a particular upstairs window to the disbelief of the ground party and the FAC's. Rolling in for the first attack, the crew was instead told to pull off to make way for an F-4 strike. Again and again, the gunship crew prepared to fire, only to be called off.'

After two hours. Hall and his disgusted crew headed back for Ubon, having fired not a single shot. Hall's combat tour was interrupted by two weeks of emergency' leave. Afterwards he returned to An Lôc with his now-veteran crewmates. Hall quickly realized that in the interval, the men on the ground at An Lôc had learned something of the effectiveness of the AC-130. No longer were there delays in applying the Spectre's firepower. From a bunker in the rubble, an American voice asked for a single 40mm round at an easily-seen fountain; verifying the burst, the voice next called for a second round at an intersection two blocks east. Finally, the voice prescribed a particular house and corner. Hall's crew thereupon destroyed the building with 20mm, 40mm and 105mm fire. The crew expressed concern during the firing, after learning that friendly forces were directly across the street. The voice below assured them that all was going well, excitedly calling for the crew to 'keep it coming.'

Lieutenant Colonel Stephen Opitz related how his crew pinpointed the enemy on one night mission over An Lôc. The AC-130 pilot called for the friendlies on the ground to identify their position with green flares. Green flares promptly appeared from several quadrants of An Loc, indicating the enemy was listening in. The pilot then called for red flares. After several red flares appeared, the American controller on the ground called out: 'I've got no red flares, hit 'em all.' Opitz and crew complied, using 20mm with effect.

Vital for the successful employment of the gunships were the several US Army advisors on the ground at An Lôc, who day after day directed the AC-119 Stingers and AC-130 Spectres to targets by voice radio. Crewmen learned the voice of 'Zippo' Smith at Lôc Ninh and invited him to attend one of the monthly parties at Ubon. All were relieved by the news that Smith had successfully exfiltrated after the fall of Lôc Ninh. AC-130 crewmen lavishly praised one Army Colonel at An Lôc who

stayed on the air for weeks and seemed especially skilled in directing the gunships to rewarding targets. The use of street and house directions for precision attacks became standard procedure, in nearly all cases either killing the enemy troops or forcing them from cover. AC-130 crewmen arriving at An Lôc knew to expect to be asked whether or not they carried the 105 cannon - the 'big gun.' Since the 105 mm could penetrate and stop tanks, those gunship crews with only the 40mm weapon were often frustrated by their ineffectiveness against enemy armour. Opitz on one occasion watched as his ship's fire splashed against and exploded on the sides of a Communist T-54. The enemy tank moved steadily closer to the friendly position, the ears of its crewmen no doubt ringing but otherwise unharmed. Finally, the friendly radio transmission ended, indicating that the position had been smashed and overrun. With heavy hearts, Opitz and his drained crewmates returned to base.

On 18 June the first AC-130 ever downed in South Viêtnam - AC-130A 55-0043 Spectre II - was shot down in the A Shau Valley, a Communist infiltration route south-west of Huê, by a Strela SA-7A heat-seeking, surface-to-air missile. Two AC-130 gunships had been lost over Laos in March to SA-2 SAMs and one had been hit by an SA-7 but not downed over An Lôc in Military Region III to the south. SA-7s brought down several A-1 Skyraiders and FAC aircraft in the Northern provinces during April and May. Spectre II was operating southwest of Huê at an altitude that should have protected it from the Strela. The target was in mountainous terrain - in a valley with hills around it that reached up to 3,500. The SA-7 was fired from the side of one of the hills. Sergeant William B. Patterson had the job of watching for missiles and AAA fire. He lay on the aft cargo door, actually hanging out into the airstream so he could get a good field of view below the aircraft. It was dark and Patterson spotted the tell-tale flash of light when the missile was fired. It arched up toward the aircraft in a smooth curving trajectory, the motor burning with an eerie blue-white light, holding straight to its course, not porpoising back and forth the way SA-7s usually did. When the missile was 2-3 seconds away, the crew fired a decoy flare, but the SA-7 kept boring right in, hitting the right inboard engine. There was a loud explosion and a flash of fire as the missile struck. The aircraft shuddered, rose up at the nose slightly and then settled down; the #3 engine separated from the wing. The flight engineer called on intercom that they were losing altitude, the pilots worked to pull her up. Someone else was calling out on the UHF radio that Spectre II had been hit by a missile.

Patterson rolled back into the aircraft, unhooked the restraining strap which kept him from falling out and reached for his chest-pack parachute. At about that time, the right wing came off and the aircraft started into a cartwheeling roll. Patterson managed to hook only one side of his parachute to his body harness, in his haste attaching it backwards, when fresh explosions blew him into the blackness outside. Fortunately, Patterson was an experienced chutist, with a hobby of skydiving. The sergeant lived to tell how he somehow found the rip-cord in the darkness and of his harrowing descent and landing - his chute still only half-connected. Three men of the fifteen aboard Spectre II that night survived. They were picked up from the A Shau Valley the next morning by the Air Force Jolly Greens.

Beginning in 1967 the C-130s of the 374th Tactical Airlift Wing flew twenty-eight 'Commando Lava' sorties into the A Shau Valley to air-drop 120 tons of defoliants so as to deny the NVA and VC

forces their entry corridor into South Viêtnam. 'Commando Lava' was dangerous work, because the C-130s had to drop down to 200 feet in order to release the chemical compound, thus heightening the risk of being knocked out of the sky by SAM missiles. Unfortunately the mud-making operations - first conceived by William H. Sullivan, the US ambassador to Laos - were no more of a hindrance to the Communists than the annual monsoon and they simply covered over the worst-affected parts of the route with gravel or bamboo matting.

Meanwhile in 1965 in a similar attempt, 'Banish Beach' missions were first flown by C-130s in an effort to deprive the Viêt Công of forest sanctuaries by starting forest fires with almost simultaneous drops of fuel drums. There were also 'Commando Scarf' bombing missions in which the C-130s carried small XM-41 anti-personnel mines; and in southern Laos, CDU-10 noisemakers were dropped by C-130s as part of the interdiction campaign.

AC-130A 56-0490 *Thor* of the 16th SOS, 56th SOW was shot down 25 miles north-east of Pakse, Laos on 21 December 1972 killing Captain Harry Roy Lagerwall and thirteen of his crew. The aircraft had found three trucks near Ban Laongam, 25 miles west of Saravan in southern Laos. It was firing at the target from an altitude of 7,800 feet when it was

AC-130U 90-0163 *Bad Omen* the first AC-130U Spooky gunship to retire from the active fleet flew from Hurlburt Field following a small ceremony on 21 September 2015 to the 309th Aerospace Maintenance and Regeneration Group at Davis-Monthan AFB.

hit by 37mm AAA. The aircraft may have been hit in a fuel tank as it exploded and crashed in flames. Two of the crew managed to bail out and were rescued by a 40th ARRS HH-53 some hours later, located by the night vision devices on board another AC-130 and the LNRS equipment on board the helicopter.[6]

55-0014 *Jaws of Death* survived, ending its career in 1995 and therefore being allocated to the Robins AFB museum in 1996. 55-0029 *Midnight Express* was retired in 1994, while 55-040 was retired in 1976. 55-046, better known perhaps as *Proud Warrior* and which in 1957 had been loaned to the USMC for in-flight refuelling tests, was retired in 1994. 56-0469 *Grim Reaper* also survived the horrors of Viêtnam and since 1995 has been used as a ground trainer at the 82nd TRW at Sheppard AFB, Texas. 56-0509 *Raids Kill Um Dead* was damaged at An Lôc South Viêtnam on 23 December 1972; however, it was repaired and later assigned to the 711th SOS. In 1995 and now named *Ultimate End,* this AC-130A finished its days at the Hurlburt Field Memorial Air Park.

Meanwhile in April 1970 the decision was taken to convert two C-130Es to AC-130E prototype gunships. The C-130E's higher gross weight, stronger airframe and increased power offered greater payload and longer loiter time than the original AC-130A gunships. As a result of experience gained in Viêtnam, more advanced avionics were fitted and what was known as 'Pave Aegis' armament configuration was created by installing a 105mm howitzer in place of one of the 40mm cannon in the port parachute door, while retaining the two 20mm cannon forward of the port undercarriage fairing. The howitzer was later attached to a trainable mounting controlled by AN/APQ-150 beacon-tracking radar.

In February 1971 nine more C-130E conversions not dissimilar to 'Pave Pronto' AC-130As were ordered. However, by the time that the first AC-130Es were completed in June and July 1971 they represented such a leap forward in avionics over the earlier 'Pave Pronto' gunships that they became known as 'Pave Spectre IV'. All eleven 'Pave Spectre' AC-130Es served in Southeast Asia, entering combat in the spring of 1972 when they helped repulse the Viêt Công offensive. AC-130Es

AC-130U sensor operator.

AC-130 gunship firing a broadside at dusk.

proved most effective tank killers during night operations and on night interdiction sorties along the notorious Hồ Chi Minh Trail. On 30 March 1972 AC-130E 69-6571 'Spectre 22' of the 16th SOS, 8th TFW at Ubon with a fifteen man crew was shot down near An Lôc, South Việtnam. 'Spectre 22' had spotted a convoy of trucks on the Trail 35 miles north of Muang Fangdeng in southern Laos. The aircraft destroyed three of the trucks and was about to fire again to make sure of the kill when it was hit by ground fire. The aircraft was flying at 195 knots and 7,500 feet when 57mm anti-aircraft shells hit its starboard wing and fuselage. The AC-130 caught fire when fuel leaking from the starboard pylon tank ignited. Captain Waylon O. Fulk headed northwest towards Thailand in the hope of reaching Ubon but he and Captain E. N. Bolling and the thirteen other crew were forced to abandon the aircraft which crashed about fifteen miles southeast of Saravan. An HC-130 soon arrived on the scene and took over as on-scene commander of what proved to be a massive and complex rescue mission.[7] Numerous aircraft including 'Nail' FACs and other Spectres conducted a radio and visual search throughout the night to locate the survivors in preparation for a pick-up

attempt at first light. It was discovered that two of the survivors had bailed out soon after the aircraft had been hit and were forty miles to the east of the main group of survivors. At first light in a well-coordinated operation four HH-53s from the 40th ARRS picked up thirteen men from the main group, one of whom had a broken leg. A few minutes later two Air America UH-34D helicopters protected by A-1 Skyraiders rescued the two other survivors from a well-defended area near the Trail to the east. Unfortunately, the successful rescue of the entire crew of Spectre 22 was overshadowed by the attempted rescue of 'Bat 21' that followed in the next few days.[8]

On 18 June an AC-130A was downed by a SA-7 shoulder fired SAM which struck the No.3 engine and blew off the wing. On 21/22 December AC-130A was downed while truck hunting along the Hồ Chi Minh Trail at 7,800 feet by 37mm AA. Although the 57-mm fire known in Laos was not as severe at An Lôc, the gunship crewmen detested equally the concentrations of 37-mm fire. The 37-mm had higher projectile velocity, which reduced the effectiveness of evasive action, while its greater rate of fire gave substantial weight in barrage. The SA-7 became the greatest concern for the gunship crews, although alertness, evasive action and the use of decoy flares held down the frequency of hits. Crews reported as many as six or seven SA-7 firings on certain missions. High threat sectors were identified and avoided when possible. One AC-130 was hit and severely damaged by a SAM on 12 May, after sighting four other launchings the same day. The crew barely managed an emergency landing at Tân Sơn Nhứt. The only sure defence against the SA-7 however, was in altitude. The higher altitudes meant some loss in AC-130 weapon effectiveness - the 20mm became almost useless because of loss of projectile velocity at this distance, while the accuracy of the 40- and 105-mm appeared only slightly affected.

In June 1973 all remaining AC-130Es were upgraded to AC-130H standard when they were re-engined with T56-A-15 turboprops. The AC-130H also differed from the AC-130E in having its 7.62 miniguns omitted. In 1978 AC-130H aircraft were retrofitted with an in-flight refuelling receptacle and other improvements. Each AC-130H/U is crewed by five officers: pilot, co-pilot, navigator, fire-control officer and electronic warfare officer - and nine enlisted men: flight engineer, low-light TV operator, infra red detection set operator, five aerial gunners and a load master.

In July 1987 Rockwell was awarded a contract to cover the research and development of a new AC-130U Spectre gunship to replace the Special Operation Squadrons' ageing AC-130A. Thirteen new C-130H airframes fire-control radar, derived from the APQ-70 carried by the F-15E Strike Eagle, AN/AAQ-117 forward-looking infra-red (FLIR) mounted under the port side of the nose, or turret-mounted Bell Aerospace all-light-level TV (ALLTV) in the port main undercarriage sponson for true adverse weather ground-attack operations. The 'Black Crow' truck-ignition sensor and radome and separate beacon-tracking radar used on earlier gunships were omitted. Observer stations are included on the three under fuselage chaff and flare dispensers (Capable of dispensing 300 chaff bundles and either 90 MJU7 or 180 M206 1R decoy flares), Texas Instruments AN/AAQ-117 FLIR countermeasures and ITT Avionics AN/ALQ-172 jammer, are all fitted to increase survivability in a low-to-medium-threat environment. Delivery to the 16th SOW began in 1994, at which time the eighteen AC-130Hs were transferred to the AFRes 919th SOW at Duke Field, Florida whose AC-130As were retired. The AC-130Us or 'U-boats' as they are affectionately known by crews provide other special operations' roles, including escort, surveillance and reconnaissance/interdiction in addition to the primary precision fire support

AC-130H 69-6573 *Heavy Metal* gunship is directed to a parking spot on the ramp in February 1995. US forces are bringing in personnel, materiel and equipment to support Operation 'United Shield', which is the withdrawal of United Nations peacekeepers from Mogadishu, Somalia. Thirty-two AC-130J 'Ghostrider' aircraft based on the MC-130J; 32 aircraft are being procured to replace the AC-130H. [USAF photo by A1C Randy S. Mallard]

AC-130U 89-0514 *Maximum Carnage*.

mission. All eighteen AC-130Us are operated by the 4th SOS, 16th SOW, at Hurlburt Field, Florida.

In 1990 the Air Force Reserve's 711th SOS deployed some AC-130As to Turkey for Operation 'Proven Force', the 'second front' for the coming war with Iraq. On 7 January 1991 the joint task force (JTF) was activated at Ramstein AB, Germany and one of its components, the Special Operations Task Force, was to seek and rescue downed Allied pilots. On 17 January three EC-130s from the 43rd ECS, 66th ECW, at Sebach AB, Germany were among the European units that deployed to Incirlik AB, Turkey. Eight AC-130 gunships meanwhile and six MC-130E 'Combat Talon Is' were deployed to Saudi Arabia for

Operation 'Desert Storm' missions in the Gulf War, which began on 16 January. (While defending a USMC force under attack by Iraqi forces on 31 January, AC-130H 69-6567 call-sign 'Spirit 03' in the 16th SOS was shot down (probably by a hand-held SAM) 68 miles south-south-east of Kuwait City with the loss of all fourteen crew).

'Combat Talon Is' of the 8th SOS delivered the 15,000lb BLU-82/B 'Big Blue' fuel-air explosive bomb, the largest and heaviest conventional bomb in the USAF inventory. (One of the largest conventional weapons ever to be used the BLU-82B was outweighed only by a few earthquake bombs, thermobaric bombs and demolition (bunker buster) bombs. (Some of these include the 'Grand

MC-130 82-04272 Fulton 7th SOS conducting training for special air operations and related activities.

Slam' and T12 earthquake bombs of late WWII and more currently, the Soviet Air Force FOAB and USAF GBU-43/B Massive Ordnance Air Blast bomb and the Massive Ordnance Penetrator). On 15 February 'Combat Talons' began dropping BLU-82 'daisy-cutters' (as they were nicknamed in Việtnam) on Iraqi minefields as a prelude to the ground offensive. The 'Big Blues' were also used by MC-130Es of Special Operations Command against Iraqi troop concentrations with devastating effect. Eleven BLU-82Bs were palletized and dropped in five night missions during the 1991 Gulf War, all from Special Operations MC-130 Combat Talons. The initial drop tested the ability of the bomb to clear or breach minefields; however, no reliable assessments of mine clearing effectiveness are publicly available. Later, bombs were dropped as much for their psychological effect as for their anti-personnel effects.[9]

'Bombs' containing 16,000,000 leaflets were also dropped by 'Combat Talon' and HC-130N/P aircraft, with messages telling Iraqi soldiers how to surrender to the ground forces; other 'PSYOP' missions dropped leaflets telling Iraqis that more BLU-82s were on the way. EC-130Es helped to psychologically prepare the battlefield for 'Desert Storm', the 193rd SOW being one of the first special operations' units to be sent to the Gulf region. On 22 November the unit began 'PSYOP' operations, broadcasting the 'Voice of America' into Iraq, Kuwait and Saudi Arabia. A crash modifications programme, lasting several weeks, upgraded the EC-130Es so that the 'Commando Solo' aircraft could broadcast in the local TV format for this region. The 193rd SOG's leaflet drops and broadcast readings from the Koran and testimonials from Iraqi prisoners were instrumental in persuading Iraqi troops to surrender. When surveyed, Iraqi PoWs indicated that PSYOP radio broadcasts reached 58 per cent of the military target audience; of those, 46 per cent indicated that the broadcasts had an influence on their decision to surrender.

In June and July 1993 Somalia pushed the war in Bosnia off the world's front pages as American air units fought to prevent General Mohamed

Captain Thomas Bernard, a 36th Airlift Squadron Hercules pilot performing a visual confirmation with night vision goggles during a training mission over Kanto Plain, Japan, 14 October 2015. Yokota Air Base aircrews regularly conduct night flying operations to ensure they are prepared to respond to a variety of contingencies throughout the Indo-Asia-Pacific region. (USAF photo/Osakabe Yasuo)

An MC-130E from the 711th Special Operations Squadron, 919th Special Operations Wing, drops the last operational BLU-82 (Bomb Live Unit bomb) at the Utah Test and Training Range on 15 July 2008. The BLU-82B/C-130 weapon system, known under programme 'Commando Vault' and nicknamed 'Daisy Cutter' in Vietnam and in Afghanistan is an American 15,000 lb conventional bomb, delivered from either a C-130 or an MC-130. The BLU-82 was retired in 2008 and replaced with the more powerful, 11-ton GBU-43/B or MOAB ('mother of all bombs'), which was first dropped on 13 April 2017, on an Islamic State stronghold in eastern Afghanistan, which killed 36 ISIS militants. It is the largest non-nuclear bomb ever used in combat.

Farrah Hassan Aidid and his supporters retaking control of Mogadishu. Aidid's fighters were blamed for the killing of twenty-three Pakistani UN peacekeepers on 5 June. AC-130H gunships and Cobra helicopters of a US Army quick-reaction force were used in day and night actions against Aidid and his supporters in Mogadishu. In a one-hour attack on 11/12 June the 'Spectre' gunships and Cobra helicopters destroyed Aidid's radio station as American soldiers led attacks on his command headquarters and weapons caches. 'Spectres' attacked ammunition dumps and garages housing 'technicals' close to Aidid's residence. While conducting a routine mission in support of UN

forces on 14 March 1994, AC-130H 'Spectre' 69-6576 call-sign 'Jockey 14' in the 16th SOS, 56th SOW crashed in the sea four miles south of Malindi, Kenya after takeoff from Mombasa after a howitzer round exploded in the gun-tube and caused a fire in the left-hand engines. Eight crew members died. Three of the six survivors stayed with the aircraft during the crash-landing while the other three parachuted to safety.

The USAF has also used AC-130 gunships in Operation 'Uphold Democracy' in Haiti in 1994. AC-130s took part in Operation 'Assured Response' in Liberia in 1996 and in Operation 'Silver Wake' in 1997, the evacuation of American

AC-130A 53-3129 *First Lady,* the first production C-130A to come off the line. AC-130H 69-6576 *Preditor, Bad Company, Widow Maker,* which was lost on 15 March 1994 over the Indian Ocean off the coast of Kenya, near the town of Malindi with the loss of eight crewmembers. Aircraft and crew were supporting the ongoing operations in and around Mogadishu, Somalia.

non-combatants from Albania. The AC-130U gunship set a new record for the longest sustained flight by any C-130 on 22 and 23 October 1997, when two AC-130U gunships flew 36 hours nonstop from Hurlburt Field, Florida to Taegu Air Base (Daegu), South Korea, being refuelled seven times in the air by KC-135 tankers. The two gunships took on 410,000lbs of fuel. Gunships also were part of the build-up of US forces in 1998 to compel Iraq to allow UNSCOM weapons inspections. AC-130s took part in the NATO missions in Bosnia and Herzegovina and Kosovo during the 1990s.

The US has used gunships in Operation 'Enduring Freedom' during the War in Afghanistan, 2001–2014 and the Iraq War (Operation 'Iraqi Freedom'), 2003-2011. AC-130 strikes were directed by Special Forces on known Taliban locations during the early days of the war in Afghanistan. The day after arriving in Afghanistan, the AC-130s attacked Taliban and Al-Qaeda forces near the city of Konduz and were directly responsible for the city's surrender the next day. On 26 November 2001 Spectres were called in to put down a rebellion at the prison fort of Qala-i-Janghi. The 16th SOS flew missions over Mazar-i-Sharif,

AFRC WC-130J 97-5305 at Dobbins AFB. The WC-130 provides vital tropical cyclone forecasting information and is the primary weather data collector for the National Hurricane Centre, supplemented by the National Oceanographic and Atmospheric Administration's WP-3D Orion. They penetrate tropical cyclones and hurricanes at altitudes ranging from 500 to 10,000 feet above the ocean surface depending upon the intensity of the storm.

Konduz, Kandahar, Shkin, Asadabad, Bagram, Baghran, Tora Bora and virtually every other part of Afghanistan. The Spectre participated in countless operations within Afghanistan, performing on-call close air support and armed reconnaissance. In March 2002 three AC-130 Spectres provided 39 crucial combat missions in support of Operation 'Anaconda' in Afghanistan. During the intense fighting, the gunships expended more than 1,300 40 mm and 1,200 105 mm rounds.

Close air support was the main mission of the AC-130 in Iraq. Night after night, at least one AC–130 was in the air to fulfil one or more air support requests (ASRs). A typical mission had the AC–130 supporting a single brigade's ASRs followed by aerial refuelling and another 2 hours with another brigade or SOF team. The use of AC-130s in places like Fallujah, urban settings where insurgents were among crowded populations of non combatants, was criticized by human rights groups. AC-130s were also used for intelligence gathering with their sophisticated long-range video, infrared and radar sensors.

In 2007 when US Special Operations forces used the AC-130 in attacks on suspected al-Qaeda militants in Somalia, Air Force Special Operations Command (AFSOC) initiated a programme to upgrade the armament of AC-130s. The test programme planned for the 25 mm GAU-12/U and 40 mm Bofors cannon on the AC-130U gunships to be replaced with two 30mm Mk 44 Bushmaster II cannons. In 2007, the Air Force modified four AC-130U gunships as test platforms for the Bushmasters. These were referred to as AC-130U Plus 4 or AC-130U+4. AFSOC, however, cancelled its plans to install the new cannons on its fleet of AC-130Us. It has since removed the guns and re-installed the original 40 mm and 25mm cannons and returned the planes to combat duty. Brigadier General Bradley A. Heithold, AFSOC's director of plans, programs, requirements and assessments, said on 11 August 2008 that the effort was cancelled because of problems with the Bushmaster's accuracy in tests 'at the altitude we were employing

Pilot and co-pilot from the 73rd Special Operations Squadron prepare to return to base an AC-130W 'Stinger II' after a live-fire mission in support of 'Emerald Warrior' at Hurlburt Field, Florida, 27 April 2015. The AC-130Ws are conversions of former MC-130W 'Dragon Spear' MC-130Ws. (USAF photo by Senior Airman Cory D. Payne)

it'. There were also schedule considerations that drove the decision, he said. There were also plans to possibly replace the 105mm cannon with a breech-loading 120 mm M120 mortar and to give the AC-130 a standoff capability using either the AGM-114 Hellfire missile, the Advanced Precision Kill Weapon System (based on the Hydra 70 rocket), or the 'Viper Strike' glide bomb.

In May 2009, following a lapse of plans to acquire and develop an AC-27J 'gunship light' to replace the aging, operations-stressed AC-130 inventory, the Air Force began exploring an option of converting MC-130Ws into interim gunships. The 'Dragon Spears' are equipped with a Bushmaster II GAU-23/A 30mm gun (an improved version of the MK44 MOD0 30mm gun), sensors, communications systems and precision-guided munitions in the Precision Strike Package. The PGMs are to be in the form of the Gunslinger weapons system, a launch tube designed to deploy up to ten GBU-44/B 'Viper Strike' or AGM-176 'Griffin' small standoff munitions in quick succession. Initial supplemental funds to the 2010 Defence Authorization Bill were for two kits to be installed in 2010. On 17 November 2009 a contract was awarded to Alliant Techsystems to produce 30 mm ammunition for use by the 'Dragon Spear'.

In September 2010 the Air Force awarded L-3 Communications a $61 million contract to convert eight MC-130W 'Combat Spear' special-mission aircraft to give them a gunship-like attack capability. Under the terms of the deal, L-3 will perform modifications that will allow the aircraft to take the weapons kits, which are called 'precision strike packages'. MC-130Ws fitted with the weapons will be known as Dragon Spears. Air Force Special Operations Command is converting all twelve MC-130W aircraft to 'Dragon Spears' in order to relieve the relentless operational demands on its regular AC-130 gunships until new AC-130Js enter the fleet. The MC-130W 'Dragon Spear' went from concept to flying with a minimum capability in less than 90 days and from concept to deployment in eighteen months. Its success led to the William J. Perry Award and it will be the model for the AC-130J gunship programme.

The first converted MC-130W arrived in Afghanistan in late 2010. It fired its first weapon one month after arriving, killing five Taliban with a 'Hellfire' missile. By September 2013, fourteen aircraft had been converted into gunships. The conversion adds a sensor package consisting of day/night video cameras with magnification capability. The weapons currently consist of ten 'Griffin' missiles and four 'Hellfires', with an optional 30 mm autocannon. The use of missiles allow the gunships to operate during the daytime because they can fly above the range of ground fire. The cannon is available but optional, as missiles provide sufficient firepower and less weight would need to be carried.

As of July 2010 there were eight AC-130H and

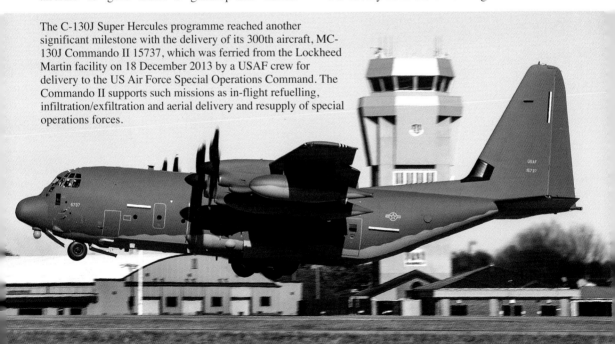

The C-130J Super Hercules programme reached another significant milestone with the delivery of its 300th aircraft, MC-130J Commando II 15737, which was ferried from the Lockheed Martin facility on 18 December 2013 by a USAF crew for delivery to the US Air Force Special Operations Command. The Commando II supports such missions as in-flight refuelling, infiltration/exfiltration and aerial delivery and resupply of special operations forces.

AC-130J 'Ghostrider' The US Air Force's newest gunships will enter service later than expected because of plans to load extra weapons on the aircraft.

seventeen AC-130U aircraft in active-duty service. The MC-130W 'Dragon Spear' was renamed the AC-130W 'Stinger II' in 2011. In March 2011, the US Air Force deployed two AC-130U gunships to take part in Operation 'Odyssey Dawn', the US military intervention in Libya, which eventually came under NATO as Operation 'Unified Protector'.

The Air Force launched an initiative in 2011 to acquire sixteen new gunships based on new-built MC-130J 'Combat Shadow II' special operations tankers outfitted with a 'precision strike package' to give them an attack capability and increase the size of the gunship fleet to 33 aircraft, a net increase of eight after the planned retirement of eight aging AC-130Hs. By September 2013 fourteen MC-130W 'Dragon Spear' aircraft had been converted to AC-130W 'Stinger II' gunships. The 'Stinger' gunships were deployed to Afghanistan to replace the aging AC-130H aircraft and provide an example

WC-130J-97-5309 *NOAA's Ark*. The most important function of these reconnaissance aircraft is to collect high-density, high-accuracy weather data from within the storm's environment. This includes penetration of the centre or hurricane eye of the storm. This vital information is instantly relayed by satellite to the National Hurricane Centre to aid in the accurate forecasting of hurricane movement and intensity.

Air Force Special Operations Command has decided to augment the existing fleet on AC-130H/U gunships in the short term by outfitting a portion of the MC-130W 'Dragon Speer' aircraft with a Precision Strike Package (PSP), similar to but more elaborate than the USMC's Harvest Hawk kit, which would give these Hercules, dubbed 'AC-130W 'Stinger II' the ability to perform Close Air Support (CAS), ISTAR (Information, Surveillance, Target Acquisition and Reconnaissance), armed over-watch and support Special Forces missions without having to buy an entirely new aircraft. A single Bushmaster 30mm cannon is fitted to the forward port side of the fuselage, along with a pair of highly capable AN/AAQ-38 FLIR turrets both under the nose and under the port forward fuselage sponson-like structure. Also, a modular Battle Management System (BMS) and advanced communications system, including the latest video and information datalinks are tied to a series of missionized control stations mounted inside the spacious cargo hold. The 'Stinger's' real sting comes from its ability to lob GBU-176 'Griffin' air-to-ground missiles, or GBU-44 'Viper Strike' munitions off of its rear ramp. This simple but effective rear ramp arsenal configuration is affectionately called 'Gunslinger.' Ten of the low-yield 'Griffins' or 'Viper Strikes' can be carried in the cradle mounted on the ramp at any given time, although there is room for more to be stowed in the hold until needed. Outboard wing pylons carry AGM-114 'Hellfire' missiles and 250lb guided GBU-39 Small Diameter Bombs.

for the new AC-130J 'Ghostrider'. Modifications began with crews cutting holes in the aircraft to make room for weapons and adding kits and bomb bases for laser-guided munitions. Crews added a 105mm cannon, 20-inch infrared and electro-optical sensors and 250lb bombs on the wings. The AC-130J will follow the path of the 'Dragon Spear' programme, along similar lines to the USMC 'Harvest Hawk' programme.

On 9 January 2013 the Air Force began converting the first MC-130J 'Combat Shadow II' into an AC-130J 'Ghostrider'. The first AC-130J entered service in 2017. The Air Force decided to add a 105 mm cannon to the AC-130J in addition to the 30mm cannon and smart bombs because the shells are more accurate and cheaper than dropping SDBs. AFSOC is interested in adding a directed energy weapon to the AC-130J. Other potential additions include an airborne active denial system to perform crowd control and deploying small unmanned aerial vehicles from the common launch tubes to provide remote video feed and coordinates to weapons operators through cloud cover. By

2018 AC-130 gunships will have been providing close air support for special operators for fifty years. Although the aircraft have been kept relevant through constant upgrades to their weaponry, sensor packages and countermeasures, they are not expected to be survivable in future non-permissive environments due to their high signatures and low airspeeds. Military analysts, such as the Center for Strategic and Budgetary Assessments, have suggested that AFSOC invest in more advanced technologies to fill the role to operate in future contested combat zones, including a mix of low-cost disposable unmanned and stealthy strike aircraft.

Perhaps the most dangerous element of AC-130 gunship operations is the relatively low altitude at which the aircraft must operate, exposing themselves to enemy ground fire. Gunpowder technology still limits the effectiveness of the airborne weapons platforms used by the US Special Forces. Lockheed Aircraft Service Company began exploring some new hypervelocity weapon technologies developed in the Strategic Defence

Initiative Organization (SDIO) or 'Star Wars' programme that promises to increase dramatically the effectiveness of airborne gunships. Craig H. Smyser, principal investigator of advanced weapons systems studies, has written: 'Low projectile velocities mean less energy on target and less accuracy because the slow-moving projectile must spend more time subject to the distorting effects of wind and weather, requiring pilots to fly closer in than might be safe.'

Directed energy devices such as lasers and particle beams are considered not 'mature' enough for tactical applications to gunships, but hypervelocity weapons such as hypercannon, coilguns, electrothermal, light-gas and liquid-propellant guns, developed for the 'Star Wars' applications, could effectively be used aboard gunships of the future. A study has shown that a 4,600hp, turbine-powered, 150mm hypervelocity electro-magnetic rail-gun and all its support equipment, could be accommodated onboard an AC-130. Hypervelocity guns would enable an AC-130U gunship (and a C-5 for that matter) to operate at stand-off distances at altitudes over 15,000 feet - well above the range of 37mm and 57mm AAA fire and IR missiles. Target accuracy remains high because the high projectile velocities of the 'Star Wars' weapons are virtually unaffected by the distorting effects of wind and weather.

This is the future. Then, as now, the part played by the mysterious Hercules of AFSOC may well never be fully told. However, when called upon to deploy specialized airpower, or to deliver special operations, or to conduct psychological and counter-measures operations, as well as a host of other covert activities. Special Operations Command is ready - anytime, anywhere.

The first AC-130J 'Ghostrider' gunship arrives at Hurlburt Field in Florida on 29 July 2015. Both the AC-130W and AC-130J lack the heavy armour of their predecessors, which will enhance their range and operating altitude but hurt in the down-low survivability department. Like the AC-130W, the AC-130J 'Ghostrider' features Integrated Helmet Mounted Sights (IHADSS) for the pilots: the same 30mm ATK GAU-23/A auto cannon and 105mm howitzer; 'Gunslinger' rear ramp modification weapons system for AGM-176 'Griffin' missiles and/or GBU-44/B 'Viper Strike' munitions (10 round magazines); wing mounted AGM-114 'Hellfire' missiles; GBU-39 Small Diameter Bombs (SDBs) and/or GBU-53/B SDB II, along with the same command and control interfaces and a high-power synthetic aperture radar pod that can provide live targeting for SDB IIs and other weaponry. All these systems can be reverse-upgraded into the AC-130W fleet and can be easily modified back into an MC-130 special operations transport and visa-versa if needed. The fleet of AC-130s will grow to 45 airframes and can be rapidly increased as required. These include 17 AC-130Us, twelve AC-130Ws and 16 AC-130Js.

Line up of MC-130H aircraft (87-0024, the nearest) at RAF Mildenhall in November 2014.

Chapter 8 Endnotes

1   Quoted in *US Air Force Special Operations Command* by Rick Llinares and Andy Evans (SAM Publications 2010).

2   It was transferred to the outdoor Air Park at the National Museum of the United States Air Force at Wright-Patterson AFB, Ohio in 1976 and converted back to AC-130A configuration in the late 1990s.

3   *Vietnam Air Losses* by Chris Hobson (Midland Publishing 2001).

4   *Vietnam Air Losses* by Chris Hobson (Midland Publishing 2001).

5   After overrunning the ARVN bases at Tân Cảnh, Đắk Tô and the Firebases along Rocket Ridge the PAVN turned their attention to the base and to Ben Het Camp which blocked the avenues for attack on Kontum. The base had been subjected to artillery fire since 24 April, but from midday on 6 May the volume of fire increased dramatically with over 500 rounds systematically destroying the base bunkers and an infantry assault by the PAVN 64th Regiment penetrated the perimeter. At 19:00 the two US advisers at the base were evacuated by helicopter. The attack was repulsed and the ARVN continued to hold for a further 3 days during which time US airpower, including gunships and 16 B-52 strikes, was concentrated on the attacking PAVN. On the night of 7 May the PAVN attempted another assault but were again repulsed suffering 300 killed. On the morning of 9 May the ARVN abandoned the base in the face of a PAVN tank and infantry assault, only 97 ARVN and their dependents reaching safety in Kontum.

6   *Vietnam Air Losses* by Chris Hobson (Midland Publishing 2001).

7   It involved seven HH-53s, eight A-1s, three HC-130s, eleven flights of strike aircraft (seven of which made attacks), four EB-66s, six F-105s, fourteen 'Nail' FACs, three 'Raven' FACs, three 'Air America' helicopters, four AC-130s and an F-4 Fast FAC. *Vietnam Air Losses* by Chris Hobson (Midland Publishing 2001).

8   The rescue of Bat 21 'Bravo' the call sign for Iceal 'Gene' Hambleton, from behind North Viêtnamese lines was the 'largest, longest and most complex search-and-rescue' operation during the Viêtnam War. It began on 2 April, the third day of the Easter Offensive when the early morning flight was led by Bat 20 flown by Lieutenant Colonel Robert Singletary. Hambleton was the navigator aboard a EB-66 aircraft escorting a cell of three B-52s. Bat 21 was configured to gather signals intelligence including identifying North Viêtnamese anti-aircraft radar installations to enable jamming. Bat 21 was destroyed by a SA-2 surface-to-air missile and Hambleton was the only survivor, parachuting behind the front lines into a battlefield filled with thousands of North Viêtnamese Army soldiers.

9   In November 2001the USAF began dropping several BLU-82s during the campaign to destroy Taliban and al-Qaeda bases in Afghanistan, to attack and demoralize personnel and to destroy underground and cave complexes. It proved a very effective anti-personnel weapon and as an intimidation weapon because of its very large blast radius (variously reported as 5,000 to 5,500 feet) combined with a visible flash and audible sound at long distances. American forces used the bomb in December 2001 during the Battle of Tora Bora. On 15 July 2008 airmen from the Duke Field 711th Special Operations Squadron, 919th Special Operations Wing dropped the last operational BLU-82 at the Utah Test and Training Range. There were 225 constructed. The BLU-82 was retired in 2008 and replaced with the more powerful MOAB

Chapter Nine

Antipodean Hercules

The Royal Australian Air Force (RAAF) has operated a total of forty-eight C-130 aircraft. The type entered Australian service in December 1958, when 36 Squadron at Sydney's Richmond Air Force Base accepted the first of twelve C-130A-50-LMs, replacing its venerable Douglas C-47 Dakotas. The acquisition made Australia the overseas customer of the Hercules. In 1966 the C-130As were joined by twelve C-130Es, which equipped 37 Squadron. The C-130As were replaced by twelve C-130Es delivered from 1966 and the C-130Es by twelve C-130J-30 Hercules in 1999. RAAF Hercules' have frequently been used to deliver disaster relief in Australia and the Pacific region, as well as to support military deployments overseas. The 17th of June 1963 was a red letter day for the RNZAF when the New Zealand cabinet approved an immediate order of three C-130E aircraft, including spares and support equipment and approval in principle was also given for the eventual purchase of five maritime versions. New Zealand thus became the fifth nation to purchase the Hercules.

Following the deployment of the 1st Battalion, Royal Australian Regiment to South Việtnam in early 1965, the RAAF began fortnightly C-130 flights into the country from June that year. These flights were initially conducted by C-130As and carried high-priority cargo and passengers from Richmond to Vũng Tàu in South Việtnam via either Butterworth or Singapore. The scale of the supply flights into South Việtnam expanded in 1967 when 2 Squadron RAAF, which was equipped with English Electric Canberra bombers was deployed to Phan Rang. A large airlift codenamed 'Winter Grip' was also conducted in mid-1967 to replace two Australian Army battalions, which had completed their year-long tour of duty, with a pair of fresh battalions. The Hercules were called upon to support the withdrawal of the 1st Australian Task Force (1 ATF) from South Việtnam and Nos. 36 and 37 Squadrons undertook many sorties to fly equipment and personnel out of the country during 1971. In late 1972 C-130s were used to withdraw the last remaining Australian force in South Việtnam, the Australian Army Training Team Việtnam; the final elements of this force departed aboard two Hercules on 20 December 1972.

As well as transport operations, the Hercules flew many evacuation flights out of Việtnam to transfer wounded or sick personnel to Australia, via Butterworth, for further treatment. These flights were initially conducted as part of the regular courier service and the patients and RAAF nurses had to endure uncomfortable conditions as the aircraft had only rudimentary facilities for personnel on stretchers. Separate evacuation flights began on 1 July 1966 and continued at fortnightly intervals until 1972; more flights were made during periods in which 1 ATF suffered heavy casualties. While the flights were generally successful, only C-130Es were assigned to this task from May 1967 after an article criticising the use of noisy C-130As to transport wounded personnel was published in The Medical Journal of Australia. The C-130Es provided much more comfortable conditions and were capable of flying directly between South Việtnam and Australia when required. A total of 3,164 patients had been transported to Australia by the time the C-130 evacuation flights ended in early 1972. The Hercules also returned the bodies of servicemen killed in Việtnam to Australia.

Many of the RAAF C-130s were redeployed to South Việtnam shortly before the end of the war in 1975. The rapid North Việtnamese advance during the Spring Offensive displaced hundreds of thousands of South Việtnamese civilians and the Australian Government deployed a detachment of Hercules to Saïgon in March 1975 as part of an international aid effort coordinated by the United States. This force, which was designated Detachment 'S', had an average strength of seven C-130s and about one hundred air and ground crew

The four Hercules models (C-130s A, E, H & J) operated by the RAAF lined up at Point Cook. C-130A A97-214 (57-0507) is nearest the camera with A97-160 C-130E (65-12897) behind. (RAAF Museum)

and was initially used to transport civilian refugees away from the front lines. After South Viêtnamese soldiers were reported to have been transported alongside civilians, Prime Minister Gough Whitlam directed that the Hercules were to only carry humanitarian cargo. As the North Viêtnamese advanced on Saïgon, Detachment 'S' was moved to Bangkok in Thailand, but continued to fly into South Viêtnam each day. Overall, Detachment 'S' had carried 1,100 refugees and 900 tonnes of supplies by the end of the war. On 4 and 17 April, aircraft of the detachment flew 271 orphaned children to Bangkok as part of the US-led Operation 'Babylift'. In late April, two of 37 Squadron's C-130Es were assigned to the United Nations to transport supplies throughout South East Asia; this force was designated Detachment 'N'. The C-130Es began operations on 3 May and were mainly used to fly supplies into Laos. The aircraft transported cargo between Thailand, Butterworth, Hong Kong and Singapore; by the

time this mission ended in early June, the two Hercules had conducted 91 sorties for the UN. Aircraft of Detachment 'S' evacuated Australian embassy personnel from Phnom Penh in Cambodia, as well as Saïgon, shortly before they fell to Khmer Rouge and North Viêtnamese forces in April 1975, after which the force returned to Australia. Detachment 'N' also evacuated the Australian embassy in Vientiane, Laos, during early June 1975.

Nineteen of the RAAF's fleet of twenty-four C-130s took part in relief efforts in 1974-75 after Cyclone 'Tracy' struck Darwin. Since then, the Hercules have been involved in humanitarian missions to New Guinea, Ethiopia, Rwanda, Cambodia, Bali, Sumatra and New Zealand. They have also seen service during the Iranian Revolution in 1979, the Fijian coups in 1987, operations in Somalia in 1993, INTERFET operations in East Timor in 1999-2000 and the wars in Afghanistan and Iraq beginning in 2001. In over fifty years of Australian service, the Hercules has accumulated 800,000 flying hours. 37 Squadron became the RAAF's sole Hercules operator in 2006 when 36 Squadron transferred its C-130Hs prior to converting to Boeing C-17 Globemaster III heavy transports.

40 Squadron RNZAF at Whenuapai operates five C-130Hs, including the first three production H models which, were delivered in April 1965. The squadron's duties include flights to the Antarctic base at McMurdo. The first major operation carried out by the RNZAF C-130Hs was in July 1965 when the three aforementioned C-130Hs (followed by the other two in January 1969) airlifted the New Zealand Army's 161 Artillery battery and its equipment from New Zealand to Biên Hòa AFB in South Việtnam. Over seven days, 14-21 July, the aircraft carried ninety-six soldiers, five 105mm howitzers, fourteen laden Land Rovers, eight trailers, two water tankers and other equipment - a total of seventy tons. 40 Squadron continued regular flights in support of New Zealand's contribution to this war, flying into Saïgon and Vũng Tàu. Between 6-19 April 1975 it made three trips between Saïgon and Singapore to evacuate

New Zealand Embassy staff, refugee children and news media representatives.

'There is no doubt that the C-130E is the right aircraft for the job. It will perform effectively, efficiently and economically, in both strategic and tactical roles.' These were the words of Air Vice-Marshal Ian Morrison, Chief of the RNZAF Air Staff in August 1962. When the RNZAF entered the 1960s its heavy transport fleet consisted of three Handley Page Hastings Mk.IIIs. These aircraft were required to over the globe to meet RNZAF and New Zealand Government requirements. Delivered during 1952 and 1953, the Hastings was World War Two technology and at the end of their economical life. Furthermore, as 'tail-draggers', with only side doors for loading they were not suitable for the vast range of cargoes moved by the RNZAF. The search for a replacement heavy transport aircraft commenced as a result of the 1961 'Defence White Paper', which directed replacement of the existing transport fleet. As an interim measure, three DC-6 aircraft were purchased from Tasman Empire Airlines Limited (TEAL) to augment the Hastings.

Air Staff in Defence Headquarters, Wellington,

RAAF personnel arriving in Việtnam in the early 1960s.

Royal Australian Air Force C-130E A97-167 (65-12898) in Việtnam on 1966. Flight Lieutenant S. G. Hyland and crew departed Dobbins AFB for Australia on 22 August 1966 via Mather AFB, Hickam AFB, Nadi and arriving at RAAF Richmond. On 17 June 1967 this aircraft had an engine failure in flight and diverted to Butterworth in Malaya. In around the year 2000 this Hercules was retired to Richmond Battle Damage Repair.

commenced research into the selection of a suitable aircraft to replace the Hastings and DC-6s. One of the officers involved, Wing Commander Richard Bolt, described the process for developing the specifications for the new transport. 'I took the specifications and information on the Hercules from the Lockheed brochures and this formed the basis for the Air Staff Requirement.' The proposal also required the selected aircraft to carry out maritime surveillance using 'roll-on' maritime modules. The maritime role was later dropped when the Orion aircraft became the obvious choice for this role. The 17th of June 1963 was a red letter day for the RNZAF. 'HERCULES ARE ON!! - three now, five later.' The headlines of the RNZAF News said it all. Cabinet had approved an immediate order of three C-130E aircraft, including spares and support equipment, at a cost of £13.5 million (NZ). Approval in principle was also given for the eventual purchase of five maritime versions. By July 1964 the production of the RNZAF's first three Hercules (NZ7001-7003) was under way at the Lockheed plant at Marietta, Georgia. By then the choice had been made to take

the new C-130H model aircraft - the first production models of this variant. At that time, the primary difference, between the E and H models was the more powerful T56-A-15 engines in the H model. Three technical officers and 32 airmen commenced sixteen weeks of training at Travis Air Force Base on 17 June 1964. They then trained at various AFBs for the remainder of that year. Three aircrews were sent to the US for conversion training at the end of 1964. It was a profound shock to the aircrews when they arrived for training at Lackland AFB to find that they were scheduled to attend a school for 'language training'.

Air Commodore Carey William Adamson, a Flying Officer at the time, recalls the incident. 'We were to take a written test to establish our level of proficiency in English. This we refused to do. A senior officer was summoned and it was quickly apparent that there had been a major misunderstanding. Whoever had made up the training package for the RNZAF was not aware that New Zealanders spoke English. It was not possible to bring forward the rest of our training, so we spent the time at Lackland learning about the

A97-160 was accepted by the Royal Australian Air Force at Lockheed Marietta Georgia on 12 August 1966 and was the first RAAF C-130E to fly into Vũng Tàu, South Việtnam, departing Richmond on 5 February 1967. It performed the last flight of the RAAF's C-130Es on 14 November 2000 before being handed over to the RAAF Museum. A97-177 arrived at RAAF Richmond on 24 November 1966 after being flown from Dobbins AFB. After logging 600,000 hours of accident free service with the RAAF this Hercules was returned to Lockheed in 2000 and stripped and rebuilt to Super-E standard with dash-15 engines before being delivered to Pakistan as 4177.

Constitution, the history of the United States, the federal system of Government, the philosophy and rules of American football and the finer technical points of baseball. This information was not wasted and proved valuable in following years.'

Air Commodore Adamson also recalls the delivery flights of the Hercules. 'We went to the Lockheed plant in Georgia to pick up our new aircraft and on 1 April 1965 our crew flew NZ7002 for the first time. That was the beginning of a thirteen year personal relationship with a magnificent and elegant lady. We went on a navigational exercise on 5 April to check out cruise procedures and left for New Zealand on 8 April 1965.' The other two Hercules also headed home that day.

Navigator Bob Howe, then a Flight Lieutenant, recalls his arrival in Wellington, New Zealand on NZ7003. 'We were directed to return to Wellington first for a reception by the Prime Minister and the Chief of Air Staff. Two things stand out about the arrival: Firstly we got too close for comfort to the Hutt Valley power lines on a holding run; and secondly we knew we were home when a civil pilot, forced to hold because of our arrival,

complained 'what about us taxpayers?' Shortly after noon on 14 April 1965 the first three Hercules arrived at Wellington's Rongotai Airport, to a formal reception ceremony, headed by the Prime Minister (The Right Honourable Keith Jacka Holyoake). 'I am sure that we have chosen wisely and well,' he said of the Hercules.

In the months immediately after arrival, the three Hercules were seen above most New Zealand cities and towns as the RNZAF showed off its new acquisitions. Overseas trips were undertaken. On 29 April 1965 NZ7001 and its crew flew from RNZAF Base Auckland to Honolulu. Covering 3,840 nm in twelve hours and twenty minutes, it was the longest distance flown by New Zealand civil or military aircraft in a single day. Another major overseas trip was in May 1965, when one aircraft flew to Singapore and returned home via the Philippines where it uplifted support equipment for 5 Squadron Sunderlands.

The first major operation carried out by the RNZAF's new Hercules took them straight into a war! The three aircraft airlifted the New Zealand Army's 161 Artillery Battery and its equipment from New Zealand to Biên Hòa AFB in South

Royal Australian Air Force C-130A A97-216 (57-0508) on 26 March 1975 during loading of CAC CA-32 helicopter A17-021, which was rolled out in April 1973, being lost in 1995 after loss of LTE during landing at Gibb River, Western Australia. C-130A A97-216 was delivered to the RAAF on 3 March 1959 and operated until September 2001 when it was scrapped.

Việtnam. Over seven days the aircraft carried 96 soldiers, five 105mm howitzers, fourteen laden Land Rovers, eight trailers, two water tankers and other equipment - in total seventy tons. The first flight was made on 14 July and the last on 21 July 1965. Each aircraft stopped only for fuel and a crew change at Port Moresby, Papua New Guinea. Just twenty hours after leaving New Zealand the soldiers were in the harsh operational environment of South Việtnam. There was much public dissension over the role of the New Zealand Armed Forces in the Việtnam War. The Air Force's involvement in the carriage of the Army Artillery units was conducted in utmost secrecy before the event. Sergeant Air Quartermaster Vern Carter remembers the degree of subterfuge used to disguise the involvement.

'We were scheduled to fly to Singapore, leaving Whenuapai (RNZAF Auckland) on Monday morning 5 July 1965. We loadies were asked to come in on the Sunday morning and supervise the loading. On arrival at the Squadron hangar, there were no signs of aircraft on the tarmac. Instead we were confronted by the sight of

161 Battery's Land Rovers and artillery waiting outside. They had driven up from Papakura at 0600 hours to avoid confrontation with the Progressive Youth Movement which was opposed to the Việtnam War. Thus we learnt that our ultimate destination was a little further than Singapore and we also learnt the reason for those nasty 'plague' jabs. Loading was a doddle, though carried out inside the hangar and the seats were rigged for the accompanying gunners. The technique for landing [at Biên Hòa, Việtnam] was to spiral down from 20,000 feet, remaining within the confines of the airfield, or you could get shot at by the VC around the perimeter of the field. When the aircraft commenced descent, the gunner's staff sergeant leapt to his feet and bellowed 'Load weapons'.

'Whoa,' yelled a startled Air Quartermaster. 'Not on my aircraft you don't.' He visualised everyone disappearing through a small hole in the side of the still pressurised aircraft. The first confrontation of the war! 40 Squadron Hercules were to continue regular flights in support of New Zealand's contribution to this war, flying into Saïgon and Vũng Tàu.

Acting Sergeant (later Squadron Leader) Warren Dale who was awarded the Việtnam Medal for duty was an Air Quartermaster on RNZAF Hercules transport flights operating between Singapore, Vũng Tàu and Saïgon.

'Our Hercules' were new and well capable of the work. Our course of air quartermasters were among the conversion courses to be trained in New Zealand by the RNZAF crews who had trained and brought the aircraft home from the United States. Vern Carter and Jock Scott (who both went on to become Master Air Loadmasters) made a good job of our training and we were confident because of this good solid grounding and the quality and capability of our aircraft and equipment. It was a time of contrasts; from seeing the mist still gathered just under the top of the jungle canopy as we flew low level over the Mekong Delta in the peace in the early morning just after dawn to the busy, somewhat dirty day-to-day business of an operational airfield. The air and the ground would shudder with the thudding beat of dozens of Iroquois and helicopter gunships lifting off in streams for their morning missions.' The RNZAF contribution during the conflict saw 40 Squadron airlift New Zealand troops to South Việtnam and 41 Squadron freighters began regular re-supply

missions from Singapore. In 1967 the first RNZAF helicopter pilots commenced duties with 9 Squadron RAAF in Việtnam. Other pilots served with USAF squadrons as Forward Air Controllers, bringing a total of thirty pilots who served in Việtnam between 1967 and 1971; ten of these received decorations for gallantry.

'Getting to know our troops and gunners over the 2-3 days from New Zealand into South Việtnam was a highlight. Watching good, solid, quiet and determined New Zealand soldiers unloading their weapons, artillery and stores and going calmly about their business when we arrived was always impressive. We would sometimes lend the gunners aircraft ear defenders, for a few short months, as they looked to be better than the gear they had. Occasionally, we would collect the same people after their tour and remember each other. They were changed, but there was always a cheer as we lifted off for the flight home. Unfortunately, we needed to bring out some of them in their coffins which were a sobering reminder of the real war that our people were facing.

'The war in Việtnam touched the public consciousness like no war previously, due in large part to the powerful then-new medium of television. It brought war - its sacrifice and horror

C-130A A97-215 (57-0508) of 37 Squadron RAAF passing Sydney Harbour Bridge and the Opera House. The aircraft was delivered to the RAAF on 3 March 1959, being broken up for spares at Fort Lauderdale and scrapped in December 1997.

- into the living rooms of ordinary kiwi families. People questioned New Zealand's role in the engagement and protests were widespread. Our servicemen were not immune to these protests and were often the easy target of unpopular government policies. I was comfortable with our engagement in Việtnam. I saw it as New Zealanders helping to defend a small country threatened by insurgency and invasion by larger and more powerful enemies. By the same token I was comfortable with the demonstrations. We felt that the demonstrators' freedom to do this was part of being New Zealanders and the sort of thing that our duties in Việtnam were intended to defend.'

Between June 1964 and December 1972 over 3,400 New Zealand military personnel served in the Republic of South Việtnam. Of that number 37 died in active service, including one RNZAF serviceman Sergeant G. S. Watt and 187 were wounded.

Meanwhile, in July 1965 a Hercules made the first around-the-world flight for this new RNZAF type, completing a circuit of the globe in 85 hours. Back home they assisted 3 Squadron Bristol Freighter aircraft in redistributing civilian prisoners throughout New Zealand after prison riots at Mount Eden (Auckland) and Paparua (Christchurch). The Hercules were beginning to show their versatility. On 12 September New Zealand Prime Minister Keith Holyoake used

NZ7003 on a VIP trip from Rarotonga to Wellington. It was the first of many overseas VIP missions the Hercules flew until the Boeing 727s took over the role on their arrival in 1981. Towards the end of 1965 the three Hercules' of 40 Squadron were busily engaged on a wide range of worldwide tasks. In October 1965 they provided support to 14 Squadron Canberras in a major international exercise in Australia. The first paradrops were made over RNZAF Auckland and training exercises to develop supply dropping techniques were carried out over Matamata airfield. In December the RNZAF's first six Bell Sioux helicopters were delivered from the United States by Hercules. They went to Hobsonville at RNZAF Auckland, the home of 3 Battlefield support Squadron (3 BSS). In June 1966 the Hercules began delivery of five new Iroquois helicopters to 3 BSS. 'The first flight out of Christchurch, the first ever made to the Antarctic by an RNZAF aircraft, left at noon on Wednesday 27 October and the last flight landed there at 5.25 on Saturday, 30 October 1965.'

This statement in the *RNZAF News* was the first comment on what has become the annual sojourn of 40 Squadron to the great white continent. Air Commodore Carey Adamson, then a young Flying Officer co-pilot, was on that first trip. He recalls this historic flight: 'We had to deliberately fly past a point of no return to a destination with no

C-130H NZ7002 of 40 Squadron RNZAF at Chittagong Airport Bangladesh during the April 1972 reilef operations.

C-130E A97-180 (65-12904) of 37 Squadron RAAF at Sydney Airport on 19 October 1988. Eight years earlier this aircraft (and A97-178) operated Red Cross relief flights to Kampuchea. The aircraft was one of twelve C-130Es delivered to the RAAF in 1966-67. (MWB)

alternate. We had heard horror stories of the destination weather closing in with no warning and shutting down the airfield in a matter of minutes. Although we knew all the theory, we were not sure what landing on the ice would actually be like. When the coast of Antarctica came into sight, the intercom became silent as everyone took in the grandeur of the scenery and the alien nature of the continent. After seven hours and ten minutes the first RNZAF flight to the Antarctic ended with an uneventful landing at Williams Field. We had proved that we now had the means to support our own people with our own aircraft.'

During this first venture to the deep-south, Hercules NZ7003 travelled 12,900 miles on round trips between Christchurch and Williams Field (McMurdo), carrying a total of 75,000lb of miscellaneous cargo for the New Zealand Antarctic Research Programme (NZARP) and for the United States 'Deep Freeze' programme. 'It was different and challenging flying,' Captain of the flight, Wing Commander Allan Wood AFC said. 'It was with joy and pride that we watched the first RNZAF Hercules land at McMurdo Sound, Antarctica' said Mr. M. M. Prebble, the leader of the New Zealand Party at Scott Base. In 1968 the New Zealand Government announced it had approved the purchase of a further two Hercules. These new aircraft (NZ7004 and NZ7005) were officially accepted at Dobbins AFB during the first week of January 1969 and arrived in New Zealand on the 9th.

On 28 July 1969 the Squadron had all five Hercules in the air for the first five ship formation over Auckland city. During May - June 1969, Hercules carried out flights to the Cook Islands in support of a Government requirement to assist this island nation. These flights were typical of those still carried out today by the Hercules to various island nations of the South Pacific. One of the first occasions the Hercules showed its skills to the New Zealand public was in April 1968. A severe tropical storm disrupted commercial shipping and Hercules' were used to carry passengers over Cook Strait. Up to ninety people a time were carried on the twelve-minute flight between Wellington and Blenheim. The geographical nature of New Zealand, with Cook Strait dividing the land mass, made for an interesting industrial dispute situation. New Zealand Railways ran a ferry service between the two main islands. The link was treated as an extension of the national highway system, so when threatened by industrial action, the Government used other means to ensure the link was maintained. In late 1969 a Hercules and three Bristol Freighters carried priority freight across the Cook Straight when industrial action halted the ferry service. Code named Operation 'Pluto', 1,750 tons of freight were transported over 22 days. The operation has been regularly repeated, with the range of cargo expanded to include light vehicles and passengers. The most recent was in April 1991.

40 Squadron's motto is *Ki Nga Hau E Wha* ('To the Four Winds'). During the 1970s the men, women and Hercules of 40 Squadron lived up to this motto by visiting a wide range of countries. The Hercules had become a very important part of the projection of New Zealand's foreign policy. In addition to the usual military work carried out during this decade, many new tasks for New Zealand's Ministry of Foreign Affairs were undertaken. Some of the decade's highlights are recalled here.

One of the first major deployments in the early

C-130A A97-206, which was delivered to the RAAF on 18 November 1958, at Jacksons Field, Port Moresby in Papua New Guinea in company with Ansett-ANA DC-6B VH-INS. In November 1993 this Hercules was purchased by Total Aerospace Miami and broken up for parts. (Maurice Austin Collection)

1970s was to the People's Republic of Bangladesh in early 1972. Replying to a worldwide call for assistance to the war ravaged country, Detachment Commander, Squadron Leader Noel Rodger and the crew of NZ7002 under the command of Flight Lieutenant Peter Hensby-Bennett left Auckland on 23 February. During a fourteen day airlift in Bangladesh more than one million pounds of urgently needed food was distributed throughout the country. Another detachment, led by Squadron Leader Peter Tremayne, followed. Hercules NZ7002 returned to Bangladesh, captained by Flight Lieutenant Colin Harris, spending three weeks airlifting 3.1 million pounds of supplies. Flying conditions were harsh, with long days, extreme temperatures and no internal air traffic organisations to co-ordinate the many international aircraft crisscrossing the country. For its efforts the RNZAF was awarded the Red Cross Medallion for Meritorious Service. During regular overseas operations Hercules NZ7004 made the first non-stop flight from Changi (Singapore) to Whenuapai, on 12 May 1970. Captained by Wing Commander Mervyn Hodge, Officer Commanding 40 Squadron, the aircraft made the 5,290 mile flight in fourteen hours 45 minutes. All five Hercules visited the Far East on many occasions during this decade, flying missions in support of Exercise 'Vanguard' (a 75 Squadron RNZAF exercise) and

the New Zealand Army Battalion based at Singapore. On 20 October NZ7005 appeared out of the hangar wearing the new 'Kiwi' roundel, adopted by the RNZAF to clearly identify New Zealand military aircraft. 'As our most prominent ambassadors, it was appropriate that a Hercules should be one of the first types to carry the new national marking'.

Throughout the seventies the Hercules were pressed into service as VIP and VVIP transport aircraft, carrying these people around New Zealand and the South Pacific. Initially, a C-130 VIP Rig with plush seats mounted on a pallet was used. The pallet had screens around it with an open top. At least one Royal referred to it as 'the horse box'. On 1 October 1978, NZ7002, under the command of Squadron Leader Carey Adamson, flew to Tuvalu to uplift Her Royal Highness the Princess Margaret, who had fallen ill during a visit there. The Princess was flown to Sydney for treatment. A fully enclosed VIP module was developed by the Squadron, mounted or a large pallet 'liberated' from the Canadians. Another Princess, Princess Anne, also travelled by RNZAF VIP Hercules. Squadron maintenance flight commander, Flight Lieutenant Alan Gill, remembers the rush to complete the module in time. 'The box arrived the day before the scheduled flight. Much effort was expended to get a satisfactory air-conditioned airflow through the enclosed room. Work continued through the night to complete the fit in time for the 0900 departure. After the mammoth effort, Princess Anne apparently spent very little time in 'the box'. Probably the lack of windows and the carpet glue smell led her to decide that the flight deck was a more enjoyable vantage point.'

With some improvement in East-West relations, New Zealand decided to establish an Embassy in Peking. NZ7002 captained by Wing Commander Mervyn Hodge, set out for China on 22 July 1973 with a cargo of furniture and equipment for the new Embassy. The aircraft stopped at Canton to collect a Chinese navigator, radio operator and interpreter for the final leg of the journey. It was a very wet day in Peking on 25 July, but the crew quickly assisted local personnel in unloading the cargo before beginning the trip home. On 5 December Hercules NZ7002 arrived in Moscow after a six hour flight from England. Captained by Wing Commander Mervyn Hodge, the aircraft carried equipment for the New Zealand Embassy being built in Moscow. It was the first RNZAF aircraft to land in the Soviet Union and was the first of three flights made by New Zealand Hercules to the Soviet Union's capital city. To enter Russian airspace each flight needed a Russian navigator and radio operator. One of the crew was a loadmaster named Sergeant Warren Dale. He recalls an unusual incident at Copenhagen while collecting the Russian escorts: 'The tarmac was

covered in a deep layer of clear ice. Our fancy little wooden chocks wouldn't hold the aircraft - it slid happily off down the tarmac, chocks and all, immediately the brakes were released - the Danes fixed that with the meanest-looking set of spiked chocks I've ever seen.'

On 25 December 1974, when most Hercules crews were enjoying an antipodean summer, a cyclone hit Darwin on the northern coast of Australia. New Zealand's Prime Minister, the Right Honourable Wallace Rowling, offered immediate air assistance and on 27 December a Hercules with two crews was on its way to Darwin. 40 Squadron had a close affinity with Darwin, as it had been a major staging post for the Squadron since the mid 1950s. During the next five days the Kiwi crews flew 65 hours, carrying urgently needed equipment to Darwin and evacuating residents to safer areas. With the impending collapse of South Việtnam in early 1975, a Hercules Detachment, under the command of Wing Commander A. E. 'Tommy' Thomson (CO 40 Squadron), made three trips between Saïgon and Singapore between 6 and 19 April 1975 to evacuate New Zealand Embassy staff, refugee children and news media representatives. In 1977 and 1978, 40 Squadron Hercules flew into Burma. Here was a country shut off from the world for many years, now seeking assistance from New Zealand on a number of technical education projects.

On 27 January 1977 NZ7005 captained by

C-130A A97-213 (57-0506) which was delivered to the RAAF on 5 January 1959 and C-130E A97-168 (65-12899), which was accepted at Lockheed Marietta Georgia on 26 August 1966, in formation. A97-213 was purchased by Total Aerospace for parts in January 1995. Wings and tails removed, A97-168 is currently used as a training aid sitting in a hanger for loadmaster, air dispatcher, air movements and aero medical evac training. External power has been added so the cargo area and ramp work as they did previously. (RAAF via Nich Wauchope)

One of five 40 Squadron RNZAF C-130Hs, which included the first three production H models and were delivered in April 1965, crossing a remote Pacific island. The squadron's duties include flights to the Antarctic base at McMurdo.

Squadron Leader Peter Bevin headed for the northern city of Myitkyina with an ambulance and machinery for a school. Further flights carrying other aid equipment were made to Myitkyina in March 1978 and January 1980. Navigator, Flight Lieutenant Terry Gardiner, remembers the hospitality shown by local 'armed civilians' at Myitkyina. 'By unmistakable gestures, they insisted on entertaining us with afternoon tea before we left. This consisted of sweet biscuits, cakes and beer served to us in a fairly ramshackle airport building which appeared to have been left untouched since the end of World War Two. Our Captain looked askance at the beer and then at the size of the cannons draped across our hosts' shoulders and made his wise decision. The rest of the crew were to drink; he would abstain and trust that it would not prove too much of a provocation. It didn't. The return flight in my memory has a warm mellow hue.'

When the Iranian revolution reached its peak in 1979, Hercules NZ7004 captained by Flight Lieutenant Ray Robinson flew to Teheran at short notice to evacuate NZ Embassy staff. RNZAF Hercules had previously visited Iran in January 1976, transporting material for the New Zealand Embassy in Teheran.

New Zealand provided an Army component to monitor the truce in Zimbabwe during 1979. On 20 December Hercules NZ7003 captained by Flight Lieutenant Scott Glendinning flew through Australia, Cocos Island, Mauritius, Durban and Salisbury with the main body of troops. They were recovered from Zimbabwe by Hercules in March 1980. In July 1979 the RNZAF's most senior Hercules, NZ7001, travelled to Greenham Common, England to take part in the International Air Tattoo. The theme for that year was the 25th anniversary of the first flight of the Hercules. In a line-up of 26 Hercules representing fourteen nations, the RNZAF Hercules was judged best aircraft on display. It was a very proud crew headed by Squadron Leader Trevor Butler, which brought home the prestigious Concours-d'-elegance trophy. The Hercules had undertaken a standard freight/passenger task to the United Kingdom before being meticulously prepared for the line-up. Another award also went to the Kiwis - Warrant Officer S. Peyton won the trophy for best crew chief. Throughout the decade, the RNZAF also enjoyed successes at 'Bullseye' competitions and at 'Volant Rodeo' in the United States.

Throughout the 1970s Hercules carried Iroquois helicopters and relief aid to a number of

New Zealand's South Pacific Island neighbours struggling to recover from cyclones. Other flights carried injured patients to New Zealand for treatment. Often a crew would be called out at short notice to evacuate a seriously ill patient from somewhere in the Pacific. RNZAF medical staff provided medical assistance on these flights. Closer to home, NZ7003 made an airdrop of young trees to the Chatham Islands during April 1978. These were planted to assist the survival of the rare Chatham Island Robin.

Constant demands on such a small Hercules fleet, was tremendous. Often there were only three or four aircraft available due to servicing. Meeting requirements meant dedication from the Squadron's small maintenance team. One of the maintenance flight commanders was Flight Lieutenant Alan Gill. He recalls the degree of effort required to keep the fleet in the air.

'The NCOs were the backbone of the maintenance operation. Their dedication in ensuring serviceable aircraft were available to taskings is something I will never forget. The nature of 40 Squadron's tasking saw aircraft departing in the morning, returning in the evening and needing to be ready again the next day. The night shift was busy and the day shift was sometimes just cleaning up the mess from the night before. The 'groundies' very rarely went on the aircraft to see what it was all about. My predecessor had argued for a maintenance position on the crew for some flights and also for a training exercise base in Fiji. That maintenance position enabled the ground crew to observe that long flights through various time zones were mostly hard and tiring work. Late arrivals and early departures, invariably the norm, left little time to enjoy the 'exotic places'.

'Allowing the ground crews to see air crews at work enabled better empathy between them and

C-130E A97-172 which was accepted at Lockheed Marietta Georgia on 10 October 1966, which was used in the Tasmanian 'Bushfire Relief' operations on 9 September 1967. This aircraft made the first direct scheduled service from Butterworth to Richmond without a stopover on 6 May 1967. In service with 37 Squadron, at some stage this aircraft was returning from New Zealand after a major service and an engine seized. On its continued flight to Richmond a second engine gave up and had to divert to RAAF Fairbairn where, having just pulled up on the tarmac, the third and fourth engines just gave up. The reason given was fuel contamination. A97-172 sat for about a month while the tanks were dried out. A97-172 was retired to Holsworthy Army Barracks on 28 March 2000 for loading and parachute training.

consequently provided a more cooperative dialogue and work arrangement.'

The decade ended on a sad note when an Air New Zealand DC-10 crashed on Mount Erebus in Antarctica. All 257 people on board the 29 November 1979 flight died. Within hours, Hercules NZ7004 captained by Flight Lieutenant Scott Glendinning was on its way to the southern continent, carrying a civilian police contingent and an air accident investigation team. The Hercules then recovered to Christchurch ending 28 hours of flying for one crew.

Other Hercules had the unenviable task of recovering bodies back to Christchurch. This whole operation greatly affected the crews and support personnel involved. As the Squadron history records, it was a sad way to end what had been a very successful year.

When the Hercules fleet entered the 1980s they and their crews were seasoned campaigners of military air lift operations. This decade continued to provide challenges and changes in emphasis. With the introduction of the two Boeing 727 tri-jets into the squadron, the Hercules crews could concentrate more on tactical airlift, paratrooping, aerial delivery and heavy freight movements. However, the responsibility of moving personnel both internally and externally remained an important task. March 1980 was a typical month with eleven overseas tasks, ten internal tasks and the commencement of a Hercules conversion course, put heavy demands on the Squadron and its aircraft. Tropical cyclone 'Wally' in Fiji during April saw the Hercules complete six return flights to Fiji carrying two helicopters and approximately 75,000lbs of tents and blankets.

The RNZAF has provided Hercules air support to cultural activities in New Zealand and neighbouring South Pacific countries. One such task was in July 1980, when Hercules NZ7005 captained by Wing Commander Ken Gayfer (then CO 40 Squadron) flew to Papua New Guinea (PNG) in support of the South Pacific Festival of the Arts. The extremes of the climate, topography and lack of air traffic control facilities were matched by the variety of passengers and freight carried. Now an Air Commodore, Wing Commander Gayfer recalls one colourful occasion.

'The first task was to convey a PNG Cabinet Minister and his wife, plus twenty or so locals to a remote part of PNG where there was to be an official ceremony connected with the festival. I assessed the status of the Minister to warrant VIP treatment and accordingly saluted him on board. He was dressed in a smart business suit. On arrival I climbed out and raced to position myself by the steps so as to provide the same courtesy. I noticed a welcoming group of fifty women was arranged

C-130A A97-207 (57-0500) *The Wizard of OZ* was delivered to the RAAF on 25 November 1958. The RAAF has the distinction of being the only recorded operator who spun the C-130 when, on 4 July 1968 it was spun during a demonstration of stalls and spins by Flight Lieutenant Bruce Clark, who was one of the CFI's on 36 Squadron at the time but he held the stall too long and the aircraft lost over 6,000 feet and spun six times. The Hercules, which received an ultrasonic inspection, flew at 20 knots slower than the rest of the fleet and it was suspected the tail-plane was slightly bent. *The Wizard of OZ* was broken up some time after September 2001. The aircraft is seen here at RAAF Richmond in September 1965. (John Bennett)

C-130H Hercules A97-007 *Licence To Deliver* on 36 Squadron unloading at Jackson Field, Port Moresby in Papua New Guinea during the late 1970s. This Hercules was delivered to the RAAF in September 1978 and was retired from service in August 2012.

in neat rows in order to complete a ritual tribal dance of welcome, clad in only grass skirts. Then to my astonishment the Minister appeared down the aircraft steps wearing only a loincloth and a massive headdress, followed by his wife in similar minimal attire to that of the women dancers! They had changed in the aircraft just prior to landing.'

In March 1981 a commercial airline strike in Australia stranded thousands of civilian passengers on both sides of the Tasman. The RAAF and RNZAF were tasked to move the backlog of passengers across 'the ditch'. 40 Squadron Hercules flew around the clock for four days using four aircraft and four crews, moving approximately 800 passengers between Whenuapai, Richmond and Wigram. Military bases were used each side of the Tasman to avoid further escalation of the industrial situation. On 11 April HRH The Prince of Wales on completion of a brief New Zealand tour flew from Christchurch to Canberra in VIP rigged NZ7002 captained by Wing Commander Ken Gayfer. The flight returned to Whenuapai having safely delivered its Royal passenger to Canberra. The introduction of the Boeings to 40 Squadron in July 1981 saw most VIP roles passed to these newcomers. However Royalty did again travel on a standard Hercules, when HRH Prince Edward flew on NZ7004. The journey from

Christchurch to Antarctica and return, in December 1982 was captained by Squadron Leader Trevor Butler. In May 1981 NZ7004 flew to Dobbins AFB in the United States to undergo the first Outer Wing Modifications required by Lockheed. All five of the Hercules had completed this programme by the end of October 1981. During 1984 and 1985 the fleet underwent a Fuselage Improvement Programme at the RNZAF's engineering facility at Woodbourne. An avionics upgrade was also started in conjunction with this programme.

From July to September 1981 a controversial Rugby Tour by the South Africans caused civil disturbances at each venue. Hercules' were used to transport police contingents to the venues. This event coincided with the requirement to position and recover aircraft in the USA for wing modifications. Even the Base Commander of RNZAF Auckland, Group Captain Peter Adamson, returned to the cockpit to assist when a shortage of crews prevailed during this hectic period. A 'first' for the Squadron occurred during Operation 'Ice Cube 81' in November. An engine change on a Hercules was required at McMurdo in Antarctic and the aircraft remained on the ice at Williams Field, near McMurdo Station for several days during the change.

Between 1982 and 1986 the RNZAF supplied

Royal Australian Air Force C-130A A97-208 (57-0501), seen here at Greenham Common in 1979, was sold to the French Government on 4 September 1983. (MWB)

personnel to the Multi National Force of Observers (MFO) based at El Gorah in the Sinai, to operate Iroquois helicopters. In support of this deployment NZ7001 under the command of Squadron Leader Trevor Butler left Whenuapai on 3 August 1982 for El Gorah. This was to become a regular task for the Squadron over the next four years.

'On behalf of our people and children, a very sincere thank you. You have saved our lives.' These were the words of Mr Pau Toke, chairman of the Penrhyn Island Council, to the crew of NZ7004 on completion of a mercy mission to the island. This mission began on 11 September 1982, when NZ7004 under the command of Captain Don Stone (a USAF exchange officer on the Squadron), flew from Whenuapai to Rarotonga. From there 5,000 gallons of fresh water was carried in two sorties to Penrhyn Island, 727 miles north of Rarotonga. The island was suffering from a drought and a call for immediate assistance was made to the New Zealand Government by the Prime Minister of the Cook Islands. Once again it was Hercules of 40 Squadron that sprung to the rescue.

Pitcairn Island, a remote island in the South Pacific, is mostly populated by descendants of mutineers from HMS *Bounty*. On 22 February 1983, Hercules NZ7004 (captained by Squadron Leader Trevor Butler) over flew the island on its way back from the United States. The primary reason for this flight was to assess the feasibility of airdropping a

bulldozer onto this small rugged island. The island's first mail drop was made during the flight. Once back at Whenuapai, planning commenced to airdrop a 28,000lb bulldozer. On 30 May 1983 NZ7005 captained by Squadron Leader Trevor Butler, headed for Pitcairn. The co-pilot was Captain Mark Barrels USAF. Along for the ride was Group Captain Mason, the British Defence Attaché to New Zealand.

The actual airdrop mission was launched from Tahiti on 31 May 1983 during a nonstop 3000 kilometre flight. The bulldozer was broken down into two loads, with the first drop made just after dawn. Winds ebbed low enough for the load to descend under six 100 foot diameter cargo parachutes. Following a 'streamer' run to gauge the strength of the residual wind, the command 'green light' was given to extract the load. It was released over a football field drop zone in a small valley with sharp cliffs and ocean at either end. The load roared out of the aircraft with the rollers screaming and protesting at the weight and speed at which the bulldozer accelerated. Anxious loadmasters, Flight Lieutenant Warren Dale and Flight Sergeant Dave Neilson, moved to the ramp and monitored the sequence of parachutes as they deployed. They were rewarded with the sight of a fireworks display as the parachute ground release cartridges ripple fired. The bulldozer landed perfectly and was quickly joined by the second platform containing its cab and blade assemblies. Almost the entire population of the island was standing on the hills of the valley to see the loads come in. The people were rewarded with the sight of an immaculate airdrop performance and the bulldozer starting up - it was dropped with fuel and a battery ready for immediate service. It also arrived with newspapers and fresh fruit installed - courtesy of 40 Squadron.

Spare cargo space on international Hercules flights is often offered to charitable institutions for free carriage of goods and supplies. Some of the wide range of charitable goods carried by Hercules are: medicines, vaccines, hospital equipment, library books, school desks, chairs, kitset classrooms, sewing machines, clothing, generators, solar power panels, outboard motors, boats, bicycles, building material, roofing iron, refrigerators, tractors, along with lots of toys and teddy bears for children. When an aircraft carrying such goods arrives at a remote island airfield, the reception is overwhelming. A loadmaster recalls one welcome. 'Everyone came to thank us,' he said. They sang, danced and gave us floral leis and headpieces to wear. We looked really colourful as we took off from the coral runway. The only problem in departing was clearing the children away from the aircraft before we started the engines. We used to save up our flight rations and have carefully timed lolly scrambles at a safe distance from the aircraft.'

The hot and humid climate of Western Samoa was the setting for a major New Zealand Defence Force exercise, 'Joint Venture 1988'. Most of the RNZAF's Hercules deployed to the tropical island during April and early May 1988. The effort to lift support material for 75 Squadron Skyhawks, 3 Squadron Iroquois, New Zealand Army units and the RNZAF's base camp in Western Samoa, placed a huge demand on the Hercules fleet. Operating from the main camp at Faleolo, the Hercules detachment flew many missions around the islands in support of the exercise. Regular deployments of this nature have allowed validation of the RNZAF's deployable equipment pack-ups and ability to move away from the home base of Whenuapai at short notice.

The summer of 1989/90 marked the 25th season that RNZAF Hercules had travelled to Antarctica through Operation 'Ice Cube'. As in previous years, the Hercules carried a wide range of freight and passengers of many nations to and from Williams Field at McMurdo Station. During the return trip on some flights 'penguin counts' and 'iceberg surveys' were carried out by New Zealand scientists. (In November 1984 NZ7002 captained by Squadron Leader Murray Sinclair, air dropped a scientific laboratory at Vanda Station, together with CDS system fuel and spares).

The 1990s started in traditional fashion with two devastating cyclones through the Pacific Islands to the north of New Zealand. The first was Cyclone OFA which ravaged Western Samoa, Nuie, the Tokelaus, the northern Tongan islands, American Samoa and Tuvalu in February 1990. The RNZAF provided an Orion aircraft to fly reconnaissance over the Tokelaus. This revealed that 45 percent of homes had been destroyed. On 13 February a Hercules was despatched to Apia (Western Samoa) with food, emergency building materials and Air Force engineers and equipment to re-establish communications with the outside world. The Hercules then began air dropping supplies to outlying islands. A further Hercules followed with specialist equipment to fix broken water mains and a number of generators to restore power to essential services. While this group of island states was recovering from this disaster, Cyclone 'Peni' arrived in the Cook Islands, causing damage to a number of small island communities. Hercules support for Cyclone 'Peni' involved one aircraft departing Whenuapai on 5 March, spending six days in the Cook Island area flying more than 8000 nautical miles and carrying almost 200,000lbs of freight. Within four days of commencing operations from Rarotonga, the aircraft had delivered thousands of pounds of civil aid to ten destinations within seven of the fifteen islands making up the northern and southern chains of the Cooks group. As well as the air crew, ground crews and movements teams spent long hours preparing loads for delivery.

With 1990 opening with a flurry of activity, the rest of the year seemed to settle down to the usual round of internal and overseas taskings, maintenance programmes and training. In September the New Zealand Government agreed to provide assistance to the large number of refugees trying to escape the Middle East, as the political situation deteriorated. Hercules NZ7002 was sent to Egypt with 16 tonnes of milk powder and then flew on to Amman, Jordan, where it carried refugees from the area. Two flights were completed to Karachi, Pakistan and another to Manila in the Philippines on the way home. A 40 Squadron Boeing 727 also diverted from a UK task to assist with the refugee flights. Towards the end of 1990 the Hercules crews were looking forward to a quiet Christmas; perhaps the cyclones would stay away for a change. However, another 'cyclone' was whirling its way through Kuwait! Along with many other nations, New Zealand responded to the call for help to this small nation when the Gulf crisis erupted. The NZ Government agreed to a Detachment of two Hercules and 46 personnel joining an RAF Hercules Squadron based at Riyadh (Saudi Arabia).

As the rest of the Air Force began the Christmas rundown in December 1990 40 Squadron personnel were frantically arranging last minute requirements to support a detachment of two aircraft in an operational area for an unspecified duration. Finally, the green light and on 20 December 1990 NZ7001, captained by Flight Lieutenant Tony Davies, followed by NZ7002 under the command of Flight Lieutenant David Wake, lifted off from Whenuapai. Arriving in Riyadh on 24 December, the Detachment wasted no time and commenced its first mission on 27 December. Working as part of the RAF Hercules Squadron, the Kiwi Hercs had flown almost 300 hours by the end of the first seven weeks. Tasking included the transportation of supplies and personnel to various locations during the build-up to the land war. It was a big adjustment for the New Zealanders to realise a chemical attack could be a reality. And then the Scud attacks began. Flight Lieutenant Rex Fraser remembers his feelings during those attacks: 'It's quite scary when you see missiles exploding outside your window and you're trying to hurry to put your gear on (NBC kit) in the dark. Everything is for real and you've got to know what to do and do it quickly.'

On 14 January 1991 another Hercules, NZ7003 under the command of Wing Commander 'Bob' Henderson, (CO 40 Squadron), left Whenuapai with a further eight aircrew personnel to boost the RNZAF's contribution. NZ7002 returned to New Zealand on 20 January. In his diary, Wing Commander Henderson records some of his impressions of the Detachment's actions: 'Monday

23 January. Thirteen days after leaving New Zealand. Flew today to Lzah and Qaisumah (Hafar al Batin) by the border. Lzah is a rough strip cut from the desert rock to the north of Jubail on the coast. We found the strip by using the aircraft's inertial navigation system and the co-pilot identified it as we went through about 200 feet, by saying 'there's a windsock'. Then flew at 500ft along the 'pipeline' - the road from Jubail inland to Qaisumah. There were literally hundreds of vehicles on the road and helicopters flying below us, along the road. Very impressive. This flying is rather exhilarating. Our extra aircrew arrived this evening about midnight. All looking rather hyped up in their 'marine' haircuts. The lucky beggars were spared an air raid tonight!'

NZ7004 replaced NZ7001 on 1 March and on 12 April, NZ7003 and NZ7004 touched down at Whenuapai, returning some of the detachment to a welcome from the New Zealand Prime Minister, the Right Honourable Jim Bolger. A RAF TriStar and another Hercules carried the balance of personnel and equipment back to New Zealand.

While the focus of attention had naturally been with the Hercules Detachment in the Gulf, the RNZAF's remaining Hercules had carried out a wide range of routine tasks in New Zealand and overseas. While on a standard flight in support of a 'Vanguard' exercise redeployment from Malaysia, a Hercules was diverted to carry 10 tonnes of milk powder and medical supplies to cyclone torn Dacca in Bangladesh. Another Hercules also flew charitable freight to various Pacific Island nations and to Papua New Guinea.

On 17 April 1991 a Hercules was despatched to Wellington to help with operation 'Pluto Nine' which had started the previous day. By the time the operation finished on 19 April, four Andovers and one Hercules had carried 819 passengers and 338 cars during 160 flights between Wellington/Woodbourne/Wellington. In June the RNZAF took back the Depot Level Maintenance (DLM) of the Hercules fleet. It was decided that this work, carried out by Air New Zealand since 1977, could be undertaken more efficiently and economically at RNZAF Woodbourne's maintenance depot. An ingenious bogey arrangement was developed which allowed each Hercules, with main wheels removed, to be lowered and moved sideways into the hangar. A

Hercules major re-fit takes about ninety days and involves both RNZAF and civilian engineers employed at the depot.

The annual cyclone season started early for 40 Squadron, when in mid December Cyclone 'Val' hit Western Samoa. A Hercules on stand-by since 10 December left early on the morning of the 12th for Faleolo (Western Samoa). On board was a 3 Squadron Iroquois which had not been assembled upon return from the Antarctic. A second Hercules quickly followed with an Air Loading Team, communications equipment and operators, Army personnel, media representatives, tarpaulins and oxygen cylinders for the local hospital. A third Hercules carried emergency supplies, fuel and a 400KVa generator in a 20 feet shipping container. It arrived on 14 December and was followed throughout the remainder of the month by a further four flights. So much for a quiet Christmas!

During the first part of 1992 the Hercules of 40 Squadron followed a fairly quiet routine. There was the usual activity in the Antarctic at the beginning of the year, support to the annual Army exercise in the Waiouru training area, winning of the annual 'Bullseye' competition in Canada for the second year in succession and delivery of a 3 Squadron Iroquois to England for Exercise 'Helimeet 92' - all before June 1992. Between 10 and 20 June the Hercules were busy carrying helicopters, material and personnel between New Zealand and Faleolo, in support of the first major tropical exercise held in three years. Once again external influences disrupted 40 Squadron's plans for a quiet Christmas break. On 23 December the New Zealand Government's offer to provide a Detachment of three Andovers and 69 personnel in Somalia, as part of the Unified Task Force, was accepted. The New Zealand endeavour, code named Operation 'Samaritan', was to take place in early January 1993. Over the Christmas break, 40 Squadron technical staff prepared three Hercules and a Boeing to deploy the Detachment to Mogadishu. Just down the tarmac Whenuapai, Base Auckland, 42 Squadron staff were busily preparing the three Andovers and myriad of stores and support material that the detachment would

Supplier Flight Sergeant Ray Loxley of 1 ATS Detachment at Williamstown on 30 September 1999 marshalling C-130H A97-007 *Licence To Deliver* on 36 Squadron. (RAAF, Sergeant Bill Guthrie)

RAAF personnel carry out preventative maintenance on C-130J A97-450 *450 Pearl* of 37 Squadron RAAF, which carries 'Hercules 50 years' artwork on the tail, in the Middle East in 2009.

require for up to six months away from home.

On 2 January 1993 three Hercules and a Boeing headed for Somalia. The three Hercules rendezvoused with the Boeing in the Seychelles prior to the final leg into Mogadishu. On 5 January 1993, the Boeing with the majority of personnel arrived at Mogadishu and one hour later the first Hercules, NZ7001 under the command of Flight Lieutenant Tony Davies, arrived. The following day the remaining two Hercules arrived. NZ7002 (Flight Lieutenant Mike Morgan) and NZ7004 (Flight Lieutenant Dennis O'Connor) disgorged the mountains of equipment required by the detachment. The Hercules stayed on the ground long enough to unload and refuel before heading out of the extremely busy airfield. The next Hercules trip to this war-torn country was on 3 February when NZ7001, under the command of Wing Commander Bob Henderson, lifted off from Whenuapai for the re-supply trip to Mogadishu.

The crew of the Hercules joined the detachment in hosting a traditional Maori hangi to celebrate New Zealand's national day of celebration (Waitangi Day) on 6 February. Total flying time for the round trip was 56 hours.

The Andovers were withdrawn in May 1993 and three Hercules transported the detachment back home. Other support flights for the NZ Army supply platoon at Mogadishu have since been flown.

During late March 1993, two Hercules, crews and support staff spent two weeks low-level tactical training at RNZAF Wigram. Between four and six sorties were undertaken per day over the South Island in the event known as Exercise 'Skytrain'. These included the dropping of equipment at various drop-zones and night flying. The experience gained during 'Skytrain' was used the following month during the 'Bullseye' competition in Australia. However the Canadians beat the Kiwis by a narrow margin and the trophy was reluctantly surrendered for the first time in three years. It was also the first time a Royal Air Force team had entered.

On 13 May 1993 NZ7002 captained by Flight Lieutenant Dennis O'Connor left New Zealand with 25,000 ration packs gifted b; the NZ Government to refugees it Bosnia. The aircraft delivered the Ration Packs to Frankfurt where they were forwarded to Bosnia by the UN. During May the Hercules' autopilots were replaced with a new automatic flight control system. This process was carried out at the Repair Depot at Woodbourne with the last aircraft fitted by the end of the year.

The 1993 year ended with twelve flights to Antarctica. The 4 Squadron Detachment operated from Christchurch International Airport, alongside its USAF (141), USN (LC-130) and US National Science Foundation (LC-130) counterparts. Also based at Christchurch was; RNZAF Mobile Air Loading Team, supplemented by New Zealand Army personnel, providing support for all aircraft

KIW44/NZ7003 C-130H on 40 Squadron RNZAF with troops of the 25th Airborne Brigade JBER during Exercise 'Talisman Sabre' in 2015.

on route to Antarctica.

During one flight, the weather closed in and the Hercules, well beyond the Point of Safe Return (PSR) diverted to an Italian airfield at Terra Nova, Antarctica. Following a very warm welcome and overnight stay with the Italians, the Hercules continued on to Williams Field. On another flight, 13,000lbs of explosives were air dropped in three areas of the polar plateau for seismic investigations by scientists at the ice. This operation was a first for the Squadron.

Christmas 1993 was relatively quiet for the Hercules crews and support personnel. Tasks included a routine trip to Somalia to transport New Zealand Army personnel and an emergency flight to Sydney with monsoon fire-fighting buckets and technicians to help extinguish huge bush fires threatening Sydney suburbs. The buckets and personnel were returned in early January.

During the first half of 1994 40 Squadron Hercules carried out the usual range of internal and external tasks. In April two Hercules, two Andovers and one Iroquois supported by 130 personnel carried out tactical air training during Exercise 'Skytrain'. This year's pre-'Bullseye' practice paid off with one of the crews under the command of Flight Lieutenant Robert Purvis winning back the 'Bullseye' trophy for the RNZAF.

The most rewarding task during the first half of 1994 was from 4-8 June when a Hercules was involved in the search for eleven yachts hit by a severe storm in the Pacific. A total of 21 people were plucked from their vessels during the five day mission. As the full extent of the searches began

unfolding 5 Squadron RNZAF sought assistance from 40 Squadron. A Hercules and crew of ten personnel spent twelve hours in the air, locating three vessels. Winds of up to 80 knots and thrashing rain made for a challenging flight. It was thanks to the professionalism and dedication of the crew that the mission proved successful.

By June 1994 each of the five Hercules in the RNZAF had flown the following total hours: NZ7001 19,636.3; NZ7002 20,243.6 NZ7003 20,327; NZ7004 16,651.3; NZ7005 160,69.5.[1]

As of 2008 the Squadron began modernising its Hercules aircraft with new avionics, centre wing refurbishment, aircraft systems upgrade and complete re-wiring and replacement of major parts and interior to extend their life expectancy (for NZ$234 million). The package for each aircraft was known as the Life Extension Programme (LEP). Initially two aircraft were completed in Canada however the programme ran into difficulties when the company tasked with carrying out the refurbishments went into receivership. The remaining aircraft were then completed by Safe Air in Blenheim, New Zealand. The Hercules fleet now operate with glass cockpits and had one of the most extensive upgrades ever completed on this type of aircraft anywhere in the world. The last Hercules aircraft to be upgraded NZ7002 was completed by the end of 2015.

The new millennium brought with it a fresh set of the challenges for the streamlined RNZAF. New Zealand's decision to join the 'war on terror' following the 9/11 terrorist attacks on the United States led to a succession of air deployments to the Middle East during the early 2000s. When the

C-130J-30 A97-450. delivered in 2000, is in service with 37 Squadron and carries the nose art *450 Pearl* and 'Hercules 50 years' artwork on the tail.

Christchurch earthquake struck on 22 February 2011 the RNZAF (along with army and navy) responded within a few hours. On the afternoon of the quake, an RNZAF Orion flew over the city taking photographs of damaged infrastructure, while a Boeing 757 arrived with search and rescue teams and medical personnel. Other RNZAF aircraft helped deploy police and medical personnel and evacuate casualties and tourists. Three months after the attack on the Twin Towers, two Hercules from 40 Squadron carried elements of the NZSAS to Pakistan following the invasion of Afghanistan. Another detachment was sent to Kyrgyzstan in 2003 to fly cargo and personnel into Afghanistan, while 5 Squadron Orions carried out surveillance flights around the Gulf region in 2003–2004 during the invasion and occupation of Iraq. These deployments signalled the beginning of a new operational era for the RNZAF. Humanitarian and peacekeeping operations in the Pacific and Middle East reinforced the importance of strategic and tactical air transport, maritime surveillance and helicopter support for army and naval forces. They also exposed the limitations of the air force's ageing equipment. In 2002 the government announced a major upgrade programme that has seen the modernisation of the Hercules and Orions and the renewal of the helicopter fleet.

The Hercules fleet was due to be replaced by 2018. The Boeing 757s were also upgraded with new avionics and more powerful engines. A cargo door was also fitted to allow pallet loading and an aero medical facility if needed. In 2015 the RNZAF was looking to replace the C-130 Hercules fleet as well as the Boeing 757s. This is due to take place over the next five years due to the C-130s and Boeing 757s reaching the end of their flying life. A replacement for the Boeing 757s looks likely to be the C-17 Globemaster and the replacement for the Hercules fleet being either the Embraer KC-390, the A-400M, or the Lockheed Martin C-130J Super Hercules.

In November 2011 Australia gave four ex-RAAF C-130Hs worth an estimated $30 million to Indonesia for humanitarian and disaster relief work. The Hercules aircraft would cost about 25 million Australian dollars in maintenance to restore them to airworthiness and were due to be sold on the open market. The Australian Defence Force agreed to give them to the Indonesian military following a request for more resources to boost disaster relief in the region. On 9 May 2012 it was announced that the RAAF's eight remaining C-130H Hercules operated by 37 Squadron at RAAF Richmond were to be retired early to save $250 million in operational and maintenance costs.

The passing of the C-130H in RAAF service was marked by a fly over of the Blue mountains almost on the edge of Sydney to Cronulla a beachside suburb and an orbit of Sydney harbour in a shuddering lap of honour to say thanks for the 34 years of service during wars, floods, fires, droughts and disasters. It evoked the following impassioned response from an Australian journalist who flew on board one of the two 'Hercs' from Richmond Air Force Base: 'I'm sweaty, shaking and being sick for the third time and I've been looking forward to this day all week. The man next to me is also being persistently ill into his vomit bag and I have no idea where the ground is outside the gyrating tin can I'm stuck in. I'm honoured and excited to be here. It's the last flight of the RAAF's work horse the C-130H Hercules at Richmond Air Force Base, with all twelve in the Australian fleet being decommissioned to make way for the newer C-130J model. For an aircraft that's served our troops for 34 years the atmosphere is fitting - every second person I see is doing Movember so the base is alive with moustaches, aviators and one guy is even wearing knee-high khaki socks and shorts.

'On the plane we take up position on what passes for seats. The first trouble I run into is when I can't figure out how the seatbelt works. They show me that, then how to find the emergency exits, the oxygen bags (weird in themselves - think putting a chicken bag on your head) and the sick bags... which seem to be liberally sprinkled around the plane.

'And then the C-130H starts her last show. 'She starts like an old dancer. A slow side to side shimmy builds in the steel frame as the three metre long propeller blades start to turn. It speeds up to a shake as we taxi along the runway. Jarring, but not particularly uncomfortable. Then she starts to sweat - a diesel and kerosene smell creeping in from the engines as we bounce our way along the tarmac. The take off is faster than any I've been a part of. Pilot Tony Charles tells me afterward that Hercs are made to lift off from short or improvised runways. 'You get up to speed pretty quickly,' he says. 'It's not a long smooth start like a passenger jet.' It needs to be - Australia's fleet of Hercules have travelled enough kilometres to go around the world fifty times over carrying millions of tonnes of cargo along the way.

Maintained by 37 Squadron at RAAF Richmond, NSW the RAAF operates twelve C-130J-30 Hercules and are supported by eight Boeing C-17A Globemaster IIIs at RAAF Amberley, Queensland and ten Alenia C-27J Spartans.

'They've taken medical aid to victims of the Bali Bombings and Boxing Day tsunami, fodder to cattle during the Queensland floods and supplies of condoms to PNG to combat the spread of AIDS. They've even tried their hand at fire fighting. And they're nothing like a passenger jet.

'We lurch into a sprint from a standing start, bumping across the runway and into the air moments later, cartwheeling and shuddering through the entire 90 minute farewell to a trusted old friend. The hot air tosses us around so much we would be confined to our seats on a commercial

flight. Not the case here - I get up and wander around. It's a ton of fun, like being on a flying jumping castle that's made out of steel. It looks clumsy from outside but flying these planes takes immense skill and breeds a special sort of love from the pilots. Tony Charles says the Hercules' last flight was like losing a friend. 'There are a few tears about the place,' he says.

'We dive and bank; only it's not the banking from car ads. A C-130H banks the same way someone turns around when they hear a sudden noise behind them, which tends to leave your stomach back where you started a moment ago. The camera man across from me already looks ill. He's leaning back with his eyes closed holding a fresh sick bag in his lap. Ha, trust TV news to cave first.

'I'm invited up to the cockpit and watch as we cruise over the blue water of Sydney Harbour. The crew wave to the photographers and camera men

On 19 November 2012 the RAAF celebrated 34 years service of the C-130H Hercules with a two-ship retirement flight by A97-005 *Cherry* and A97-008 (which once carried 'Hercules 50 years' artwork on the tail and *You Sent Us To Arabia* on the nose) over Sydney (inset). Departing RAAF Richmond they formed a loose formation and flew along Sydney's southern beaches at a reported altitude of 150 metres. Separated by 600 metres, they then orbited the Sydney Harbour area for 20 minutes before departing to the North and the town of Barrenjoey, where they headed west to the Blue Mountains before returning to base. A97-005 was acquired by Indonesia (TNI-AV) and serialled A-1334. It crashed on approach to land at Wangmon, Papua on 18 December 2016. All thirteen aboard perished.

crowded onto the lowered ramp of the second Hercules above us.

'I return to the back of the plane and concede I'm going to be ill. It's the smell - a rich, thick mess of sweat, kerosene and diesel fuel. The plane is painted black so it sucks up the heat until I feel like I'm being smoked, marinated in it while I'm shaken around. The guy beside me is next to go, vomiting into a bag he has doubled-up for the occasion. Doubling up the bag is a good idea. I think I'll do that. Just in case. 'If you're going to do it you get it out of the way early,' he tells me. 'That's the trick.' 'Two down from me one of the female journos starts as well. I wonder how the crew is all still so cheerful and if this is a right of passage. After this will I be immune to motion sickness?

'Out the window I see sky, then water, then sky, then earth, then sky, buildings, sky, buildings, ocean, buildings, blur, blur, blur. 'Eyes closed, no that's worse. Eyes open. This seatbelt mystified me. Sky, water, sky, sky, ground, sky. The cameraman across from me is trying to climb into his vomit bag head first. It's puffing in and out like someone trying not to hyperventilate only I can see wet stuff inside of it. My time has come. Eventually five out of eight of us are bested by the Hercules.

'To my credit I didn't bargain with god but I did make a 'well if you're already going to the shops' request of him that if he was going to help the other journos he might want to see to me while he was at it. But there is something precious about the Hercules. The C-130H is a much loved part of the Air Force family - moving and supplying troops through some of our toughest campaigns. While it will now always be linked in my mind to a less-

than comfortable experience to thousands of others has been a symbol of hope, relief and salvation. For the Special Forces in Afghanistan the C-130s were their ticket to safety and their supply line during hard times. For the victims of the 2004 Boxing day tsunami the C-130s were Australia's first on the scene bringing supplies and aid to the disaster's victims and showing them we would stand with them. For the Australian public during the 1989 pilot's strikes the C-130s were there to transport them for four months after they were stranded away from home - action that won them a Queensland Tourism Award. They even flew the Iraqi Soccer Team out of Iraq to compete in the 2004 Olympics…where they went on to defeat the Ollyroos in the quarter finals. Well, I suppose even trusted friends can make mistakes. Members of the RAAF tell me they'll miss the C-130H, that it's a 'part of history'.

'Being ferried from the pass gate to the air strip my driver tells me she hopes the C-130s get a 'proper send off'. They've earned it. It's a symbol of everything that's dependable and reliable in the air force, literally the 'first to arrive, last to leave'. When I text my father, ex-air force himself, he replies: 'Bastard. Say goodbye for me!' Those are fond words from dad. And when I tell I failed to escape the trip unscathed he's just as dry. Ha ha. Welcome to the wonderful world of the C130. It's much better up front.'

Twelve C-130J-30s were received by 37 Squadron during August 1999 and March 2000. The RAAF celebrated 800,000 Hercules flying hours in September 2014. The C-130Js had by this time accumulated over 100,000 hours and they are expected to remain in service until 2030.

Chapter 9 Endnotes

1   *Charles - 130H A RNZAF News Special* July 1994.

Chapter Ten

Conflict, Comfort, Relief, Hope and Enduring Freedom

WHOOMPF!
Alarmed, Captain Mark A. Naumann exclaimed 'What was that?'
He didn't wait for an answer -'Did we take a hit? Did any pieces fly off?' Fortunately it was nothing
more than an air pocket. overseas.

In August 1990 conflict arose in the Persian Gulf after talks between the representatives from Iraq and Kuwait did not resolve grievances over oil pricing. On 2 August President Saddam Hussein of Iraq massed seven divisions, totalling 120,000 troops and 2,000 tanks, along the Iraq/Kuwait border and invaded Kuwait in the early morning hours: on 8 August he announced that Kuwait was the nineteenth province of Iraq. Immediately after the invasion President George Bush had placed a US economic embargo against Iraq and the United Nations Security Council had quickly followed suit. On 7 August, when Saddam Hussein had refused to remove his troops from Kuwait, President Bush had set the US contingency commitment 'Desert Shield' in motion, ordering warplanes and ground forces to Saudi Arabia, saying the country faced the 'imminent threat' of an Iraqi attack. More than 55,000 Air Force personnel would ultimately be despatched to the Gulf, including more than 180 aircraft and 5,400 personnel assigned to USAFE units. During the period 16 to 28 August fifteen C-130Es from Military Aircraft Command's 37th Tactical Airlift Squadron became the first European-based USAF aircraft deployed to south-west Asia.

The US Central Command HG, which would direct the coalition of allied forces against Iraq under the command of Army General H. Norman Schwarzkopf, immediately set pre-planned preparations in motion. CENTCOM'S function was to co-ordinate US force deployment to the Gulf region to help defend Saudi Arabia and provide security to other Arab states. Lieutenant General

Charles A. Horner USAF, the allied coalition's supreme air commander began co-ordinating all air actions related to the build-up and within days had established HQ Central Command Air Forces (Forward) in Saudi Arabia. From his HQ, the air actions which ultimately would bring an end to the war were put into operation.

More than 145 Military Airlift Command (MAC) C-130 Hercules were deployed in support of 'Desert Shield' and 'Desert Storm': these aircraft moved units to forward bases once they arrived in theatre. One of their first tasks was to move the 82nd Airborne Division from its staging area to positions near the Kuwait border. In late August 1990, President Bush signed an order authorizing members of the armed forces reserves to be called up for active duty. Throughout the campaign, AFRes and ANG members flew and maintained aircraft, including those used in strategic and tactical airlift operations, as well as tanker support. In addition, a small USMC tanker task force was established using KC-130Fs, KC-130Rs and KC-130Ts, based at Bahrain and Al Jubail, while the USN operated a few C-130Fs for logistics support and the EC-130Q in the communications relay role. Finally, it should not be forgotten that Australia, France, Saudi Arabia and South Korea also sent C-130 transports and KC-130 tankers to the Gulf and that help was sent by the RAF and RNZAF.

Efforts by the UN Security Council to find a peaceful resolution with Iraq proved futile. On the morning of 15 January 1991, an eleventh-hour appeal by the council for Iraq to withdraw from

 Local Kenyan workers watch a C-130 Hercules in the 314th Air Lift Wing, Little Rock AFB, Arkansas delivering relief supplies to Wajir, Kenya for Operation 'Provide Relief'. (USAF)

Kuwait was met with silence and at twelve noon the deadline for peace had passed. Next day at approximately 19:00 hours Eastern Standard Time Operation 'Desert Storm' began, the allied forces answering Iraq's silence with attacks by strike aircraft based in Saudi Arabia and Turkey. By the time the ceasefire came into effect on 3 March MAC C-130 transports had, since 10 August 1990, flown 46,500 sorties and moved more than 209,000 personnel and 300,000 tons of supplies within the theatre. They provided logistical support, medical evacuation of the wounded and battlefield mobility once the fighting started.[1] During the '100-Hour' ground campaign, MAC C-130 transports flew more than 500 sorties a day.

One of the Gulf War's most immediate consequences was the disintegration of Iraq. Civil unrest erupted among Iraq's Shiite and Kurdish minorities and Hussein used his military ruthlessly, crushing the uprisings with helicopters and what armour his army had left. In the northern part of

the country, 500,000 Kurds made their way to the Turkish and Iranian borders. On 5 April the UN condemned Iraq and President Bush ordered US European Command to assist Kurds and other refugees in the mountains of northern Iraq. The following day, JTF 'Provide Comfort' was formed and deployed to Incirlik, Turkey to conduct humanitarian air operations in northern Iraq.

On 7 April USAF aircraft began dropping food, blankets, clothing, tents and other equipment, while at the same time Iraq was warned not to carry out any kind of activity north of the 36th parallel, where Kurdish refugees had gathered. Eventually, thirteen countries took part in 'Provide Comfort' and another thirty were to provide various types of material assistance. By 8 April USAF aircraft had dropped approximately 27 tons of relief supplies to the Kurds; on 9 April, the mission expanded to sustaining the refugee population for thirty days. Two days later 'Provide Comfort' took on the additional responsibility of providing temporary settlements for the Kurds. By 6 June the last mountain gap had closed and the refugee population was in the security zone, or 'safe haven'. The UN assumed responsibility for relief operations the following day. The last coalition ground forces let Iraq on 20 July and 'Provide Comfort' ended on 15 July; the emphasis then shifted to preventing a recurrence, with Operation 'Provide Comfort II'.

In 1992 those USAFE C-130Es based at the relatively small Rhein-Main AFB, billed as the 'Gateway to Europe' during its lifetime and which shared the city's busy international airport five miles south of Frankfurt, took part in relief operations to the Soviet Union, East and West Africa and Bosnia. The C-130E element was provided by the 37th 'Blue Tail Flies' Airlift Squadron, 435th Airlift Wing, 17th Air Force whose primary mission is the tactical airlift mission within the European theatre.

In April 1992 USAFE transports took part in Operation 'Provide Hope II', a long-term effort to aid cities in the former Soviet Union. On the 4 and 5 May 1992, following a 30 April coup in Sierra Leone, a US European Command Joint Special Operations Task Force rescued 438 people from Freetown, Sierra Leone. The 37th ALS contributed

nine C-130 sorties, carrying 302 evacuees to Dakar, Senegal. From the 12 August to 9 October, three 435th ALW C-130Es were deployed from Rhein-Main to Luanda, Angola, to be used to relocate government and rebel soldiers during Operation 'Provide Transition', a multi-national UN effort to support democratic elections following the civil war in Angola. The C-130s flew 326 sorties, carrying 8,805 passengers and 265 tons of cargo during the operation.

On 3 July 1992 the 37th ALS flew the first two C-130s in the first 'Provide Promise' mission; these were laden with humanitarian relief supplies from Rhein-Main, their objective the war-torn city of Sarajevo. The flights were not without hazard: on 3 October an Italian Air Force C-130 was hit by a missile 21 miles west of Sarajevo and was lost with its four-man crew and at least two USAF C-130s received small-arms fire at Sarajevo Airport. Undeterred, C-9 Medevac missions began on 2 February 1993; they took place twice a month and in March the operation expanded to include the airdrop of relief supplies in Bosnia-Herzegovina. On 27 February a USAF Hercules first dropped about a million leaflets in less than forty minutes over eastern Bosnia, telling residents and refugees that the airdropped relief was on its way and

C-130H CNA-OL of the Force Aérienne Royal Morocainé (Royal Maroc Air Force) taking off from Mogadishu on 1 March 1993 during the Provide 'Relief' operation. (MWB)

C-130E of the 711th SOS, 919th SOG from Duke Field, Florida and C-130H 74-2067 of the 772nd ALS, 463rd TAW from Dyess AFB, Abilene, Texas at Moi International Airport, Mombasa, Kenya, 28 February 1993. Operating from August 1992 to February 1993,'Provide Relief' was a multi-nation air-relief operation in Mombasa, Kenya, involving, at its height, sixteen USAF and USAFE C 130s, with transports from six other nations. It delivered supplies to refugees in neighbouring Somalia while Operation 'Restore Hope' protected the relief efforts. (MWB)

cautioning people of the dangers of being too close to the drop zone. Night after night Bosnian refugees stood in the open and waited for the 'parcels from God' to drop.

On 14 August 1992, the White House, prompted by continuing reports of heavily armed, organized gangs stealing food and famine relief supplies from humanitarian organizations in the famine-ravaged east African state of Somalia, announced that US military transports would support the multi-national UN relief effort. Ten C-130s and 400 personnel were deployed to Moi International Airport, Mombasa, Kenya, in Operation 'Provide Relief'. a multi-nation air operation involving the US, Great Britain, Germany, France, Italy, Belgium and Canada, under the leadership of the United Nations in Nairobi. Operation 'Provide Relief' began in late August 1992 and continued until the end of February 1993, by which time multi-national efforts had restored stability to the refugee locations in the country and it was possible to convey supplies over secure land routes from the Somali ports of Mogadishu and Kismaayu directly to the relief locations.

By the end of 1992 clans of opposing beliefs

fighting for food, territory and ethnic revenge had created such a climate of violence in Somalia that 'Provide Relief' workers were prevented from providing aid in areas of greatest need. This came to a head on 8 December and in response, President Bush, implementing Operation 'Restore Hope', sent American troops to protect the relief efforts. At the peak of the operation in January 1993, Joint Task Force 'Provide Relief'/Restore Hope' included 1,007 Air Force, Marine, Army and Navy personnel as well as flying units from Germany to the UK, three German C-160 Transalls and five Marine KC-130 tankers sharing the ramp space, with occasional C-141s and C-5s. By 25 February 1993 the multi-national unit had flown 1,924 sorties to Somalia and 508 to Kenya and had carried over 28,000 tonnes of food for international relief organizations who operate feeding centres and clinics for the Somali people in both Kenya and Somalia.

On 28 February Colonel Thomas Samples, CO of the Air Component at Mombasa and the Dyess crew made the final US food flight from Mombasa to Mandera loaded with three pallets of powdered milk and bottled water. Other loads during the six-month period had included wheat, beans, rice, maize, various flours, cooking oil and a corn and soya preparation called 'Unimix'. The food used to arrive by ship in Mombasa and was then trucked to the 'Provide Relief' operations centre at Moi Airport. 28 February also saw the departure of two ANG C-130s with their support equipment and personnel. Operation 'Provide Relief' really made a big difference. The C-130s operated from austere, dusty runways, sometimes littered with rocks and as short as 3,000 feet, but without a single accident or mission lost due to a maintenance problem - although several incidents occurred at outlying fields between helicopters and fixed-wing aircraft.

WOC (Wing Operations Command) Mombasa, as it was officially called (for Wing Operations Centre), continued to operate as an air component under the JTF Headquarters in Mogadishu, Somalia, moving support supplies, including food and water for the troops, construction items, equipment and personnel throughout Kenya and Somalia. The MAC transport fleet at Mombasa consisted of four C-130Hs of the 463rd TAW, 773rd ALS, from Dyess AFB at Abilene, Texas. The 773rd, which is part of Air Mobility Command, replaced its sister squadron, the 772nd ALS, which redeployed Stateside in the second week of February.

On 1 March Captain Paul Britton, check pilot Captain Mike P. Brignola, from Westchester, Pennsylvania and the three-man flight crew boarded the sweltering cabin of the C-130 for an 'Absolution' trooping and supply mission to combat units to Kismaayo and Mogadishu. Almost at once

the cabin and massive hold filled with refreshing icy blasts from the air-conditioning system; cargomasters sealed the rear ramp door and soldiers and Red Cross girls on board settled down into the rows of sideways-facing seats for the 510-mile flight up the coast to Mogadishu. Tail-number, souls on board and fuel endurance were relayed to ground control. All around the field were aircraft of every size and type: light aircraft, airliners, Southern Air Transport L-100 Hercules and a few German and Belgian C-160s and 130s were parked on the apron. An all-white Hawker Siddeley 748 of the Royal New Zealand Air Force which had flown in from Auckland looked like a polar bear in the desert. Highly colourful Kenyan Air Force Puma and Tucano aircraft threaded their way to the ramp, adding to the spectacle. An African Safari Airways DC-8 roared noisily into the air.

The C-130 rumbled along the uneven concrete to the threshold; permission to take off was sought and given. The four massive 4,508-shp Allison T56-A-7 turboprops lifted the C-130H effortlessly into the cloudy sky and the nose-wheel engaged in the well beneath the cockpit with a reassuring thump. Soon the C-130 was on its briefed course at a cruising altitude of 17,000 feet at 200-300 knots. Over the Indian Ocean it flew parallel to the lush green coastline of Kenya, then the Murrum red desert floor of Somalia. It was essential that the aircrew gave frequent position reports so as to avoid flying into any conflict, because the E-2C 'King Control' had been withdrawn in December. Before entering Somalian airspace, all aircraft gave

C-130Hs of the 772nd ALS, 463rd RTAW from Dyess AFB, Abilene, Texas and C.Mk.1P XV185 and C IP XV293, the two RAF Hercules used in Operation 'Vigour' at Moi International Airport, Mombasa, Kenya, 28 February 1993, the day before they routed home to Lyneham. In three months these two RAF Hercules and four crews of 38 Group delivered 3,500 tons of supplies to all areas of Somalia, flying just short of 1,000 hours in the process. (MWB)

a position report on 127.45MHz and loadmasters frequently joined the crew on the flight deck for a quick look or consultation. Down below, the islands of Jofay and Koyaama appeared and then the navigator pointed into the heat haze past the islands: ' Kismaayo!' he said, above the thundering clamour of the four engines and rushing slipstream.

Captain Britton checked his map and UHF contact with Kismaayu, call-sign 'Tailpipe Kilo', was established. Bill Murray, the flight engineer, sat like a father confessor immediately behind the two pilots. He smiled and then shouted that the C-130 would be going straight in and turning before landing. Armed battles had taken place in Kismaayo on 22 February between an Aidid backer, warlord Omer Jess and his rival Hersi, known as 'Morgan', who had taken over the town from the Belgians. At least eleven people had been killed and Jess's USC/SSDF forces had retreated from the city they had controlled since shortly after the 1991 overthrow by Rebels of Somali dictator Mohammed Siad Aarre. Britton put the C-130H into a 45-degree descent; it lost altitude rapidly and the altimeter passed through several thousand feet until it read '1'. The young Texan concentrated intensely as he dived for the single paved runway. Up to now the only threat had been a high flying stork or crane - birds such as these caused the deaths of two light-aircraft pilots in 1991. Down and down the C-130 plummeted, until finally Captain Britton levelled off and the Hercules zoomed along the runway at a very exciting 150 feet at 260 knots. He was not showing off however: this procedure was designed to scatter any cattle, camels or the odd Somali who might have decided to cross the runway. But none had and the C-130 whizzed past the control tower and assembled multitude of Cobra helicopters. Captain Britton peeled off to the left at the end of the runway in a beautiful 'fighter' turn and circled for an assault landing. He pulled up within 3,000 feet using the powerful reverse thrust, in doing so producing quadraphonic sound all around the flight deck.

The Hercules' massive four-bladed props were still turning as cargo-masters eased the pallet out - and the C-130 was off again, trundling down the length of the runway in the other direction this time. The pilot's seat was taken now by Captain Mike Brignola. He pointed out a herd of camels to the left - they were not disturbed by the subsequent

take-off, which was remarkable, since taking off from rudimentary Somali airstrips in the intense heat with four, let alone two engines, called for strong nerves. Once off safely and when they had reached 100 nautical miles distance away, contact was made with Mogadishu approach and their intention stated. At sixty nautical miles Mogadishu approach placed the Hercules under positive radar control for a radar service to Mogadishu International. The heart-stopping landing at Kismaayu had been dramatic, but Mogadishu produced an incredible view for an awestruck observer. Dark grey warships were anchored offshore of the war-torn Somali capital. Large breakers pounded the beaches and sand-coloured Humvees and construction vehicles dotted the landscape inland of the dunes. It looked like a scene from a Normandy beachhead, except that Marines were jogging around the airport perimeter and handball games were in full swing on the beach.

The C-130 taxied to just in front of the tower and the troops and supplies were disembarked. A long file of 'grunts' took their place, flopping wearily into the bucket-seats in the cargo hold. A Nigerian C-130 taxied out, returned along the runway at speed and turned sharply onto 270 degrees, away from the town as machine-gun fire had been reported in the area.

At 0535 hours Captain Britton followed exactly the same pattern and the C-130 was off again and climbing away without incident. The faithful Allison turboprops beat a pulsating rhythm and the tension in the cockpit evaporated with the diminishing heat as the C-130 climbed gradually to 23,000 feet. The crew settled back as the Hercules droned above the coast at a steady 300 knots. Copies of *Stars and Stripes* were being read until the sun went down below the right wing and the orange-red instrument lights and green computer CRTs began to light up the pilots' smiling faces.[2] Darkness descended. The stable Hercules headed 'home' and the crew relaxed, knowing that after their exertions, in a few hours they would be enjoying 'field conditions' again at their plush hotel in Mombasa.[3]

For the relief operation from Rhein-Main to Bosnia, the 37th ALS were joined by C-130E/H crews on TDY (temporary duty) from the 317th ALW and the 40th ALS, 23rd Wing - both from

Above: 1st Lieutenant Ross Becker, 815th ALS, 403rd ALW, AFRes at the controls of C-130E 62-1834, a 96th TAS, 934th Air Guard, AFRes aircraft on TDY at Rhein-Main, as it crosses the Alps en route to Sarajevo on 23 March 1994. (MWB)

Below: 1st Lieutenant Eric L. Meyers at the controls of C-130E 62-1834 en route to Sarajevo. (MWB)

Pope AFB North Carolina - as well as other stateside-based, active duty AFRes 'mix and match' rather than a 'hard' crew. On 23 March 1994 C-130E 62-1834 was used for a 'Provide Promise' flight (UN Flight 17) to Sarajevo; the aircraft was crewed by AFRes personnel. Pilot and airplane commander 1st Lieutenant Ross Becker, pilot 1st Lieutenant Eric L. Meyers and Captain Thomas D. Mims, navigator were from the 815th Airlift Squadron, 403rd Wing, at Keesler AFB, Biloxi, Mississippi Staff Sergeant Ronald A. Downer, the flight engineer, 327th AS, 403rd Wing, was from Willow Grove Air Reserve Station at Horsham, Pennsylvania. It was Ross Becker's sixteenth mission to Bosnia, Eric Meyers' sixty-seventh and Mims' twenty-third. Staff Sergeant Dorothy 'Bobbie' Bach - in the 60th ALW from Travis AFB, the Sat Comm operator at the 'black box' - was flying her 100th air-land/airdrop mission to Sarajevo; she wore a patch commemorating the event on the arm of her flight suit.

Brigadier General James Eldon Sehorn, director of operations, HQ 14th AF (AFRes) at Dobbins AFB, Georgia, was also on board; he wore the red triangular 'Flying Jennies' badge on his jacket. General Sehorn began his air force career in 1963 in primary pilot training. Upon graduation in 1964, he was assigned as an F-100 Super Sabre pilot at RAF Wethersfield, England. He then volunteered for F-105 Thunderchief duty in South-East Asia and was assigned to the 469th TFS, 388th TFW at Korat RTAFB, Thailand. He received combat-crew training for the F-100 in 1965 and the F-105D in 1967. On 14 December 1967 when the Ham Rong ('Dragon's Jaw') Bridge was once more the target for an F-105 on a 'Wild Weasel' strike, Captain Sehorn's aircraft F-105D 59-1750 *The Flying Anvil IV* was lost when it was hit by AAA as it pulled up off the target.[4] He ejected and was captured to spend over five years as a PoW in the notorious Hỏa Lò prison built in Hànôi by the French in 1896 which American PoWs held there until 29 March 1973 would nickname the 'Hànôi Hilton' or the 'Hànôi Slammer', as General Sehorn described it. Captain Sehorn was only on his seventh mission when he was shot down. After repatriation on 14 March 1973 he continued his military career and eventually retired with the rank of Brigadier General in the Air Force Reserve.

Staff Sergeant David A. Caldwell, flying his

fortieth mission to Bosnia and assistant load-master senior airman Eric J. Hebb on his twenty-fifth mission, both from Pittsburgh, were from the 758th ALS, 911th ALG, AFRes. A miner for fifteen years, Dave Caldwell worked in the construction industry during the summer months, between tours of duty; this was his fourth tour in Germany. He did not disguise his delight in being able to make a worthwhile contribution to events in Bosnia by delivering food and medical supplies, his reassuring no-nonsense approach no doubt handed down from his father who served in Patton's 7th Armoured Division in World War II.

UN 17 lifted off from Frankfurt with a take-off load of 23,000lb. Vibration and noise were intense - it was like sitting in a tube train running without wheels. David Caldwell and Eric Hebb - brave men - were unseen in the rear of the hold. Tied with green webbing, the bundles of food and medical supplies stacked securely behind the raised ramp looked like goods wagons behind railway buffers.

UN 17 levelled off and headed towards Augsburg, then Innsbruck, Vicenza and Ancona. From the flight deck the snow-covered Alps looked stunning, their black, jagged peaks protruding menacingly through the high cloud layers below. Radio chatter crackled through the headphones: there was mention of 'Magic' (AWACS) and 'egress' speeds out of Sarajevo in the event of an emergency. General Sehorn was in discussion with the engineer. After delivering the load to Sarajevo the C-130E would fly on to Split on the Aegean coast in Croatia and deliver more supplies before returning to Sarajevo with another load. This was to be the pattern throughout the day, finishing in a third flight to Sarajevo when the fuel remaining would determine whether the C-130E would return to Split to refuel or be flown straight home. The general discussed the arrival at Sarajevo with the pilots, querying the predictability of the flight plan - it was long and slow into the Bosnian enclave and he wondered if a fast run in wouldn't be better. Ross Becker explained that the very nature of the mission was its predictability: 'That's the idea and that's what has been agreed,' he said. The crew had only been together for two weeks, but it did not show: they worked well.

Nearing the war zone, camouflaged flak vests were donned; the crew pressed the front Velcro strip firmly. Flying down high valley walls, the C-130E skirted snow-covered mountain peaks. In front a Hercules toppled over on its left wing and disappeared into the murk for landing as Ross Becker took his turn for Sarajevo Airport. In the distance the long runway appeared: behind it appeared to be a solid mountain wall and the Hercules a sitting duck for any bored sniper or anti-aircraft gunner.[5]

Landing was accomplished without incident, however, though ears ached with the descent and the pressure squeezed the yellow ear-plugs until the pain moved to the cheekbones. It could now be seen that some of the white-walled and orange-roofed houses which had looked so picturesque from high altitude were in fact burned-out hulks, with blackened openings where windows had once looked onto pleasant vistas. UN 17 raced past them, hit the runway perfectly and taxied to the shattered terminal building. Nearby, a white and blue Ilyushin IL-76 was parked and a French Air Force Transall taxied in. Evidence of the terrible war was everywhere.

David Caldwell said, 'You should have been here in December - it was like the Fourth of July!' White UN trucks and carriers milled around and forklift drivers wearing blue UN helmets unloaded the pallets; in minutes these were all pushed along the rollers in the floor and out of the Hercules. General Sehorn clambered over the top and helped two soldiers push out the pallets too!

Take-off for Split was made in sunshine and blue sky and soon the deep blue waters of the Croatian coast appeared again. Near Split the crew was advised to look out for a Triple A emplacement, fortunately friendly; it tracked every plane in. The C-130E dashed across the built-up area of Split. It was eerie: there were no boats or surfers offshore and certainly no tourists and on a road in the distance just two cars could be seen travelling along it. The runway at Split was covered in black tyre marks where a Hercules had burst a tyre but taxied in without problems.

UN 17 was loaded and took off again. Climbing away, the mission seemed almost routine now and but for the flak vests it could almost have been a training flight. Dave Caldwell said that in the event of an emergency the load could be jettisoned in ten seconds. The only drama came on the last flight of the day into Split when 62-1834 sprang a hydraulic leak and had to be left at the

View from C-130E 62-1834 of the 96th TAS, 934th AG, AFRes on TDY at Rhein-Main, Germany as it crosses the Alps en route to Sarajevo on 23 March 1994. (MWB)

Croatian airport. The crew hopped aboard C-130H 91-1231 (the 2,000th Hercules, which was rolled out on 16 May 1992) for the flight 'home' to Rhein-Main - at last they could relax. Caldwell got out his hammock and draped it across the width of the Hercules and soon he was swinging gently to and fro as the aircraft headed back to Germany. The hangar door welcomed the C-130 with appropriate letters: 'MISSION SUCCESS'.

In addition to the air-land missions, as of March 1994 over 2,720 airdrop missions (which had begun on 28 February 1993) had been flown and over 31,000 bundles had been dropped. The normal method used was the high-velocity Container Delivery System (CDS) in which supplies and equipment were delivered from an aircraft in flight using a stabilizing parachute, approximately 26 feet in diameter when opened. At first two parachutes had been used per bundle, but after well in excess of 25,000 parachutes had been used and since they could not be recovered, each CDS bundle was fitted with just one 1950s-style, G-12 low-velocity parachute because the manufacturer could produce only fifty a month - enough for just two nights' work. The parachute deploys automatically after exiting the aircraft and ensures that the bundle remains upright; it cushions the

bundle's impact, as does the corrugated honeycomb cardboard base.

Airdrops have to be made from very low altitudes and as such are vulnerable to small arms' fire and the risk of ground collision in mountainous terrain. In Bosnia, drops were often thwarted by bad weather conditions and the possibility that the DZ could be immediately overrun by unfriendly forces before food could be offloaded from pallets. Worse, in May 1993 six people were killed and eight injured by aid crates parachuted into Goradze and Srebrenica. Moreover, at one DZ, five people were killed in the fight around the parachute, whilst at another, a woman and child lay dead beneath a pallet. Clearly, other methods had to be tried and to this end the tri-wall aerial delivery system (TRIADS) was first used on 20 March 1993, over Srebrenica: in this method individual HDR packets packed into 4 x 31 feet cardboard boxes are 'fluttered' onto DZs. The boxes have walls made of three layers of cardboard and self-destruct after leaving the C-130 because the ties holding them together are pulled apart: individual HDRs then scatter into the air and fall to the ground, in much the same way as a leaflet drop. On the night of 23/24 August 1993 USAFE C-130s flew over Mordar and discharged in a 'free fall', 13,440 individual MRE (Meals Ready to Eat) packs weighing approximately 20lb, in boxes designed to open in mid-air, spreading the packages inside a wide area.

A typical high-velocity CDS airdrop mission was flown by six Hercules on the night of Thursday 24/Friday 25 March 1994 to Bjelimići, Bosnia. One of the C-130Es was 64-0529 - UN call-sign 43 - from the 43rd Wing at Pope AFB, North Carolina, commanded by Captain Michael P. Brignola, flying as check pilot for the mission pilot, 27-year-old Captain Darren A. Maturi, an American of Italian extraction from Virginia, Minnesota, who occupied the left seat. Darren had graduated in the top 15 per cent at flying school and though this qualified him to fly jet fighters, he had chosen transports. He had no regrets and in the past eighteen months had flown drops into Turkey, the Gulf and Angola, as well as to Bosnia; he was also the co-pilot aboard the first Bosnian airdrop mission on 1 March to Cerska, when three C-130s had dropped supplies in a drop zone 1,138 yards wide and 1,935 yards long.[6]

Captain Brignola gathered the flight crew of nine around him outside the Hercules and went through the AAA and SAM avoidance procedures, Chaff dispensers and inert heat-sensitive flares being standard equipment; then everyone climbed aboard. Into the rear fuselage went the loadmasters, Staff Sergeant David T. Marko from Woburn, Massachusetts; Staff Sergeant Mike T. Norton from Chicago, Illinois. Technical Sergeant Barney 'Joe' Ivy and AFRes loadmaster from West Memphis, Arkansas also went to gain experience. On the flight deck all the crew, apart from Sergeant Jim A. Carezas, the satellite communications operator, also in charge of oxygen supply, were from the 37th Airlift Squadron; Jim Carezas was from Travis AFB. During a typical airdrop mission the C-130 travelled about 1,500 air miles, which takes around six hours; and on a typical day, four USAF C-130s would fly to Sarajevo and twelve would make airdrop missions.

A great Frank Sinatra fan, Darren Maturi donned his red-and-white cap with his 'Frank Rules' badge; the cap was a present from Colonel

Pilot 1st Lieutenant Ross Becker and co-pilot 1st Lieutenant Eric L. Meyers (right), also from the 815th ALS, 403rd ALW, their flak jackets on now, and Staff Sergeant Ronald A. Downer, flight engineer, 327th ALS, 403rd ALW, maintain a close watch as the C-130E wends its way through the steep mountain passes in Bosnia near the end of the flight into Sarajevo on 23 March 1994. (MWB)

On arrival at Sarajevo C-130E 62-1834 is unloaded and UN passengers disembark after its arrival from Rhein-Main. Brigadier General James E. Sehorn, director of operations, HQ 14th AF (AFRes) at Dobbins AFB, Georgia, who was 'hitching a ride' on this flight, was first off the aircraft to help with the unloading! On 14 December 1967 flying a F-105 on a 'Wild Weasel' strike in the war in SE Asia, the then Captain Sehorn was shot down and captured and spent over five years as a PoW in the notorious Hỏa Lò prison otherwise

Harry Andersson, a family friend who flew F4U Corsairs in the US Marine Corps on Guadalcanal in World War II. Navigator was Captain Mark A. Naumann, from Minnesota. Most navigators appear intense and Mark was no exception, his glasses making him look even more studious as he studied at his small table the large green scope, portable GPS NAVISTAR, maps and papers marked 'SECRET'. Flight engineer Staff Sergeant Robert A. Higginbotham, from Mooresville, Indianapolis, sat pensively studying dials and gauges.

The sun dropped behind the far side of the airport as UN 43 taxied out. In the lead were Captain David A. Peiffer and his all-41st ALS crew. His Hercules was equipped with AWADS (Adverse Weather Aerial Delivery System) and was thus able to navigate to its own release point. There were six Hercules in the 'package': two

AWADS and their wingmen. Darren Maturi was to have led to gain lead experience - what was termed 'spreading the wealth' - but an enforced delay aboard Captain Warren H. Hurst's C-130, who was to have been the No. 2, meant that he flew his slot. Hurst's co-pilot was Captain Catherine A. Jacob,

Right: Welcome to War-torn
Sarajevo! (MWB)

Below: C-130E 62-1834 is
reloaded with supplies at Split,
Croatia for another flight to
Sarajevo. (MWB)

one of three female pilots in the 37th ALS; Hurst
would catch up as the mission progressed. To the
left, Captain Gallagher nosed out to take the third
slot, then a fourth with Captains Mike Hampton
and Ed Brewer at the controls. Hampton's aircraft
was an AWADS-equipped Hercules. Captain Jones,
who was to have flown the fifth slot, had a
malfunction and the spare aircraft, piloted by
Major Douglas D. Delozier, filled in.

Peiffer was soon climbing away into leaden
skies and UN43 followed. Darren Maturi opened
the throttles and the C-130 rumbled along the
runway; there was a slight judder as it gained
height and the wheels were retracted. The orange
scope of the AN/APN-169A SKE (Station-Keeping

Equipment) atop the instrument panel showed a
reassuring line of five red blips with a circle (us)
behind the lead blip. To the left of the SKE, the
flight command indicator, or the 'fluter phone',
waited to be used to pass commands to the other
aircraft. The layer of black cloud grew wider. On
intercom Darren Maturi said, 'We are now entering
the 'bumpy zone'!' Peiffer's white-flashing tail-
navigation lights disappeared into the cloud; he
turned and Maturi turned also. The conga-line on
the SKE followed a fraction later. At 7,000 feet the
C-130 started to pick up icing and leading-edge de-
icers had to be turned on; only the faithful line of
red blips following on the SKE lit up the console.

Priorities for drops over Bosnia were provided

by US European Command (EUCOM) from the UNHCR office in Geneva. EUCOM would pass the information to Joint Task Force at Naples, where a targeting board convened daily to assess information and determine where formations would drop. The information was then passed to planners and schedulers at Rhein-Main who put together the actual mission. Airdrops had concentrated mainly on Mostar recently due to the large numbers of refugees there.

West of Munich Captain Maturi followed Peiffer in the turn; applying 20 degrees of bank. Intercom conversation was staccato, short and to the point. Darren Maturi and Mike Brignola agreed that it is harder to be element leader, which they were, than formation leader. At this point Jim Carezas, the sat-comm operator, informed Captain Mark A. Naumann that a fighter pilot has reported triple A in the area. However, it was made on VHF in the clear, so the two pilots agreed that it could not be too sensitive. On intercom someone said, 'On some nights I hear word of twenty sightings - let's press on.'

The moon was high above as the C-130 skimmed the clouds below. Misty gossamer trails scudded past, while in front huge clouds loomed like polar ice caps; Darren Maturi banked away slightly to avoid turbulence. There was a city below: lights, lots of them. There were no stars visible, only the twinkling of Peiffer's nav' lights. Captain Maturi had got a little high, so he banked lightly to the left; the blips followed obediently like carriages being pulled by a locomotive. There was a brief, tantalizing glimpse of the Alps in a rare shaft of moonlight, though the pilots were seemingly oblivious to the majestic sight. They were thinking ahead, fully aware of the dangers a full moon presented over the drop zone.

Full moon out there.'

'Means we'll be visible over Bosnia.'

'Yeah, could do with some cloud.'

On the interphone came a chilling reminder of the recent shooting down, on 28 February, by F-16Cs, of four Serbian SOKO G-4 Super Galeb jets - the first confirmed violation of the UN aid resolution by fixed-wing aircraft since NATO began Operation 'Deny Flight' in April 1993: 'Unidentified aircraft land immediately or I will have to take action. You are in violation of UN Resolution 816.' Nothing further is heard and the

pilots showed no more concern in their voices than they did before. Mark Naumann cut in, 'Twenty minutes off our combat checklist'.

The formation headed inexorably into Croatian and then Bosnian airspace. Somewhere out there F-16 escort fighters were patrolling, protecting their 'assets', as the C-130s are termed. Apart from the Hercules there was another, smaller 'package' of French and German Air Force Transalls heading for their drop zone at Tesanj.

The crew donned their flak vests. Darren Maturi discarded his lucky cap, put on his light-blue helmet and clamped his oxygen mask on. Everyone followed suit. Thumbs up showed that everyone's oxygen system was working normally as Carezas turned the controls to depressurize the cabin and the hold. Everyone was now breathing pure oxygen. Navigation and cabin lights were extinguished and the cockpit was bathed in a red hue; Captain Mark A. Naumann called out the time to the IP (Initial Point) and Higginbotham checked the fuel gauges above his head.

WHOOMPF!

Alarmed, Mark Naumann exclaimed, 'What was that?' He didn't wait for an answer -'Did we take a hit? Did any pieces fly off?' Fortunately it was nothing more than an air pocket.

The DZ was Bjelimići, south-west of Sarajevo. Captain Mark Naumann explained the drop procedure: 'AWADS enables us to make airdrops at night or in bad weather when we cannot visually see the drop zone. We have a GPS NAVISTAR navigational computer so we can programme radar targets into the computer, call up the targets and it projects cross-hairs onto the radar scope over the targets; we can then see if the cross-hairs are accurately placed on the target. If not, the navigator can manually move the cross-hairs over the target to update the navigational computer. Then we fly off the navigational computer to the release point to make the drop. The rear ramp is lowered. Coming into the drop we slow down a certain distance out, making a series of warning calls - thirty seconds slow down, five seconds slow down, then the slow-down call itself, slowing to our drop zone air-speed, which is 140 knots.

Captain Mark Naumann made a one-minute advisory call. He added 'Confidence high - 'Dee Zee' ahead,' and sends a 'Down Prep' on the SKE system, which our followers receive. He then made a ten-second call and sent another 'Down Prep' which our wingmen following us received.

Through all of this he has been evaluating wind speed and altitude and passing on flight directions to Darren Maturi. The biggest variable that occurs after the load exits is the wind. For example, a ten-knot cross-wind airdropping at, say, 10,000 feet, causes the load to drift about 800 yards over the ground. The Hercules is travelling at about 100 yards per second, at a drop airspeed of 140 knots. Captain Mark A. Naumann used his equipment to evaluate the winds, speed of aircraft and all of these sorts of parameters, forecast versus the actual, to come up with the CARP, or computed release point. Maturi eased the control column back to reduce his airspeed and raised the nose about 8 degrees to allow the CDS to exit from the rear cargo door.

Once Captain Naumann had the DZ in the crosshairs he informed the pilots: 'Green light, Green light, Green light!' Mike Brignola threw the switch that released the cargo-restraining strap and the extraction process was set in motion: slowly at first the six pallets of food bundles, medical boxes, clothing, blankets and tetanus serum, slid down the rollers towards the black void. The small chemical green pen-lights which stay lit for more than eight hours to aid recovery of the CDS on the ground, swung pendulously on the webbing straps. It took only about four seconds but it seemed longer - and then suddenly they were gone. Each bundle was attached to a conventional 26 feet ring-slot parachute, opened by static line; the parachutes bring the bundles in at about 60 mph. Special packing techniques ensure the survival of the contents: on one occasion, 4,000 glass vials of penicillin were dropped near a hospital and not one broke!

Captain Jim Stockmore had the opportunity to observe an allied air-drop; here is his eye-witness account of it: The effort was well organized, with strict control measures in place. Prior to the drop, a crew of about sixty local residents under the control of the local police chief, Hurem Sahic, were in place around the drop zone. Most of the crew had walked the rugged uphill route from Zepa, a 15-kilometre trek, which takes about three hours by foot. They now huddled around a small fire, attempting to stay warm in the wind and snow on the high, flat drop site.

Before the drop, small sorties of NATO aircraft went over the area, an indication that the C-130 Hercules aircraft were not far behind. The window for the drop had been passed the day before, through the UNMO CAPSAT communications net, the only link to the outside world. Within the announced time-window, the aircraft arrived over the drop zone. An eerie silence fell on the hilltop.

The crew knew instinctively that at any moment the pallets would drop somewhere in the area. The rate of descent - about 50 mph - also meant that any one of them could be crushed to death; however, through experience they had learned where to position themselves to minimise the threat. Even so, their silence was indicative of their anxiety.

The pallets began to hit with a loud thud. Three struck the south side of the drop zone ahead of the others; then minutes later, a ripple of impacts, similar to the sound made by dud artillery rounds, echoed across the field. There was a chorus of cheers from the crew and after waiting about fifteen minutes to ensure there were no more drops, they rushed to find the pallets. Each was guarded throughout the cold night by a member of Hurem's crew.

'The Bosnians expected fifty-six pallets, based on the information passed though the UNMOs. Altogether, three US planes dropped a total of forty-one CDS bundles and by 0500 hours, thirty-five pallets had been found. Three had come down without fully deployed parachutes, but without damage to the contents. Hurem's crew made inventories of the contents of the pallets and loaded them on Ukrainian trucks for the trip down the hill to Zepa. On arrival the cargo was again inventoried, then warehoused and distributed by the local government. Two persons were arrested for attempting to enter the drop zone and pilfer cargo.'

Meanwhile, in the six C-130s leaving the area above, the loadmasters confirmed, 'Load clear!' Down below, Bosnia was illuminated by many hundreds of lights - and aboard UN43, Captain Brignola remarked on how strange it was that a country at war had so much electricity. The total flight-time was going to be around six hours by the time the C-130 touched down at Frankfurt and upcoming vacations were discussed to help while them away.

At last the two parallel runways at Frankfurt appeared; their green landing and red exit bars glowing against the skyline. Minutes later the C-130 was down and one by one the superb Hercules were marshalled into position by ground signallers using illuminated batons. Engines were cut and the cabin lights came on. Another six cargoes of supplies had been delivered to Bosnia and for the crews a day of rest would be taken before it all began again - if not here, then somewhere else in Europe, or the Far East, or Africa: wherever the US air forces would be needed next.[7]

From September 2001 until December 2005, when it closed, Rhein-Main continued to provide support for transient C-130, C-141 Starlifter, C-17 Globemaster III, C-5 Galaxy, KC-135 Stratotanker, KC-10 Extender and Air Mobility Command-chartered civilian airliners supporting both US military activities throughout Europe, as well as a waypoint for air mobility operations throughout Southwest Asia towards the wars in Afghanistan and Iraq. Now based at Ramstein, the 37th Airlift Squadron in the 86th Airlift Wing routinely performs airdrop and air-land missions, delivering equipment, supplies and personnel 'on target, on time'. The current fleet consists of one C-40B, two C-20Hs, five C-21As, two C-37As and fourteen C-130Js.

The airlifters can train and deploy paratroops, transport a fire truck, helicopter, boat or other vehicles, evacuate wounded as a flying hospital, or serve as a troop carrier, cargo aircraft or humanitarian responder. The speedy crews can switch tasks in mid-mission, flying cargo in and troops out, for example, transforming their aircraft from one mode to another in 45 minutes or less. They do all of this with a minimal flight crew of three or four, managing a geographical responsibility that spans much of Europe and Africa from their base in southern Germany. And

Above: Captain Darren Maturi (left) and Captain Mike Brignola in front of C-130E 64-0529 just before take-off from Rhein-Main for the night airdrop at Bjelimici, Bosnia on 24/25 March 1994. (MWB)

Left: Captain Mike Brignola (centre, right) brief the crew of C-130E 64-0529 in the 41st ALS, 43rd ALW, from Pope AFB just before the 'off' at Rhein-Main for the night air drop at Bjelimici, Bosnia on 24/25 March 1994. (MWB)

that's not all. With a rugged airframe and four powerful Rolls-Royce AE 2100 turboprop engines, the 86th's C-130Js get in and out of places that other larger airlifters simply can't. Short, unimproved air strip? No problem - let a little air out of the tyres to soften the landing and the C-130Js will get the job done.

Pilot Brian Shea of the 37th Airlift Squadron, comments: 'The 'Herc' is an iconic aircraft and we are still exploring its capabilities. This plane is such a beautiful mix of technology and time-tested reliability. Our squadron has tackled airdropping entire army units across Europe, hauled massive amounts of cargo across Africa and fulfilled the varied niches in between without hesitation.'

C-130Js will unload personnel or cargo from the back ramp, then take off again and head to the next stop on their journey. A tour can last up to several weeks before returning to Ramstein.

But for all the missions the 86th performs, one of them tops all - air evacuation of wounded soldiers on the ground, said Colonel Raymond E. Briggs, commander of the 86th Maintenance Croup.

'We might be down in Africa hauling stuff or doing a mission. All of a sudden, we have to do an air evac,' he explained. 'We have to get them out.'

The new 'J' models added length to the cargo hold; it carries more weight, takes off quicker and lands shorter with reverse propeller capability. Its cargo compartment is designed for quick reconfiguration, making it an ideal platform for anything from palletised-cargo movement to emergency medical evacuation. For the men and women of the 86th Air Wing, aeromedical evacuation is considered job No. 1.

The new airlift unit began flying with C-130E aircraft and at one point, had nineteen of the type in its fleet. The legacy warhorses, powered by Rolls-Royce T56 engines, performed well for years. The new C-130J aircraft began arriving at the 86th in 2009 - and the bigger, faster, stronger Super Hercules brought a definite upgrade in power. Its four Rolls-Royce AE 2100 engines provided the equivalent of adding a fifth T56 engine to a legacy C-130. That extra power is appreciated on many of the 86th's missions, which are frequently into risky, unprotected landing zones.

Technical Sergeant Francis Gilson, 86th Aircraft Maintenance Squadron, a flying crew chief, recalled one mission, to an undisclosed location, where no one wanted to stay any longer than necessary.

The sun dips below the horizon as Captain Darren Maturi taxies out at Rhein-Main. Captain Mike Brignola, in the right-hand seat, checks the details. Note the AN/APN-169A SKE (Station Keeping Equipment) scope mounted atop the instrument panel. (MWB)

'We unloaded all our stuff and said, 'Bye, we are out of here.' I can't tell you any more than that,' he said, recalling how grateful they were for a rapid departure. 'The C-130J is the most versatile aircraft, especially the places we go to.' We go to places in the middle of forests, a little dirt air strip. You're flying around and you see this little strip and you say, 'we're going to land there?'

But in addition to military operations, the 86th has assisted with humanitarian efforts in several countries, including the Ebola response in western Africa, Nigerian elections and earthquake relief in Haiti.

'We were the second flight down there to open up the base. It was a great experience to help the people of Haiti, who were devastated by the earthquake.'

Whatever the mission, the crews count on their engines every day. They don't want to think about them or worry about them. They just want to start up the engines and go fly whatever and wherever they are assigned - and then return safely.[8]

Iraq's invasion of Kuwait in 1990 had ended in Iraq's defeat by a US-led coalition in the Persian Gulf War (1990–91). However, the Iraqi branch of the Baʿth Party, headed by Ṣaddām Ḥussein, managed to retain power by harshly suppressing uprisings of the country's minority Kurds and its majority Shīʿite Arabs. To stem the exodus of Kurds from Iraq, the allies established a 'safe haven' in northern Iraq's predominantly Kurdish regions and allied warplanes patrolled 'no-fly' zones in northern and southern Iraq that were off-limits to Iraqi aircraft. Moreover, to restrain future Iraqi aggression, the United Nations (UN) implemented economic sanctions against Iraq in order to, among other things, hinder the progress of its most lethal arms programs, including those for the development of nuclear, biological and chemical weapons. (See weapon of mass destruction.) UN inspections during the mid-1990s uncovered a variety of proscribed weapons and prohibited technology throughout Iraq. That country's continued flouting of the UN weapons

The tri-wall aerial delivery system (TRIADS) first used on 20 March 1993 over Srebrenica. In this method individual HDR packets packed into 4 x 31 feet cardboard boxes are 'fluttered' onto DZs. The boxes have walls made of three layers of cardboard and self-destruct after leaving the C-130 because the ties holding them together are pulled apart: individual HDRs then scatter into the air and fall to the ground, in much the same way as a leaflet drop.

ban and its repeated interference with the inspections frustrated the international community and led US President Bill Clinton in 1998 to order the bombing of several Iraqi military installations (code-named Operation 'Desert Fox'). After the bombing, however, Iraq refused to allow inspectors to reenter the country and during the next several years the economic sanctions slowly began to erode as neighbouring countries sought to reopen trade with Iraq.

On the evening 19 March 2003 one day prior to the onset of combat operations, Air Force F-117 stealth fighters struck the Dora Farms complex southwest of Baghdad based on intelligence that Saddam Hussein was in the area. Unfortunately, the attack was not successful. Combat operations began the next day and the USAF participated in air strikes on key targets in and around Baghdad, launching more than 1,700 coalition air sorties and missile launches against Iraq. Similar to Operation 'Enduring Freedom', during the first six weeks of operations 68 percent of weapons employed were precision guided munitions. Because Turkey refused to allow the Air Force to use its air bases to deliver troops and supplies into Northern Iraq, Coalition Forces needed an airfield in Iraq. On 26 March C-130 and C-17 aircraft dropped nearly 1,000 paratroopers of the 173rd Airborne Brigade as well as members of the Air Force's 86th Contingency Response Group onto Bashur airfield near Erbil in Northern Iraq to help secure the airfield. That marked the first time that the C-17 had been used in a combat airdrop. On 6 April CENTAF leadership declared air supremacy over all of Iraq and on 16 April the first humanitarian relief flight landed at Bashur airfield.

Coalition Air Forces flew nearly 1,000 Intelligence, Surveillance and Reconnaissance (ISR) sorties during the initial weeks of Operation 'Iraqi Freedom', collecting 42,000 battlefield images and more than 3,000 hours of full motion video. As of April 30, 2003, coalition air forces numbered 1,801 aircraft, 863 of which were U.S. Air Force fighters, bombers, tankers, special operations and rescue aircraft, transport aircraft and ISR and command and control aircraft. In the first six weeks, coalition air forces flew more than 41,000 sorties and the USAF accounted for more than 24,000 of the total. Likewise, Air Force C-130 aircraft transported over 12,000 short tons of

materiel during the initial stages of the operation, while Air Force tankers flew more than 6,000 sorties and disbursed more than 376 million pounds of fuel. At the end of April 2003, the Air Force had approximately 54,955 active duty personnel in Iraq, 2,084 Air Force Reserve personnel and 7,207 members of the Air National Guard. In addition, the Civil Reserve Air Fleet (CRAF) was called upon for only the second time in its history (the first had been during Operations 'Desert Shield' and 'Desert Storm'). Although only active for four months, the CRAF moved nearly 100,000 troops to the Area of Operations (AOR).

The Air Force also employed Global Mobility Task Forces (GMTF) during Operation Iraqi Freedom. The GMTF accompanied advanced forces and made determinations on whether or not captured airfields could be quickly converted for coalition use as logistics hubs or as close air support bases. The success of those teams in identifying suitable bases led to the first basing of coalition aircraft inside Iraq on 4 April 2003 when USAF A-10s were based at Tallil airfield.

Major combat operations were declared over on 1 May. However, Iraq remained unstable, with little security and massive looting. The situation continued to deteriorate and coalition forces soon found themselves facing an insurgency caused by a number of factors, including lack of infrastructure and basic services for citizens, as well as ethnic and religious tensions among various groups. Since 2003 the USAF has maintained a continuous presence in Iraq. Air Force operations during that period, although classified as security, stability, transition and reconstruction operations, remained at a high operations tempo. The Air Force provided constant combat air patrols in support of ground forces and as well as providing airlift, ISR, aerial refuelling, aeromedical evacuation and combat search and rescue capabilities. Air Force Joint Terminal Attack Controllers (JTACs) provided command and control for close air support missions, while the Air Force performed a range of other missions usng civil engineers, security forces, logistics readiness personnel and dozens of other Air Force specialties. Similar to Operation 'Enduring Freedom', this also included hundreds of Airmen filling 'in lieu of' taskings to perform tasks with the Army. Finally, remotely piloted aircraft (RPA) also filled the skies of Iraq

C-130H 91-1231, the 2,000th Hercules built, readied for the return flight from Split to Rhein-Main on 23 March 1994 after technical problems with C-130E 62-1834 meant that it was not worth risking life and limb crossing the Alps in that aircraft.

and were heavily relied upon by military leaders at all levels because of the real time situational awareness and persistent ISR presence they provided. The Air Force also surged its assets when required. For example, during the period January to April 2005, when the Marines increased their forces in Iraq, the Air Force supported that surge with 325 inter-theatre airlift missions and 1,059 intra-theatre missions, completing what Marine Corps historians believed to be the largest troop rotation in US military history. Likewise, when the Army 'surged' forces into Iraq in late 2007 and 2008, the Air Force supported those operations with increased airlift and close air support missions.

Chapter 10 Endnotes

1   The role played by the Special Operations' AC/EC/MC/HC-130s in the Gulf War is covered in Chapter 5, while the part played by RAF Hercules is covered in Chapter 8.
2   Major Paul Britton retired from the USAF in 2001 as a C-130/U-2 instructor and became a captain/check pilot with Southwest Airlines.
3   On 3 October 1993 120 Delta Force Commandos and Army Rangers were dropped into the heart of Mogadishu. Their mission was a fast daylight raid to kidnap lead terrorist Mohammed Farrah Aidid, who had been killing UN workers delivering food to starving Somalis. Aideed's goal was to control the country by controlling all the food. The US raid went off with clockwork precision, until the unexpected happened. Two of the Black Hawk helicopters, the soldiers' airlift out, were shot down. The mission abruptly changed to a rescue operation. Surrounded by Somali militia, a fierce fire-fight ensued that left American troops trapped and fighting for their lives. The ordeal left 18 American soldiers dead, 70 wounded, with 3,000 Somali casualties.
4   This raid and another on the same target on 18 December put five consecutive spans of the bridge out of action for many months causing significant disruption to the flow of supplies into Hànôi although a pontoon-type railway bridge was constructed a few miles away by April 1968. *Vietnam Air Losses* by Chris Hobson (Midland Publishing 2001).
5   On 3 September 1992 an Italian Air Force (Aeronautica Militare Italiana) G.222 transport was shot down when approaching Sarajevo airfield, while conducting a United Nations relief mission. It crashed eighteen miles from the airfield; a NATO rescue mission was aborted when two USMC CH-53 helicopters came under small arms fire. The cause of the crash was determined to be a surface-to-air missile, but it was not clear who fired it. Everyone on board - four Italian crew members and four French passengers - died in the crash.
6   Darren was a C-130 Instructor/Examiner from 1989 to 1998 and is now a Cathay Pacific 747-400/747-8 captain.
7   C-130E 64-0529 was put into storage at AMARC on 20 December 2006.
8   Adapted from *The Ramstein Workhorse* by George McLaren, Rolls-Royce *the magazine*, June 2015.

C-130J C.5 ZH889 on 9 September 2001 flown by Wing Commander Rick
Hobson. Lyneham received the first of 25 C-130J C.5 Hercules on 23 November
1999, to be operated by XXIV Squadron and 30 Squadron. The J worked side by
side with 29 refurbished C-130Ks flown by 47 Squadron. Lyneham was the RAF's
principal transport hub until the station closed on 31 December 2012, when
Lyneham was designated as a Master Diversion Airfield.

Chapter Eleven

That Eagles
May Fly

Five in the morning, May 21 1982, seven weeks into the Falklands conflict. The Argentine radar operator at Rio Grande airbase, on the island of Tierra del Fuego, is looking forward to his bed. Outside, rain is blowing across the deserted airfield. The blip appears out of nowhere, 25 miles out to sea, coming in fast and low. Suddenly alert, the operator calls over his duty officer, but the blip has already faded. Out over the South Atlantic, two Hercules transports of 47 Squadron battle through the night. Buffeted by strong headwinds, they skim the waves at 50 feet to evade detection. The co-pilots peer through night vision goggles, guiding the pilots towards the coast, one lapse enough to cause disaster. Night vision is in its infancy, the devices a secret gift from the Americans. Tension mounts as landfall over Argentina approaches, the conclusion of a 13 hour flight from Ascension Island involving two mid-air rendezvous with Victor tankers. Behind the crews, in the cavernous holds of the Hercules, sixty men of B Squadron, 22nd SAS Regiment, ready their weapons and vehicles, Land Rovers bristling with machine guns. This is a one way mission, the best outcomes being escape to neutral Chile, or capture. The worst outcome is all too obvious. Minutes later, the C130s slam down on the runway at Rio Grande. The rear doors are already open, the lowered ramps scraping the ground. In an instant, the Land Rovers are charging straight for the apron where four French-built Super Étendard fighters of the Argentine navy stand. Some of the SAS fling charges into the engine intakes while others search for the Étendard pilots, who are to be shot on sight. Another group search for the weapon that above all others threatens Britain with defeat in the South Atlantic: the Exocet. Moments later, the first charges explode. Gunfire erupts. The world dissolves into chaos.

Operation 'Mikado' was a plan to use the SAS to attack the Argentine's Super Étendard bases at Tierra Fuego. Had it happened, Operation Mikado would have been the most dramatic raid staged by Britain since the Second World War, a desperate coup de main intended to remove the Exocet (French for 'flying fish') threat to the Royal Navy task force seeking to retake the Falklands. Throughout its very long and distinguished history, RAF Transport Command - renamed Air Support Command (motto *Ut Aquilae Volent*) on 1 August 1967 and later reduced to a group of Strike Command - boasted one of the finest indigenous transport fleets in the world.

By late 1967 only two transport squadrons of Hastings remained in service with the RAF, while Beverleys were finally withdrawn from RAF service at the end of the year. The decision to go for the Hercules was not difficult, particularly when it was agreed that British companies like Marshall of Cambridge (Engineering) Ltd and Scottish Aviation could be permitted to sub-manufacture avionics equipment and other components and since the only home-produced contender had been cancelled. The version chosen for issuing to RAF Transport Command was essentially the C-130H-130 airframe with 4,508 eshp T56-A-15 engines. Britain's subcomponent contribution was politically as well as financially expedient and so significant that it led to the RAF Hercules production versions being given their own designation. Thus the C-130K was born. In RAF service the new transport would be designated the Hercules C.Mk.1. In 1965 the British Government placed an order for 66 C-130Ks, making the RAF the second-largest Hercules user after the USAF (Iran later received 64 C-130s).

The first C-130K (65-13021/XV176) flew at Marietta, Georgia on 19 October 1966 and remained in the US for six months of flight-testing. On 16 December the second aircraft (XV177) became the first Hercules delivered to Marshalls, the prime contractor responsible for the support and co-ordination of all engineering development. This, together with the third aircraft (XV178) underwent Service trials at the A&AEE (Aircraft and Armament Experimental Establishment) at Boscombe Down in February and March 1967 respectively. 36 Squadron, which had flown the Hastings at Colerne moved to Lyneham, Wiltshire and became the first squadron in the RAF to begin re-equipment with the C.Mk.1 in July and August 1967. Six more were operated by 242 OCU at Thorney Island in Hampshire, which had received its first C.Mk.1 in April. C.Mk.1s were flown out to Singapore to equip a second ex-Hastings squadron (48, at RAF Changi) in October 1967. Final deliveries to the RAF of the C.Mk.1 were made in 1968. During February, May and June Nos. 24, 47 and 30 Squadrons converted to the Hercules, 24 joining 36 Squadron at Lyneham and the other two being based at RAF Fairford. In 1970 70 Squadron at Akrotiri, Cyprus became the sixth Hercules squadron when it began receiving C.Mk.1s that November. In January 195 70 Squadron returned to England and 48 Squadron left Changi in September, both to join the Lyneham Wing, although the latter disbanded there in January 1976. 36 Squadron disbanded in November 1975. These developments left four front-line Hercules squadrons (Nos. 24, 30, 47 and 70) and the OCU at Lyneham (which in July 1992 was renumbered 57 (Reserve) Squadron).[1]

The Hercules' range of over 4,500 miles carrying a payload of nearly 20,000lb or 2,500 miles with 45,000lb gave the RAF a transport equally suited to tactical and strategic roles. Introduction into service for any aircraft type is never straightforward and in 1969 Marshall's discovered that the service use of contaminated fuel

C-130K C.1 XV177 the first Hercules for the RAF, which was handed over on 19 December 1966 and (left) on arrival at Marshalls of Cambridge.

had corroded many of the C.Mk.1s' integral wing tanks. This resulted in eleven Hercules being withdrawn from front-line squadrons and each had its 48 feet long tanks either completely or partially replaced with new components manufactured by Lockheed. In 1972 XV208 was taken out of service with 48 Squadron and delivered to Marshall's for extensive modification as the Hercules W.Mk.2 for weather reconnaissance and research by the Royal Aircraft Establishment's Meteorological Research Flight at Farnborough. Once completed, Snoopy, as this aircraft was affectionately known, flew on 31 March 1973. Snoopy ceased operations with the UK Met Office (Met Research Flight) on 31 March 2001. During 1972-85 Marshall's modified the Hercules' outer wing structure, wing joints and engine truss mounts to extend the life of the C.Mk.1 airframes. When a structural test programme conducted by Marshalls in January 1975 revealed a major failure in the test aircraft, the decision was taken to modify all the C.Mk.1s with a redesigned centre section; this had been first introduced by Lockheed for the USAF's C-130A, E and HC-130H aircraft in 1968. Marshall's completed this modification in 1979. In addition to all of this work, beginning in 1976, Marshall Engineering began major servicing of the RAF Hercules fleet, dealing with each aircraft on a three-year cycle. For three years, from 1976-79, all the C.Mk.1s were also put through an anti-corrosion programme to extend their service life.

In 1978 the MoD had funded a 'stretch' programme to bring thirty C.Mk.1s up to C.Mk.3 standard to increase the available cabin volume by 37 per cent and raise capacity from 92 to 129 infantrymen or from 64 to 92 paratroops, (which could, if necessary be dropped by the 'ultra low-level airdrop' (ULLA) method only yards above the ground). This decision followed Lockheed's success in extending the commercial L-100-20 and -30 by using a 5 feet 'plug' forward of the wing and a 3.3 feet 'plug' aft. XV223 was therefore flown back to Marietta late in 1979 to become the prototype of the Hercules C.Mk.3. XV223 first flew in modified form on 3 December 1979. It returned to Britain in January 1980 to undergo Service trials with 'B' Flight at the A&AEE. Plugs were manufactured by Lockheed and shipped to Marshall's where the remaining 29 C.Mk.1s were stretched to be brought up to C.Mk.3 standard. All were completed by the end of November 1985.

In 1970 RAF Hercules assisted in earthquake relief operations in Turkey and Peru and cyclone relief operations in East Pakistan. During the 1971 war between India and Pakistan, in eighteen sorties between 10 and 12 December, Hercules transports evacuated 909 British and friendly foreign nationals from West Pakistan and 434 from a bomb-cratered runway in East Pakistan. In 1972 Lyneham's Hercules helped with typhoon relief in the Philippines, earthquake relief in Nicaragua, as well as reinforcement of Belize to counter threat of invasion by that country. In March 1973, 46 Group was involved in Operation 'Khana Cascade', the biggest airlift since Berlin in 1948, in which Hercules dropped almost 2,000 tons of grain, maize and rice to Himalayan villagers in Nepal. (In 1980 the RAF Hercules returned, in 'Khana Cascade 80'.) In 1973 also, Hercules assisted in famine relief in Sudan, Mali and West Africa and deployed UN peacekeepers to the Middle East after the Yom Kippur war.

RAF C.1 XV199 of the Lyneham Wing, RAF Air Support Command in the early high- gloss sand/brown upper surface and black under surface scheme. Sixty-six C-130K models were purchased by Great Britain for the RAF. The first flew on 19 October 1966 and as the Hercules C.MK.1, entered service with 242 OCU at Thorney Island in April 1967.

242

In 1974 Hercules dropped relief supplies to St. Helena and gave assistance to cyclone relief in north Australia and famine relief in North Africa. 1974 was also the first year that the Hercules first began deploying troops to Northern Ireland. In July, during the war in Cyprus, the RAF airlifted 13,430 service and civilian families by Hercules, VC 10s, Britannias, Belfasts and Comets. One Hercules alone airlifted 139 people from Dhekelia to Akrotiri. On 10 March 1975 Hercules' of 48 Squadron evacuated civilians from Phnom Penh, Cambodia. An evacuation of the British Embassy in Saïgon was made under fire. Emergency reinforcement of Belize and earthquake relief in the Van region of Turkey was carried out, but all RAF units in Cyprus, except a few Whirlwind helicopters but including transports were withdrawn to the UK. In 1979 Hercules' evacuated Western nationals from Iran, assisted in earthquake relief in Yugoslavia, supported the Red Cross in

Kampuchea and delivered civil relief to Nicaragua during the civil war there. For three months during 1979-80 six Hercules were used in Operation 'Agila' to resupply British forces in Rhodesia (later to become Zimbabwe) stationed there to help monitor the ceasefire and the setting up of free elections after a long and bloody civil war. Main operations were flown from the capital, Salisbury and about five other towns, as well as remote air drop zones (DZs). The latter posed the biggest threat to air operations. There had been no time to fit the RAF Hercules with defence against infra-red guided surface-to-air missiles (SAMs), but the main danger came from Patriotic Front small arms and anti-aircraft artillery (AAA). The 'Fat Alberts' were flown at lo-lo altitudes of 250 feet at a speed of 210 knots to minimize the SAM threat. Operations were flown without accident, although there were a few near-misses, the main problem being a few bird strikes. On 3 August 1981 a

Nepalese children at Surkhet sift grain spillage from a delivery just brought to them by C.Mk.1 XV200 of 46 Group (RAF) Transport Command during the March 1973 Operation 'Khana Cascade'. This aircraft became the C.Mk.1P prototype in April 1982. (RAF)

stretched C.MK.3 of 70 Squadron left Lyneham to rescue British holidaymakers stranded in the Gambia following an attempted coup. Operating from Dakar, Senegal the RAF crew under the command of Squadron Leader Rod Caffady evacuated approximately 200 refugees from Banjul airport during the following week. On 31 October 1984 the RAF flew a detachment of two Hercules, four aircrews and fifty ground staff at short notice to Addis Ababa to assist in the distribution of famine-relief supplies in Ethiopia. Within hours of arriving in Addis Ababa the RAF detachment was in action flying up-country, delivering grain into some of the toughest and most inhospitable airstrips in the world. The RAF transports were joined in due course by military aircraft from five other nations. Operation 'Bushell' as it was called was initially intended as a three-month effort (by year-end the Hercules had ferried more than 3,500 tons of supplies) but it continued into 1985, making it the longest sustained relief effort ever. It involved aircraft from Nos. 47 and 80 Squadrons, specially trained in low-level air-drop techniques, with crews rotating regularly. The tropical heat and the altitude of the Ethiopian plateau posed problems similar to those which the RAF had experienced in Rhodesia in 1980.

On 2 April 1982 Britain suddenly had a war on its hands in the South Atlantic when Argentinean forces invaded the Falkland Islands. The UN attempted to persuade the ruling junta in Buenos Aires that it should withdraw its forces of occupation from the islands, but to no avail. Even though the British government had already decided to mount Operation 'Corporate' to retake the islands, Britain's action was legitimized by the UN following this failure to resolve the situation diplomatically. On 3 April eight Hercules left Lyneham and staged through Gibraltar to Wideawake airfield on the British-owned island of Ascension (4,260 miles from Britain and 3,915 miles from Stanley). One aircraft carried a six-man team from the UK Mobile Air Movements Squadron (UK MAMS) in order to establish an airhead for the Hercules fleet from the UK. Apart from the need to organize, equip and deploy a large naval task force to repossess the islands, one other major consideration centred on how the very long-range supply mission could be best carried out. On 21 April the first airdrop by Hercules from Ascension Island to ships of the Task Force took place. In the first three weeks 163 flights were made by Hercules aircraft and they delivered almost 1,500 tons of stores and equipment for the Task Force. In addition, two chartered Boeing 707s and even some ex-RAF Belfasts supplemented the RAF effort.

These supporting operations posed no immediate problems to the RAF. Hercules crews were already familiar with this route, staging through Gibraltar (southbound) and Dakar (northbound), where they ground-refuelled for the legs to and from Ascension Island. However, the range performance of 47 and 70 Squadron's Hercules was such that provision for in-flight refuelling would have to be made if they were to support the Task Force as far as Port Stanley in the Falklands. In the interim, beginning on 16 April, the Engineering Wing at Lyneham adapted and began fitting surplus 825 Imperial gallon auxiliary tanks intended for use in Andovers and Argosys, subsequently held in store, in the forward fuselage of the C.Mk.1s. This added 13,200lb of fuel to the Hercules' standard 63,000lb, increasing the range by approximately 1,000 miles and extending the maximum endurance by about four hours. The converted aircraft became known as LR.2s and adaption was completed in just five days. A further increase in range was gained by installing four tanks in the forward fuselage instead of two and these aircraft became known as LR4s. The first LR version was deployed to Ascension on 4 May.

Meanwhile, on 15 April Marshall of Cambridge was urgently directed, as a matter of high priority, to design, install, test and fit, 15 feet in-flight refuelling probes to 25 C.Mk.1s, which, when completed, would be designated C.Mk.1Ps. On 30 April Marshall also received word from the MoD that it should prepare a trial installation for a Hercules tanker using the standard Flight Refuelling Ltd hose-drum unit (HDU, or 'hudu') ML17B, which British Aerospace were using to help convert six Vulcan K.Mk.2 tankers at Manchester. In all, six modified C.Mk.1s, designated C.Mk.1Ks, would be required to serve as tankers. In-flight refuelling conversion on this scale had never been attempted before, except for a small number of EC-130Es in the USAF which had received underwing probes. The Vulcans were the only aircraft already 'probed', but their in-flight refuelling systems had not been used for fifteen years and crews were not current in the refuelling technique. Since no new probes could be made in the time available, Marshall Engineering produced a probe installation fashioned from a standard Flight Refuelling Ltd probe with a Mk.8 nozzle fitted to a surplus Vulcan. Using as the prototype C.Mk.1P XV200 (which was at Cambridge for routine engineering), it was installed in the upper forward fuselage of the Hercules, offset to starboard. The in-flight refuelling pipe (of 3 inches diameter) was routed along the upper surface of the fuselage to enter the wing trailing edge-to-fuselage fairing on the starboard side, where it connected with the vertical ground refuelling pipe. The latter was modified to have a 'Y'-branch, adjacent to which a non-return valve was included to isolate

the in-flight refuelling system when the aircraft was refuelled on the ground. Another non-return valve was fitted just aft of the probe to contain fuel in the event of nozzle failure at the weak link, which could result from excessive side loads during air-to-air refuelling. Two floodlights were fitted to the side of the co-pilot's instrument panel and positioned to illuminate the probe from the right-hand windows and the refuelling control

Right: On 18 June 1982 Flight Lieutenant Terry Locke and his crew on 70 Squadron set a new world duration record for the Hercules in C.Mk.1P XV179 on an airdrop mission to East Falkland lasting 28 hours 4 minutes. (Marshall Aerospace)

Below" Hercules C-130K C.1 XV203 with a Vulcan and three Phantoms on Wideawake Airfield on Ascension Island during the Falklands War. XV203 was delivered to the SLAF (Sri Lankan Air Force) as CR-880 in June 2009.

Hercules C-130K C.1 XV205 at the time of the Falklands War in 1982. Unconfirmed reports indicate that at or just prior to Wednesday 29 August 2007 this aircraft, from RAF Lyneham now having been converted to C.1P standard, was landed heavily at night on a rough airstrip in the Afghan desert and was badly damaged and could not be recovered. It was being used to transport SAS units and was equipped with highly classified satellite and high frequency radio communications suites. Because of the presence of Taliban troops in the area, some equipment was removed and the Hercules was blown up.

panel was located above the navigator's station on the flight deck.

Marshalls completed this first C.Mk.1P in just ten days. XV200 made its first flight fitted with the probe installation on 28 April and was delivered the next day to the A&AEE. The aircraft passed its first test with flying colours on 2 May when it successfully transferred fuel to a Victor K.2 and on 5 May XV200 was redelivered to 47 Squadron at Lyneham. Problems during trial 'prods' with Victor K.2s were gradually eliminated and a new air-to-air refuelling 'toboggan' technique was adopted. The Victor's minimum speed at 23,000 feet (the Hercules' optimum range-height with load) was 264 mph, compared with the transport's maximum speed at high all-up weight of 242 mph. This meant that the Victor had to approach the Hercules from above and astern, the latter beginning a 500 feet-per-minute descent as soon as visual contact was made. The Victor then slowly had to overtake, allowing the Hercules to move into the six o'clock low position to engage the drogue and continue the descent at about 500 feet per minute for fifteen minutes at a speed of 270 mph.

XV200 reached Wideawake on 12 May and the first Hercules' air-refuelled, long-range, airdrop

sortie to the Total Exclusion Zone (TEZ), imposed by British Forces around the Falklands went ahead on 16 May. The operation, to drop 1,000lb of special stores and eight members of the SAS, a total distance of 7,247 miles, was made by Flight Lieutenant Harold Burgoyne's crew in the Hercules. Burgoyne wrote:[2]

'Oh, wouldn't it be great to have a nice, safe job like being on a front-line fighter squadron!'

'The line was delivered by Flight Lieutenant Bob 'Bumper' Rowley, the co-pilot of XV200 as it slowly taxied past the two Quick Reaction Alert F-4 Phantom fighters parked off the edge of Runway 14, Wideawake airfield, Ascension Island early on the morning of 17 May. Across the cockpit, in the captain's seat, I smiled and have both aircraft a wide berth as I gingerly moved past them in the darkness. Just behind us, our flight engineer, Flight Sergeant Steve 'Slug' Sloane, wiped the grit from his eyes and passed his last fuel reading to Flight Lieutenant Jim Cunningham, who duly completed his navigator's log and placed it in his bag. As the aircraft came to a halt on its parking slot, my loadmaster MALM Mick Sephton opened the door, stepped down on the tarmac and gratefully filled his lungs with the fresh, salt-laden Island air. I called for the 'Shut-Down Checks' and, as the propellers of the Hercules slowly wound to a halt and the all-pervading noise faded, I extracted my aching body from my seat, stretched stiffly and reflected inwardly on what my crew had just been through in the lead up to our record-breaking flight of 24 hours and five minutes from Ascension to the Falkland Islands and return.

'It seemed a long time ago, yet it was barely 46 days since that fateful day, 2 April, when it all began...

'All personnel of 37 Squadron, RAF Lyneham, were eagerly looking forward to the Easter weekend and a well-earned break after a particularly busy exercise period. The news of the Argentine invasion had not made much of an impact. After all, the Falkland Islands were over 4,000 miles from any usable airfield; well outside the operating range of the C-130 Hercules aircraft and thus unlikely to have any impact on our activities. However, others had different ideas.

'Two of our five crews were hastily detached to Ascension Island to begin a steady programme of parachute re-supply drops to the ships of the British Task Force as they steamed steadily southward. Simultaneously, the remaining three crews began an intensive programme of mission rehearsals and developing the new techniques that would be required to meet the operational plans

The famous 'Blue Falcons' parachute display team after dropping from their Hercules.

being developed at the Northwood HQ of Operation 'Corporate'. New equipment such as Inertial Navigation Systems and Night Vision Goggles (NVG) arrived daily and were fitted, trialled and tested. To increase the range, four ex-Andover aircraft fuel tanks were mounted in the cargo compartments of several aircraft and experimental trial flights of over twelve hours were commonplace. In three weeks, we completed a trials and training programme that would have taken almost two years in peacetime.

'Towards the end of April it became apparent that our main job was going to be the re-supply of the Task Force, which by then was at the extreme range of the Ascension-based Hercules, even those fitted with the auxiliary fuel tanks. A means of further extending the range of the aircraft to the 4,000 nautical miles required had to be quickly evolved and the answer was Air-to-Air Refuelling (AAR).

'The necessary extra equipment was fitted to a Hercules in record time and on the morning of 6 May 'The Boss' and I plus a composite crew, assembled in a briefing room at the Aeroplane and Armament Experimental Establishment, Boscombe Down, to prove the system and learn how to conduct AAR operations under the tutelage of Test Pilot Squadron Leader John Brown.

'Five days later all was complete. In that time we cleared the Hercules to refuel from a Victor tanker at weights above 155,000lb (the normal maximum take-off weight of the C-130) on four and three engines. Two-engine AAR had been attempted but had proved impossible at the extreme weights involved; but I vividly recall my excitement at flying the aircraft for the first time in my ten years on the Hercules with two engines actually shut down!

'Already an experienced RAF Qualified Flying Instructor and with all of four trips and five hours experience under his belt, Max Roberts was nominated as the first Hercules AAR Instructor and set about teaching AAR to other pilots and forming what would become the Lyneham Tanker Training Flight. Meanwhile, my crew hopped on a VC10 and detached to Ascension Island to start re-supplying the task force using our newly acquired, but 'unrefined', skills.

'On our arrival at Ascension on the morning of

In 1972 C-130K C.1 XV208 was taken out of service with 48 Squadron at Changi, Singapore and the aircraft returned to the UK in 1973 with a damaged main spar. It was delivered to Marshalls for extensive modification as the Hercules W.Mk.2 for weather reconnaissance and research by the Royal Aircraft Establishment's Meteorological Research Flight at Farnborough. Once completed, Snoopy, as this aircraft was affectionately known, flew on 31 March 1973. 'Snoopy' remained at Farnborough until experimental flying ceased; it then moved to Boscombe Down where it was operated by DERA until the aircraft was taken out of service in April 2001. Snoopy's last weather trip was on 28 March 2001 returning from a successful trip to Tromsö in northern Norway looking at the Arctic ice pack and its effect on global climate and satellite meteorology. Snoopy served with MRF from 1972 and flew over 1,800 research sorties from Rio de Janeiro and the Solomon Islands to the Polar ice caps. XV208 was scrapped on 14 April 2015 at Cambridge.

14 May, Wideawake airfield appeared initially to be a scene of total chaos. Apron space was at a premium with Victors, Nimrods, VC10s, Hercules and even a visiting USAF C-141 apparently shoehorned into their parking slots whilst overhead a never-ending stream of buzzing helicopters went about their business. The predatory shape of a lone Vulcan bomber parked just off the runway seemed to preside over this hive of activity and its Shrike anti-radar missiles slung menacingly under the wings only added to the sinister image. It was hot, dusty and the noise level was ear shattering.

'After extracting our bags from the VC10, we were driven the three miles over the stark volcanic plains of Ascension Island and up the winding hill road to the relative calm and marginally cooler surrounds of the bungalow in 'Two Boats' settlement which would be home for the next few months.

Pilot, Flight Lieutenant Jim Norfolk and navigator, Flight Lieutenant Tom Rounds had already flown several long-distance sorties to the Task Force and passed on a wealth of knowledge and experience regarding naval procedures, weather and especially the techniques of operating the Hercules as its limits.

'On 15 May I was asked to report with my crew to the Air Transport Ops at the airhead where we were briefed on our first AAR mission. This was to be an airdrop of eight parachutists and 1,000lb worth of stores to a ship, the RFA *Fort Austin* at a position approximately sixty miles north of Port Stanley airfield.[3] The drop was scheduled for mid-afternoon of the following day which, since transit time would be almost thirteen hours, meant a take-off time of 0230, less than twelve hours ahead. Time had suddenly become very much of the essence!

'Because our overstretched ground crew were working all out to unload and refuel the constant stream of transiting aircraft, it was left to the aircrew to prepare our aircraft. My loadmaster (ALM) Mick Sephton and flight engineer, 'Slug' Sloane, aided by two other ALMs, Pete Scott and

Roy Lewis, departed to start the lengthy process. Fuel tanks were filled, aircraft equipment checked, survival suits, life jackets and parachutes transferred from another Hercules and the 1,000lb load prepared and carefully rigged for parachuting. At the same time the pilots and navigators started flight planning. Three hours later, as the sun sank behind Green Mountain preparations were complete with the exception of the all important fuel and AAR plan. As nearly all the Victors were still airborne, refuelling as Vulcan en route to attack the Falklands, we had no way of knowing how many tankers would be available for our task until some hours later. My navigator, Jim Cunningham, volunteered to stay in the AAR planning cell and complete the planning, thereby allowing the rest of the crew to return to Two Boats to catch what sleep we could.

'Back at Wideawake the crew rushed through an intelligence brief and then rejoined Jim Cunningham at the flight planning tent who had worked throughout the evening to complete his work. With Jim Norfolk's help and the experience he had gained on his previous flights, I managed to work through the aircraft's performance manual and calculated all the required speeds for our expected take-off weight.

'Unfortunately, as this weight was above the

Phantom FG.2 of 23 Squadron from Stanley taking on fuel from a C.Mk.1K during a sortie in December 1982. After the Falklands War 23 Squadron occupied Port Stanley airfield until reduced to a Flight of four aircraft in 1988, reforming at Leeming with Tornado F3s. (Mick Jennings)

C-130K C.1 XV296 (66-13539) refuelling two of the four Phantom FGR2s of 1435 Flight providing the defence of the Falkland Islands. In 1982 a detachment of Phantoms began providing the air defence of the islands once the airfield at Stanley was capable of operating Phantoms following the victory over Argentina. On 31 October 1988, when 23 Squadron converted to the new Tornado F.3, the Falklands-based Phantoms took the designation 1435 Flight.

maximum weight shown in the various performance graphs those speeds had to be extrapolated and were in fact nothing more than educated guesses. What I did know was that if we lost an engine during the take-off, the remaining three engines would be unable to produce enough power to keep us flying and would, therefore, be taking us directly to the scene of the crash! However, Jim Norfolk assured me that he had already made several take-offs at this weight and I was confident that the aircraft wouldn't let us down.

'It was a strangely quiet atmosphere as we completed our mission briefs, walked out to the aircraft and set about our individual pre-flight tasks. Survival suits were unpacked, parachutes checked, flak jackets issued and everything positioned ready for immediate use. I went into the freight bay to check on progress and was immediately struck by the lack of space. The four Andover fuel tanks filled the main cargo area, while the boxes containing the parachutists'' equipment filled the ramp area. The chemical toilet that normally sat there had been removed and now sat in the middle of the freight bay between the forward and aft fuel tanks and offered no privacy to anyone who might have cause to use it. The eight troopers had found space in the webbing seats adjacent to the fuel tanks and were trying to create an area that might offer some comfort during the

thirteen hours that they were going to be on board.

'As the last few minutes before departure ticked away, there was little of the normal friendly 'banter'; everyone seemed engrossed in their own little world, all pre-occupied with their individual thoughts. However, at the appointed time, the familiar ritual of the pre-start checks concentrated minds; the sleeping Hercules was slowly nursed into life and, with a 'Good Luck' from the Air Traffic Controller, we were cleared for take-off.

'As I released the brakes, I noted the time as 0220 and wondered when we would be back on Ascension, but those thoughts quickly vanished as the aircraft gathered speed. As I anticipated, the take-off roll was much longer than normal but in answer to my tentative pull on the control column, XV200 rose slowly into the warm night air. I had never flown the Hercules this heavy before but the aircraft seemed to behave as normal; the only really noticeable difference was that everything seemed to be happening a little slower than usual. I wanted to have plenty of speed in hand before attempting any manoeuvering at this weight so, following a long period of acceleration, I slowly eased into a gently turning climb and, as the aircraft settled on course, the Southern Cross appeared off the nose, clearly visible among the myriad stars twinkling in the deep purple-black of the night sky.

'Having stabilised in a cruise-climb at just under 16,000 feet, the next few hours passed fairly

C-130J ZH889, which was delivered to the RAF in May 2000, flown by Wing Commander Rick Hobson over Wiltshire from RAF Lyneham on 9 September 2001. (MWB)

C-130J ZH889, which the author photographed air-to-air over Wiltshire on 9 November 2001 photographed (quite by chance) by same at Gibraltar on 21 February 2012! (MWB)

routinely although the crew were kept busy with hourly fuel calculations and checks. ALM Mick Sephton opened the galley and amazingly, produced freshly made egg and bacon sandwiches which were gratefully received and swiftly despatched. Dawn broke around 0600 and this, combined with copious amounts of hot, sweet coffee, restored the energy levels in preparation for the airborne refuel.

'During the six-hour transit, we burned off about 30,000lbs of fuel, which allowed us to climb to just over 22,000 feet and as we approached the re-fuelling point I noted with some relief that area was clear, apart from some cumulo-nimbus clouds far below. They wouldn't be a factor - or so I thought!

'As I pondered the job ahead of me I was roused from my reverie by the harsh intrusion of the radio call from the approaching Victor. Having taken off from Ascension some time after the Hercules the much faster tanker had gradually closed the gap and was now only five miles behind. My co-pilot, Bob Rowley made a radio call in reply and after confirmation that all was ready, the delicate airborne ballet of air-to-air refuelling began.

'Following the UK trials, it had been established that the AAR would have to be conducted at a minimum speed of 230 knots but the fully laden Hercules would be unable to maintain this speed in level flight. Therefore, the refuel would have to be done in a descent to allow both aircraft to maintain the required speed and ideal refuelling position - about 20 feet apart.

'The slim, elegant shape of the Victor swiftly overtook the ungainly Hercules, stabilised itself just forward of the Hercules' right wing and, on Rowley's command, both aircraft began a gradual descent of about 500 feet per minute. Trying to keep my control inputs to a minimum, I carefully manoeuvred into a line astern position about twenty feet behind the Victor's trailing refuelling hose and began my hook-up run. Under Bob's calm directions and with the engineer monitoring the engines, the two giants slowly closed until the refuelling probe on top of the Hercules and the Victor's dancing basket were only ten feet apart.

'AAR has been described as 'trying to spear a rolling doughnut' and this was no exception. Time and again I edged my aircraft forward but each time failed to get the probe into the basket. Although I was getting frustrated with my inability to find the target, I had to put that aside and keep on trying but I was conscious that valuable fuel was being used up and the formation was getting lower and lower. Finally, as we passed through 17,000 feet and with my self-induced pressure becoming almost unbearable, at the sixth attempt a successful contact was made and fuel began to flow.

'Transferring the required 37,000lb of fuel took thirty minutes and, towards the end, it was a real touch and go situation. By that time both aircraft had descended to Around 2,500 feet and we were dodging around the cumulo-nimbus clouds that I had assessed earlier as not being a problem!

'Just maintaining contact in the turbulent, low-level air was proving very difficult and I knew that if I accidentally disconnected early I would not have the power to reconnect and the mission would be lo0st. Luckily, the tanker captain was on top of his game and skilfully led us around the worst of the big clouds and showers. After what seemed like an eternity, flight engineer Steve Sloane announced that the refuel was complete. With an enormous feeling of relief, I eased back on the power and with a soft clunk and a slight spray of fuel from the refuelling bracket, a clean disconnect was achieved.

'I watched as the Victor completed a sweeping turn away from us and eased back northwards to Ascension and then noticed that Bob had steadied our aircraft and that the compass needle had settled once more on south, towards the Falkland's Total Exclusion Zone (TEZ). To avoid detection by the Argentinean radar on the hill overlooking Port Stanley, the descent to the *Fort Austin* was initiated about 250 miles north of the Falkland Islands. The specially devised 'Combat Entry Checklist' was completed to set the aircraft up in its best fighting configuration and, as the Hercules levelled at 2,000 feet, the paratroop doors were opened and our two army despatchers from 47 Air Despatch Regiment checked in on the intercom from their observation positions.

'Conditions were not ideal. It was a grey, foreboding day with a cloud base of about 2,500 feet and a visibility of about six kilometres which decreased markedly in the widespread, squally showers. It was bitterly cold and as Bob Rowley established contact with the Royal Navy, the sea temperature was reported as two degrees. Luckily, the wind speed was just within limits for the drop and as the parachutists were wearing immersion suits it all looked reasonable. As we homed towards the ship, our hastily-installed, primitive, hand-held Radar Warning Receiver chirped and squawked indicating that several radars were illuminating the aircraft although, thankfully, no fire-control radars had 'lock-on'.

'I spotted the Austin at about two miles out, riding on a grey sea and with its recovery boat already in the water. This part of the mission turned out to be straightforward and went almost exactly to plan. With minimum delay, the parachutists were despatched on the first run and the stores on the second and, as we turned back north into the gathering dusk, a faint voice on the radio confirmed that all the parachutists were safe and that the stores were on board Fort Austin.

'By the top of the climb, darkness had descended and a new problem had arisen. Unforecast headwinds had developed, seemed likely to continue for some time and, as this had fuel implications, a solution was required. It was Jim Cunningham, who offered a possible way out using a technique borrowed from sailing ships - tacking. Jim suggested that instead of applying drift to our heading we should allow the aircraft to

be blown east by the wind and then turn hard into it until track was regained. I thought it sounded a bit strange but the alternative options of ditching in the Atlantic Ocean short of Ascension or diverting to the South American mainland were not terribly inviting, so I elected to give it a try. Amazingly, it worked and thereafter the procedure was repeated until the wind eventually abated about two hours later.

'As we continued the 11-hour night flight back to Ascension, seats were swapped and meals eaten but more to combat encroaching fatigue than from hunger. Games were devised but we discovered that there is a limit to 'I-Spy'. Meanwhile, the BBC World Service continued to provide hourly updates on the overall progress of our operation to restore the Falkland Islands to their rightful inhabitants.

'About an hour from Ascension, it seemed that the most demanding and potentially hazardous portions of the flight had now passed and we allowed ourselves to relax. However, this air of calm was shattered when Jim Cunningham announced that he had a contact on the radar at our 10 o'clock position about five miles distant! Our intelligence briefs had mentioned the remote possibility of an Argentine Air Force Boeing 707 being equipped with air-to-air missiles and sent out on patrol. Indeed, we had heard a rumour that this aircraft had already 'intercepted' a reconnaissance

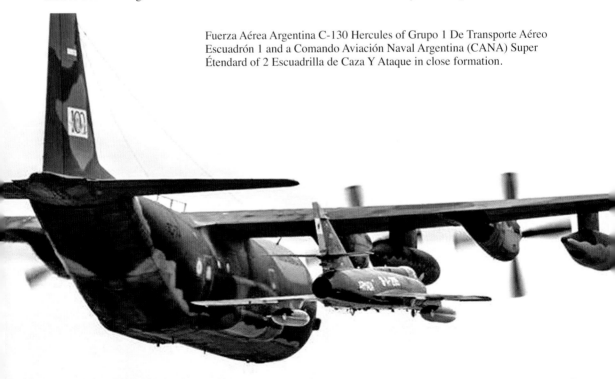

Fuerza Aérea Argentina C-130 Hercules of Grupo 1 De Transporte Aéreo Escuadrón 1 and a Comando Aviación Naval Argentina (CANA) Super Étendard of 2 Escuadrilla de Caza Y Ataque in close formation.

A C-130K refuelling from a VC10.

flight by one of our own aircraft, although on that occasion nothing further had developed. I acquired a visual sighting almost immediately and confirmed it as a group of lights that appeared to be an aircraft in a left bank and turning towards us. I was well versed in fighter evasion techniques and immediately disengaged the autopilot, reduced the power and started a high bank angle, high 'G' turn towards the threat. Jim Norfolk had shot forward to my side and it was his timely intervention that avoided a possible catastrophe as he identified the lights as a string of refuelling Victors on climb out from Ascension. What had appeared to my eyes as an aircraft in a turn was in fact a mass formation of tankers setting out on another 'Black Buck' mission which had not been known about when we had been briefed some 27 hours earlier!

'Following these hair-raising few minutes, the approach and landing were straightforward by comparison. However, fatigue ensured that everyone monitored everyone else very closely as XV200 finally touched down on Wideawake's runway some 24 hours and five minutes after take-off.

'I was given the news by the Ascension Ops Officer that things hadn't changed greatly in the time that we had been away - all the bars were shut and transport was unavailable. At 0300 the only way back to our accommodation at Two Boats was to wait until a vehicle was available or to try hitchhiking back up the hill. Oh well, I thought, never mind. I'm pretty sure that some of the other crews would still be around in the bungalow putting the world to rights over another 'Irish coffee' and the most wide-awake drunks in the South Atlantic would, no doubt, have ensured at least one beer was waiting in the fridge. Wouldn't they?...'

For this extraordinary achievement, Harry Burgoyne was awarded the Air Force Cross.

Each of the other 24 C.Mk.1s, fitted with two internal auxiliary tanks, was converted to the same standard as XV200; the last being delivered on 25 October 1982. Meanwhile, Marshall Engineering was also required to fit CMA 771 Omega navigation equipment (similar to that installed in the USAF C-130H) to RAF Hercules for use on the long over-water flights in the Atlantic. This involved mounting the display and control panel in the navigation station and the small antenna in the upper rear fuselage on the port side behind the fin. XVI79, which had been delivered to Cambridge for the probe modification became the first RAF Hercules to be fitted with the navigation device. Also, installation of the HDU Mk.17B in the fuselage of six C.Mk.1K tankers proceeded apace. XV296 was fitted out first, the HDU installation being sited on the rear loading ramp with the auxiliary carriage and drogue deployment box on the cargo door so that the Hercules could remain pressurized while not refuelling. (Much later, Marshall Engineering retrofitted a system which

enabled in-flight refuelling to take place while retaining pressurization.) Fuel supply to the HDU came from the C.Mk.1K's main tanks (and not from the cabin auxiliary tanks) by tapping the standard fuel dump pumps, refuelling pressure being supplied by a bleed-air turbine-driven fuel pump. Two ram-air intakes and a pair of exhaust ducts were mounted in the sides of the pressure hull to provide cooling for the HDU components. Standard external tanker lights were fitted, together with their switches adjacent to the in-flight refuelling panel above the navigation station.

XV296 successfully deployed its drogue in two flights from Cambridge on 8 and 10 June. On the

11th the aircraft was despatched to the A&AEE to make its first dry coupling with a Harrier. However, the HDU projecting from the rear ramp caused some buffeting and the HDU oil cooler overheated. XV296 was therefore returned to Marshall Engineering, where strakes added to the loading ramp solved the buffeting defects and a third ram-air intake solved the air cooler problem. On 21 June XV296 carried out an entirely successful in-flight refuelling, transferring 5,900lb of fuel to a Buccaneer at 1,000lb/minute. XV296 returned to the A&AEE on 22 June and was equally successful in 'wet' coupling with Hercules, Nimrod, Sea Harrier and Phantom aircraft. The

tanker was delivered to Lyneham on 5 July, but problems with the heat exchangers persisted and it was eventually decided to introduce alternative heat exchangers. With this final modification four C.Mk.1Ks (XV296, XV210, XV204 and XV192 *Horatius*) were delivered to Lyneham by 26 July. The first operational use of a C.Mk.1K was made early in August, seven weeks after the Argentinean surrender at Port Stanley, during a round trip from Ascension. (By the end of the year, two were based on Ascension Island and two at Stanley. The two remaining tanker conversions were completed in early 1983.)

Meanwhile, on 3 June 1982 the RAF notched

An RAF 'loadie' maintains a close watch on C.130K C.3 XV299 of the Lyneham Wing from the ramp of his Hercules. C.1 XV299 was delivered to 30 Squadron on 26 April 1968.

up its 10,000th hour of Hercules operations since 'Corporate' began. In fourteen weeks of operation, the UK MAMS teams at Ascension handled over 18,000 tons of freight and 42,000 passengers, all without loss. On 18 June Flight Lieutenant Terry Locke and his crew on 70 Squadron set a new world duration record for the Hercules in C.Mk.1P XVI79 on an airdrop mission to East Falkland lasting 28 hours 4 minutes.

The Fuerza Aérea Argentina (Argentine Air Force) had nine Hercules - two C-130Es and five C-130H transports and two KC-130H 'Chancha' ('Mother Sow') tankers of Grupo 1 de Transporte Aero at Rio Gallegos in its operational strength. The KC-130H tankers were used extensively in support of the Skyhawks and Super Étendards and frequently operated in a pair. The two C-130s, TC-61 and TC-63, with the C-130Hs TC-64 to TC-68 were primarily used from Comodoro Rivadavia. The FAA operated these Hercules transports on thirty-one resupply sorties, mostly under cover of darkness at very low level, in appalling weather, to the Port Stanley garrison from 1 May until 13 June, less than twenty-four hours before the surrender. They carried 400 tons of cargo in and brought out 264 casualties, plus a captured RAF Harrier pilot who was evacuated to the mainland. Two airdrop sorties were also flown to remote locations on the Islands. Grupo 1 operated one of its C-130Hs (TC-68) as a bomber on 29 May, when the fuel-laden 15,000-ton *British-Wye* was the target for a salvo of eight bombs. One of the bombs hit the ship but fortunately failed to explode, bouncing off into the sea. (A week later, on 8 June, a US-leased oil tanker, coincidentally named *Hercules*, on its way round Cape Horn in ballast, was also hit and again the bomb failed to explode - but this time the weapon finished up lodged below decks and the ship eventually had to be scuttled.)

The Falklands had only three airfields with the longest and only paved runway at the capital, Stanley. Though the newly-designated 'Aerodromo Malvinas' was too short to support fast jets. IA-58 Pucará's (an Argentinean-built counter-insurgency aircraft) and lightly-loaded C-130 Hercules could operate from half the length of the Stanley runway. Hercules transport night flights brought supplies, weapons, vehicles and fuel and airlifted out the wounded up until the end of the conflict. The only Argentine Hercules that was lost in the conflict was shot down on 1 June when TC-63 was intercepted by a Sea Harrier of 801 Squadron from the carrier HMS *Hermes*, fifty nautical miles north of Pebble Island in daylight when it was searching for the British fleet north-east of the islands. The C-130E had departed Comodoro Rivadavia that morning at about the same time that a C-130H (TC-66) left Port Stanley for a long homeward run. The two aircraft were in occasional radio contact until about 1340Z, by which time the fighter controller on the British frigate HMS *Minerva* in San Carlos Water detected intermittent 'skin paints' to the north of Pebble Island by search radars when the Hercules 'popped up' for a quick radar sweep. Although low on fuel, two 801 Squadron Sea Harriers piloted by Lieutenant Commander Nigel 'Sharkey' Ward and Lieutenant 'Stevie T' Thomas were diverted from the return leg of a routine CAP over Pebble Island. 'Sharkey' Ward picked up the target on his own radar and began a tail-chase after the C-130E below cloud. Possibly warned by Argentine ground radar at Stanley, the C-130E made off at high speed and low level towards the mainland but was easily caught by the Sea Harrier. Worried by his low fuel state, 'Sharkey' Ward fired his first Sidewinder out of range and it fell short but he hit with his second, which started a fire between the port engines. Unable to wait to see if the missile had taken out such a large target, he emptied 240 rounds of 30mm cannon into the Hercules at close range and saw a wing off break off before the aircraft crashed into the sea in flames, fifty miles north of Pebble Island eight minutes after it was detected. All seven crew were killed. 'Sharkey' Ward and Steve Thomas had only 45 gallons of fuel left for their 180 mile transit to Invincible. They landed-on safely which was just as well because both pilots did not have enough fuel for a further circuit.

The final battles made Stanley's runway untenable for Hercules aircraft until 24 June, when the first RAF Hercules landed with a UK MAMS team aboard whose mission was to help restore the islands' war-torn economy. Next day a Hercules flown by Harry Burgoyne landed at Stanley to triumphantly return Rex Hunt, the former governor, to the Falkland Islands. Between 15-28 August the runway at Port Stanley was closed for landings while it was repaired and extended, so the Hercules had to make the 7,830-mile round trips without landing. These usually required around four in-flight refuellings. To enable a single Hercules to reach Port Stanley, the primary C-130 flew from Wideawake accompanied by a C.Mk.1K tanker, followed by a pair of Victor K.2s. The primary Hercules would be refuelled by the Victors before they returned to Ascension to be refuelled themselves, the Hercules tanker would then refuel the primary Hercules which would fly on to Port Stanley, while the C.Mk.1K also returned to Wideawake. The Victor K.2s would then take off and rendezvous with the primary Hercules on its return flight.

The Hercules carried mail and supplies on these air drops and picked up mail using an air-snatch technique devised at Brize Norton six weeks before. This involved trailing a grappling hook from the Hercules' lowered ramp and engaging a nylon rope, suspended between two 22 feet poles on the ground, to which the mailbag was attached.

Often the unsung and largely unheralded role performed by the RAF Hercules fleet in sustaining the Task Force is understated and overlooked. That the Hercules was able to operate over such vast distances and in such inhospitable climes in the first place is due entirely to the engineering staff at Marshall Aerospace and at Lyneham, while the professionalism of the air- and ground-crews in the Lyneham Wing is unsurpassed. In all, 2,004 RAF personnel received the South Atlantic Campaign

medal and 74 honours for the South Atlantic Operation were bestowed on members of the RAF, including fifty 'in-theatre' meritorious and gallantry awards.

Lessons learned in the Falklands were manifold and many have since been put to excellent use around the world. From April 1986, four (later two) C.Mk.1Ks of 1312 Flight have been stationed at RAF Mount Pleasant. Beginning in 1986 Marshall Engineering began fitting in-flight refuelling probes to the thirty C.Mk.3s to convert them to C.Mk.3P configuration. Starting in 1987 C.Mk.1Ps and C.Mk.1Ks began receiving AN/ALQ157 IR jamming equipment and chaff/flare dispensers. At least five C.Mk.1Ps were fitted with Racal 'Orange Blossom' ESM pods beneath their wing-tips to give some degree of surveillance capability.

Nine years after the Falklands War the RAF was faced with an even bigger logistics challenge when Iraq invaded neighbouring Kuwait on 2 August 1990, quickly overran this small Arab kingdom and massed its armies on the border with Saudi Arabia. King Fahd of Saudi Arabia invited friendly nations to assist in the defence of his country and the UN response led to the largest deployment of military hardware since World War II. The RAF involvement is described by Squadron Leader C. E. Cook BSc: 'RAF Lyneham's contribution to Operation 'Granby' began before

RAF C-130J aircraft delivering UK aid to Iraq.(MoD)

even the first drumbeat of war had finished sounding in Whitehall. The first three crews departed on the morning of 8 August using spare seats that happened to be available on a VC-10 bound for Akrotiri, Cyprus on a normal peacetime task. These crews were to found a pool in Cyprus that was to remain there without break right through into May of the following year. Within three days the lift to the Gulf began in earnest and 25 aircraft were committed, slipping through Cyprus to Gulf stations as these were established. This was in addition to much of the normal tasking which had been the Station's pre-planned lot, although plenty of a lowly nature was cancelled to release the crews and aircraft for the unexpected effort.

'Initially, the lift was out of Lyneham, as we positioned all the equipment and personnel needed to support our own operations. Gradually, however, the thrust altered as the fighter squadrons began to deploy and the focus of the operation moved to Coltishall and Marham in Norfolk. The crews were flying long days, frequently in excess of 19 hours and working out of Cyprus either to the Gulf and back to Cyprus, or to the UK and back, in a single duty period. Few aircraft came through Lyneham at this time, creating something of an unreal air on the Station about the whole operation. By this stage Lyneham personnel were scattered across the whole of the Middle East, although there was more a feeling of optimism as each day seemed to bring the end of the operation apparently nearer. This

false hope, however, was swiftly dispelled as more and more units were added to the list of those deploying. By the end of August the work rate had increased and it became apparent that we were in for a long haul. August indeed proved busy in the extreme, producing a total of hours flown at 2.8 times the original planned rate.

'In September, deployment was no longer the complete air transport operation. By this time the units already deployed were crying out for re-supply and deliveries of equipment that had been forgotten in the initial rush and, thus, a daily schedule began moving supplies and rations to Bahrain and Dubai. Within a week, though, its destinations had increased to include Seeb and Thumrait in Oman and Riyadh as well, with the schedule keeping Arabia on the left one day and on the right the next, as the route was reversed. Tasking throughout September was up-and-down as one deployment was completed and the next was not ready to go. Crews were brought home from Cyprus in reaction to an apparent lull only, in some cases, to turn round after a single night at home to return for a further effort.

'At the start of October the Army started to move in force. Most of the troops came from Germany, which meant again a change of focus for the Operation. Fortunately, a measure of sanity imposed itself into the arrangements and all of the aircraft routed through Lyneham to change crews and avoid the long crew duty times that had featured so strongly in the early days. This phase

C-130J-30 ZH872 taking off from Camp Bastion in Afghanistan. (MoD)

opened interesting doors to us as Austria, a country we normally avoid, offered overflying rights to our aircraft, although not without creating confusion with the Italians, who could not get used to our continuing straight on at the top of Italy instead of turning left for France. The intensity of operations continued as the build-up of the Army developed and the first of the strange items of equipment, which eventually became so familiar, began to appear. The area around the outbound freight hangar gradually assumed the air of a junkyard as the normal storage areas were unable to cope with the volume of freight and boxes, cartons and equipment were piled haphazardly in the open air awaiting their return.

'The end of October saw another record in the number of hours flown by the Hercules fleet in a single month. Despite 25 hours more than August's total, there still seemed no real sign of a let-up. Instead, the first Hercules detachment in the theatre formed when three aircraft, six crews and twelve each of engineers and movements personnel under a detachment commander established themselves at Riyadh International Airport. Whilst the TriStar took over the movement of freight and personnel from the UK to Riyadh, its aim was to distribute from there to all the Gulf stations. Not least amongst the mass of freight moved by this route was mail, which meant that once again the sound of Albert meant the arrival of 'Blueys' (Forces Air Mail letters) from those back home to cheer the weary days for the troops upon the ground.

'Throughout November and into December operations continued. Despite confident assertions, the promised break for Christmas never materialised. Over Christmas Day itself, of our own we had only four crews in Cyprus plus the Riyadh detachment, although a total of 141 Lyneham people were scattered throughout the many Gulf locations. By now we were being assisted by many other nations and civilian cargo aircraft from Spain, Belgium, Nigeria and even Rumania, to name but a few. The roll call of strange loads continued with a complete desert cinema, water osmosis treatment plants, aardvarks and giant cobras featuring in the manifests. Amongst these wonders the mundane continued and all the facilities for a tented city to sleep over a thousand people passed through the gates on their way East. Unfortunately, the promised football

pitch never appeared, although this was much to the relief of our loadmasters upon whom would have fallen the task of watering it during its transit.

The effort continued into January, but on the outbreak of the air war we, paradoxically, had our first real break for five months. In deference to the danger for unarmed transport aircraft, the skies of Saudi Arabia were closed and for one glorious 24-hour period, there was no tasking or movement of any kind. Then, as the scope of our air superiority became apparent so we eased back into action. By now the detachment in Riyadh had grown considerably, with seven aircraft and fourteen crews working round the clock both into the major air bases and to up-country rough strips in direct support of the Army. Despite the brief surcease, January proved to be another record month as over 7,500 hours were flown in support of the Operation alone.

'The pace quickened, as it now became apparent that the ground war would soon follow and the lists of forgotten 'must-haves' continued to grow. Then, at last, it happened - but was as soon over. Our major role after the ground war started was to have been casualty evacuation, but little was required and, fortunately, the elaborate plans were not needed. Within days the emphasis changed entirely and the noises were all about returning items and personnel home, the freight stored in the open at Lyneham began to disappear back to the depots and a further air of unreality settled on the Station. Before the homeward rush began, however, other firsts were notched up as we flew the first fixed-wing aircraft into Kuwait itself, delivering firstly the men to secure the Embassy and then, a mere two days later, returning the Ambassador himself to his rightful place. Lyneham's work was far from complete. Most of the equipment was to come home by sea, but still an enormous amount was too expensive or valuable to be left too long. In addition, the plight of the Kurds led to more effort as we launched into the new Operations of 'Provide Comfort' and 'Haven' to bring succour and protection to the refugees in Northern Iraq and Turkey.

'By May something of a real calm at last descended. The main Operation was definitely complete but still our contribution, muted but nonetheless there, continued. A schedule ran every other day to Turkey in support of the Marines then extending into Iraq itself, as the Americans opened the small airfield of Sirsenk in the Anatolian Mountains. Meanwhile, our gulf detachment, now reduced to two crews and one aircraft, moved to Bahrain to continue until the end of June and 50,000 flying hours later when it was all over.'[4]

The RAF Air Transport Detachment (ATD) at King Khaled International Airport, Riyadh, was formed on 30 October 1990 with three Hercules and six crews, plus engineering, movements and support personnel from RAF Lyneham. Under the command of Wing Commander Peter Bedford its task was to provide 'in-theatre' transport wherever and whenever it was needed by British and other coalition forces in the Gulf. Two Hercules and three crews of 40 Squadron RNZAF joined the ATD on 23 December 1990 and was expanded to four crews in mid January, making a total of about sixty RNZAF personnel during the war period. In the main, support equipment tor operational squadrons was airlifted direct from normal operating bases in the UK, with station Mobility Flight personnel playing a major role in the planning and preparation for airlift. Lyneham and Brize Norton movers prepared and loaded the majority of the air freight and it was here that the strain of the huge out-load task was felt the most. The initial basis of operations was a 'hub and spoke' system, with RAF TriStars and VC-10 C.1.s feeding the 'hub' at King Khaled with freight and passengers and the Hercules flying out on the 'spokes', carrying the freight and passengers to locations within the theatre of operations. These included Seeb and Thumrait, both in Oman, Minhad in the United Arab Emirates, Bahrain and Saudi Arabian airfields such as Dhahran, Tabuk, Jubail and Qaisumah and to other airfields and strips within the theatre of operations. From August 1990 to the end of February 1991 over 46,000 Army, RAF and Royal Navy personnel were moved out to the Gulf by air alone, along with over 46,000 tonnes of equipment.

The unit was expanded on 14 January 1991 to seven Hercules and fourteen crews with proportionally more engineering and movements' personnel, which brought the total number of people to about 200. The increase in size occurred just before the start of the air war on 17 January. That month over 7,500 hours were flown in support of the operation alone.

The beginning of 'Desert Storm' saw the Hercules using short strips - natural surface airfields - for moving troops of the 1st British Armoured Division. These flights employed 'combat loading', a procedure in which the aircraft fuselage is left empty of seats and the troops sit on the floor. During this time crews became expert in the skills of desert low flying. Their role then was to have been CASEVAC (Casualty Evacuation) from the field hospitals back to Riyadh for onward flights to the UK, but thankfully, little was required and fortunately the elaborate plans were not needed. The unit began to operate into Kuwait International Airport on 28 February and an ATD Hercules was the third fixed-wing aircraft to land there after the airport was reopened. Subsequently, the crews had the horror of having to fly into the thick black choking smoke that emanated from the burning Kuwaiti oil wells. From the beginning of March the Hercules operated regular schedules from Riyadh to the big seaport at Al Jubayl (Saudi Arabia), the Tornado bases at Tabuk (northwest Saudi Arabia) and Muharraq (Bahrain), as well as Dubai and Kuwait City and as required between various desert airstrips, like LZ05 in Kuwait and the desert airfield at Qaisumah (northern Saudi Arabia). Many tons of equipment and large numbers of homeward-bound personnel were carried on these flights, contributing to the records already broken by the RAF's Hercules fleet since August 1990.

By the time the fighting was over, the Airlift Co-ordination Centre (ALCC) at HQ, Strike Command at RAF High Wycombe had despatched over 2,250 RAF and 550 civil air transport flights. In the main, these carried deploying forces and their equipments, or the vast quantities of supplies which were required to sustain them. In total the combined RAF/RNZAF Air Transport Detachment at Riyadh flew 2,990 hours on 2,231 sorties, delivering 19.9 million pounds of freight and over 22,800 passengers. Before the homeward rush began, the ATD notched up other firsts, as they flew the first fixed-wing aircraft into Kuwait itself, delivering the men to secure the British Embassy and then a mere two days later, returning the Ambassador himself to his rightful place.

With the ending of the Gulf War most of the equipment used in the conflict was to come home to the UK by sea, but still an enormous amount was too expensive or valuable to be left too long. By

C-130K Hercules C.3 XV307 (66-13550) taxiing for takeoff at the Royal International Air Tattoo, RAF Fairford, Gloucestershire on 17 July 2006. (Adrian Pingstone)

May the main operation was complete, but the Hercules mission continued with a schedule every other day to Turkey in support of the Marines, then extending into Iraq itself, as the US forces opened the small airfield of Sirsenk in the Anatolian Mountains. The RAF Hercules detachment, now reduced to two crews and one aircraft, moved to Bahrain; there they continued until the end of June 1991 and 50,000 flying hours later, when it was all over. In July the plight of the Kurds of Northern Iraq, following their failure to overthrow Saddam Hussein, led to more effort and the RAF launched in to Operation 'Warden' (the UK contribution to the US-led 'Provide Comfort' relief operation for the UN 'Safe Haven').

Where there is famine or when warring factions use food - or lack of it - as a weapon, as in the case of Bosnia, inevitably the UN High Commission for Refugees (UNHCR) attempts to provide the innocent bystanders with the basic essentials for survival. Lacking any resources, they quite naturally ask individual nations to contribute aid. In the case of the UK, that request comes to the Foreign 6k Commonwealth Office who, if they agree, will inevitably 'contract' the MoD to do the task, who in turn order Strike Command, who pass it to 38 Group and their Hercules' fleet. The activities and personnel involved in 38 Group's response to humanitarian tasks involved three very different categories: Operation 'Martock', the evacuation of British Nationals from Luanda in November 1992; Operation 'Vigour', the UK contribution to US-led Operation 'Provide Relief' involving the delivery of aid to Somalia, and Operation 'Cheshire', the on-going provision of humanitarian aid to the people of Sarajevo. In August 1992, the multi-national air operation known as 'Provide Relief' was launched to airlift supplies to feeding centres and clinics for Somali refugees. By 25 February 1993 28,050.86 tonnes of food had been delivered by the American, German and Royal Air Forces based at Moi International Airport, Mombasa in 1,924 sorties to Somalia and 508 to Kenya. During Operation 'Vigour' in three months two Hercules and four crews of 38 Group delivered 3,500 tons of supplies to all areas of Somalia, flying just short of 1,000 hours in the process.

Operation 'Cheshire' began in the summer of 1992 when the UN asked nations to provide aircraft to deliver aid to Sarajevo. The UK Government responded with an offer of one Hercules and a 47 Squadron aircraft began flying into Sarajevo three times a day from 3 July 1992. Group Captain D. K. L. McDonnell OBE, Head of Air Transport and Air-To-Air Refuelling Branch, HQ 38 Group at High Wycombe, has written the following account of the operation:

'Regrettably, the aircraft are regularly tracked by radar-layed AAA and occasionally pick up transmissions from potentially hostile systems. Clearly they are at their most vulnerable during approach and departure at Sarajevo; therefore the ground situation is continuously monitored. As at the end of October 1993 the RAF had delivered 12,500 tons of aid to Sarajevo in 880 visits and flown close to 2,000 hours in the process. This represented 18 per cent of all aid delivered by air -

not bad when we represent only 12 per cent of the aircraft dedicated to the airlift ... We have been fortunate so far, in that there has been little damage to our aircraft - only two bullet holes. Others have been less so; for instance, the Italians lost a G.222 to missile fire in 1992 and it was only through the quick reaction of the crew that the Germans did not lose a C-160 in February 1994 [there were no UK casualties during the course of Operation 'Cheshire', but there were more than 260 security incidents involving other relief aircraft]. The hazards are evident. Our hope is that we shall continue to get the balance right and not exceed it. We get it wrong at our peril'.

A Hercules crew of 47 Squadron, with two Hercules from the French and US air forces, carried out the last relief flight (IFN 94) into Sarajevo on 9 January 1996. The RAF contribution to the airlift, the longest in history, was immense: a total of 1,977 sorties carried 28,256 tonnes of relief supplies into the city over the 1,279 days of operation and overall, the UN effort totalled

160,370 tonnes of aid and included flights from the air forces of Canada, the US, Germany and France.

Meanwhile, in 1995 Hercules crews from Lyneham were involved in relief missions to the tiny Caribbean island of Montserrat which was threatened by volcanic eruptions. About 3,000 of the island's 12,000 inhabitants left Montserrat for Antigua and surrounding islands. The first appeal for assistance was answered by a Hercules which left Lyneham in early August. This aircraft, crewed by 47 Squadron, spent a week in the area of relief duties. Its first flight carried food parcels and soft toys for children and thereafter three flights each day took in food, fold-up beds, pillows and tents; the aircraft finally returned to Lyneham on 10 August. Following a second personal request from the island's governor, forty Royal Marines were flown from Lyneham on 24 August to help the beleaguered islanders. The aircraft flew to Goose Bay where it changed crew before flying on to Antigua.

In addition to the humanitarian and logistics

An RAF C-130 waits on the tarmac at a Middle Eastern airfield prior to taking off. This image was a winner in the RAF Photographic Competition 2008 for photographer Sgt Pete Mobbs.

operations, there are other operational considerations each and every year which involve the RAF Hercules fleet. Each year Exercise 'Dynamic Mix' - involving land, sea and air forces from several NATO nations takes place in the Mediterranean. In order to support the substantial British participation in the exercise, a large amount of engineering equipment has to be transported to Turkey. As well as the equipment needed for the day-to-day operations of the Tornados, a spares back-up is also required to provide replacement parts for aircraft and bulky ground engineering equipment. A large proportion of this equipment is sent by sea, but smaller items of equipment and the support passengers, including engineers and suppliers as well as aircrew, all travel from Brize Norton to Akinci AB, Turkey in up to six Hercules.

The overworked Hercules fleet had, by the early 1990s, reached a point whereby if the humanitarian and logistics support roles were to continue to function in times of extreme crisis, then replacement of the RAF's senior citizens was due. (The RAF has been operating the C-130K since 1967.) The UK is the largest operator of C-130s outside the US, with a fleet of sixty C.Mk.1, C.Mk.1P and C.Mk.3P versions and it has the highest utilization rate of any operator because of its rigorous training schedules, worldwide commitments and involvements in many peacekeeping and humanitarian tasks. In 1992 an LS82 project team was set up to oversee the Hercules replacement project. The subsequent decision to opt for the C-130J model was an obvious one and twenty-five of the existing fleet were scheduled to be replaced by C-130Js/-30s. Of these, the first fifteen were the stretched C-130J-30 version, an option being held on the last ten to switch all or some of them to the shorter version, should requirements change for which this version would be better suited. They were re-designated Mks 4 and 5 respectively. With these aircraft the RAF became the first operator of these new versions.

During the 2003 invasion of Iraq (Operation 'Iraqi Freedom'), the C-130 Hercules was used operationally by Australia, the UK and the United States. After the initial invasion, C-130 operators as part of the Multinational force in Iraq used their C-130s to support their forces in Iraq. In 2002 the new US president, George W. Bush argued that the vulnerability of the United States following the September 11 attacks of 2001, combined with Iraq's alleged continued possession and manufacture of weapons of mass destruction (an accusation that was later proved erroneous) and its support for terrorist groups - which, according to the Bush administration, included al-Qaeda, the perpetrators of the September 11 attacks - made disarming Iraq a renewed priority. UN Security Council Resolution 1441 passed on 8 November 2002 demanded that Iraq readmit inspectors and that it comply with all previous resolutions. Iraq appeared to comply with the resolution, but in early 2003 President Bush and British Prime Minister Tony Blair declared that Iraq was actually continuing to hinder UN inspections and that it still retained proscribed weapons. On 17 March, seeking no further UN resolutions and deeming further diplomatic efforts by the Security Council futile, Bush declared an end to diplomacy and issued an ultimatum to Ṣaddām, giving the Iraqi president 48 hours to leave Iraq. The leaders of France, Germany, Russia and other countries objected to this buildup toward war.

The Second Persian Gulf War, 2003-11 in Iraq consisted of two phases. The first of these was a brief, conventionally fought war in March-April 2003 in which a combined force of troops from the United States and Great Britain (with smaller contingents from several other countries) invaded Iraq and rapidly defeated Iraqi military and paramilitary forces. It was followed by a longer second phase in which a US-led occupation of Iraq was opposed by an insurgency. The 30 January 2005 RAF shoot down of C.3 XV179, call sign 'Hilton 22', which was probably shot down by Sunni insurgents, killing all ten personnel on board was, at that time, the largest single loss of life suffered by the British military during Operation 'Telic', the British Campaign in Iraq 2003-2009. XV179 took off from Baghdad at 1622 local time. It was to fly at low level to Balad to deliver freight and the single passenger Acting Lance Corporal Steven Jones of the Royal Signals. Six minutes later it reported a fire on board, Jones, stating: 'No duff, no duff. We are on fire, we are on fire' and it was confirmed 'missing' at 1655. American Apache helicopters located the crash site 45 minutes after the distress call. As the site was in a hostile area, the priority was for human remains, personal effects and classified material to be recovered at the time. Part of the right wing had been detached and it was found over a mile from the crash site. The investigating team was only able to spend a short time at both sites. By 3 February the site had been looted and the wreckage taken; it was decided not to attempt to recover the wreckage from the looters. Those killed included eight crew from RAF Lyneham in Wiltshire, another RAF serviceman and one soldier. The Board of Inquiry report in December 2005 identified the lack of a fire-suppressant system as a contributory factor. In September 2006 Channel 4 News aired an article criticising the Ministry of Defence for having fitted only one C-130 with a foam fire-suppressant system. The RAF had ordered a retrofit of this system to all front-line C-130s, a system which could well have prevented the loss of XV179 and its crew. On 12 February 2007 C.4 ZH876 was seriously damaged during a landing incident in the Maysan Province of Iraq near the Iranian border. The aircraft was subsequently destroyed as it was deemed too dangerous for coalition forces to repair and recover it. This was the first C-130J loss for any nationality since the new variant entered service in 1999. Although it is acknowledged that this was not a Special Forces aircraft, it carried secure communications equipment that could not be compromised.

After violence began to decline in 2007 the United States gradually reduced its military presence in Iraq, formally completing its withdrawal in December 2011. On 30 April the United Kingdom formally ended combat operations. Britain handed control of Basra to the United States Armed Forces. On 28 July Australia withdrew its combat forces as the Australian military presence in Iraq ended, per an agreement with the Iraqi government. On 29 June 2009 US forces withdrew from Baghdad. On 30 November 2009, Iraqi Interior Ministry officials reported that the civilian death toll in Iraq fell to its lowest level in November since the 2003 invasion.

In December 2001 the International Security Assistance Force (ISAF), which aimed to assist the Afghan Transitional Authority in creating and maintaining a safe and secure environment in Kabul and its surrounding area, was created. It went on to comprise 37 nations. In 2003 NATO assumed command of ISAF; Stage One and Two of ISAF expansion saw ISAF move into the North and West of Afghanistan. This support came in a number of different forms and comprised about 850 RAF personnel. Tactical reconnaissance and close air support is provided by Tornado GR.4 force; in-theatre airlift is provided by the RAF C-130s and supplemented by Comms Fleet aircraft, including the HS.125 and BAE 146; air refuelling support for Coalition aircraft was provided by the VC-10, while the Sentinel R1 and MQ-9 Reaper played a large part in delivering ISTAR support. RAF Chinook and Merlin Helicopters formed part of the Joint Helicopter Force in Afghanistan and were the backbone for the provision of tactical mobility for Land forces. Essential support was given by the RAF Strategic Air Transport fleet with the Voyager and C-17 moving essential men and material into and out of the region.

Operation 'Herrick' was the codename under which all British operations in the War in Afghanistan were conducted, 2002-2014. It consisted of the British contribution to the NATO-led International Security Assistance Force (ISAF) and support to the American-led Operation 'Enduring Freedom' (OEF). Since 2003 Operation 'Herrick' had increased in size and breadth to match ISAF's growing geographical intervention in Afghanistan. Operation 'Herrick' superseded two previous efforts in Afghanistan. The first of these was Operation 'Veritas', which consisted of support to the war in Afghanistan in October 2001. The last major action of this was a sweep in east Afghanistan by 1,700 Royal Marines during Operation 'Jacana', which ended in mid-2002. The second was Operation 'Fingal', which involved leadership and a 2,000 strong contribution for a newly formed ISAF in Kabul after December 2001. Command was subsequently transferred to Turkey several months later and the British contingent was scaled back to 300. Since then, all operations in Afghanistan were conducted under Operation 'Herrick'.

On 24 May 2006 Hercules C.1 XV206 of 47 Squadron Special Forces Flight was carrying the new British ambassador, Stephen Evans when it crash landed at a dirt landing strip outside the town of Lashkar Gar in Helmand Province after hitting a landmine on roll-out which holed the port external fuel tank and set the number two (port inner) engine on fire. All nine crew and 26 passengers aboard safely evacuated, but the airframe burned out. It was later revealed that the Hercules was carrying a large number of SAS troops as well as a large amount of cash described as being one million dollars in some sources and as 'more than £1 million' by others, while the MoD only admitted to a 'sizeable amount of cash'. The money was apparently destined for local warlords in exchange for their influence and intelligence.

In December 2012 Prime Minister David Cameron announced that 3,800 troops - almost half of the force serving in Helmand Province - would be withdrawn during 2013 with numbers to fall to approximately 5,200. Combat operations were projected to end sometime during 2014. Between 2001 and 12 December 2014 a total of 453 British military personnel have died on operations in Afghanistan. The UK ceased all combat operations in Afghanistan and withdrew the last of its combat troops on the 27 October 2014.

Sixty-one year old Air Chief Marshal Sir Glenn Torpey GCB CBE DSO, commander in Operation 'Telic' and Chief of the Air Staff from April 2006 to July 2009 admitted that the 19-year operation in the Gulf, which began in 1990 and ended in June 2009 and the war in Afghanistan had taken its toll on the RAF, from which it would take years to recover. Referring to the Second Gulf War, the former fast jet pilot in the late 1970s and 1980s who saw active service during the Gulf War on the Tornado and then went on to higher command, highlighted the difficulties of targeting and destroying mobile Surface-to-Air and Surface-to-Surface missiles and the way this forced a change to the start of the campaign. 'Gaining air superiority is not, therefore, plain sailing. It needs investment and training. The introduction of Typhoon will significantly enhance the RAF's air-to-air capability but the aircraft also has a significant multi-role capability and in time will take over the offensive role from the Tornado GR.4. Looking more broadly, the RAF's frontline is undergoing a significant modernisation programme, including more C-17s, Sentinel R.Mk.1, Harrier GR.9, more helicopters, Nimrod MRA.4, A400M, FSTA, Reaper (Remotely Piloted Air System) and, in time, JSF (Joint Strike Fighter). As a consequence, I believe we currently have the capabilities required to fulfill our key roles, which I would summarise as: gaining control of the air; rapid deployment and sustainment; battlefield mobility; precision strike and offensive support; ISTAR; Force Protection; and Command and Control. More to the point, there are few other Air Forces in the Western World that have such a range of capabilities - aside from the USAF - and this gives the UK a unique ability to deploy rapidly over strategic distance, either to conduct offensive operations or deliver humanitarian relief.

'The C-130 force, the VC 10s, TriStars and C-17s are all doing a tremendous job in sustaining the strategic air bridges to Iraq and Afghanistan. The C-130s are also playing a vital intra-theatre role, transporting troops and freight to a variety of austere locations,; indeed, during the last troop rotation in Afghanistan the C-130 force flew 350 sorties into the gravel strip at Camp Bastion in Helmand Province. Improving the robustness of our Air Transport force is one of my top priorities. The new C-130J fleet is proving a great success. The aircraft's increased performance is paying real dividends in the hot and high conditions in Afghanistan and the crews love the glass cockpit and the increased reliability associated with a new aircraft. Our C-130Ks have served us extremely well over many years but will gradually be phased out as the A400M starts to come online. The C-17s have been an outstanding success and I am delighted that we have decided to buy the initial four we had on lease and to procure an additional two aircraft, which should be with us in 2008. The aircraft is vital for transporting large, outsized loads and like the C-130J has proved to be very reliable. In simplistic terms, a C-17 carries about four times the load of a C-130, with A400M carrying about twice the load of a C-130. Once the modernisation programme is complete the Air Transport force will consist of 25 C-130Js, 25 A400M and at least six and ideally eight C17s. This coupled with the air-to-air refuelling and passenger carrying capability of FSTA will provide the RAF with a robust, modern transport fleet capable of global reach.

'As is well known, we are currently flying our C-130s and support helicopters at a very intensive rate in Iraq and Afghanistan and our people are doing a tremendous job under extremely difficult conditions. We have sufficient helicopters to carry out today's task, but we could always use more. The procurement of an additional six Merlins from

Stores for the first contingent of RAF personnel to deploy on Opeation 'Ellamy' arrive on C-130Ks at an air base in the Mediterranean as part of the UK contribution to help enforce the no fly zone over Libya. The role of the team from RAF Coningsby in Lincolnshire accompanied by specialist air movements staff from 1 Air Mobility Wing at RAF Lyneham in Wiltshire, was to unload cargo and passengers.

Denmark is a very welcome initiative and these aircraft, together with the decision on the eight Chinook Mk3s, will provide a significant boost in our rotary-wing capability. The C-130Ks and Js are a vital part of the tactical mobility jigsaw, without which it would be impossible to prosecute the campaigns in Iraq and Afghanistan. All these air assets are operating in high threat areas and we have spent a considerable amount of money on added protection systems, including defensive aid suites, extra armour and machine guns.'

Chapter 11 Endnotes

1   Four aircraft were written off between 1969 and 1973: XV180 operated by 242 OCU stalled on a three-engined take-off from RAF Fairford on 24 March 1969. XV216 of 242 OCU crashed in the sea after take-off from Melovia, Italy on 9 November 1971. XV194 on 48 Squadron veered off the runway when landing at Tromsö, Norway on 12 September 1972 and was scrapped for parts. XV198 on 48 Squadron crashed when an engine failed on a three-engined touch-and-go training flight at Colerne on 10 September 1973.

2   *The first operational C-130 air-to-air refuel in the South Atlantic* by Squadron Leader Harry Burgoyne AFC; *Spirit of the Air* (Vol.2, No.4 2007.)

3   When the Falklands War began, this Royal Fleet Auxiliary was deployed in the western Mediterranean for the annual 'Spring Train' exercise, and received orders to head south, taking part in the landings at San Carlos Water as a stores and ammunition ship. When the order to head south was given, several warships including the Type 22 frigates HMS *Broadsword* and HMS *Brilliant* and the aircraft carriers HMS *Hermes* and HMS *Invincible* had the WE.177A nuclear weapon deployed aboard. Some newspaper reports also named RFA *Fort Austin*. The MoD explored various options to transfer these nuclear weapons from the frigates to the safety of the deep magazines aboard *Fort Austin*, *Hermes* and *Invincible*. The presence of these nuclear warheads in territorial waters around the Falkland Islands would break the UK obligation to the Latin-America Nuclear Free Zone. After the conflict ended, weapons were transferred at sea to the two RFAs *Fort Austin* and *Resource* for transport back to the UK.

4   *Albert's Granby - A Herculean Task, Royal Air Force 92. No.4.*

Chapter Twelve
The 21st Century Hercules

The design objective of the C-130J is to provide a replacement that makes good economic sense for any twenty-year-old Hercules. Buying a new C-130J is more cost-effective in the long run than extending the service life of old airplanes.

Al Hansen, Vice President for Airlift Programs at LASC, speaking in April 1994.

In 1991 Lockheed-Martin began designing a state-of-the-art Hercules for the 21st century. British industry participation started in the early 1990s, with a partnership between just two companies and Lockheed-Martin. By January 1998 almost fifty British firms were supporting the C-130J project on a risk-sharing basis and more than £470 million of orders had been placed in the UK. British companies have played an integral role in the development and production of the C-130J, sharing in all orders, irrespective of customer. The aircraft's new, more powerful and efficient propulsion

system is largely produced by British companies including Dowty Aerospace, GKN Westland, Lucas Aerospace and Rolls-Royce.

The most dramatic changes in costs and performance is that the C-130J has two crew instead of four. Also, the avionics are modern state of the art and there is the new Allison AE-2100D3 two-spool powerplant, complete with oil-bath engine starter and new modular gearbox. The T56 has been an outstanding performer - pilots trust it and like its responsiveness - but the AE-2100 has added a new dimension to the C-130J: full

C-130J final assembly line.

Brigadier General Mark Dillon, commander, 86th Airlift Wing (Motto, 'Virtus Perdurat'), pilots a C-130J to Morón, Spain from Ramstein AB, Germany, on 12 January 2010. Morón provides refueling for aircraft en route to Europe, Africa and the Middle East and also serves as a NASA Transoceanic Abort Landing (TAL) Site. (USAF)

authority, digital electronic control is incorporated; there is 29 per cent more take-off thrust; and 15 per cent better fuel economy. The engine is also modular and lighter in weight. Coupled to it is the Dowty-designed composite R391 scimitar-shaped six-bladed propeller unit, replacing the all-metal four-bladed propeller on the C130H. This new propeller is lighter, has fewer parts and delivers 13 per cent mote thrust. (The new propeller subsequently proved extraordinarily successful in live-firing tests, which analysed its ability to sustain damage from direct attack or shrapnel.) Other innovations include Mk.IV carbon brakes coupled with an automatic braking feature and a new anti-skid system to shorten landing distances. A new modular wheel and integral self-jacking struts greatly reduce the time required to change a wheel and make it possible to replace tyres at remote sites without ground-support equipment. A new nose-gear strut improves the stability to taxi on rough airstrips. An updated electronic system with two new converters provides stable power to all avionics and electronic loads.

A new fuel system has a single cross-ship manifold, with half as many fuel-control valves. Foam installed in the dry bays provides added safety and survivability. Because the new engine/propeller combination and reduced drag increase range by 20 per cent, there is no real need for external fuel tanks, although the C-130J can carry an additional 18,700lb of fuel in external tanks if required. Lockheed has relocated the in-flight refuelling probe from the centre of the fuselage to the left side over the pilot's head; this is designed to make it easier for the co-pilot when in-flight refuelling is being performed, than in earlier versions. Lockheed-Martin also plans a boom tanking version for refuelling USAF-type aircraft and this will be offered as future modification. A variable speed basket on the probe-

and-drogue refuelling system will permit in-flight refuelling of an F/A-18 and a Bell-Boeing V-22 using the same basket, rather than the two separate baskets at the outset.

Cruising at an average of 310 knots, at up to 30,000 feet, the 'old' C-130 burned approximately 5,000lb of fuel every hour. The C-130J and C-130J-30 have a maximum internal fuel load of 45,900lb the maximum is reduced by slightly over 2,000lb when foam is introduced into the tanks - though international C-130Js are not normally equipped with the foam. Lockheed estimated the range of the C-130J to be about 3,000 nautical miles without external tanks. The C-130J-30's added length added 3,729lb to the aircraft's empty weight and reduced payload by the same amount. However, the stretch C-130J can carry two additional pallets as compared to the C-130J and ninety-two paratroops as opposed to sixty-four for the standard C-130J.

The cockpit is still approached via a near-vertical ladder, (although there is no fold-down floor panel to cover the ladder well) and the two crew-rest bunks remain at the rear of the cockpit. Although the flight engineer and navigator stations have been eliminated, there is provision for a third crew member (check-out pilot, etc) to sit behind

the centre console between the two pilots to monitor the flight, or to operate the aircraft's systems, as required. The superb 'greenhouse' windowing, providing unparalleled all-round vision, has also been retained (although two in the nose have been blanked off). The galley has been turned through 90 degrees to face into the cockpit instead of over the ladder as previously. The control yokes, the nose-wheel steering wheel and the parking-brake handle, are all throwbacks to the familiar C-130s of yore - but all this said, the C-130J cockpit is still revolutionary because in terms of electronics on the aircraft, it is a wholly different world. The systems include a digital autopilot, a fully integrated global positioning system, colour weather and ground-mapping radar and a digital map display, plus an advisory caution and warning system that allows for fault detection.

Mission effectiveness has been infinitely improved thanks to a mission computer allied to electronically controlled engines and propellers, databus architecture and digital avionics. The new configuration includes the USAF-developed Self-Contained Navigation System (SCNS). System architecture is centred around dual Electronic Flight Instrumentation System (EF1S) M1L-STD-1553B databuses with analogue and digital

C-130J 97-1351 *Pride of Balitmore II* in the 135th AS, Maryland ANG which, along with C-130J 98-1357 was the last to leave the Maryland ANG on 13 September 2011 for re-assignment to the USAF's 48th AS.

Above: EC-130J Commando Solo.

Left: US Military personnel assigned to the 4th Psychological Operations Group, 193rd Special Operations Wing, Pennsylvania Air National Guard broadcast television and radio programming from onboard an ANG EC-130J 'Commando Solo' Hercules in support of Operation 'Iraqi Freedom' in March 2003.

interfaces. (Replacing the conventional wiring systems with this data-bus architecture reduced wire assemblies by 53 per cent and wire terminations by 81 per cent. The new design reduced line-replaceable units by 53 per cent.) A new Digital Avionics Flight Control System (DAFCS) is installed for the autopilot and flight director system. An Integrated Diagnostic System (IDS) offers fault detection and isolation and is integrated with the ACAWS greatly to improve maintenance troubleshooting. The 'virtual systems' on the aircraft cover automatic thrust control and engine monitoring. The Lucas Aerospace full-authority, digital engine-control (FADEC) for the Allison AE2100D3 engines provides automatic starting cycles, with automatic shutdown for overspeeding and warnings should other malfunctions occur. It has also meant that the need to line up all four engine powers by setting each power lever is no longer necessary.

Engine status is present on one of the four flat-panel, liquid-crystal (LCD), head-down (HDD) colour displays on vertical bars, while system data is presented as digital readouts on the display. The Westinghouse AN/APN-241 weather/navigation radar display - which equipment includes the only proven forward-looking wind shear mode available today - presents the primary navigation plan, showing the aircraft proceeding along a flight-plan course on a map overlay. Eight different navigational tasks are carried out automatically. An Enhanced Traffic Avoidance System (E-TCAS) and a Ground Avoidence System (GCAS) are also fitted. A second display presents Advisory Caution and Warning System (ACAWA) messages and SKE-2000 (Station Keeping Equipment) information. The fourth display presents all information necessary to fly the aircraft. Two flight dynamics holographic head-up (HUD) displays permit both pilots to maintain a constant out-of-the-window view while monitoring all the data necessary to control the aircraft. All the panels and consoles in the cockpit have been redesigned and the aircraft is compatible with night-vision imaging systems. As a fail-safe, there are two mission computers, although one computer is capable of doing all tasks.

Much of the protracted flight-test programme has concentrated on proving the complex software systems. Lockheed tested the systems heavily in the laboratory and then released the software loads in a staged process involving a flight simulator and the test aircraft. There are almost 600,000 lines of software code in the aircraft and Lockheed-Martin were determined to carry out more comprehensive testing on this aircraft than on any military or civil aircraft before.

N130JA, the C-130J (Hercules C.4/ZH865) prototype, was rolled out of Lockheed's huge hangar at Marietta on 18 October 1995 in front of distinguished guests from the US and Britain, with Air Marshal Sir John Allison, deputy C-in-C of Strike Command, the guest of honour. One of the most interested observers was Group Captain Brian Symes, station commander at Lyneham, where the first squadron to receive the aircraft was 57, followed by 24 Squadron. A diminutive figure in the crowd turned out to be 82-year-old Willis Hawkins, the chief engineer of the original C-130; in 1951 his late boss, Kelly Johnson, had

F-35B STOVL and a KC-130J in August 2009 during trials of the F-35B BF-2 (2nd STOVL flight test aircraft) uploading fuel into the aircraft at 10,000, 15,000 and 20,000 feet at speeds of 200-250 knots.

reluctantly signed the right bit of paper, saying the aircraft was 'too ugly' to succeed! What Johnson would have had to say about this new generation of tactical transport aircraft is open to question. Sir John Allison greeted Hercules ZH865 as a milestone aircraft, the latest example of a line which would go down in aviation history as one of the truly great designs.

ZH865 flew for the first time on 5 April 1996. In-flight refuelling tests were carried out in January 1998. A new airflow difficulty emerged when it was found that the aircraft's tail-fin iced up in freezing conditions. Lockheed came up with a solution, however: a pneumatic rubber boot wrapped around the foot of the tail-fin; this was during 'cold-weather' trials Argentina in mid-1998. (Lockheed-Martin had rejected the Falklands for 'cold-weather' trials, apparently because the islands have only one runway, in favour of Rio Gallegos, 400 miles from the Falklands base at Mount Pleasant and the home of Argentina's Exocet force in the 1982 Falklands War.)

The MoD was originally promised that the first production versions for launch customer, the RAF, would begin arriving in the UK in November 1996. Orders received by January 1998 had reached eighty-three firm contracts and sixty-two options for C-130Js, with Italy ordering eighteen aircraft, the RAF twenty-five, the Royal Australian Air Force twelve and the USAF, AFRes and ANG, twenty-eight and the USMC, seven. The MoD took delivery of the first aircraft on 26 August 1998, later joined by the second aircraft on 30 November; the third followed on 22 April 1999. The first of the C-130Js was officially received by the RAF's Transport Wing at Lyneham, Wiltshire on 23 November 1999, more than two years behind schedule. (The station closed on 31 December 2012 with the majority of its personnel and other assets having moved to RAF Brize Norton). According to some Press reports the delays were such that Lockheed-Martin was forced to present the RAF with a 'free aircraft!'[1] From March 2000 Italy began receiving twelve C-130Js. Between

Royal Canadian Air Force C-130J-30 601 making its first flight. Seventeen stretched model Hercules are operated by 436 Squadron at 8 Wing Trenton, Ontario.

C-130J-30 *Frigg* 08-5601 of 335 Skavdronen of the Luftforsvarets (Royal Norwegian Air Force).

2002 and 2005 ten 'stretched' C-130J-30s were delivered. Australia received a dozen C-130J-30s during August 1999 and March 2000 to replace twelve C-130Hs.

In 2014 Lockheed Martin launched an updated civilian version of its C-130J Super Hercules transport, which is designed to operate out of 2,000 foot-long dirt strips in high mountain ranges and have the ability to transport more than 40,000lbs of cargo and supplies.

On 4 February the Bethesda, Maryland-based company announced that it had kicked off the certification process on 21 January, when it filed a notification letter with the US Federal Aviation Administration. Production of the LM-100J Super Hercules began in April 2016. The company expects to receive FAA certification by 2018, following a one-year flight test programme and plans to deliver the first example that same year. The timing comes amid a period of spending cuts by the C-130J's primary US military customers, making the new civilian LM-100J an attractive source of potential non-military Super Hercules revenue, says the company. 'This would give us

stability in [the Super Hercules] production programme and supply chain,' Lockheed says, adding that the new aircraft meshes with a broader effort to diversify revenue. The company hopes the aircraft, which will have a base price of around $65 million, will follow the success of its predecessor, the civilian L-100 Hercules. Lockheed sold roughly 115 of those aircraft, which were based on the first-generation C-130, between 1964 and 1992. Now, however, many L-100s are approaching the end of their life cycles, sparking demand for new civilian freighters, it says. 'We see a natural progression of being able to recapitalise those fleets with an aircraft [that has] better reliability, better capability [and] better maintainability, safety and performance.'

The LM-100J is modelled after the latest-generation C-130J Super Hercules, which has been in production since the early 1990s. Unlike previous updates to the C-130, Lockheed says it took a 'revolutionary approach' with the J model, giving it digital avionics and making a series of design changes to improve performance and reduce operating costs.

KC-130J BuNo166765 of VMGR-352 'The Raiders' at Miramar, California in a formation with another Hercules. 'The Raiders' were the first to deploy the 'Harvest Hawk', during October 2010 in Afghanistan. The first weapons engagement was on 4 November supporting the 3rd Battalion, 5th Marine Regiment in Sangia when one 'Hellfire' missile was fired and five enemy insurgents were killed.

'All of those concepts are flowing to the LM-100J,' Lockheed says. When it first developed the original C-130J, it also received a type certificate for a civilian version. But primary customers were militaries and Lockheed says it lost the civilian certificate as the aircraft's military avionics, communications and navigation equipment evolved.

Described by the company as a 'civil multi-purpose air freighter,' the new LM-100J will have modern avionics and a 'digital back end' system with a loadmaster computer station that will assist with loading and weight and balance. The cargo compartment will be 15 feet longer than the L-100, providing space for two additional pallets and the aircraft will be able to carry 33% more payload on a 2,500 nm flight, say Lockheed.

The LM-100J, which has the ability to fly 2,200 nm with a 40,000lb payload, has about 50% more range than the L-100, according to Lockheed. Its top speed will be 355 knots; 10% faster than its predecessor. In addition, the LM-100J will be operated by two flight crew (instead of three for the L-100), will burn 15% less fuel and have maintenance costs that are 35% less. LM-100Js will be built at Lockheed's Marietta, Georgia facility and will be powered by four Rolls-Royce AE2100D turboprops, which will provide 30% more power than the L-100's Allison T-56 power plants, the company says. Lockheed estimates it can sell 75 to 100 LM-100Js over twenty years, a level of demand similar to that for the original L-100. Though the company declines to name prospective customers, it says oil, gas and mineral exploration companies are interested. Such companies must transport heavy equipment like generators and earth moving equipment to remote outposts not linked to railways or roads. They need rugged aircraft that can operate from 'austere', unpaved runways. The LM-100J will help bring stability to the Super Hercules programme, as the US government trims its defence budget, says Lockheed. In fiscal year 2014, the US Navy received $69 million for procurement of tanker-variant KC-130Js; almost half of the $134 million the service requested, according to budget documents. Likewise, the US Air Force requested $1.4 billion but received $1.3 billion for the procurement of C-130Js, including special-mission MC-130Js and search and rescue HC-130Js. '[The LM-100J] adds another capability towards the Hercules portfolio that hasn't existed in a while,' Lockheed says. 'It looks really promising.'

This where we came in!

Chapter Endnotes

1   *The Lockheed-Martin C-130 Hercules* by Peter C. Smith (Crécy Publishing Ltd, 2010).

Appendix I

Commercial and Humanitarian Operators

In 1959 Lockheed announced that Pan American Airways had ordered twelve GL-207 Super Hercules for delivery in early 1962 and that Slick Airways was to receive six later in the year. They were to differ from the C-130B in being 23 feet 4 inches longer, with wingspan increased by 12 feet 5 inches and were to have a maximum take off gross weight of 204,170lb. The intention was to power the Super Hercules with 6,000 eshp Allison T61 engines and in 1960 a GL-307 version with 6,445 eshp Rolls-Royce Tynes and gross weight of 230,000lb was also proposed. Moreover in that same year a jet-powered version with four 22,000lb thrust Pratt and Whitney JT3D-11 turbofans, a 250,000lb gross weight and with a maximum cruising speed of 564 mph at 20,000 feet was put forward. However, Pan American and Slick cancelled their orders for GL-207s and these other versions did not progress beyond the initial study phase. Since then, all commercial versions of the C-130 have been straightforward developments of the production aircraft. To date, civil Hercules have been produced in three versions: L-100, L-100-20 and L-100-30.

A total of 114 L-100 commercial models have been built. They differ from the military Hercules in that the underwing fuel tanks have been omitted and most military equipment removed, although the aircraft can be fitted with retractable combination wheel-skis. The L-100 demonstrator (382-3946 N1130E) made a very impressive first flight on 20/21 April 1964, when it remained airborne or 25 hours 1 minute; and all except 36 minutes of this time were flown using just two of the 4,050 eshp Allison 501-D22 engines (the commercial version of the C-130's T56). N1130E was used to obtain a type certificate on 16 February 1965. It was subsequently modified to Model 382E/L-100-20, being 'stretched' with a 5 feet fuselage plug forward of the wing and a 3.3 feet plug aft to bring cabin-hold volume from 4,500 cubic feet to 5,335 cubic feet. Eight more L-100s were later stretched to become L-100-20 models. Only one unmodified L-100 (4144) remains in service, with

Pakistan air Force. This aircraft and another unmodified L-100 (4145), were acquired by the Pakistan Government for Pakistan Airlines in October 1966 and were given the registrations AP-AUT and AP-AUU respectively. Both the aircraft subsequently passed to the Pakistan Air Force, but AP-AUU was lost on 30 April 1968 when it crashed near Chaklala and was written off.

The first commercial L-100 operator was Alaska Airlines which, on 8 March 1965 put into service the Hercules demonstrator, on lease from Lockheed. It later leased four more L-100s and purchased one, but by the end of the 1960s had disposed of all of them. Twenty-one production aircraft (Model 382B) were built. The first delivery of L-100, to Continental Air Services took place on 30 September 1965. L-100s did not carry underwing fuel tanks and had most military equipment removed. They could be fitted with retractable combination wheel-skis. Aft doors were an optional fit. Twelve converted L-100s, stretched 15 feet were followed by fifty-three new-build examples. The first L-100 versions were severely limited in cargo-carrying capacity, so to rectify this situation Lockheed produced the L-100-20 version. Twenty-seven L-100-20s have been produced; nine of them modified from L-100s, with their fuselage stretched an additional 8.3 feet by fitting a 5 feet plug forward of the wing and a 3.3 feet plug aft. 4129 and 4150 were modified likewise (but with 4,050 eshp 501-D22s instead of 4,510 eshp 501-D22As) to become Model 382F/L-100-20s.

The L-100-20 was certificated on 4 October 1968 and entered service with Interior Airways one week later. Eight L-100-20s were later modified to L-100-30 configuration. 4412, an ex-Kuwaiti L-100-20, was modified as the experimental HTTB (High Technology Test Bed) for the C-130J etc., as part of a multiphase development programme to obtain STOL data for use in designing aircraft to meet USAF requirements for an advanced tactical transport. Phase 1 began on 19 June 1984, with the first flight of the modified L-100-20 which was then specially

Above: Coulson Flying Tankers (Lynden Air Cargo) L-100-30 (L-382G) N405LC/13, seen here during a test drop without retardant mixture) is among some of the biggest 'Large Air Tanker' (LAT) fire fighting aircraft down under and they have become familiar sights in Australian skies during the summer seasons, being regularly contracted to spend the hot, dry months to fight the devastating bush fires.

Right: A C-130 MAFFS air-tanker dropping retardant on Waldo Canyon Fire on 28 June 2012. (S/Sgt Stephany Richards USAF)

Left: The US Forest Service's large Modular Airborne Fire Fighting System being rolled into the back of C-130H 37311 of the 152nd 'High Rollers' Airlift Wing - Reno, Nevada ANG, one of three ANG units (and one from the USAFRes) each stationed around the Western US (the others being the 153rd AW at Cheyenne, Wyoming; the 302nd AW at Colorado Springs, Colorado and the 146th AW. MAFFS equipment can drop up to 3,000 gallons of water or fire retardant in six seconds through a nozzle on the rear left side of the aircraft.

Left: 'Tanker 130', Hawkins & Powers first Hercules fire-fighting aircraft (C-130A 56-0538 N130HP) which crashed due to structural failure on 17 June 2002, while fighting a fire near Walker, California. All three crew members were killed.

ANG C-130E 61-2359 with Modular Airborne Fire Fighting System in the 115th AS at Channel Islands ANG Station, California makes a Phoschek fire retardant drop on 28 October 2003 during the devastating wildfire that burned 108,204 acres of land in the Simi Hills and south-eastern Simi Valley in eastern Ventura County and western Los Angeles County, California. Pilots flying eight C-130s dropped 129,600 gallons of retardant during 48 sorties and 32 flying hours as of 29 October. (USAF)

instrumented and fitted with a head-up display, a dorsal fin extension and lateral strakes (horsals) ahead of the stabilizers. For Phase II trials, it was fitted in 1968 with double-slotted flaps, drooped wing leading edge, wing spoilers, extended chord ailerons and rudder and a high-sink-rate undercarriage. Prior to Phase III, the HTTB received a steerable turret housing an FLIR (forward-looking infra-red) and a laser ranger and was later re-engined with 5,250 eshp T56A-101 propeller-turbines.

Five L-100-30s (4950, 4952 - configured as a dental clinic - 4956/57 and 4960) were modified for use in Saudi Arabia as airborne hospitals. In 1992 and 1993 respectively, 4950/HZ-MS05 and 4957/HZ-MS10 were demodified to L-100-30 with their hospital equipment removed. Two other L-100-30s were sold to Armoflex for purported use in Benin, but finished up in the hands of the Libyan government. The L-100-30 entered service with Saturn Airways in December 1970.

In an effort to boost the Hercules' commercial market, Lockheed had proposed and continues to

L100 prototype (3946) N1130E at Fairbanks International Airport with Alaskan Airline markings. Alaska Airlines leased the first L-100 and it was christened the *City of Fairbanks* upon its arrival in its new home. Alaska Airlines later purchased five L-100s. (Lockheed Martin Aeronautics archives)

market, a number of derivatives, including the L-100-50 (with a fuselage stretched by another 20 feet), the L-100-PX passenger transport with 100 seats, the L-100-30QC cargo/passenger convertible and the L-100-30C combined cargo/ passenger version. It also announced in January 1980 its decision to proceed with development and production of the L-400 Twin Hercules, a smaller and lighter version powered by two 4,910 eshp Allison 501-D22Ds; however, this decision was later rescinded and development of the L-400 was shelved.

Algeria

Three L-100-30s have been operated by Air Algerie, Algiers: 4880/7T-VHG has been operated since May 1981 and 4886/7T-VHL since July 1981; 4883/7T-VHK was operated form June 1981 until August 1989, when it was written off after a ground loop during landing at Tamanrasset. Two other L-100/-20s have been leased.

Angola

Twenty L-100, -20 and -30 have been operated by Angola Air Charter, Luanda and TAAG Angolan Airlines, Luanda. L-100-20 (4176) (D2-FAF) was damaged whilst landing at Sao Thome on 15 May

1979 while operating with TAAG and was written off. L-100 (4222) L-100-20 (D2-THA), bought by TAAG in October 1979 made a wheels-up landing at Dondo, Angola on 8 June 1986, fire and was written off. L-100-20, also sold to TAAG (D2-EAS) at the same time, was shot down near Menongue, Angola on 16 May 1981. (D2-THB) on lease to Transafrik, was hit by a missile at Menonque, Angola, on 5 January 1990, crash-landed and was written off. L-100-30 (4679) (D2-TAD) was damaged beyond repair by fire from overheated brakes landing at Malenge, Angola on 7 April 1994. L-100-30 (4839) D2-EHD of ENDIEMA operated by Transafrik and chartered by the UN was lost after take-off from Huam-bo, Angola on 2 January 1999 with all nine passengers and crew (possibly shot down by UNITA). This aircraft had previously been damaged by UNITA taking off from Luena in February 1993.

Argentina

L-100-30 (4891) was operated by Lineas Aéreas del Estade (LADE), Buenos Aires.

Bolivia

The Fuerza Aérea Boliviana's Grupo Aéreo de Transporte 71, based at BA General Walter Arze, La

Paz, is operated on a peacetime basis as an internal domestic airline: Transporte Aéreo Boliviano (TAB).

Canada
L-100-30s operated by Canadian Airlines International, Vancouver and Northwest Territorial Airways, Yellowknife, (leased).

China
Two L-100-30s operated by China Air Cargo, Shanxi, for fish charter Tianjin-Japan.

Ecuador
One L-100-30 operated by the government of Ecuador.

Ethiopia
Two L-100-30 operated by Ethiopian Airlines, Addis Ababa.

France
L-100-30 operated by EAS Air Cargo, Perpignan.

Gabon
L-100-30 operated by Air Gabon, Libreville. L-100-30 operated by the Republic of Gabon government.

Indonesia
L-100-30 operated by Merpati Nusantara Airlines, Jakarta and Pelita Air Service, Jakarta.

Libya
L-100-20s and -30s operated by Libyan Air Cargo. L-100-20 and -30 operated by Jamahiriya Air Transport, Tripoli.

Mexico
Two ex-USAF C-130H military (56-0487 and 56-0537) and two ex-USAF RC-130As (57-0517 and 57-0518) were operated by Aeropostal, Mexico City. C-130A 56-0487 was sold in 1994 and both RC-130As were withdrawn from further use in 1996. L-100-30 operated by Petroleos, Mexicanos (Pemex), Mexico City.

Morocco
The fourteen C-130 military transports operated by the Royal Maroc Air Force carry civilian-style registrations; these are worn with the aircraft construction number; on the fin.

Netherlands
L-100-30 leased by Schreiner Airways, Leiden.

Netherlands Antilles
Frameair (TAC Holidays) has leased four L-100-30s at various times and purchased one (5225); the latter was damaged in August 1993 during lease to TAAG Angola Air Charter, when a hand-grenade detonated accidentally in a cargo compartment while the aircraft was on the ground. It was sent to Luanda for repair;

Angloa Airlines L-100-20 setting off on its delivery flight.

L-100-30 Hercules 1216 of the United Arab Emirates Air Force.

HZ-129-044 Royal Saudi Air Force Hercules in Saudi Arabian Airlines markings waits to depart RAF Fairford following the Royal International Air Tattoo on18 July 2011.

it is now in Mozambique. A second L-100-30 (5307) was contracted in February 1992 but not purchased; it went to the Canadian Armed Forces instead.

Philippines
C-130A operated by Aboitiz Transport.

Sao Thome
L-100-20 and -30 operated by Transafrik. L-100-30 (4561) Sao Thome registered S9-CA0, belonging to Transafrik, was lost after take-off from Huambo, Angola, 26 December 1998. All fourteen aboard, including eight members of the UN Observer Team were killed (possibly shot down by UNITA).

Saudi Arabia
A fleet of five L-100-30s and one C-130H-30 medically-configured Hercules were operated by Saudi Special Services, Jeddah, in conjunction with 1 Squadron (one is configured as a dental clinic). In 1992 and 1993 two were demodified to L-100-30, their hospital equipment removed.

South Africa
SAFAIR Freighter (Pty) Ltd, Johannesburg, have operated nineteen L-100-20s/L-100-30s at various times; these are also available as a military reserve airlift asset. SAFAIR is a wholly owned subsidiary of Safren - Safmarine and Rennies Holdings Ltd the independent holding company which has grown to be one of Africa's giants in the fields of aviation, shipping, cargo services and security. The airline operates its charter services on Boeing 707 and Hercules aircraft and operates freight and passenger charter flights across the length and breadth of the continent. Its facilities at Jan Smuts Airport, Johannesburg is fully equipped to accommodate Airbus, Boeing 707 and Boeing 737 jets as well as L-100 aircraft. SAFAIR's Hercules are leased by private individuals and businessmen as well as some of the largest corporations on the continent. Approximately six remain in operation with SAFAIR, or on lease from the company. On 17 July 2014 at Farnborough - ASL Aviation Group, owner of Safair, the South African-based C-130 operator, became the first commercial operator of the LM-100J when it signed a letter of intent with Lockheed Martin for up to ten LM-100Js. First deliveries were expected in late 2018 pending the completion of FAA certification.

Sudan
Of the six C-130Hs operated, one aircraft has occasionally been seen in civilian guise wearing the markings of Sudan Airways and varying registrations.

Tunisia
Two C-130Hs, which wear quasi-civilian markings.

Uganda
L-100-30 (4610) was purchased in August 1975 by Uganda Airlines (5X-UCF) and was operated by Uganda Air Cargoes, Kampala , from August 1981 until September 1985 when it was impounded and from September 1987 until April 1993. It is operated by Medecair Foundation.

United States of America
Advanced Leasing Corporation (L-100-30); Aero Firefighting Services, Anaheim, CA (C-130A); African Cargo Inc, Miami, FL (C-130A); Butler Aircraft Co, Richmond, OR (C-130A); Flight Cargo Leasing Inc, Dover, NY (L-100-30); Hemet Valley Flying Service Inc, Hemet, CA (C-130A);

UN L-100-20 Hercules at Entebbe in Uganda.

IEP IEPO, Chatsworth, CA (C-130A). Military Aircraft Restoration Corporation, Anaheim, CA (C130A); National Aeronautics and Space Administration (NASA), Moffett Field, CA, (NC-130B) and Wallops Island, VA (EC-130Q); National Oceanic and Atmospheric Administration, Miami, FL (L-100-30, EC-130Q); National Science Foundation (EC-130Q). Pacific Gateway Investments, Orange, CA (C-130A); Pacific Harbor Capital Inc, Portland, OR (C-130A); Pegasus Aviation Co (L-100-30); Rapid Air Trans, Washington DC (LC-100-30); Snow Aviation International Inc. Columbus, OH (C-130A); Southern Air Transport, Miami, FL (L-100-20/-30); T&.G Aviation, Chandler, AZ (C-130A). TBM Inc., Redmond, OR (C-130A). World Wide Trading Inc., Delray Beach, FL (L-100-30).

Yemen
Yemenia, Sanaa (C-130H).

Zambia
Five L-100s have been used by the Zambian government and Zambia Air Cargoes and possibly the air force, too. 4109 was destroyed in a ground collision with 4137 at Ndola on 11 April 1968. 4209, operated by ZAC from April 1964 until 1969, was sold by the insurance company to AIA; it was destroyed on the ground when the cargo exploded at Galbraigh Lake on 30 August 1974, 4101 was operated on lease by ZAC from August 1968 until early 1969. It was modified to L-100-30 configuration in 1972 and, after being operated by several users, was destroyed on the ground at Caafunfo, Angola, during a UNITA guerrilla attack on 29 December 1984. C/No. 4129 *Alexander* was bought by ZAC in 1966 and sold to Maple Leaf Leasing in 1969. It was rebuilt as L-100-20 and enjoyed a colourful career with St. Lucia Airways, operating as 'Juicy Lucy' transports to UNITA and 'Grey Ghost' in Tepper Aviation; it crash-landed at Jamba in Angola on 27 November 1989.

Lockheed Martin's LM-100J completed its debut flight from Marietta, Georgia on 25 May 2017, just over three months after the commercial freighter was rolled out at the site.

Appendix II

World Military User Directory

Algeria

The Al Quwwat Ali Jawwiya al Jaza'eriya (previously Force Aérienne Algerienne) received two C-130H-30 (CT) Combat Talons in July and August Ten C-130Hs and five C-130H-30 (CT)s were delivered between 1982-84 and an eighth C-130H-30 (CT) was delivered in November 1990. The ten C-130Hs and eight C-130H-30 (CT)s are shared between 31, 32, 33 and 35 Escadrilles.

Argentina

Three C-130Es were delivered to the Fuerza Aérea Argentina in 1968. However, TC-62 was lost on 28 August 1975 when a bomb exploded by the side of the runway during take-off from Tucuman; and during the Falklands War in 1982 one C-130E was shot down by a Sea Harrier on 1 June - this was replaced by a former Lockheed L-100-30 demonstrator in December. Five C-130Hs were received between 1971 and 1975, one of which - TC-68 - was used as a bomber in the Falklands War and two KC-130H tankers in 1979. Five ex-USAF C-130Bs were delivered to the FAA between 1992 and 1994. The 1 Escuadrón de Transport, Grupo 1 de Transporte Aero at BAM El Palomar, Buenos Aires, is the FAA Hercules operator.

In February 2014 Argentina's Defence Ministry announced plans to modernize its Air Force fleet of C-130 Hercules aircraft. The Air Force has five C-130s. 'Modernizing the fleet of aircraft and making sure they are well-maintained is a high priority', said Defence Minister Agustín Rossi. The Air Force first obtained C-130 aircraft in 1969. In April 1970 the Air Force used some of the aircraft to provide supplies to the Marambio Antarctic Base, which is the country's primary military base in the region. The base was founded on 29 October 1969. It is named after famed Air Force Vice Commodore Gustavo Argentino Marambio, who was one of the first pilots to fly over the Antarctic region. Over the years the Air Force has continued to use the C-130 aircraft to supply the base. The aircraft is known for performing well in frigid conditions. Temperatures at the base are often below zero. The modernization will be a cooperative effort between Argentina and the United States. An Argentinean C-130 will be taken to the United States to be modernized, officials at the Defence Ministry said. Once that plane is modernized, it will be brought back to Argentina. The modernized aircraft will serve as a model and the rest of the fleet will be modernized in Argentina. The modernization will cost an estimated $166 million (USD), according to published reports. Once the aircraft are modernized, they should last until at least 2040. The Air Force has used the aircraft primarily to transport supplies. Once the modernization is complete, the Air Force will be able to use the aircraft to conduct search and rescue missions with sophisticated infrared radar; transport paratroopers; and conduct missions at sea.

Air Force officials plan to use the modernized aircraft for different types of missions, said Richard Gadea, an Argentinean military analyst. 'Argentina's plans for the refurbished Hercules include supplying deliveries to areas affected by natural disaster, evacuating victims and fighting forest fires,' Gadea said. The modernized C-130s will be useful in responding to natural disasters in Argentina and in other countries. The Argentinean military has a long tradition of providing humanitarian aid to other countries which are struck by natural disasters, Gadea said. For example, the Argentinean military provided humanitarian assistance to Haiti after that country was struck by a devastating earthquake in January 2010. That 7.0 magnitude earthquake killed between 100,000 and 160,000 people and destroyed or severely damaged 250,000 homes and 30,000 commercial buildings, authorities said. The C-130 aircraft is useful for providing humanitarian aid because it performs well over long distances and requires relatively little maintenance. 'This is a legendary plane that has made history in Latin America and the world over,' Gadea said. 'It is a technological marvel and it has endured through the years in very demanding conditions and all climates.'

Fuerza Aérea de Chile (FACh) C-130H CH-02 of Grupo 10.

Belgium

The Force Aérienne Belge operates twelve C-130Hs, delivered in 1972 and 1973. They are flown by the Smaldeel (Squadron), Groupement de Transport/15 Wing, at Brussels-Melsbroek. These aircraft have been used for United Nations operations and famine relief duties with the Red Cross in Ethiopia and the Sudan and may be seen in overall white or specially marked finishes. The C-130s have also been involved in the Open Skies treaty verification programme.

The FAB played a key role in dropping food in Ethiopia. Having already experimented with such drops without parachutes at low level in 1973-74 during another Sahel country's drought period, the FAB refined its VLAGES (Very Low Altitude Gravity Extraction System) food-drop technique in Ethiopia in 1985-86. A total of 677 live food drops was made at Mehoni (near Maychew) and Sekota (in Wollo Province). The overall success rate was 96.7 per cent, but during the last drop months, an average loss of less than 2 per cent was recorded due to further refinements in bagging procedures and drop techniques.

Grain is put into 55 or 110lb nylon bags, these are then put into bags of 35 inches in size, which in turn are put into two outer bags of 47inches). When the bags strike the ground, the inner bags generally tend to burst and the contents spread into the larger middle bag; should the middle bag also split, the outer bag will, in most cases, retain the grain. After improving the flying and re-bagging techniques, post-impact damage was reduced in many cases to zero or almost zero losses.

When approaching the drop zone, the speed of the airdrop is 125 knots and the altitude 50 feet radar altimeter. At that moment the nose attitude is higher. At the 'Green On' given by the navigator, the retriever will tighten the cable and the knife will cut the straps holding the load. The load starts moving. When the pallets move towards the ramp, the straps running along the tight cables will cut the D ring of the pallets. Bags leave the pallet and fall on the ground.

The Belgian Air Force Hercules' airdropped food using the VLAGES technique in southern Sudan, flying from Lokichokio in northern Kenya. Although the technique had to be slightly modified again - because of the terrain at the drop zones the delivery altitude had to be changed from 70 to 60 feet agl - the results stayed as successful as before, with an average of only about 2 per cent loss rates. Drop loads ranged from twelve to sixteen tons, in a single pallet row, single passage airdrop.

Bolivia

The Fuerza Aérea Boliviana's (FAB) Grupo Aéreo de Transporte 71 based at BA General Walter Atze, La Paz operated on a peacetime basis as an internal domestic airline known as Transporte Aéreo Boliviano (TAB). However, it doubles as the main tactical support element of country's military forces, in which role it is known as the Transporte Aéreo Militar (TAM). Of the eleven ex-USAF C-130As and C-130Bs delivered to FAB as from October 1988 only two C-l 30Bs remain in service. Five C-130A/Bs were withdrawn from use and two were lost in crashes in 1989 and 1994. Two new-build C-130Hs were acquired in 1977 and one L-100-30 in 1979. Of these, C-130H TAM-90/CP-1375 crashed into the water after a night take-off from Panama-Tacumen on 28 September 1979 and L-100-30 TAM 92 was shot down near Malanje, Angola, on 16 March 1991 while on lease to Transafrik.

Brazil

Since 1965 the Forca Aérea Brasileria C-130Es, seven C-130Hs and one KC-130H) at various times. C-130E 4093 crashed on landing with high sink rate on 26 October 1966 and C-130E 4091 was written off on 21 December 1969 at Recife. One C-130E has been put into storage, another (4290) crashed on approach in fog to Santa Maria AB, Brazil on 24 June 1985 and 4293 was destroyed at Formosa, 37 miles north-east of Brasilia on 14 October 1994 when the ammunition load caught fire in the air. Five Es, six C-130Hs (C-130H 4998 having crashed into the sea on approach to Fernando de Noronha Island, Brazil, on 14 December 1987) and the KC-130H remain in service. These are flown by the 1st Esquadrão of the 1st Transport Group 'Coral' at Galeão Airport, Rio de Janeiro and the 2nd Esquadrão, 1st Tactical Transport Group 'Gordo', at Campos dos Afonsos, Rio de Janeiro. The C-130Hs are tasked with serving the Army's 1st Parachute Division. Ski-equipped aircraft also support the Brazilian mission in Antarctica.

CC-130H (130330/73-1591 in 435 TRS pictured taking off with JATO rockets was delivered on 16 October 1974. On 29 March 1985 130330; the lead aircraft as part of a mass fly over which included two other C-130s and other Air Force aircraft marking 61 years of the RCAF was involved in a mid-air collision with CC-130H 130331 over CFB Edmonton, Alberta during battle break recovery when hit on the underside by 130331. Ten crewmembers (likely five crew on each aircraft) were killed. The third C-130 (130333) landed safely. The first of 17 new J-model CC-130s began arriving in 2010 to replace the oldest aircraft in the Hercules fleet.

CC-130T 130339 refuels a pair of CF-188s during a Canada to Iceland flight on 4 April 2011 to join a Task Force at Keflavik AB.

Cameroon

Two C-130Hs and one C-130H-30 (4933/TJX-AE, later TJX-CE) have been flown by the l'Armée de l'Air du Cameroon. The aircraft were delivered in August and September 1977 and based at Douala have been used in support of counter-insurgency (COIN) operations from Batouri, Garoua and Yaounde and also for civilian passenger purposes. C-130H 4747 (TJX-AC) burned on the ground at Marseilles in December 1989 and in 1997 was to be shipped to Bordeaux for repairs.

Canada

Four C-130Bs were received in October-November 1960 and issued to 435 Squadron RCAF. 10304 was lost in April 1966 when the forward cargo door opened in flight, striking the port inner propeller which threw it over the fuselage, severing the tail control cables before striking both the starboard propellers. The aircraft belly-landed in a wheat field in Saskatchewan. The three surviving C-130Bs were returned to Lockheed in 1967 and these were acquired in 1969 by the Columbian Air Force (two were later lost). Meanwhile, twenty-four C-130Es had been delivered to the RCAF. These were followed by fourteen C-130H models, diverted from the USAF's 1973 Appropriations for Tactical Air Command and delivered between October 1974 and February 1975.

During the period 1967 to 1993, five C-130Es have been lost, as have three C130Hs in 435 Squadron (two of which were involved in a mid-air collision on 29 March 1985). One of the C-130Es and one of the C-130Hs were lost in accidents involving LAPES operations.

The current RCAF transport fleet consists of 26

E's and H's and the first of 17 C-130J (CC-130J) tactical aircraft arrived on 4 June 2010. In 1996 two L-100-30 aircraft (5320 and 5307) were modified to C-130H-30 - locally designated as CC-130s; they serve with the following squadrons on strategic and tactical transport, search-and-rescue and training duties: 413 Transport and Rescue, Greenwood, Nova Scotia; 418 (Air Reserve) Transport and Rescue, Namao; 424 Transport and Rescue, Trenton, Ontario; 426 Transport Training, Trenton (no aircraft permanently assigned: it also operates CC-130s for the tactical Air Lift School and Transport Operational Test and Evaluation Facility); 429 Transport, Trenton; 435 Transport and Tanker, Namao; 436 Transport; 437 Transport and Tanker, Trenton.

Chad

This former French colony's Hercules fleet has been built up as from 1983 when the country became involved in a war with its northern neighbour Libya; it reached a peak of seven aircraft. The former RAAF C-130A (3208, A97-208) was obtained by France's Securité Civile in November 1983. Four ex-USAF C-130As were acquired during the 1980s, though two of these were lost in crashes in 1986 and 1987 and two more were sold in 1991. Two new-build models, a C-130H and a C-130H-30, were acquired in 1988 and 1989 respectively. These and the surviving C-130A, remain in service with the Force Aérienne Tchadienne at Merino Benitz air base near Santiago.

Chile

The Fuerza Aérea de Chile operates C-130s with Grupo de Aviacon 10 at Santiago-Merino Benitez. The fleet consists of two C-130Hs which were

Fuerza Aérea Colombiana (Colombian Air Force) C-130H (L-382) of the Grupo de Transporte Aéreo 81 at El Dorado, Bogotà at Farnborough in July 2012.

delivered in 1972 and 1973 and four ex-USAF C130Bs acquired in 1992, the latter retain their former 'European One' camouflage.

Colombia

In 1969 the Fuerza Aérea Colombiana bought three ex-RCAF C-130Bs, which had been returned to Lockheed in 1967. Two of these were subsequently in August 1969 and October 1982. Eight C-130Bs were also required and of these five remain in service. Two new-build C-130Hs were delivered in 1983. The FAC Hercules' are operated by the Escuadrón de Transporte at Eldorado Airport, Bogata.

Denmark

The Kongelige Danske Flyveaabnet's (Royal Danish Air Force, RDAF) escadrille 721 of the Flyvertaktisk Kommando (Tactical Air Command) at Værløse uses three C-130Hs to provide support or the Danish Air Force and Army since delivery during the months April-July 1975. The first of three C-130J transports for the RDAF was delivered to its new home base in northern Jutland on 1 March 2004.

Ecuador

The Fuerza Aérea Ecuatoriana's (FAE) small Hercules fleet serves with Ala de Transporte II at Quito-Mariscal Sucre. Four ex-USAF C-130Bs were obtained in the 1970s; these were joined by three new-build C-130Hs, the first two being delivered for service with Escuadrilla 11 in July and August 1977. The second of these (4748) was lost when it crashed into the Pinchincha Mountains in Ecuador on 12 July 1978 (4812, a replacement, was delivered in April 1979). The first (4743), also crashed into a mountain, 9 miles from Marisal Sucre airport near Quito on 29 April 1982, during a go-around after a missed approach. An L-100-30 was obtained in July 1981.

Egypt

The Al Quwwat AH Jawwiya Ilmisriya (the Air Force of the Republic of Egypt, EAF) received twenty-three C-130Hs between 1976 and 1982 and three C-130H-30s in 1990. The first six C-130Hs were diverted from the USAF's 1976 Appropriations and were delivered during December 1976 and January 1977. The first C-130H delivered (SU-BAA/4707) was written off after it had its nose burned out during Egypt's commando-style assault against terrorist hijackers who had taken a number of Egyptian nationals hostage at Larnaca airport, Cyprus, on 19 February 1978. A second C-130H (SU-BAH, which was carrying a cargo of ammunition) was lost when it hit the ground after take-off from Cairo-West on 29 May 1981. Two of the C-130Hs are now configured as VC-130H VIP transports and two serve as ECM/ELINT platforms or airborne command posts. The other twenty serve in the transport role. Egypt will receive two C-130Js in 2019.

Egyptian Air Force C-130H SU-BAC 1272 (76-1600) delivered in January 1977. On 24 February 2009 it sustained substantial damage during a night time touch-and-go landing.

France

The l'Armée de l'Air has five C-130Hs (including two ex-Zaire Air Force machines which were impounded in February 1982 at Milan-Malpensa) and nine C-130H-30s that were delivered between 1987 and March 1991. All are flown by the Escuadrón de Transport 2/61 at Orléans-Bricy. On 29 January 2016 France placed an order for two C-130J transports and two KC-130Js equipped for in-flight refuelling of helicopters. The first two aircraft will be delivered between the end of 2017 and early 2018, with the two refuelling versions due in 2019.

Gabon

The Force Aérienne Gabonaise has just three Hercules (an L-100-30 was sold in 1989): a C-130H, an L-100-20 and an L-100-30 (the presidential aircraft), operated by the Escadrille de Transport at Libreville-Leon M'Ba Airport.

Germany

In January 2017 Germany purchased up to six C-130Js which, together with the C-130J of the French Air Force to form a joint air transport squadron.

Greece

Four C-130Hs were acquired by the Ellinki Aeroporia (Royal Hellenic Air Force) and delivered between September 1975 and June 1976 for service with 356 Mira (Squadron), 112 Ptérix, of Air Materiel Command. Greece withdrew from NATO following Turkey's invasion of Cyprus and it was not until 1977 that the US export of arms was resumed when eight C-130Hs, diverted from the 1975 USAF Appropriations, were sold to the RHAF. C-130H 4724 crashed into Mount Billiuras during its landing approach to Nea Anchialos on 5 February 1991 and 4729 hit a mountain on approach to Tanagra air base on 20 December 1997 whilst searching for a crashed Ukrainian airliner near Athens. One of the C-130Hs was withdrawn from use in 1997. Meanwhile, in 1992, five ex-USAF C-130Bs were acquired to supplement the Hercules fleet. The fourteen C-130Hs that remain in service continue to be flown by 356 Mira at Eleusis. Some are equipped for fire-fighting missions with the MAFFS system and a few are modified for electronic surveillance duties.

Honduras

During 1986-89 the Fuerza Aérea Hondurena received an ex-USAF C-130D (57-0487) and four ex-USAF C-130As. The C-130D crashed near Wampusirpi, Honduras on 14 August 1986, while one of the C-130As was withdrawn in 1991. The Escadrilla de Transporte operates the three remaining C-130As at Tocontin Airport, Tegucigalpa.

Indonesia

In 1958-59 the Angkatan Udata Republik Indonesia received ten C-130Bs diverted from Tactical Air Command's production allocation for that year and these entered service with No. 31 Squadron at Jarkarta-Halim, Java. T-1307 was lost on 3 September 1964 when it crashed in Malaya and T-1306 was lost a year later, on 21 September 1965, when it was believed to have been 'frightened down' by an RAF Javelin. Two C-130Bs were modified to KC-130B. In September 1980, 32 Squadron received the first stretched C-130H-30 (4864) from the production line. C-130H-MP (TNI-AU/4898) crashed into volcano Sibyak on 21 November 1985. Some of the L-100-30 models were leased or sold to Pelita Air Service. The Tantara Nasional Indonesia-Angkatan Udare (TNI-AU) still operates most of the total of twenty-five Hercules it has received. 31 Squadron at Jakarta-Halim operates the survivors of the sixteen C-130Bs delivered in 1960 and 1961, 1975 and 1979 and also the L-100-30, while 32 Squadron at Malang flies the remaining H and H30 models (TNI-AU/4927 crashed after takeoff from Halim-Perdanakasuma, Jakarta, on 5 October 1991).

On Tuesday 30 June 2015 an Indonesian C-130 was carrying more than 120 people when it crashed near a residential area. Military personnel and their family members, students and other civilians were among those on board the C-130 that went down shortly after takeoff in Medan on the Indonesian island of Sumatra. The transport had 122 people aboard 110 passengers and twelve crew members when it took off from Soewondo Air Force Base in Medan, according to Supriatna. No survivors were found. Engine trouble might have been to blame. Major General Fuad Basya, an Indonesian military spokesman said that the aircraft, built in the United States in the 1960s, had been inspected and cleared to fly before it took off from Medan. The plane was carrying people and logistical supplies to bases on other Indonesian islands. It began its multi-stop journey Tuesday in Jakarta, the capital and had made two stops along the way to Medan, in Pekanbaru and Dumai. Sometimes, Indonesian civilians also hitch rides on military flights to get to islands which might otherwise be inaccessible. The C-130 hit a busy road that connects Medan with the highland tourist resort of Brastagi. The crash site is about five kilometres (3 miles) from the air base.

Iran

Beginning in 1962, the Nirou Havai Shahanshahiye Iran (Imperial Iranian Air Force, IIAF) took delivery of four C-130Bs, 28 C-130Es and thirty-two C-130Hs (the last two being delivered in May 1975) making it the third largest user (with 64 aircraft) of the Hercules after the US and the RAF. The C-130Bs were used for about four years with 5 Air Transport Squadron at Mehrabad before being purchased by Pakistan pending delivery of seventeen C-130Es in 1965-66 (eight) and 1968 (nine). C-130E 107/4118 was destroyed following a lightning strike on 18 April 1967. C-130E 5-112/4154 crashed while simulating two-engines out in Shiraz on 7 April 1969. In 1970-71, eleven more C-130Es were delivered. In the mid-1970s, five C-130Es were subsequently disposed of, again to Pakistan. Four IIAF C-130Hs were modified for covert signal monitoring and electronic reconnaissance along the Iranian border with the Soviet Union, as part of the Ibex ELINT-gathering network; the electronic equipment was installed in pods carried outboard of the outer engines. Following the Islamic revolution, the arms embargo imposed on Iran has taken a toll of the remaining fleet and only a handful are believed to be still flyable (since February 1974, seven Iran Air Force C-130s have been lost).

India

On 28 March 2014, Indian Air Force C-130J-30 KC-3803 crashed near Gwalior, India, killing all five personnel aboard. The aircraft was conducting low level penetration training by flying at around 300 feet when it ran into wake turbulence from another aircraft in the formation, which caused it to crash. IAF ordered six 13 C-130Js in early 2008, exercising options to buy six more aircraft in July 2012 and six more on 20 December 2013.

Iraq

The IAF ordered six C-130J-30s in July 2008.

Israel

During 1971-72 the Heyl Ha'Avir (Israeli Defence Force/Air Force, IDAF) acquired twelve C-130Es - all recently disposed of by the 313th, 316th and 516th Tactical Airlift Wings, USAF - and gave them dual military/civil registrations to disguise their military purpose. Starting in October 1971 and ending in September 1976, the IDAF took delivery of ten C-130Hs and two KC-130H tankers. After the outbreak of the Yom Kippur War in 1973, twelve more ex-USAF C-130Es were delivered.

Ten C-130Hs are still in use on transport duties and are operated by 103 'Elephant' Squadron and 131 'Yellow Bird' Squadron at Nevatim. (4X-FBD) is known to have been lost in a crash at Jebel Halal on 25 November 1975 and others have been placed in storage.

The Israeli Government placed orders for four C-130Js with options for a further five. The Israeli Air Force is to purchase nine C-130J-30s.

C-130H (L-382) of the
Jordanian Air Force.

Right: Kōkū Jieitai (Japan Air
Self-Defence Force or
JASDF) C-130Hs in
formation. (JASDF)

Italy

The Aeronautica Militaire Italiana's 50th Gruppo of the 46 Aerobrigata at Pisa-San Giusto continues to fly the Hercules on strategic airlift duties, using twelve C-130Hs from a batch of fourteen delivered in 1972. In June 1978 three were used on fire-fighting duties. 46-10 (4492) was lost when it flew into Monte Serra 9 miles east of Pisa on 3 March 1977. In 1980, 46-14 was cannibalized for spares (subsequently used for C-130H 46-09) on 23 January 1979 when it jumped its chocks during an engine run-up at Milan-Malpensa and hit a tree. Ten C-130J-30 aircraft were delivered between 2002 and 2005.

Japan

The fifteen C-130Hs of the Koku Jietai (Japan Air Self-Defence Force, JASDF) have been operated since entering service in 1984 by the 401st Hikotai (Squadron) of the 1st Tactical Airlift Group at Komaki AB. Some of the aircraft have been fitted with a locally produced Naval minelaying system.

Jordan

The Al Quwwat Almalakiya (Royal Jordanian Air Force) initially received four ex-USAF C-130Bs in 1973, followed by four C-130Hs acquired in 1978 and an HC-130H (not confirmed). Two of the C-130B models were sold to Singapore and the remaining aircraft are flown by 3 Squadron from Amman-Ling Abdullah.

Kuwait

The Kuwait Air Force originally took delivery of two L-100-20s in 1970; N7954S was destroyed on 5 September 1980 when it crashed near Montelimar in southeast France after a lightning strike and the other (4412) was sold back to Lockheed - it was used as a high technology test bed (HTTB) and was subsequently lost on 3 February 1993 when it crashed during a high-speed ground-test. Four L-100-30s were acquired from 1983; 4949/KAF322 (N4107F) was hit by ground fire at Kuwait City Airport on 2 August 1990 during the Iraqi invasion and flown to Iraq - where it was hit by a bomb which badly damaged the centre fuselage. It was transported by road to Kuwait in March 1995 but was not repaired. 4951/KAF323, 4953/KAF324 and 4955/KAF325 were evacuated to Saudi Arabia on 2 August 1990 and flown by 41 Squadron at Kuwait International Airport. The Kuwait Air Force signed a contract for three KC-130J air refuelling tankers in May 2010 with an option to purchase three more.

Liberia

The former RAAF/Bob Geldof C-130A (N22FV) was briefly registered in Liberia as EL-AJM in April 1986 during varied and frequent changes of ownership, carrying the name Wizard of Oz. The Liberian Air Force was officially declared null and void in 2005.

Libya

Eight of the sixteen C-130Hs ordered for the Libyan Arab Republic Air Force were received between 1970 and 1971, the others being embargoed in 1973 and placed in storage at Marietta. 4401 was destroyed by fire at Entebbe, Uganda on 8 April 1979. Seven of the aircraft remain in service, supplemented by L-100-20s and -30s operated by Libyan Arab Air Cargo. L-100-30 4992 eventually ended up at AFI International Ltd 'for oil exploration in Benin' and was delivered to Libya in May 1985. It was hijacked by a Libyan crew to Egypt in March 1987 and was returned to Libya. L-100-30 (5000) was sold to AFI International Ltd, registered to Benin as TY-BBU (not used) and obtained by Jamahiriya Air Transport, Libya in May 1985. The Libyan Air Force has two C-130J-30s on order for the Free Libyan Air Force.

Malaysia

The Tentar Udara Diraja Malaysia (Royal Malaysian Air Force) has received six C-130Hs (FM2401/6), delivered between 1976 and 1980; of these, FM2403/4674 crashed whilst landing at Sibu, Sarawak, on 25 August 1980, while FM2401/4656 was put into storage in April 1997. It also has three C-130H-MPs and six C-130H-30s. Nos. 14 and 4 Squadrons at Kuala Lumpur-Subang Fly the four C-130H and three C-130H-MPs respectively, in joint maritime and transport duties; the latter are distinguished by an overall light grey finish. No. 20 Squadron operates the six C-130H-30s.

Mexico

The Fuerza Aérea Mexicana has received a total of nine ex-USAF C-130As and one RC-130A since 1987 for use by Escuadrón Aéreo Transporte Pesado 302 at Santa Lucia. The RC-130A was briefly operated under a civil registration on Presidential Flight duties. Four of the C-130As were written off in 1997. An L-100-30 was sold to Protexa in September 1994.

Mongolia

The Mongolian Air Force is planning to buy three C-130Js.

Morocco

A total of seventeen C-130H transports were delivered to the Force Aérienne Royal Morocaine (Al Quwwat Ali Jawwiya Almalakiya Marakishiya, Royal Maroc Air Force) in three batches between 1974 and 1981, the last being two C-130Hs (4888 N4162M/CNA-OP and 4892 CNA-OQ) in August 1981 with an SLAR (sideways-looking airborne radar) on the left main undercarriage fairing for use in detecting Polisario infiltrations in the Western Sahara. Two KC-130Hs were also delivered in November-December 1981. Polisario rebels shot down 4537/CNA-OB over the Sahara on 4 December 1976 and 4717/CNA-OH at Guelta Zemmour in West Sahara on 12 October 1981. Several aircraft at Kenitra were fitted with under-wing Chaff and flare pods, two were equipped with an SLAR pod for

Right: C-130H (L-382) CNA-OK L-382 of the Royal Moroccan Air Force (RMAF).

Left: Nigerian Air Force C130-H30 (NAF 918) arriving at Marshalls of Cambridge for overhaul. (Samuel Pilcher)

surveillance work and 4875/CNA-OM has been modified to carry MAFFS equipment for locust spraying. Civilian-style registrations are worn, with the aircraft construction number on the fin.

Netherlands

The Koninklijke Luchtmacht received the first of two C-130H-30s in 1994 (G273 Ben Swagerman and G2775 Joop Mulder), to become the newest European Hercules operator. The aircraft are flown by 334 Squadron at Eindhoven as part of the recently expanded transport office.

Niger

The small Escadrille Nationale du Niger (Force Aérienne Niger) took delivery of two C-130Hs (5U-MBD/4829 and 5U-MBH/4831) at Niamey in 1979. 5U-MBD was put into storage during 1986, but was returned to service in 1988. It was lost on 16 April 1997 when, with two engines on fire, it crashed at the village of Sorei on its approach to Niamey.

Nigeria

The Federal Nigerian Air Force received six C-130Hs delivered in two batches of three between September 1975 and February 1976; also three 'stretched' 130H 911/4624 crashed after take-off from Lagos, Nigeria, on 26 September 1992 when three engines failed because of contaminated fuel. The eight remaining aircraft are operated from the base at Lagos-Murtala Muhammed.

Norway

Six C-130Hs were delivered to the Kongelige Norske Lufforsvaret in June and July 1969 and are still flown by Skvadron 335 based at Gardermoen. They are: 68-10952 BW-A *Odin;* 68-10953 BW-B *Tor;* 68-10954 BW-C *Balder;* 68-10955 BW-D *Froy;* 68-10956 BW-E *Ty;* and 68-10957 BW-F *Brage.* Frequently assigned to the United Nations, they consequently often bore prominent 'UN' titling. LC-130J 10-5630 (c/n: 382-5630) crashed into the western wall of Mount Kebnekaise on 15 March 2012. The aircraft

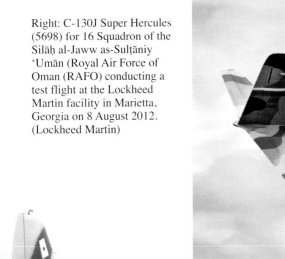

Right: C-130J Super Hercules (5698) for 16 Squadron of the Silāḥ al-Jaww as-Sulṭāniy 'Umān (Royal Air Force of Oman (RAFO) conducting a test flight at the Lockheed Martin facility in Marietta, Georgia on 8 August 2012. (Lockheed Martin)

Left; The Royal Norwegian Air Force (Luftforsvaret) C-130Hs are frequently assigned to tasks on behalf of the United Nations and are consequently seen bearing prominent 'UN' titling. C-130H (68-10956) *Ty* is pictured at Sheremetyevo 1 Airport, Moscow, on 14 August 1992. (MWB)

Portuguese Air Force (Força Aérea Portuguesa) or PoAF C-130H 16803, which was delivered in April 1978 and is one of six C-130H/H-30s that equip Esquadra 501 'Bisontes'. On September 2004 this C-130H ran off the runway at Kabul Airport, Afghanistan after what was thought to be because of brake failure. No injuries were reported.

Right: Pakistani Air Force C-130E 64-144, specially painted to highlight the sacrifices of Pakistani people and the Armed Forces in Operation 'Zarb-e-Azb' (during the 2005 Pakistan earthquake) which not surprisingly won the Concours D' Elegance trophy at Air Tattoo 2016 at RAF Fairford.

disappeared from radar over the Kebnekaise mountain range near Kiruna in Sweden. All five on board were killed. It was the last of four acquired by the Norwegian military between 2008 and 2010 and was named *Siv*. The Royal Norwegian Air Force ordered four C-130J-30s in 2007 to replace six aging C-130Hs in need of additional repairs. One of these was lost in March 2012.

Oman
The Sultan of Oman's Air Force acquired three C-130Hs in 1981 for use by 4 Squadron from their base at Muscat-Seen Airport. Two more C-130s were ordered in August 2010. Oman has ordered three C-130J-30s.

Pakistan
A mixed force of thirteen Hercules remains in service with 35 (Composite) Air Transport Wing of the Pakistan Fiza'ya; this is from a total of thirteen C-130Bs (five of which were ex-USAF and four ex-Imperial Iran Air Force), five C-130Es (all ex-IIAF) and two L-100s (bought by the Pakistan government for PIA, but operated by the PAF) delivered at various times. Seven of the twenty aircraft (five C-130Bs, one C-130E and one L-100) were lost or written off between 1965 and 1988. C-130B 62-3494/PAF 23494 crashed on 17 June 1988 after take-off 4 miles north of Bahawalpur airport, Pakistan, en route to Rawalpindi. President Zia-ul-Haq and many senior officers were killed. The remaining aircraft, which includes the world's last unmodified L-100, are operated mainly by 6 Tactical Support Squadron at Chaklala AB, Rawalpindi.

Peru
The Fuerza Aérea Peruana (Peruvian Air Force) has operated a total of sixteen Hercules since 1970, having received six ex-USAF C-130Bs, two ex-USAF C-130Ds (both of which were scrapped in August 1993) and eight L-100-20s. Two of the C-130As were converted to tankers, one of which was withdrawn from use in 1997. Only three C-130As remain in service. Of the eight L-100-20s, three were written off in crashes: 4364/FAP394 suffered an engine shutdown on take-off from Tarapoto on 19 February 1978. 4450, delivered to the FAP in April 1972 and coded 396, made an emergency landing at night with no fuel near San Juan on 24 April 1981 and was written off. 4708, delivered in December 1976, crashed at Puerto Maldonado, southern Peru on 9 June 1983. The remaining Hercules in the FAP inventory are operated by Escuadrón 841, Grupo Aéreo de Transporte 8, from Jorge Chavez Airport, Lima.

Philippines

The Philippine Air Force acquired an ex-RAAF C-130A (later sold) and seven ex-USAF C-130Bs, four of which were either withdrawn from use between 1996 and 1997, or were rendered non-operational. L-100 (N1130E), the ex-Lockheed demonstrator, was acquired by the Philippine government in 1973 and issued to the Air Force after long storage in Manila. The Philippine government also acquired four L-100-20s, two of which were for the Air Force. One L-100-20 was withdrawn from use in 1991. Three new-build C-130Hs were acquired in the period 1976-97 and issued to 222 Heavy Airlift Squadron at Mactan. The third aircraft (4761) crashed into Mount Manase 155 miles south-east of Manila on 15 December 1993 during descent towards Naga airport.

Portugal

Força Aérea Portuguesa acquired five C-130Hs, delivered from August 1977 to June 1978. Two were subsequently modified to C-130H-30 configuration. A new-build C-130H-30 was added in October 1991. Esquadra de Transporte 501 at Montijo Air Base Operates all six aircraft, all of which can be equipped with the MAFF system for fire-fighting.

Qatar

Qatar ordered four C-130J-30s in October 2008 for the Qatar Emiri Air Force.

Romania

The Romanian Air Force acquired four ex-USAF C-130Bs, which were delivered from Ogden Air Logistics Center to Romania in 1996-97 and equipped 90 Airlift at Otopeni near Bucharest. In 2004 the former IItalian Air Force C-130H MM61991.

Saudi Arabia

The first Hercules of the Al Quwwat Ali Jawwiya Assa'udiya (Royal Saudi Air Force) were nine C-130Es delivered between 1965 and 1968. Losses were 4128/RSAF453, which suffered and engine fire and crashed taking off from Medina on 14 September 1980 and 4136/RSAF454 which crashed at Le Bourget, Paris, on 1 January 1969. The C-130Es were followed by thirty-seven C-130Hs beginning with two in December 1970 and including eight delivered between October 1991 and March 1992, plus eight KC-130Hs (delivered in 1973-74, 1977 and 1980-81) and two VC-130Hs (delivered in July 1980). One of the KC-130Hs (4872) crashed landing at Riyadh on 24 February 1985. Three of the C-130Hs were modified to hospital aircraft; one was reconfigured as a VC-130H for the royal family, while 4756 and 4754 were lost in crashes on 27 March 1989 and 21 March 1991 respectively. Six L-100-30s were acquired. One (4954) was sold to Sheikh Ibrahim, a Saudi VIP and the other five (4950, 4952 - configured as a dental clinic - 4956/57 and 4960) were modified for use as airborne hospitals and operated by Saudia. In 1992 and 1993 respectively, 4950/HZ-MS05 and 4957/HZ-MS10 were demodified to L-100-30 designation and their hospital equipment was removed. Three C-130H-30s were delivered, the first in 1984 and the other two in 1992; the first of these (4986) being converted to a hospital aircraft and operated by Saudia. The standard transport aircraft are flown by Nos. 4 and 16 Squadrons at Jeddah/Prince Abdullah AB. The single VIP-configured L-100-30 and the three VC-130Hs operate from King Faisal AFB, Riyadh, alongside the three C-130H hospital aircraft and the three medically configured L-100-30s and one medically configured C-130H-30. Two KC-130Js were delivered in 2016

Royal Saudi Air Force C-130H (1623) participating in the airdrop competition over McChord Air Force Base, Washington on 23 July 2007, during 'Rodeo 2007', an Air Mobility Command readiness competition with US and international mobility air forces focusing on improving war fighting capabilities and support of the war on terrorism. (USAF)

Singapore

The first Hercules acquired for the Republic of Singapore Air Force were four ex-USAF C-130B models, two of which had also served with the Royal Jordanian Air Force. Delivered in 1977, all were converted to KC-130B transport/ tanker configuration in 1985 and 1986. In 1980 four C-130Hs were delivered, followed by a fifth in 1987, together with a KC-130H (ex-Lockheed tanker demonstrator). All the Hercules serve with 122 Squadron at Paya Lebar.

South Africa

Seven C-130Bs were delivered to the SAAF between 1962 and 1963 for issue to 28 Squadron, Air Transport Command, at Waterkloof, Transvaal, which continues to fly these to this day. A UN arms embargo on sales to South Africa meant that no further Hercules were purchased until 1996-97, when three ex-USN C-HOFs were acquired. In 1997-98, two ex-USAF C-130Bs were added. The nineteen L-100-30s operated by Safair Freighter (Pty) Ltd, Johannesburg at various times (only about six remain), have also been available as a reserve airlift asset.

At the end of May 2013 28 Squadron marked two major milestones – its 70th anniversary and the 50th anniversary of the venerable C-130BZ in service. At AFB Waterkloof, Colonel Jurgens Prinsloo CO, 28 Squadron had responsibility for the nine C-130BZs in the SAAF inventory. The SAAF C-130s were regularly flying to Sudan, the DRC and Uganda to provide logistic support for SA National Defence Force troops deployed on peace support and peacekeeping missions. One of the squadron's aircraft had gone as far north as Malta to bring home South Africans, including diplomats, rushed out of North African countries during the 2011 Arab Spring uprisings.

Seven C-130B Hercules were acquired in 1963 and when the squadron moved to AFB Waterkloof, it left its Dakotas behind to join 44 Squadron at Swartkop. In February 1968 the VIP flight was reconstituted as 21 Squadron, while the C-160Z Transall was acquired in 1969 and operated with the squadron from January 1970 until they retired in 1993. Three ex-USN C-130F aircraft were acquired in 1996 with a further two ex-USAF C-130B following in 1998. The F models were only flown for a short time before being retired. The squadron continues to fly the nine C-130B Hercules, all having been upgraded to C-130BZ configuration.

South Korea

The Republic of Korea received four C-130H-30s in 1987-88 and two batches of four C-130Hs in 1989 and 1990, for service with its Air Transport Wing at Seoul-Kimpo. The first C-130H-30 (N408M/5006) was used at Pope AFB in June/July 1987 to test LAPES etc with 'stretched' aircraft). One aircraft was deployed to serve in the 1991 Gulf War. Four C-130J-30s were delivered in 2014.

Spain

The first four C-130Hs were delivered to the Ejército del Aire Espanol (EdA) in December 1973 and early 1974; initially these were assigned to Escuadrón 301 of the Mando Aviacion Tactica (Tactical Air Command) at Valenzuela-Zaragoza. In Spanish service these were designated T-10s. The first aircraft, 4520/T-10-1, crashed into a mountain in central Gran Canaria while operating from Las Palmas, on 28 May 1980. The third aircraft (4531/T-10-3) had a fortunate escape on 15 November 1988 when it collided with an F-18 near Zaragoza and lost 30 feet of its wing: both aircraft landed safely. In 1976 three KC-130Hs (TK-10s) were delivered; in 1979-80 these were followed by three more C-130Hs and in 1980 by two more KC-130Hs. 5003, a C-130H-30 (TL-10-01) was delivered in 1988. This and all C-130 transport aircraft are flown by Escuadrone 311, Ala de Transporte 31, at Zaragoza. The KC-130Hs (TK-10s) are operated by Escuadrón 312.

Sudan

Six C-130Hs for the Silakh al Jawwiya and known as 'Sudaniya' were delivered to Khartoum between January and May 1978. One Aircraft (4766) has occasionally operated as ST-AHR and ST-AIF in the markings of Sudan Airways. The third aircraft (4769/Sudan AFI 102) is the 1,500th Hercules delivered'.

Sweden

The Svenska Flygvapnet became the first European air force to operate the Hercules, leasing C-130E 64-0546/4039 from Lockheed in February 1965 after the aircraft had been sold back before delivery to the USAF. A second C-130E joined this aircraft in Flygflottilj 7 (F7) Transportglyg-divisionen at Satenas and in 1982 both were modified to C-130H configuration. Six additional C-130H models had by then entered service. Designated Tp 84, the aircraft continue to be flown by F7 at Satenas and have been equipped with flare and chaff dispensers and armoured cockpits.

Taiwan
The Republic of China Air Force has received twenty-one C-130Hs, the first twelve having been delivered in 1986. One (5067/Taiwan1310) crashed during an attempted go-round at Tiipeh-Sung-Shan in a rainstorm on 10 October 1997. The twenty remaining aircraft (at least one of which is equipped for electronic warfare) are operated by 101 Squadron based at Pingtung AB.

Thailand
The Royal Thai Air Force received its first three C-130Hs in 1980 under the US Military Assistance Program. A C-130H-30 was delivered in 1983, followed by three more in 1988 and 1990. During 1990-92, three C-130Hs were acquired, one going to Cambodia in 1997. In 1992 also, two more C-130H-30s were acquired, one of which is presumed to be used as a VIP aircraft. Most of the Hercules are flown by 601 Squadron, part of 6 Wing at Bangkok-Don Muang.

Tunisia
Seven ex-USAF C-130Bs were acquired for the Tunisian Air Force and these were delivered between 1995 and 1998. Meanwhile, two C-130Hs were purchased in 1985: they serve with the Escadrille de Transport et Communication at Bizerte and wear quasi-civilian markings. Two C-130J-30s were received as of December 2014.

Turkey
Under the US Military Assistance Program (MAP), the Türk Hava Kuvvetleri received eight C-130Es 1964-1974 for service with Air Transport Command at Erkilet. 4100/ETI-949 in

131 Squadron crashed into a mountain during approach to Izmir, Turkey, on 19 October 1968. The Hercules were used to support the 6th Allied Tactical Ait Force of NATO Allied Air Forces Southern Europe and on relief operations. They also took part in the Turkish invasion of Cyprus in 1974, which led to an arms-sale embargo on Turkey. Seven ex-USAF C-130Bs were delivered to Turkey during 1991-92, one subsequently returning to the US and being sold to Romania. All Turkish Air Force Hercules are operated by 222 Squadron at Erkilet/Kayseri.

Uganda
L-100-30 (no further details available).

United Arab Emirates
The integrated air forces of Abu Dhabi and Dubai comprise the UAE Air Force. Two C-130Hs (4580 and 4584) delivered to Abu Dhabi in March 1975 were sold back to Lockheed in February 1984 (subsequently being acquired by Canada for the CAF) in exchange for two new C-130Hs (4983 and 4985 respectively). Two other C-130Hs were delivered to Abu Dhabi in 1981. The four C-130Hs now operate with the Transport Wing of Western Air Command from Bateen AB, Abu Dhabi. An L-100-30 (4834) was delivered to Dubai in 1979 and a C-130H-30 was delivered in 1983. Both fly with the Transport Squadron, Central Air Command, from Minchat AB, Dubai. On 25 February 2009 the UAE placed an order for 12 C-130J-30s to modernize the country's tactical airlift fleet with an option for four KC-130J tankers.

'Turkish Stars' C-130E 73-00991 support aircraft.

United Kingdom

Sixty-six C-130K models were ordered for the RAF in 1965. These were 65-13021/13044, 66-8550/8573 and 66-13533/13550 and they were essentially C-130H airframes powered by 4,508 eshp T56-A-15s with some components made by Scottish Aviation and British electronics. The first aircraft (65-13021/XV176) flew at Marietta, Georgia on 19 October 1966. Known in service as the Hercules C.Mk.1, it was the first to be delivered and was assigned to 242 OCU at Thorney Island, Hampshire in April 1967. Final deliveries to the RAF of the C.Mk.1 were made in 1968. Four aircraft have been lost and twenty-five were provided with in-flight refuelling probes and modified to C.Mk.1P standard. Six more were fitted with the air-refuelling probe and a hose-drum unit in the fuselage and were designated C.Mk.1K Hercules. XV223 was modified by Lockheed as the prototype of the Hercules C.Mk.3. with the fuselage stretched by 15 feet to increase capacity from ninety-two to 129 infantrymen, or from sixty-four to ninety-two paratroops. This aircraft first flew in modified form on 3 December 1979. Twenty-nine C.Mk.1s were stretched by Marshall Engineering, to be brought up to C.Mk.3 standard.

Following the Falklands War in 1982, Marshalls fitted an in-flight air-refuelling probe to twenty-five aircraft, which became C.Mk.1Ps. Beginning in 1986 they also began fitting in-flight refuelling probes to the thirty C.Mk.3s to convert them to C.Mk.3P configuration. Starting in 1987, C.Mk.1Ps and C.Mk.1Ks began receiving AN/ALQ 157 IR jamming equipment and chaff/flare dispensers. At least five C.Mk.1Ps were fitted with Racal 'Orange Blossom' ESM pods beneath their wing-tips to give some degree of surveillance capability.

The RAF has a total of 24 C-130J (C4/C5) aircraft. The C4 is almost the same size as the current C3 aircraft, but with a slightly shorter fuselage, while the C5 is the same size as the C1.

United States of America

The original user of the Hercules in December 1956, the USAF now has a total of 201 C-130E, C-130H and H-30 transports in its inventory, which serve with eleven Airlift squadrons in Air Combat Command (ACC); Air Mobility Command(AMC);USAFE; USAF Special Operations Command; US Pacific Air Forces (PACAF); US Air Education and Training Command (AETC); AFMC (Air Force Materiel CMD); AFRes; ANG; Air Mobility Command (AMC); US Air Combat Command (USACC); US Navy (USN); USMC and the US Coast Guard (USCG). The last named is a key component of the US Armed Forces (USCG district commanders are of USN Rear Admiral rank), with essential

HC-130H CG1717 (86-0420) coming into land at CGAS Clearwater, Florida in April 1991. This Coast Guard Hercules was registered N436NA to NASA at Wallops Island on 26 March 2015. (MWB)

Right: EC-130Q BuNo 159469 was delivered to VQ-4 at Patuxent River in July 1975 for airborne communication with USN nuclear submarines. This aircraft was re-designated TC-130Q before being released to AMARC in September 1991. On 10 September 1997 Derco Aerospace sold the aircraft to the Netherlands for spare parts. (Lockheed)

wartime/readiness responsibilities under the US Navy Maritime Defense Zone (MARDEZ), it carries out combat and combat support tasks for the USN, which include SAR, port security, harbour defence, antisubmarine warfare (ASW), logistic support and surveillance interdiction. Apart from SAR, the USCG is part of the international ice patrol: in the average year, 200 to 400 icebergs are located and tracked in the 45,000 square miles of North Atlantic sea lanes patrolled by CG C-130s.

The following roles are becoming increasingly important for the Hercules: enforcement of immigration and sea traffic laws and treaties (ELT), drug-traffic interdiction and also marine environmental protection (MEP) - CG Hercules on offshore and port area surveillance detect oil contamination resulting from offshore drilling operations, tankers, spillage and other sources. Since

1988, Operation 'Bahamas', Turks and Caicos Islands (OPBAT), a multi-national effort of law enforcement and military agencies, has stemmed the flow of illegal drugs smuggled into the US through the Caribbean; in 1997, a record year for drug seizures, OPBAT netted 12,163lb of marijuana and more than two tons of cocaine.

USCG aircraft are normally funded through the USN Appropriations; the first four Hercules, ordered under the designation R8V-1G (later SC-130B), were delivered between December 1959 and March 1960. Two more SC-130Bs were delivered from January to March 1961, by which time the aircraft were re-designated HC-130G. Then three more were delivered to the CG in March and April 1962 and another three (now re-designated as HC-130Bs) between December 1962 and February 1963. All were withdrawn from use in the 1980s.

EC-130E 63-7869 of the 193rd Special Operations Squadron, 193rd Special Operations Group, Pennsylvania ANG over Harrisburg, Pennsylvania on 1 May 1980. Built as a C-130E, 63-7869 was converted to an EC-130E in April 1979 and modified to an EC-130H 'Commando Solo' in January 1993.

Right: The 'Blue Angels' C-130T BuNo164763 Hercules passing the New York skyline.

The 'Blue Angels' C-130T BuNo164763 Hercules taking off with JATO rockets.

The 'Blue Angels' Honour Guard takes the salute.(USMC photo by Staff Sergeant Oscar L. Olive)

In August 1966 the CG received its first EC-130E (4158, later redesignated HC-130E) and this was used until the mid-19808. In 1968 three HC-130Hs were delivered and another nine followed, in 1973, 1974 and 1977. One HC-130H (4757) crashed 2.5 miles south of Attu in the Aleutian Islands on 30 July 1982 while trying to land in bad weather. In 1983 and 1984, eleven HC-130H-7s were received and between 1985 and 1987 a further eleven HC-130Hs were added. In 1988 one additional HC-130H (5121) was delivered, to COS Clearwater, Florida and then modified in 1991 to EC-130V; it was transferred to the USAF in 1993. On 24 January 1992, HC-130H-7 CGI706, based at Kodiak, Alaska, lost a propeller in flight and suffered fuselage and wing damage, but managed to land safely. Three months later, on 24 April, HC-130H 1452 (67-7183) was attacked by Peruvian Su-22s while on an anti-drug mission and suffered extensive damage; it was repaired, but was consigned to AMARC in 1993. Thirty CG C-130H and H-7 aircraft and the HC-130J version are in the USCG inventory at the following CG stations: Barbers Point, HI (HC-130H); Borinquen, Puerto Rico (HC-130H); Clearwater, FL (HC-130H); Elizabeth City, North Carolina (HC-130H); Kodiak, Alaska (HC-130H); Sacramento, McClellan AFB, California (IIC-130II).

Uruguay
Between 1992 and 1994 the Fuerza Aérea Uruguaya acquired three ex-USAF C-130Bs, although the last (3541) was never used and was withdrawn from use in August 1996. The two remaining aircraft are flown by the Regimento Tactico 1 at Montevideo-Carrasco.

Venezuela
The original order intended for the Fuerza Aérea Venezolana and placed in 1969, was for six C-130Hs for service with Escuadrón de Transporte 1 at Caracas, four to be delivered in 1970 and two in 1975. Four were delivered to the FAV in 1971 for operation by Escuadrón 62 at Matacay-El Libertador and the other two duly arrived in 1975. However, 4408/FAV7772 24 de Julio crashed on night approach to Lajes, Azores, in bad visibility and high winds on 27 August 1976; and 4406/FAV3556 crashed attempting a three-engined take-off from Caracas airport on 4 November 1980. Two further C-130H models were delivered, in December 1978 and 1988, as an attrition replacement for the two crashed aircraft.

Việtnam
As part of Operation 'Enhance Plus', thirty-five C-130As were speedily transferred from ANG squadrons in the US and delivered to the Republic of Việtnam Air Force (South Việtnam) in November 1972. By April 1975, when the country was overrun, three C-130As had been lost, nineteen were flown to Thailand, but thirteen were captured in 1975 and entered service with the 918th Regiment, Việtnamese People's Air Force. Some were kept flying by cannibalizing others and were used as makeshift bombers in the invasion of Kampuchea in 1978. A few may have been given to the former USSR. Attempted sales of surviving airframes in the early 1990s were unsuccessful.

Yemen
In August 1979 the Yemen Arab Republic Air Force received two C-130Hs donated by Saudi Arabia; they are operated by Yemen Airways.

Zaire
Only one (4411/9T-TCA) of the seven C-130Hs which served with the Force Aérienne Zairoise (1971 to 1997, now The Air Force of the Democratic Republic of the Congo) remain in service: with 191 Escadrille of 19 Wing d'Appui Logistique at N'Djili Airport, Kinshasa. Initially, three C-130Hs were delivered in 1971, then three more in 1975 and the seventh (4736/9T-TCG) in 1977. 4422/9T-TCD crashed at Kisangani, Zaire, on 18 August 1974, but all the rest were used during the war of 1977 which followed the invasion of Shaba by foreign mercenaries. Subsequently, 4569/9T-TCE crashed during a three-engined take-off with maximum load from Kindu, Zaire, on 14 September 1980. Then 4736/9T-TCG crashed near Kinshasa, Zaire on 19 April 1990 because a propeller blade broke off. Finally 4416/9T-TCB and 4588/9T-TCF were impounded at Milan-Malpensa airport in October 1994, the latter going on to serve with the French l'Armée de l'Air (as did 4589/9T-TCC after 1995).

Zambia
Though no Hercules has officially served with the Zambian Air Force, five L-100s have been used by the Zambian government and Zambia Air Cargoes and possibly by the air force, too.

Twenty-one USAF C-130J Super Hercules roll down the runway at Dyess Air Force Base, Texas on 21 June 2014 when the aircrews from multiple units flew a large formation. More than 500 manning hours and 200 maintainers in the 317th Airlift Group generated twelve aircraft for the large-scale launch when C-130Hs and Js joined more than fifty other aircraft across 14 other wings and seven major commands to take part in the largest 'Joint Forcible Entry Exercise' led by the US Air Force. The 21-ship formation, of both the C-130H Legacy and C-130J Super Hercules models from eight Air Force installations travelled to Nellis AFB, Nevada, in support of the JFE.

Appendix III

Models and Variants

YC-130-LO (Model 082-44-01)

The two prototypes/service test aircraft (53-3396/53-3397) were the only two Hercules built at Burbank; they were powered by four 3,250eshp Allison YT56-A-1A axial-flow propeller turbines driving three-blade Curtiss turbo-propellers. The first aircraft was used initially for static tests and the first flight was made by 53-3397 at the Lockheed Air Terminal on 23 August 1954. The YC-130s were later operated by Allison for engine tests and were re-designated NC-130s in 1959. 53-3396 was disassembled in October 1960 and 53-3397 in 1962.

CM30A-LM (Model 182-44-03)

This was the first production version, of which 204 were built at Marietta in Georgia. These differed from YC-130s in that they had provision for two 450-US gallon (1,703-litre) external fuel tanks outboard of the outer engines and were powered by 3,750eshp Allison T56-A-1A or T56-A-9 engines. The original Curtiss three-blade propellers were fitted to the first fifty or so C-130As, but during the course of production these were replaced, first by Aeroproducts propellers and finally, in 1978, by Hamilton-Standard four-blade units. All C-130As had provision for four 1,000lb thrust Aerojet 15KS-1000 JATO (jet-assisted take-off) bottle on each side of the rear fuselage to improve short-field performance, thus reducing take-off ground run at the design mission weight of 108,000lb (from 1,000 to 790 ft. Rough-field tests proved that the side hinged nose-gear doors were easily damaged and starting with the fifteenth production aircraft, these were replaced with units sliding fore and aft of the wheel well.

The first twenty-seven C-130As were delivered with a 'Roman nose', but beginning with the twenty-eighth production aircraft, the now familiar 'Pinocchio' nose' radome was added to house AN/APN-59 search radar in place of the earlier AN/APS-42. (The last ten of the first twenty-seven were retrofitted with the new radome also.) Other production changes included the installation of a crash position indicator in an extended tail-cone; wing centre-section modifications

to extend the life of the airframe; the installation of the Tactical Precision Approach System; and the deletion of the upward-hinged, forward cargo door. Provision was made later for some C-130As to carry two 500-US gallon (1,893 litre) auxiliary fuel tanks in the fuselage, while others were equipped to carry a 450-gallon (1,703 litre) non-jettisonable pylon tank beneath each wing outboard of the engines.

The C-130A was first flown at Marietta on 7 April 1955. Starting in October 1956, 192 C-130As were delivered to the USAF and fourteen modified RC-130As were acquired. Beginning in December 1958, twelve C-130As powered by T56-A-lls were delivered to the RAAF, who operated the type for twenty years. Thirty-five C-130As were modified to AC-130A, C-130A-H, DC-130A, GC-130A, JC-130A, NC-130A, RC-130A, TC-130A, C-130D, C-130D-6 and RC-130S configurations. Two C-130As (55-046 and 55-048) were temporarily fitted with underwing refuelling pods for evaluation by the USMC.

In 1986 a NC-130A (55-022) belonging to the 4950th Test Wing, Aeronautical Systems Division (ASD) was modified as a sensor and seeker testbed for terminally-guided air-to-ground missiles. For that purpose, the aircraft was fitted with a retractable, gimballed ventral turret for the airborne seeker evaluation test system (ASETS). During the same year, two C-130As were specially configured for aerial spray operations to replace the unit's Fairchild UC-123Ks. The last C-130As in military service equipped the 155th TAS, Tennessee ANG; they were replaced by C-141Bs in 1991. Outside the military, many have been converted for civil use and as forestry tankers.

AC-130A-LM

54-1626, an early production JC-130A was first evaluated as a 'gunship' under Project 'Gunboat', beginning on 6 June 1967. The AC-130A, sometimes referred to as 'Plain Jane', was modified by the Aeronautical Systems Division, Air Force Systems Command, at Wright-Patterson AFB, Ohio to carry four General Electric 20 mm M-61 cannon mounted on the port side of the fuselage, to fire obliquely downward. The following were also installed: Starlight Scope (a night observation device), side-looking radar, a computerized fire-control system, a beacon tracker, DF homing instrumentation, FM radio transceiver and an inert tank system; in addition, a semi-automatic flare dispenser and a steerable 1.5 million candlepower AN/AVQ-8 searchlight containing two Xenon arc lights (infra-red and ultra-violet) were mounted on the aft ramp. 'Plain Jane' was battle-tested in south-east Asia during October-December 1967 and from February-November 1968. It proved so successful that the Pentagon awarded a contract to LTV Electrosystems of Greenville, Texas, for the modification of seven more JC-130As to AC-130A configuration. Delivered between August and December 1968, they differed from the prototype in being fitted with improved systems, including the AN/AAD-4 SLIR (side-looking infra-red) and AN/APQ-136 moving target indicator (MTI) sensors and an AN/AWG-13 analogue computer. Used in the fighting in south-east Asia, the AC-130As proved very effective, especially against vehicles along the Hó Chi Minh Trail at night.

C-130A (55-0011) was modified under the 'Super Chicken' or 'Surprise Package' programme to meet a requirement for improved all-weather capability and with larger guns. The 'Surprise Package'/'Cornet Surprise'/'Super Chicken' AC-130As carried two 7.62 mm guns, two 20mm cannon forward and two 40mm Bofors clip-fed cannon aft of the wheel fairing. An AN/ASD-5 'Black Crow' truck ignition sensor was installed in the prototype, but was not originally included in the subsequent aircraft. Also fitted were Motorola AN/APQ-133 beacon tracking radar and an AN/ASQ-24A stabilized tracking set containing ASQ-145 LLLTV (low light-level television).

Nine further C-130As were modified to the AC-130A 'Pave Pronto' configuration with AN/ASD-5 'Black Crow' truck ignition sensor reinstated; also the AN/ASQ-24A stabilized tracking set with AN/AVQ-18 laser designator and bomb damage assessment camera, SUU-42 flare ejection pods, dual AN/ALQ-87 ECM pods under the wings and some other improvements. The earlier AC-130As were retrospectively brought up to 'Pave Pronto' and 'Pave Pronto Plus' standard. In south-east Asia the AC-130As used their laser designation/rangefinder equipment to mark targets for F-4 Phantoms carrying laser-guided bombs (LGBs). Five were destroyed in combat between 1969 and 1972.

The eighteen C-130A/JC-130As modified as gunships were 53-3129, 54-1623, 54-1625/1630, 55-011, 55-014, 55-029, 55-040, 55-043/044, 55-046, 56-469, 56-490 and 56-509.

CM30A-II-LM

Twelve C-130A-II COMINT/SIGINT (communications intelligence/signals intelligence gathering) versions obtained, beginning in late 1957, by modifying C-130As (54-1637, 56-0484, 56-0524/0525, 56-0528, 56-0530, 56-0534/0535, 56-0537/ 0538 and 56-0540/0541). Each was fitted with direction finders, pulse and signal analysers, receivers and recorders and was capable of accommodating twelve to fifteen ECM operators. Up until about 1971 the C-130A-IIs were operated by the 7406th Operations Squadron, 7407th Combat Support Wing, at Rhein-Main AB in West Germany and from Athens, Greece on Operation 'Creek Misty' and other eavesdropping missions along the Iron Curtain and in the Middle East. 56-0528 was shot down by Soviet fighters over Armenia during an eavesdropping sortie on 2 September 1958. All remaining C-130A-IIs were replaced by C-130B-IIs in 1971.

DC-130A-LM

In 1957 two C-130As (57-496 and 57-497) were modified as drone directors to carry, launch and direct remotely piloted vehicles (RPVs) such as the Ryan Firebee drone. These were followed in the 1960s by 56-491, 56-514, 56-527, 56-461 and 57-523 (an ex-RL-130A) and a C-130D (55-021). Originally these were designated GC-130A but from 1962 all were known as DC-130A. The DC-130A carries four drones beneath the wings, with specialized guidance equipment operators in the fuselage. The first two DC-130As were transferred to the USN as BuNos 158228/158229. Many had their original Pinocchio nose' replaced with an extended (thimble) nose radome housing the AN/APN-45 and some had an added microwave guidance system in an undernose (chin) radome. Beginning in 1969 five DC-130As were transferred to the USN and to VC-3, where they were given BuNos 158228, 158229, 560514, 570496 and 570497. Following Navy service, the last three were operated under contract first by Lockheed Aircraft Service and then by Flight Systems Inc. from

Mojave Airport, California.

QC-130A-LM

Initial designation given to the DC-130As, later applied to permanently grounded Hercules that are, or have been, used as instructional airframes.

JC-130A-LM

Sixteen C-130As (53-3129/53-3135, 54-1624, 54-1627/54-1630, 54-1639, 56-490 56-493 and 56-497) modified in the late 1950s and early 1960s to track missile; during tests over the Atlantic range. Based at Patrick AFB, Florida at least eleven were used in conjunction with submarine-launched Polaris ballistic missiles. Six (54-3129, also 54-1627 to 54-1630 and 56-490) were later modified to become AC-130A gunships, while the remainder were converted to NC-130A and RC-130S configuration.

NC-130A-LM

Five C-130As (54-1622, 54-1635, 55-022/ 023 and 56-491) temporarily used for special tests by the Air Force Special Weapons Center at Kirtland AFB, New Mexico. Three subsequently reverted to C-130A standard. The NC-130A designation was then used in 1968 to identify Air-borne Seeker Evaluation Test System (ASETS) Aircraft.

TC-130A-LM

The nineteenth C-130A modified to serve as the prototype for the proposed crew trainer version. The USAF had no requirement tor a dedicated Hercules training aircraft and so it was modified again, to become the prototype for the RC-130A (see next entry).

RC-130A-LM

During the mid-1950s TC-130A 54-1632 was modified as a prototype photographic-mapping aircraft. Equipment fitted included electronic geodetic survey apparatus, cameras and a darkroom for in-flight photo processing. Its success in this role led to the last fifteen C-130As (57-0510/0524) being delivered in March 1959 to RC-130A standard, to the 1375th Mapping and Charting Squadron, 1370th Photomapping Group at Turner AFB, Georgia. This unit, redesignated 1370th Photomapping Wing in 1960, later moved to Forbes AFB, Kansas; it was inactivated here in June 1972. All except 57-0523 (which became a DC-130A) were remodified to C-130A configuration, stripped of their survey equipment and served as transports with AFres and ANG units.

C-130B-LM (Model 282)

The second production series of the Hercules, more powerful version than its predecessors, due largely to the implementation of 4,050eshp T56-A-7 engines which drove four-bladed Hamilton Standard propellers. Other major improvements included a stronger landing gear and additional tanks in the wing centre section, inboard of the engines; these tanks increased the internal fuel capacity from 5,250 to 6,960 US gallons (19,873 to 26,346 litres) and meant that the pylon tanks could be deleted. The forward cargo door was permanently sealed and a deeper cockpit with bunks for a relief crew was fitted. These improvements, plus in some aircraft the strengthening of the wing centre section to improve fatigue life, increased the gross weight from 124,200 lb to 135,000 lb. Those aircraft fitted with an AN/URT-26 crash position indicator had the same extended tail-cone as similarly modified C-130As. A Tactical Precision Approach System was also installed.

The first aircraft (57-525) was flown at Marietta on 20 November 1958 and the C-130B first entered service with the 463rd TCW at Sewart AFB, Tennessee, in June 1959. A total of 231 C-130B versions were built, beginning in December 1958, comprising as follows: 118 C-130Bs for Tactical Air Command; forty-three C-130Bs for overseas customers (Canada, Indonesia, Iran, Jordan, Pakistan and South Africa); and seventy basically similar aircraft which were built as HC-130Bs for the US Coast Guard, WC-130Bs for the USAF and as GV-1s (KC-130Fs), GV-1Us (C-130Fs) and UV-1Ls (LC-130Fs) for the US Navy and US Marine Corps. Thirty-seven USAF aircraft were modified as C-130B-H.S (RC-130Bs) JC-130Bs, NC-130Bs, VC-130B and WC-130Rs, while two Indonesian aircraft (T-1309/T-1310) were modified as tankers with underwing refuelling pods and became KC-130Bs. From 1988 Singapore also operated three KC-130Bs (720, 724 and 725). (The five new-build WC-130Bs (62-3492/3496) were remodified to C-130B configuration.) Aircraft basically similar to the C-130Bs were built as C-130BLs (LC-130Fs), WC-130Bs, GV-1s (KC-130Fs), GV-1Us (C-130Fs) and R8V-1Fs (SC-130B/HC-130Bs).

C-130B-II

Thirteen 'Sun Valley' IP C-130Bs (58-711, 58-723, 59-1524/1528, 59-1530/1533, 59-1535 and 59-1537) modified as electronic reconnaissance aircraft. They carried long-focal-length oblique cameras and reconnaissance systems and entered service in May 1961 with the 6,091st Reconnaissance Squadron at Yokota AB, Japan (556th RS from 1 July 1968). They replaced the unit's 'Sun Valley' and 'Smog Count' Boeing RB-50Es used on photo surveillance duty along the Korean DMZ (demilitarized zone). All thirteen C-130B-IIs were subsequently remodified as C-130Bs by removal of all reconnaissance equipment.

C-130BL-LM

Designation assigned by the USAF to the first four 'ski birds' acquired for and on behalf of, the US Navy to assist in Antarctic exploration as part of Operation 'Deep Freeze'. In USN service the aircraft were originally designated UV-1L, but they were subsequently redesignated LC-130Fs in September 1962.

HC-130B-LM

Originally designated R8V-lGs (USN) and SC-130Bs (USAF) prior to 1962, these twelve search and rescue aircraft were redesignated HC-130B in September 1962. All twelve were delivered to the US Coast Guard (USCG serials 1339/1342 and 1344/1351). They differed from C-130Bs in having the crew rest-bunks replaced by a radio-operator station and on-scene commander station, clear-vision panels fitting over the parachute doors after the cabin was depressurized and provision for carrying life rafts and rescue kits. By using just two engines once the search area was reached, HC-130Bs could remain on station for up to seven hours. The HC-130Bs remained in service for almost twenty years before they were put into store at MASDC in the early 1980s.

JC-130B-LM

Fourteen C-130Bs (57-525/529, 58-713/ 717, 58-750, 58-756 and 61-962/963) modified for aerial recovery of satellite capsules. Six were operated by the 6593rd Test Squadron, Air Force Systems Command at Hickam AFB, Hawaii, for aerial recovery of capsules ejected by Discovery military satellites. (Tracking equipment was carried in a radome atop the JC-130B fuselage and a retrieval system was trailed from the rear cargo ramp to snatch the capsule parachute while

in flight.) At least one JC-130B was used to evaluate the Fulton STAR (surface-to-air recovery) personnel retrieval system which was later fitted to the HC-130H and MC-130E. One JC-130B was modified as a VC-130B VIP transport before this aircraft and most of the other JC-130Bs were converted back to C-130B configuration.

KC-130B-LM

Two Indonesian Aircraft (T-1309/T-1310) and three Singapore aircraft (720, 724 and 725) modified as tankers with refuelling pods containing hose-and-drogue assemblies in place of underwing tanks.

NC-130B-LM

Lockheed-developed STOL version of the Hercules, initiated after the US Army expressed an interest in a short -take-off-and-landing aircraft. C-130B 58-712 was converted as a STOL prototype to test a boundary layer control system, having a rudder of increase chord and single-hinged flaps in place of Fowler flaps. Air bleeds from two Allison YT56-A-6s operating as gas generators located under the outer wing panels in place of the external tanks were blown over the flaps and rudder to enhance lift and controllability. However, the US Army cancelled its requirement for the proposed C-130C production before 58-712 flew on 8 February 1960 in STOL configuration. In all, the NC-130B logged twenty-three hours of flight before being placed in temporary storage. The STOL system was later removed and the aircraft fitted with standard wings and rudder from a damaged Hercules for delivery to NASA as N929NA (later N707NA), to take part in the 'Earth Survey' Programme. One JC-130B (58-717) assigned to the 6,593rd Test Squadron was also designated NC-130B for use on special tests.
RC-130B-LM See C-130B-II entry. SC-130B-LM Re-designation of the R8V-1Gs; later they became HC-130Gs and finally HC-130Bs.

VC-130B-LM

JC-130B 58-714 temporarily modified as a staff transport before being remodified to the C-130B configuration.

WC-130B-LM

Five weather-reconnaissance aircraft (62-3492/3496) produced in 1962 for the Air Weather Service by Lockheed. That same year, they entered service with the 55th Weather Reconnaissance Squadron at Ramey

AFB, Puerto Rico where the WC-130Bs replaced Boeing WB-50Ds on hurricane- and typhoon-hunting missions in the region. In the 1970s eleven C-130Bs (58-726/727, 58-729, 58-731, 58-733/734, 58-740/741, 58-747, 58-752 and 58-758) were modified to WC-130B standard. When suitably modified WC-130E/H aircraft were obtained in the mid-1970s, most WC-130Bs were returned to C-130B configuration for service in AFRes and ANG units. 58-731, a Kaman AWRS (Airborne Weather Reconnaissance System)-equipped aircraft, was the exception, being transferred in 1975 to the National Oceanic and Atmospheric Administration (NOAA), US Department of Commerce, at Miami, Florida first as N8037 and then as N6541C.

C-130C-LM

Proposed STOL US Army version for which the NC-130B-LM (58-712) had served as a prototype. It was not built.

C-130D-LM

A ski-equipped Hercules was originally conceived in the late 1950s for service in Alaska and Greenland with Alaskan Air Command in support of the Distant Early Warning (DEW) Line radar stations. The forty-eighth C-130A (55-021) was modified to become the ski-equipped prototype, which, while retaining its wheeled undercarriage, was fitted with 5.5 feet wide Teflon-coated aluminium skis: the nose-unit skis were 10.3 feet long and the main skis 20.5 feet long. The ski-equipped prototype first flew on 29 January 1957 and underwent testing in Minnesota and Greenland - only to be returned to C-130A configuration immediately afterwards. This aircraft later became a DC-130A drone director and was issued to the US Navy as BuNo158228. In the meantime, twelve production ski-equipped C-130Ds (57-484/495) for TAC were built with late production C-130A airframes and powerplants. These were delivered to the TCS on 29 January 1959. Furthermore, two C-130As (57-0473 and 57-0474) were modified as C-130Ds but later were returned to their original configuration. Six C-130Ds (57-0484/0489) were converted to C-130D-6 standard during 1962-63 by removal of their skis. C-130D-6 (3203) The Harker (formerly Frozen Assets) stalled while overshooting at Dye III, 320 kilometres east of Sondrestrom (originally Bluie West 8), a US air base in central Greenland, on 5 June 1972 and was written off.

Beginning in the summer of 1975 the rest was assigned to the 139th TAS, New York ANG, which operated the five 'ski-birds' until their replacement by LC-130Hs November 1984-April 1985.

QC-130D/QC-130D-6

Designation given to at least three permanently grounded GC-130Ds used as instructional airframes.

C-130E-LM (Model 382)

Tactical Airlift Command's C-130A and C-130B had proved exceptional tactical transports. By 1964 the TAC needed additional C-l30 models and this requirement coincided with that of Military Air Transport Service (MATS), in June, for turbine-powered aircraft to replace part of its burgeoning fleet of obsolescent piston-engined transports. The third major production version of the Hercules was therefore designed with longer-ranged logistic missions in mind. To meet the MATS payload-range performance requirement, maximum take-off weight on the first 323 C-130Es for the USAF and the first thirty-five export models, was increased from 124,200 lb for the C-130A to 155,000 lb (or to 175,000 lb, by limiting manoeuvres to reduce load factors from 2.5 to 2.25) and by increasing the fuel capacity to 9,226 US gallons (34,923 litres). The latter increase was achieved by replacing the two 450-gallon (1,703-litre) underwing tanks of the C-130B by 1,360 US gallon (5,148 litres) underwing units, with the larger external tanks being moved to a position between the engine nacelles. Starting with the 359th C-130E (68-10934) the fuel capacity was increased to 9,680 US gallons (36,642 litres). The 4,050hp T56-A-7 engines used on the C-130B were retained, the increase in the C-130E's operating weight resulting in stronger wing spars and thicker skin panels, as well as strengthened landing gear. The first flight of a C-130E (61-3258) was made at Marietta on 15 August 1961 with deliveries to the 4442nd Combat Crew Training Group, TAC at Sewart AFB commencing in April 1962.

During production the first sixteen C-130Es had the forward cargo-loading door on the port side sealed; from the seventeenth aircraft onwards it was removed entirely, to be replaced by new outer skin panels. Other ongoing improvements included the fitting of the AN/URT-26 crash position indicator in an extended tail-cone, the provision of both AN/APN-169A station-keeping equipment (SKE) and the

Tactical Precision Approach System, as well as wing centre-section modifications to improve fatigue life. In 1970-71 the Adverse Weather Aerial Delivery System (AWADS) was installed aboard many tactical C-130Es. In later years, USAF, AFRes and ANG C-130Es were upgraded by the installation of a self-contained navigation system (SCNS) enhanced SKE and updated AWADS.

In total, Lockheed built 491 C-130Es including one generally similar EC-130I and four C-130Gs for the US Coast Guard and the US Navy respectively; the USA received 377 aircraft (255 for TAC and 122 for MATS) whose successor, Military Airlift Command (MAC) assumed complete control of airlift operations in the mid-1970s. (Air Combat Command uses almost all USAF C-l30s for its operations.) Some 109 additional were exported to nine overseas countries, the Canadian RCAF being the first receive them in December 1964. Argentina, Australia, Brazil, Iran, Saudi Arabia, Sweden and Turkey are the other customers, while Israel received ex-US C-130Es. Sixty USAF C-130Es were modified to fulfil seven different roles, details as follows:

C-130E-I

On 12 August 1958 during joint service tests, Marine Staff Sergeant Levi W. Woods was successfully plucked from the ground by a specially modified PB-1 using the Fulton STAR (surface-to-air recovery) personnel airborne recovery system. This provided for a line to be attached to the person to be rescued, held aloft by a helium balloon to be snatched by folding, pincer-like tines on the nose of the rescue aircraft. While the USN continued with their own Project 'Skyhook' USAF interest in the STAR system waned; until there was a pressing need to recover downed airmen and other service personnel deep in enemy territory arose during the Việtnam War.

At Pope AFB, North Carolina in 1965 trials involving a C-130E fitted with a fixed ring device on the nose proved successful. Seventeen further C-130Es (62-1843, 63-7785, 64-0508, 64-0523, 64-0547, 64-0551, 64-0555, 64-0558/0559 and 64-0561/0568) and one NC-130E (64-0572) were subsequently modified with the STAR system for special operation behind enemy lines, fitted with upgraded avionics for adverse weather operations. In 1967 they entered service with the 'Combat Spear' detachment of the 314th Troop Carrier/Tactical Airlift Wing and then with the 15th Air Commando Squadron, 14th ACW. Although the

STAR system was actively operated there is no evidence that any recoveries actually took place. Instead, the C-130-Is (now known as 'Combat Talons') were used on more conventional, but equally risky, sorties in Việtnam, flying day and night airlift and adverse weather resupply missions for Special Forces operating behind enemy lines. 64-0563 was destroyed during a mortar attack at Nha Trang on 25 November 1967, 64-0547 was shot down by a SAM in North Việtnam on 9 December, 64-0508 was shot down by ground fire during a night SAR mission near An Lộc, South Việtnam on 28 December and crashed in Laos and 64-0558 was lost in a mid-air collision with an F-102A near Myrtle Beach, South Carolina in 1972. The remaining C-DOE-Is became C-130H(CT)s and two were modified as MC-130-Ys and one as an MC-130E-C.

C-130E-II (ABCCC)

The war in south-east Asia revealed the need for ABCCC (Airborne Battlefield Command and Control Centre) aircraft, whereby a commander could directly influence and co-ordinate operations involving ground personnel and the air components and direct them in a unified manner against the enemy. This requirement led, in the early 1960s, to the C-130-II designation being applied to ten C-130Es (62-1791, 62-1809, 62-1815, 62-1818, 62-1820, 62-1825, 62-1832, 62-1836, 62-1857 and 62-1863). Each carried an AN/ASC-15 command battle staff module housing LTV communications and control systems and accommodation for up to sixteen operators. Combat deployment with the 314th TCW, operating from Đà Nẵng AB, South Việtnam began in September 1965. The C-130E-IIs were redesignated EC-130Es (see EC-130E/ABCCC entry) in April 1967.

AC-130E-LM 'PAVE SPECTRE' I

In April 1970 a decision was made to convert, at Warner-Robins Air Material Area (WRAMA), two C-130Es to prototype AC-130E gunship versions. The C-130E's higher gross weight, stronger airframe and increased power offered greater payload and longer loiter time than the original AC-130A gunships. Originally the AC-1 30Es were armed with two 40mm Bofors cannon, two M-61 20 mm cannon and two MXU-470 7.62 mm miniguns; eventually a 'Pave Aegis' array was carried, consisting of two miniguns (often deleted), two M-61 cannon and a 105 mm howitzer in place of one of the 40 mm guns. In

February 1971 nine additional conversions not dissimilar to 'Pave Pronto' AC-130As were ordered but by the time that the first AC-130Es were completed in July 1971 they represented such a quantum leap in avionics over the earlier 'Pave Pronto' gunships that they became known as 'Pave Spectre Is. AN/APN-59B navigation radar and a moving target indicator were earned in a nose radome and a head-up display (HUD) was located in the cockpit. Also fitted were the following: AN/ASQ-5 'Black Crow' truck ignition detector sensor; AN/ASQ-145(V) LLLTV; AN/ASQ-24A stabilized tracking set with a laser illuminator and rangefinder; AN/AAD-7 FLIR; AN/APQ-150 beacon tracking set; and a 2kw AN-AVQ-17 searchlight. SUU-42A/A chaff and flare dispensers were located between the engine nacelles and AN/ALQ-87 ECM pods were fitted on the outer wing pylons. The 'Pave Spectre Is' (69-6567/6577) entered service in south-east Asia in the spring of 1972 and were used to great effect against NVA tanks and vehicles using the Hó Chi Minh Trail at night. All but 69-6571, which was shot down near An Lộc in March 1972 were upgraded in 1973 to AC-130H standard.

DC-130E-LM

Seven early-production C-130E airframes (61-2361/2364, 61-2368/2369 and 61-2371) modified as launch-and-guidance aircraft for drones or RPVs (remotely piloted vehicles). Underwing pylons permitted four drones, or two drones and two external fuel tanks (on the inboard pylons) to be carried. Internally, provision was made for consoles and work stations for two launch control officers and two airborne remote-control officers. The DC-130Es differed from the DC-130As in having a chin radome containing a microwave guidance system in addition to the thimble radome which housed tracking radar. They entered service with the 408th/100th Strategic Reconnaissance Wing and were used extensively in SE Asia before being returned to C-130E configuration and reassigned to the 314th TAW.

EC-130E

This designation has been used to identify six distinct Hercules variants, although the only one built to the actual EC-130E designation was a C-130E delivered to the US Coast Guard (USCG 1414) in August 1966 for use a Loran (LOng RAnge Navigation) A & C calibration aircraft. (During development it was designated S (for 'search') C-130E, but because the 'search' prefix was considered inappropriate for an electronic calibration aircraft, this was changed to EC-130E before delivery to the USCG. Later, this aircraft was re-designated HC-130E.)

EC-130E (ABCCC)

The EC-130E designation was next used in April 1967 to identify ten ABCCC (Airborne Battlefield Command and Control Centre) aircraft previously designated C-130E-IIs (62-1791, 62-1809, 62-1815 - destroyed by a rocket on the ground at Đà Nẵng on 15 July 1967 - 62-1818, 62-1820, 62-1825, 62-1832, 62-1836, 62-1857 and 62-1863). These aircraft were operated in SE Asia by the 7th Airborne Command and Control Squadron (ACCS). (62-1809 was destroyed in a collision with an RH-53D at Posht-i-Badam, Iran during the failed attempt to rescue US hostages on 24 April 1980.) At least four remaining EC-130Es were retrofitted with 4,058eshp (de-rated from 4,910eshp) T56-A-15 engines and fitted with an in-flight refuelling receptacle atop the forward fuselage. (Despite the changes these aircraft retained their EC-130E designation and were not redesignated 'EC-130H' as is sometimes reported.) Since 1990 at least two EC-130Es received new Unisys ABCCC III capsules to replace the Việtnam era ABCCC II capsules. These have much new equipment, including upgraded satellite communications equipment, JTIDS data link and secure communications facilities. The two ABCCC III EC-130Es became operational only twelve days before Operation 'Desert Storm', during which they controlled almost half of all attack missions flown during the war. Also, they were used to co-ordinate SAR missions, flying a total of 400 hours during more than forty sorties.

EC-130E(CL), EC-130E(RR) 'RIVET RIDER', 'CORONET SOLO'

Other aircraft designated EC-130Es at one time or another are five 'Comfy Levy'/'Senior Hunter' (63-7783, 63-7815, 63-7816, 63-7828 and 63-9816) and three 'Rivet Rider'/'Volant Scout' electronic surveillance aircraft (63-7773, 63-7869 and 63-9817). The first five aircraft were modified in 1979 to EC-130H(CL) configuration for the jamming and acquisition of electronic intelligence by Lockheed Aircraft Service for the Pennsylvania ANG's 193rd TEWS (in turn, re-designated 193rd ECS and 193rd SOG) at Harrisburg. ANG personnel fly these aircraft, but it is believed that mission specialists are provided by the National Security Agency and that tasks are performed under the direction of USAF Electronic Security Command. Beginning in June 1987 all EC-130CL/RRs were retrofitted with T56-A-15 engines as well as in-flight refuelling receptacles and 1RCM jamming equipment. In June 1992 the three remaining EC-130E(CL) aircraft (63-7773, 63-7869 and 63-9817), plus 63-7783 (which was modified to EC-130E(RR) in April 1980) were brought up to 'Volant Solo' standard for 'PSYOP' missions. These were characterized by the addition of large blade aerials ahead of the fin and beneath the wing outboard of the engines. They became 'Coronet Solo' when the Pennsylvania ANG changed from TAC status to MAC control in March 1983.

Experience gained in the Gulf War revealed the need to install a new TV broadcast system suitable for operation anywhere in the world and so, in 1992-93 63-7773, 63-7869, 63-9817 and 63-7783 were modified to 'Commando Solo' configuration. The dorsal fin leading-edge blade aerial was deleted and replaced by four fin-mounted, protruding antenna pods dedicated to low-frequency TV broadcasting and a UHF/VHF antenna associated with TV broadcast signals, in two 23 feet x 6 feet pods, one mounted under each wing near the blade antennas. Other modifications include the addition of trailing wire antennas, one released from the 'beavertail' and used for high-frequency broadcasts and a second, which is lowered from beneath the EC-130E and held vertically by a 500lb weight and used for AM broadcasts. During Operation 'Uphold Democracy' 'Commando Solo' broadcasts played a vital role in avoiding the necessity for an invasion of Haiti. The 'Commando Solo' configuration is also applicable in emergency in peacetime: thus EC-130Es can be used as airborne radio/television relay and transmission stations to broadcast public information and evacuation instructions in response to natural disasters such as hurricanes or earthquakes.

HC-130E-LM
 see EC- 130E entry

JC-130E-LM
Designation applied to the first C-130E (61-2358) which in March 1964 was modified for unspecified trials at the Air Force Flight Test Center at Edwards AFB and El Centro. The aircraft was subsequently returned to C-130E standard in 1972.

MC-130E-C 'RIVET CLAMP' MC-130E-Y 'RIVET YANK' MC- 130E-S 'RIVET SWAP'
Designations applied to fifteen special operations support (SOS) C-130E-1 'Combat Talon Is' obtained by upgrading and modifying eleven C-130H(CT)s, three C-130E-Is and one NC-130E (64-571 'Night Prowler', reportedly used for ELINT). These improvements included a change to T56-A-15 engines, also the installation of an in-flight refuelling receptacle on top of the forward fuselage and AN/APQ-122(V)8 dual-frequency I/K band radar with terrain following. MC-130E-C 'Clamp' aircraft were fitted with the Fulton STAR recovery system (the 'Yank' and 'Swap' are not). Other retrofits include inertial navigation system (INS), IRCM pods, chaff and flare dispensers, radar warning receiver and a system permitting precision air drops of Special Forces teams. Their serial numbers are as follows: MC-130E-C Rivet Clamp: 64-523, 64-551, 64-555, 64-559, 64-561, 64-562, 64-566, 64-567, 64-568, 64-572. MC-130E-S Rivet Swap: 64-571. MC-130E-Y Rivet Yank: 62-1843, 63-7785, 64-564, 64-565. Operating with the 1st SOS, 64-564 was lost in a crash on 26 February 1981 near Tabones Island, Philippines, during a low-level turn. In 1992, 63-7783 was modified to 'Commando Solo' configuration. In July 1994 MC-130E-C 64-567 in the 8th SOS flew ex-President Manuel Noriega from Panama to Miami.

NC-130E-LM
Designation given to two C-130Es (64-571 and 64-572) used for trials associated with the C-130E-1/MC-130E project at Edwards AFB, California and Wright-Patterson AFB, Ohio. 64-571 became an MC-130E-S, while 64-572 was remodified in 1977 as a C-130E-I and in turn, as a MC-130E-C in 1979.

WC-130E-LM
Weather reconnaissance/hurricane-and typhoon-hunting version obtained by modifying six C-130Es (61-2360, 61-2365/2366 and 64-552/554) during the 1960s. All passed to the 815th TAS in 1989-91 for use in the transport mission role, while retaining their WC-130E configuration. They were subsequently passed to the Aerospace Maintenance and Regeneration Center (AMARC).

C-130F-LM

US Navy utility transport model corresponding to the C-130B of the USAF. Seven were delivered as GV-1Us (BuNos149787, 149790, 149793/149794, 149797, 149801 and 149805). They were re-designated C-130Fs in September 1962.

KC-130F-LM (QV-1)

Marine Corps interest in a Hercules tanker version led to two USAF-loaned C-l 30As (55-0046 and 55-0048) being fitted with hose/drogue refuelling pods; they were then evaluated by the Naval Air Test Center (NATC) at Patuxent River, Maryland in 1957. The evaluation proved successful and deliveries to the USMC began in 1960. Initially the GV-1s and GV-1Us (as they were known prior to September 1962) were powered by 4,050eshp T56-A-7 engines, but later they were modified to use the T56-A-16 version. Eventually forty-six dual-role transport/tankers were ordered, to be achieved by the conversion of C-l 30B airframes. As tankers they carried one 1,800 US gallon (6,814 litre) tank (or two of these in overload condition) inside their fuselage and 934 lb refuelling pods beneath their outboard wing panels so that they could refuel simultaneously two fighters or attack aircraft. Each pod contained a hose and drogue unit with a 91 feet hose - normally this extended to 56-76 feet - and a refuelling basket, but it did not contain fuel. These HRU pods were fitted with three coloured lights: red indicating that pressure was off; yellow that the aircraft was ready to transfer fuel; and green that fuel was flowing. In USMC service the aircraft were given Bureau Nos147572/573, 148246/249, 148890/899, 149788/789, 149791/792, 149795/796, 149798/800, 149802/804, 149806/816 and 150684/690. KC-130F BuNo149798, the twenty-third KC-130F completed, had its in-flight refuelling pods removed and was then fitted with Hytrol anti-skid brakes and modified nose-gear doors for delivery to the Naval Air Test Center, Patuxent River on 8 October 1963: here it began trials to test the feasibility of operating the Hercules as a COD (carrier onboard delivery) aircraft but was considered impractical as it required the flight-deck to be cleared of almost every other aircraft.

LCM30F-LM

Four ski-equipped aircraft (BuNos 148318/321) based on the C-130B variant, with 4,050eshp T56-A-7 engines acquired by the USAF as C-DOBLs on behalf of the US Navy, which re-designated them as UV-1Ls. (After September 1962 the UV-1L designation was superseded by the LC-130F designation). All were fitted with Navy communications equipment and skis similar to those of Air Force C- 130Ds for use by VX-6 (later VXE-6) in Operation 'Deep Freeze' in Antarctica, where they replaced Douglas R4Ds. JATO-assisted take-offs were frequently employed, but three serious accidents occurred when the bottles separated and damaged the aircraft surfaces. The worst of these happened on 1 December 1971 when BuNo148321 The Crown had to abort takeoff from Carrefour 'D-59', 746 miles from McMurdo: it sank in the ice and was abandoned. It was finally dug out in December 1986 and after temporary repairs, was flown out in January 1988 to Christchurch, New Zealand for permanent repair; it was returned to VX-6 at NAS Point Magu, California in September 1989. BuNo148318 City of Christchurch hit a snow-wall taking off from McMurdo on 15 February 1971 and burned. BuNo148319 Penguin Express was damaged when a JATO bottle broke loose during take-off from 'Dome Charlie' on 15 January 1975; it was repaired with a new wing and flown out of Antarctica in December 1976. BuNo148320 The Emperor was also damaged when a JATO bottle broke loose during take-off from 'Dome Charlie' on 4 November 1975. VXE-6 was disestablished in 1998/99 and the LC-130Fs were withdrawn from use in the Antarctic.

CQ-130G-LM

Designation describing four US Navy transport aircraft (BuNos151888/891) corresponding to the C-130Es but fitted with Navy radio equipment and powered by 4,910eshp T56-A-16 engines. They served briefly in the transport role with VR-1 at Norfolk, Virginia and with VR-21 at Barber's Point, Hawaii before being modified for strategic communications as EC-130G TACAMO aircraft (see next entry).

EC-130G(TACAMO)/TC-130G

Designation given to the four C-130Gs (BuNos151888/891) after they had been modified during the period 1966-1970 to TACAMO (TAke Charge And Move Out) configuration and fitted with 5,000 feet long, trailing antennas extending from the ventral loading ramp just below the rear fin. In this role the aircraft acted as relay stations, receiving VLF (very low frequency) and UHF communications from the National Command Authority (NCA) airborne national command posts (ABNCPs) via satellites and other emergency radio links and then retransmitting the instructions in VLF to ballistic missile submarines at sea. All four EC-130Gs were operated by Fleet Command and Control Communication Squadrons VQ-3 and VQ-4. BuNo151890 was written off at Patuxent River after being damaged by an in-flight fire in the No.1 fuel tank in January 1972. In May 1990 BuNo151891 was modified to TC-130G as a test bed for equipment being developed for the EC-130Q, including wing-tip electronic pods. After retirement from the TACAMO mission, it was intended that the EC-130Gs would be brought up to TC-130G standard for the trainer/utility transport role but none of the aircraft had retained their rear cargo ramp and from October 1991 BuNo151891 was used as the 'Blue Angels' support aircraft. 151888 and 151889 were re-designated TC-130G, but the former was sent to AMARC in 1990 and the latter was broken up in March 1994, having been used for spares while in storage at NAD Cherry Point, North Carolina from 1992-93. The original TACAMO aircraft were joined by a number of EC-130Qs, though eventually both the EC-130Gs and -130Qs were replaced by Boeing E-6A Mercury aircraft.

HC-130G

Designation used briefly only to refer to the twelve aircraft delivered to the US Coast Guard (1339/1342 and 1344/1351) in the early 1960s. The aircraft involved however, were soon redesignated (see HC-130B entry).

C-130H-LM

Initially this most numerous version of the Hercules was built with the overseas market in mind; the first three models being delivered to the RNZAF in March 1965 (the first - 4052/NZ7001 - flying on 19 November 1964) but sales only really took off when the Air Force showed interest in the early 1970s; the first models being delivered to the USAF in 1974. Fifty air forces have since bought the C-130H, making it the most widely used model of the Hercules: in total, 1,092 C-130Hs have been built. Outwardly C-130Hs were basically similar to the C-130E, but were powered by T56-A-15 engines normally derated from 4,910 to 4,508eshp. Other improvements included a redesigned outer wing and

stronger centre-wing box assembly to improve the service life of the airframe, a more efficient braking system and updated avionics. At first, provision for JATO was made but this facility was abandoned in 1975. From 1993 the Night Vision Instrumentation System was introduced and TCAS II was included in new aircraft from 1994.

Beginning in 1979 C-130Hs were delivered to the AFRes and the ANG, the first time that these reserve forces had received new-build Hercules. Some of these aircraft have been and indeed are still being used in fire-fighting missions. Specially modified aircraft are operated by the 757th AS, AFRes at Youngstown-Warren Regional Airport, ARS Ohio for aerial spraying, typically to suppress mosquito-spread epidemics. Variants obtained by modifying existing C-130H airframes include the DC-130H, NC-130H, VC-130H and WC-130H. Related models are the HC-130H, KC-130H, C-130K, HC-130N, HC-130P, EC-130Q, KC-130R and LC-130R. A Swedish C-130E (Flygvapnet 84002) was brought up to C-130H standard in 1982. Two Royal Morocaine (Royal Maroc Air Force) C-130Hs (4888 N4162M/CNA-OP and 4892/CNA-OQ) were delivered in August 1981 with SLAR (sideways-looking airborne radar) on the left main undercarriage fairing for use in detecting Polisario infiltrations in the Western Sahara.

C-130H-(CT)

Designation given to C-130E-Is fitted with T56-A-15 engines and improved electronic equipment as part of the C-130E-I Combat Talon special operations programme. Nine later became MC-130Es and -Cs and two became MC-130E-Ys.

C130H-30 (previously C-130H(S))

This version combined the features of the C-130H with the longer fuselage (15 feet) of the L-100-30. The first two C-130H-30s (4864 and 4865, TNI-AU A-1317 and A-1318 respectively) were delivered to 32 Squadron in the Indonesian Air Force in September 1980. A total of fifty-six new build and two modified from C-130H configuration were built for thirteen air forces.

C-130H(AEH)

Aircraft designed to provide medical care at remote disaster areas. Lockheed Aircraft Service, Ontario, California first modified a C-130H ordered by the Kingdom of Saudi Arabia (N4098M) as an airborne emergency hospital (AEH), complete with operating room, intensive care unit and all necessary equipment and supplies. Electrical power for the medical equipment and air conditioning on the ground was provided by auxiliary power units housed in non-standard underwing tanks and could be operated continuously for up to seventy-two hours. Since delivering this first AEH in January 1980, LAS has modified and delivered to the Royal Saudi Air Force eight other C-130AEHs of various configurations (two modified C-130Hs and six modified L-100-30s: 4954/HZ-117, 4950/HZ-MS05, 4952/HZ-MS06, 4956/HZ-MS09, 4957/HZ-MS10 and 4960/HZ-MS14), each having surgical capability. One version carries its own ambulance to transport triage teams to the scene of a disaster if it is away from where the aircraft is able to land; another can be quickly converted into a medical evacuation vehicle with the capacity to airlift fifty-two litter patients in a single flight.

C-130H-MP (PC-130H)

A multi-role maritime patrol and search-and-rescue version of the C-130H: the first three were initially produced for Malaysia in 1980 (4847, 4849 and 4866). A fourth (4898AFNI-AU AI-1322) was delivered to Indonesia in November 1981, but was lost when it crashed into Sibyak volcano. These aircraft, powered by T56-A-15 engines, were fitted with seats and a rest area for a relief crew, also searchlights on the wing leading edge, observation windows on each side of the forward fuselage, an observer station in the port paratroop door and a pallet-mounted flare launcher and rescue kit. A Hasselblad camera operating in tandem with the aircraft's navigation system and onboard computer could produce a matrix showing the time and position of any object photographed. Optional equipment included sea search radar, LLLTV, an IR scanner and passive microwave imager.

C-130H(S) subsequently re-designated C-130H-30 AC-130H-LM

In June 1973 the ten surviving AC-130Es (69-6571 having been shot down over South Viêtnam in March 1972) were provided with 4,508eshp T56-A-15 engines, thereby upgrading them to AC-130H standard. In 1978 provision was made for in-flight refuelling with a boom receptacle atop the fuselage, aft of the flight deck. Retrofits include a digital fire control computer, electro-optical (EO) sensors and target acquisition systems, including forward-looking infra-red (FLIR) and LLLTV. Fire-control computers, navigation, communications, ECM and sensor suites have all been upgraded. AC-130Hs were deployed to the Middle East for the Operation 'Desert Storm' mission in the Gulf War, 1991. 69-6567 in the 16th SOS was shot down on 31 January 1991, 110 km south-south-east of Kuwait City. They have also taken part in operations in Bosnia, Liberia and Somalia; during the latter, on 14 March 1994, 69-6576, in 16th SOS, crashed in the sea 7 km south of Malindi, Kenya after take-off from Mombasa when a howitzer round exploded in the gun tube and caused a fire in the left-hand engines. In January 1998, 69-6568 was delivered as the (MC-130P) prototype for the 'Special Operations Force Improvement' (SOFI) update programme. Eight AC-130Hs were progressively replaced by new-build AC-130U gunships.

DC-130H-LM

It was intended that two HC-130Hs (C/Nos. 4116 and 4131/65-971 and 65-979) be modified late in 1975 as drone directors, hut the ending of America's involvement in the Viêtnam War obviated the need for this and in the final outcome, only 65-979 was converted to DC-130H standard, though both aircraft were transferred to the 6514th Test Squadron. In 1998 65-971 was still flying as an MC-130P with the 5th SOS, while at the time of writing, 65-979 was still operating as an NC-130H.

EC-130H 'COMPASS CALL'/CCCCM

In the early 1980s this designation was used to identify four EC-130Hs (64-14859, 64-14862, 65-962 and 65-989) as well as twelve C-130Hs (73-1580/1581, 73-1583/1588, 73-1590, 73-1592, 73-1594 and 73-1595), modified for use as 'Command, Control and Communications Counter-measures' (CCCCM) jamming platforms. The last twelve aircraft were easily identifiable by a blister fairing on both sides of the rear fuselage and undertail 'trestle-like' antenna array. Additional ram air inlets in the undercarriage bays provided cooling air tor the onboard electronic equipment. The EC-130Hs were vital in disrupting Iraqi military communications at strategic and tactical levels in the Gulf War. At the time of writing, three of the original HC-130Hs modified to EC-130H (64-14862, 65-0962 and 65-0989) (64-14859 was remodified to C-130H standard in 1996) are among the EC-130Hs operated by the 41st, 42nd and 43rd ECSs, 355th Wing, 12th Air Force, at Davis-Monthan AFB, Arizona. As new-build C-130J aircraft are procured, priority for replacement will be given to special mission aircraft.

EC-130H(CL) 'SENIOR SCOUT'
Two C-130Hs (4735/74-2134 and 5194/ 89-1185) modified in March 1994 and January 1993 respectively for the jamming and acquisition of electronic intelligence.

HC-130H/HC-130H-7
Originally the HC-130H ('Crown Bird') designation was for forty-five USAF rescue and recovery aircraft, built to replace the Douglas HC-54s used by the Air Rescue Service in the airborne rescue mission control function. A radio operator station was installed in place of crew bunks against the aft cockpit bulkhead, the bunks being relocated to within the main cargo compartment. An observation window with swivelling seat was sited on each side of the forward fuselage. Provision was made in the fuselage for a 1,800 US gallon (6,814 litre) auxiliary fuel tank and for rescue equipment. The latter comprised three MA-1/2 kits (each kit consisting of five cylindrical bundles linked by four buoyant 210 feet polyethylene ropes; bundles one and five contained life rafts and bundles two, three and four, waterproof supply containers). Ten launch tubes were installed in the rear ramp for parachute flares, smoke and illumination signals, or marine location markers.

The first HC-130H was delivered on 26 July 1965 and all were equipped with the nose-mounted Fulton STAR (surface-to-air recovery) personnel recovery yoke (although this was often removed in service). The first Fulton STAR live pick-up and dual pick-up took place on 3 May 1966 at Edwards AFB, California. Two days later three men were plucked up from the Pacific Ocean surface, this particular exercise demonstrating the HC-130H's ability to recover the crew of Apollo spacecraft. Four aircraft (64-14858, 64-14854, 64-14857 and 65-979) were modified for in-flight recovery of space capsules after re-entry, before being assigned to the 6593rd Test Squadron at Hickam AFB, Hawaii. Subsequently they were re-designated JC-130H (64-14858), JHC-130H (64-14854 and 64-14857) and NC-130H (64-14854, 64-14857 and 65-979). At the request of NASA, all USAF HC-130Hs were fitted with a Cook aerial tracker (AN/ARD-17) in a fairing above the forward fuselage, to locate space capsules during re-entry. In fact, no spacecraft recovery missions involving HC-130Hs ever took place and no astronauts were ever recovered; but beginning in December 1965 HC-130Hs saw widespread use in SE Asia as airborne co-ordination aircraft during combat rescue missions. Using its locator beacons, the Cook aerial tracker now proved valuable in locating downed personnel.

Two HC-130Hs became DC-130H drone control aircraft, one was temporarily designated JC-130H, four became EC-130Hs and fifteen were modified as WC-130Hs. The HC-130H designation was also applied to twenty-four basically similar aircraft built for the US Coast Guard (1452/1454, 1500/1504, 1600/1603 and 1710/1715). These however, were not fitted with the ARD-17 Cook aerial tracker, nor the Fulton STAR recovery yoke and they did not carry HRU pods.

The HC-130H-7 designation was used to identify eleven US Coast Guard aircraft (1700/1709 and 1790) powered by 4,050eshp T56-A-7B engines in place of T56-A-15s. Coast Guard versions have been fitted with side-looking airborne radar (SLAR) and forward-looking infrared (FLIR) pods for drug surveillance operations. Experiments have been conducted using the Lockheed SAMSON ('Special Avionics Mission Strap On Now') system, which comprises a pod-mounted FLIR, an optical data link and a control console with display and recorder. Retrofits have included updated navigation equipment and cockpit lighting has been modified to permit operations with night vision goggles (NVGs), while most of the surviving examples were brought up to HC-130P standard with wing-mounted HRU pods containing hose-and-drogue equipment for the in-flight refuelling of helicopters. At the time of writing, HC-130Hs are serving at six Coast Guard Air Stations in the USA and at Argentia, Newfoundland, Canada.

JC-130H-LM
Designation given to HC-130H 64-14858 while it was assigned to the 6593rd Test Squadron at Hickam AFB, Hawaii, returned to HC-130H configuration and subsequently modified to HC-130P standard and finally to MC-130P in February 1996.

JHC-130H-LM

Designation given to seven HC-130H aircraft so modified during 1965-66 (64-14852/14858): all were returned to HC-130H standard in 1986-87, then some to HC-130P configuration in 1989. (64-14854 and 64-14858 also operated later as MC-130Ps, while HC-130H 64-14857 went to AMRC in 1995 and is reported to have been acquired by the Royal Jordanian Air Force in 1997. HC-130P 64-14856 crashed into the sea 70 miles west of Eureka, Caliifornia on 22 November 1996 after all its engines stopped because of fuel starvation.

HC-130(N)

Designation applied to six C-130H airframes, namely 88-2101 City of Anchorage; 88-2102, delivered in October 1990; 90-2103, delivered in November 1992 and 93-2104/2106, delivered in October 1995: they went to the Alaska ANG for the dual helicopter in-flight refuelling and rescue and recovery missions. Basically similar to the HC-130P, they have updated avionics, HRU pods beneath the wings and auxiliary fuel tanks in the fuselage.

KC-130H-LM

Twenty-two air tankers built new and six C-130Hs modified to KC-130H standard produced for Argentina, Brazil, Canada, Israel, Morocco, Saudi Arabia, Spain and Singapore fitted with wing-mounted HRU refuelling pods and one or two 1,800 US gallon fuel tanks in the fuselage hold.

LC-130H

Designation for seven ski-equipped C-130Hs: four aircraft (83-0490/0493) first delivered to the New York ANG in 1985 to replace the C-130Ds equipping the 139th TAS. 92-1094 *Pride of Grenville*, 92-1095 and 92-1096 *City of Christchurch NZ* were delivered to the 139th TAS during October-December 1995. The Navy Antarctic Development Squadron (first designated VX-6, then VXE-6 from 1969) originally operated the LC-130 aircraft. Initially, VXE-6 was home based at the Naval Air Station Quonset Point, Rhode Island and later at the Naval Air Station Point Mugu, California. Operation of the aircraft was transferred in the late 1990s to the 109th Airlift Wing of the New York ANG when Navy support of the Antarctic programme was terminated. Currently all LC-130 aircraft are operated by the New York ANG at Schenectady County Airport. Seven aircraft are

LC-130H-2 (three of these were Navy LC-130R from VXE-6 converted to LC-130H-2). Three are LC-130H-3.

MC-130H-LM 'COMBAT TALON II'

Designed to supplement and eventually replace the MC-130Es used by the 1st Special Operations Wing for 'Combat Talon' clandestine and special operations. In 1984 the USAF ordered the first of twenty-four C-130Hs (83-1212) for modification to MC-130H 'Combat Talon II' standard, with IBM Federal Systems Division handling systems integration and E-Systems installing the specialized avionics. Electronic and equipment fit included AN/APQ-170 multi-role radar (ground-mapping, navigation, terrain following and terrain avoidance), INS, high-speed low-level aerial delivery and container release system and automatic computed air-release point, as well as AN/AAQ-15 IR detection system, AN/AAR-44 launch warning receiver, AN/ALQ-8 ECM pods, AN/ALQ-172 detector jammer, AN/ALR-69 radar warning receiver, IR jammer and chaff/flare dispensers. The first MC-130H was delivered to the 8th SOS at Hurlburt Field, Florida in June 1990. All twenty-four MC-130Hs (83-1212, 84-475/476, 85-011/012,86-1699,87-023/024, 87-125/127, 88-191/195, 88-264, 88-1803, 89-280/283, 90-161/162) were delivered to the USAF by November 1991.

NC-130H-LM
Re-designated JHC-130Hs.

VC-130H-LM

Six C-130Hs modified as VIP transports for the Egyptian Air Force (4803 and 4811, in 1984 and 1979 respectively) and four for Saudi Arabia (4605, 4737 for the RSAF and N4101M/4845 and N4099M/4843 for the Saudi Royal Flight, operated by Saudia). All are distinguishable by having enlarged, relocated square fuselage windows, airline seating, galley and toilet and extra sound-proofing.

WC-130H-LM

Designation given to fifteen HC-130H/C-130Hs (64-14861, 64-14866, 65-963/965, 65-966/969, 65-972, 65-976/977, 65-980 and 65-984/985) modified as weather-reconnaissance aircraft with Fulton STAR recovery system removed (but retaining radome) and special equipment fitted. 'Swan 38' (65-0965) at

Andersen AFB on Guam was lost in the Taiwan Strait on 13 October 1974 during penetration of Typhoon 'Bess' (known in the Philippines as Typhoon 'Susang'). Radio contact with 'Swan 38' was lost after 2200 on 12 October, apparently as the aircraft was heading into the typhoon's eye to make a second position fix during its alpha pattern. There were no radio transmissions indicating an emergency on board and search teams could not locate the aircraft or its crew except for a few pieces of debris. All six crew members were listed as missing and presumed dead. The fourteen remaining aircraft were transferred to the AFRes, 65-972 being transferred to AMARC in December 1997, leaving thirteen in AFRes service at that time. The new replacement WC-130J model encountered teething problems that delayed its Initial Operational Capability until just before the 2005 Atlantic hurricane season. Between May 2007 and February 2008, all ten WC-130J procured and assigned to the 53d WRS, now the only manned weather reconnaissance unit in the Department of Defense, were equipped with the Stepped-Frequency Microwave Radiometer (SFMR or 'Smurf'), which continuously measures the surface winds and rainfall rates below the aircraft, mounted in a radome on the right wing outboard of the number four engine.

YMC-130H-LM 'Credible Sport'

Three USAF C-130Hs (74-1683, 74-1686 and 74-2065) which received 'Credible Sport' modifications in 1980 to YMC-130H configuration for possible use in the abortive Operation 'Eagle Claw' fitted with an in-flight refuelling receptacle, DC-130 type radome and downward-pointing braking retrorockets to reduce landing run. 74-1683 crashed at a demonstration at Duke Field on 29 October 1980 when the retrorockets fired too early. The two other YMC-130Hs were returned to C-130H standard in November 1984. 74-1686 was put on display at Warner-Robins AFB Museum in March 1988. As of February 2008 74-2065 was assigned to the 317th Airlift Group, 15th Expeditionary Mobility Task Force at Dyess AFB Texas.

C-130K-LM (C.Mk.l/C.Mk.lP/ C(K) Mk.l/W.Mk.2./C.Mk.3)

See Chapter Eleven

C-130L-LM and C-130M-LM

Designations not used.

HC-130N-LM

Fifteen search-and-rescue aircraft (69-5819/5833), originally for the recovery of aircrew and the retrieval of space capsules: eleven were re-designated MC-130Ps in 1996; nine of these operate in the special operations squadrons and two in the 67th ARRS. Four (69-5824, 69-5829, 69-5830 and 69-5833) remain as HC-130Ns, operating in the SAR role with the 39th RQS, 939th RQW (USAFRes), at Patrick AFB, Florida.

HC-130P-LM/ MC-130P-LM 'COMBAT SHADOW'

Twenty combat aircrew recovery aircraft (65-988, 65-991/994 and 66-211/225), designated in 1966: they are similar to HC-130H (retaining that type's AN/ARD-17 Cook aerial tracker antenna and the Fulton STAR recovery system) but fitted with underwing drogue pods and associated plumbing for in-flight refuelling of rescue helicopters. The HC-130Ps entered service late in 1966 and were immediately deployed to south-east Asia. 66-214 and 66-218 in the 39th ARRS were destroyed by satchel charges at Tuy Hoa, South Viêtnam, on 29 July 1968. 66-211 was lost when its right wing snapped in severe turbulence at low level 15.5 miles north of Magdalena, New Mexico on 2 April 1986. In February 1996 AFSOC's 28-aircraft tanker fleet was redesignated the MC-130P 'Combat Shadow', aligning the variant with AFSOC's other M-series special operations mission aircraft. At the same time as this redesignation, USAF continued to field HC-130P/N aircraft as dedicated CSAR platforms under the Air Combat Command (ACC). Nine MC-130Ps are assigned to the 9th SOS at Eglin AFB, Florida and five each are assigned to the 17th SOS, Kadena AB, Japan and to the 67th SOS, RAF Mildenhall. The 5th SOS, AFRes, at Duke Field, Florida, has five aircraft and the 58th SOW at Kirkland AFB, New Mexico has four, the latter all for training. The MC-130P's primary role is to conduct single-ship or formation in-flight refuelling of special operations forces' helicopters in a low-threat to selected medium-threat environment.

All MC-130Ps have been modified with new secure communications, night vision goggle (NVG)-compatible lighting and advanced dual navigation stations with digital scan radar, self-contained ring-laser gyro INS (integrated navigation system), FLIR and GPS. They have also received upgraded missile warning systems and countermeasures for refuelling missions in hostile environments. Fifteen have been fitted with an in-flight refuelling receptacle.

EC-130Q-LM

US Navy designation given to eighteen improved TACAMO airborne communications relay aircraft (BuNos156170/156177, 159348, 159469, 160608, 161223, 161494/161496, 161312/161313 and 161531) built with C-130H airframes, but with 4,910eshp T56-A-16 engines and delivered between 1968 and 1984. They were used to supplement and then replace, all EC-130Gs in service with VQ-3 at NAS Agana, Guam and VQ-4 at NAS Patuxent River. (BuNo156176 crashed into the sea after a night take-off from Wake Island on 21 June 1977.)

The new models were characterized externally by wing-tip ESM pods housing electronic and communications equipment and with dual trailing antennas. Extended from the tail-cone and through the rear ramp, the antennas were fitted with stabilizing cones and were respectively 26,000 feet long and 5,000 feet long. Usually, the long antenna was streamed 16,000-20,000 feet, with the EC-130Q flying in tight orbits to keep both antennas almost vertical. The TACAMO equipment was successively improved for more effective EMP (electro-magnetic pulse) 'hardening' (protection against EMP effects such as occurring in the wake of a nuclear explosion). In the late 1980s this equipment was removed from the EC-130Qs and installed in the Boeing E-6As, which supplanted them, starting with VQ-3 at NAS Barber's Point, Hawaii between 1989 and 1990, then with VQ-4 at NAS Patuxent River, Maryland 1991-92. Following the removal of the TACAMO equipment the seventeen EC-130Qs were either sold off, cannibalized or scrapped, although three (156170, 159348 and 159469) were re-designated TC-130Q in 1990 and used as trainers and utility transports. 156170 and 159469 were later transferred to AMARC and subsequently registered to Airplane Sales International. 159348 is now on static display at Tinker AFB.

TC-130Q

Three EC-130Qs re-designated as TC-130Qs in 1990 (156170, 159348 and 159469) and then used as trainers and utility transports. (See EC-130Q entry.)

KC-130R-LM

Fourteen tanker/transports (BuNos160013/160021, 160240 and 160625/160628) with pod-mounted hose-and-drogue systems for the USMC delivered between September 1975 to mid-1978. Based on the C-130H airframe and powered by 4,910 eshp T56-A-16 engines, they were fundamentally similar to the KC-130H for export customers. The KC-130R could however, carry 13,320 US gallons (50,420 litres) of fuel, compared to the earlier KC-130F which could carry 10,600 US gallons (40,125 litres).

LC-130R-LM

Six ski-equipped versions (BuNos155917, 159129/159131 and 160740/160741), based on the C-130H airframe but with 4,910eshp T56-A-16 engines. All were obtained with National Science Foundation funds to supplement LC-130Fs in the Antarctic, but were operated on the NSF's behalf by the US Navy's VX-6 (later VXE-6). 155917 crashed when landing at Amundsen-Scott South Pole Station on 28 January 1973. 159129 was damaged when the nose ski broke off on take-off from Dome Charlie, Antarctica, on 15 January 1975. The aircraft was repaired on site in January 1976 and returned to service, but was later involved in a collision with a fork-lift at NAD Cherry Point, in November 1997; it was then transferred to AMARC. 1591131 crashed at site D59, Antarctica, when it was landing with spares for LC-130F 1483 21 on 9 December 1987 and was written off. 160740 was damaged at Starshot Glacier, Antarctica, in December 1984 and was repaired in situ; in 1998 it was transferred to the 139th AS, 109th AW, ANG, at Schenectady County Airport, New York. 160741 was also transferred to this unit in 1998/1999.

RC-130S 'BIAS HUNTER'

Two (originally four) JC-130A hunter-illuminators (56-493 and 56-497) for strike aircraft flying close air-support sorties in south-east Asia at night modified in 1967 by E-Systems with BIAS (Battlefield Illumination Airborne System) as a result of a recommendation made in March 1966 as part of Operation 'Shed Light', a high-priority research and development programme initiated by the Air Force to attain a night-strike capability along the Hó Chi Minh Trail. A large fairing housing fifty-six searchlights with a combined illumination of 6.14 million candlepower was mounted on each side of the forward fuselage and various sensors, including infra-red devices, were fitted for location of the enemy. However, in a hostile environment such as SE Asia where the 'BIAS Hunters' were expected to maintain tight orbits at low altitude to illuminate their targets, the RC-130S aircraft would have soon fallen victim to enemy return fire and in 1969-70 the searchlights and other equipment were removed and 56-493 and 56-497 reverted to C-130A configuration. Both were operated by AFRes and ANG units until 1988 when 56-497 was placed in storage at AMARC. 56-493 ended its career as a logistic support aircraft with the 152nd TFTS, 162nd TFG Arizona ANG at the Tucson IAP.

C-130T Logistics Support Aircraft
Twenty examples (BuNos164762/763, 164993/998, 165158/161, 165313/314, 165348/351, 165378/379) ordered for service with Naval Reserve Fleet Logistics Support Squadrons (VR). Basically similar to the C-130H, but with 4,910eshP T56-A-423 engines and updated avionics, the first example was handed over to VR-54 at New Orleans, Louisiana in August 1991 and delivery was completed in December 1996. Aircraft have been delivered to the Naval Air Reserve Force as follows: five to VR-53, Andrews AFB, Maryland; five to VR-54, NAS New Orleans, Louisiana; five to VR-55, Moffett Federal Airfield, California; and five to VR-62, NAS Brunswick, Maine. Two C-130Ts were transferred to NAVAIRWARCENACDIV Patuxent River, Maryland for F/A-18E/F in-flight test support. In FY00, these two aircraft returned, one each, to VR-55 and VR-62 in the Naval Reserve Fleet. Today, the four C-130T squadrons and the seven C-9B squadrons work together to keep one C-9B and one C-130T forward deployed to NAS Atsugi, Japan and two C-9Bs and one C-130T forward deployed to NAS Sigonella, Italy most of the time. The C-9B aircraft can only carry a very limited load on long transit legs so C-130T deployments are a more reliable way of getting overseas. Generally the squadrons in the eastern part of the United States fill the Sigonella commitment while those in the west go to Atsugi, but there is some crossover.

KC-130T/JC-130T
Tanker version for the USMC based on the C-130H airframe powered by T56-A-423 engines rated at

4,910eshp and similar to the KC-130R, but also fitted with an updated avionics suite to incorporate a new autopilot, AN/APS-133 search radar and an inertial navigation system plus Omega and TACAN. Twenty-six KC-130Ts (162308/311, 162785/86, 163022/23, 163310/11, 163591/92, 164105/06, 164180/81, 164441/42, 164999/5000, 165162/63, 165315/16, 165352/53) were acquired and were in service with VMGR-234 'Rangers', now a reserve USMC KC-130J squadron, part of MAG-41, 4th MAW at NAS-Joint Reserve Base at Fort Worth, Texas and VMGR-452 'Yankees' at Stewart ANG base, New York who support Fleet Marine Force commitments worldwide by providing both fixed-wing and rotary-wing aerial refuelling capabilities in addition to assault air transport of personnel, equipment and supplies. The USMC has chosen the KC-130J to replace its aging KC-130 legacy tanker fleet. With the addition of the Marine Corps's ISR/Weapon Mission Kit, the KC-130J will be able to serve as an overwatch aircraft and can deliver ground support fire in the form of 'Hellfire' or 'Griffin' missiles, precision-guided bombs and eventually 30 mm cannon fire in a later upgrade. This capability, designated as 'Harvest Hawk' (Hercules Airborne Weapons Kit) can be used in scenarios where precision is not a requisite such as area denial. The AN/AAQ-30 Target Sight System (TSS) integrates an infrared and television camera, and is mounted under the left wing's external fuel tank. It is the same TSS used on the upgraded AH-1Z Viper attack helicopter. The typical load out is four 'Hellfire' missiles and ten 'Griffin' GPS guided missiles. The weapons systems operator uses a Fire Control Console mounted on an HCU-6/E pallet in the KC-130J's cargo compartment.

KC-130T-30
BuNos164597 and 164598 assigned to VMGR-452, a US Marine Corps Reserve tanker/transport unit, at Glenview, Illinois in October-November 1991, differing from previous models in having stretched fuselages, being some 15 feet longer than the standard tanker. The increased fuel capacity raises the amount that may be passed to receiver aircraft via the wing-mounted refuelling pods.

AC-130U 'SPECTRE'
Thirteen gunships (87-0128, 89-0509/14, 90-0163/67 and 92-0253) based on the C-130H airframe with

integrated avionics by the North American Aircraft Operations Division of Rockwell International Corporation. Production began with airframe 87-0128, which was flown from Marietta to Palmdale in July 1988 for fitting out. It eventually emerged as an AC-130U in December 1990 and was then assigned to the 6510th Test Wing at the Air Force Flight Test Center, Edwards AFB. Beginning in 1990 twelve more AC-130Us were delivered and all are operated by the 4th SOS, 16th SOW at Hurlburt Field, Florida. The AC-130U has greater altitude capability and combines impressive firepower, reliability and superior accuracy with the latest methods of target location. This has involved updating the sensor suite, inputs from which are processed by IBM IP-102 computers at the 'battle management center' in the rear fuselage. The 'Black Crow' truck ignition sensor and radome and the separate beacon tracking radar used on earlier gunships have both been omitted. Observer stations are included on the rear ramp and starboard forward fuselage side. Spectra ceramic armour, three underfuselage chaff and flare dispenser (capable of dispensing 300 chaff bundles and either ninety MJU7 or 180 M206 IR decoy flares), Texas Instruments AN/AAQ-117 FLIR countermeasures and ITT Avionics AN/ALQ-172 jammer, are all fitted to increase the aircraft's chance of survival in a low-to-medium-threat environment. Standard armament consists of a trainable GAU-12/U 25 mm Gatling gun in place of the AC-130H's two 20 mm cannon, one 40 mm Bofors gun and a 105mm howitzer. All weapons can be slaved to the digital Hughes AN/APQ-180 fire-control radar, AN/AAQ-117 FLIR (mounted under the port side of the nose), or to the Bell Aerospace all-light-level TV (ALLTV) (turret-mounted in the port main undercarriage sponson) for truly adverse weather ground-attack operations. Other equipment includes a HUD, combined INS and NavstarGlobal Positioning System (GPS).

EC-130V/NC-130H

Designation for the single US Coast Guard airborne-early-warning example (CGI721) modified from HC-130H configuration. Having operated several USN Grumman E-2C Hawkeye early-warning aircraft on surveillance operations intended to cut the flow of drugs into the southern USA, the US Coast Guard soon reached the conclusion that it required a platform with similar detection capabilities but possessing greater endurance. CGI721was first delivered to Clearwater CG station, Florida in HC-130H configuration in October 1988. General Dynamics carried out the conversion to EC-130V standard at Fort Worth, Texas by installing an AN/APS-125 radar dish - almost identical to the array fitted to the E-2C - above the aft fuselage section. Other modifications included additional intakes for the cooling of onboard electronic equipment, as well as unidentified antenna fairings on both sides of the forward fuselage and above the nose radome ahead of the cockpit. Pallet-mounted displays and consoles sited in the hold area allow the EC-130V to carry up to three system operators.

CGI721 flew for the first time in this configuration on 31 July 1991 and the USCG operated it from Clearwater until April 1992. That summer the white and red livery was overpainted with camouflage and the aircraft was then delivered to the 514th Test Squadron USAF as 87-0157. In October 1993 87-0157 was redesignated NC-130H and later flown by the 418th TS until January 1998. It went to the Naval Air Test Center at Patuxent River the same year for evaluation and in November 2005 was used to test the Hawkeye 2000 radar. Lockheed Martin and the USAF are now considering an airborne-early-warning version based on the latest C-130J for overseas military sales.

Opposite page: A Hercules in the 314 Airlift Wing leads Air Force 'Thunderbirds' during a flyover of downtown Little Rock, Arkansas during the base's 50th Anniversary Air Show on 7 October 2005. The show brought crowds of more than 150,000 people to the base. (USAF)

Acknowledgements

I am especially indebted to Việtnam veterans' Alan Baker; John Gargus, author of the *Son Tay Raid*, and Sam McGowan, author of *Trash Haulers: The Story of the C-130 Hercules Troop Carrier/Tactical Airlift Mission* and *C-130 Hercules: Tactical Airlift Missions, 1956-1975* for kindly allowing me to tap their fund of exceptional war stories and share them here. I am equally indebted to Robert D. Young for kind permission to feature some of his exceptional images of the Việtnam War. Thanks are also due to Graham Simons, my trusted 'wingman' for his detailed work on the images etc and for carrying out my myriad amendments to the layouts; and to Laura Hirst and Jon Wilkinson at Pen & Sword. For anyone wishing to expand on their technical knowledge of the Hercules and in-depth analysis of individual models I would refer them to two superb journals; *The Lockheed Martin C-130: A Complete History*, by my good friend Peter C. Smith and the *Lockheed Hercules Production List 1954-2014* by Lars Olausson, a retired Lieutenant Colonel of the Swedish Air Force, the thirtieth edition having been printed in March 2012.